I taste
fire,
earth,
rain

I taste
fire,
earth,
rain

elements
of a life
with a
Sherpa

Caryl Sherpa

I Taste Fire, Earth, Rain
Elements of a Life with a Sherpa

By Caryl Sherpa

10 9 8 7 6 5 4 3 2 1

Editing by Waverly Fitzgerald & Kyra Freestar
Design by Nina Barnett
Proofreading by Anne Moreau
Maps by Robert Peirce & Grace Ericson
Cover design by Chuck Pennington
Cover photograph © Caryl Sherpa
Kirtimukha images © Tibetan Art Design, India

ISBN: 978-0-9836094-2-1
Library of Congress Control Number: 2011907808

STUDIO S PRESS

P.O. Box 16212
Seattle, WA 98116-0212
info@StudioSPress.com
URL: http//StudioSPress.com

To Nima Gyalgen Sherpa,
my guide in the mountains and in life,
and to our friend Jules

KIRTIMUKHA

On the book cover, *kirtimukha* emerges from the darkness. Known as the "monster mask" or "the creature without a name," *kirtimukha* is the face of glory and majesty. Born of the blaze of Shiva's third eye, *kirtimukha* guards the threshold of Shiva's door for all eternity.

Iconographically, ferocious *kirtimukha* is shown as an animal head, missing the lower jaw, and two hands. With horns that curl out, *kirtimukha* has a mane like a lion, a snout like a pig, and whiskers like a dragon. *Kirtimukha's* mouth devours strings of jewels. A protuberance, often shown with a crescent moon and sun above, appears high on *kirtimukha's* forehead.

Kirtimukha is common in Tibetan art and was used on implements of war as a heraldic device. *Kirtimukha* appears on door handles to temples; *kirtimukha's* strings of jewels adorn temple bells, including the handheld *drilbu*, or are hung around temple pillars; friezes of *kirtimukha* faces are found high up on temple walls and beams; a single *kirtimukha* face appears over doorways.

Popular with Newari craftsman in the Kathmandu Valley, *kirtimukha* can be found carved into wood lintels or archways. Along a brick street in Kathmandu, I once photographed a small shrine that bore a *kirtimukha* at its crest. Locals had shown respect with vermilion pigment and rice grains, which covered the shrine following the morning *pūjā*.

Welcome, says *kirtimukha*, the threshold guardian. And watch your head as you enter.

CONTENTS

rain (March – April 1994)

AUTHOR'S NOTE

Tashi Delek,

Welcome to the Himalaya. This story is set in the early 1990s, and I have chosen to use spelling and place names that were used at the time to share the experience of that time period, rather than update to current transliterations or name changes since. Elevations, which change in the Himalaya as they continue to rise, are from published maps and guidebooks of the 1990s as well.

As words in Nepali, Sherpa, and Tibetan are used often, and Nepalese historical figures, religious figures, place names, ethnic groups, and the like may be unfamiliar to many readers, a glossary is provided at the back of the book for easy reference. A definition or description is typically given the first time the word or name is used. Apart from family members and public figures, all names in this book are aliases, in respect for those who shared our journey.

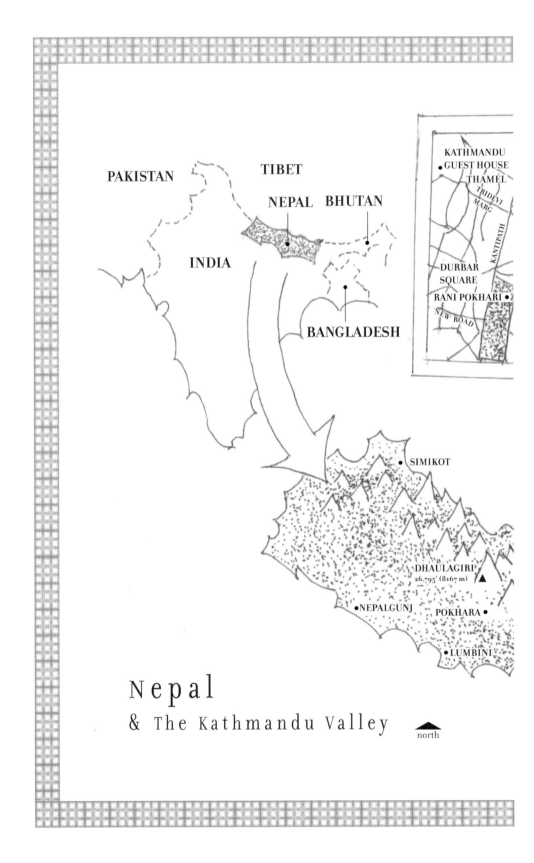

PAKISTAN

TIBET

NEPAL BHUTAN

INDIA

BANGLADESH

KATHMANDU
GUEST HOUSE
THAMEL
TRIDEVI MARG
KANTIPATH
DURBAR SQUARE
RANI POKHARI
NEW ROAD

•SIMIKOT

DHAULAGIRI
26,795' (8167 m) ▲

•NEPALGUNJ   POKHARA •

•LUMBINI

Nepal
& The Kathmandu Valley

▲
north

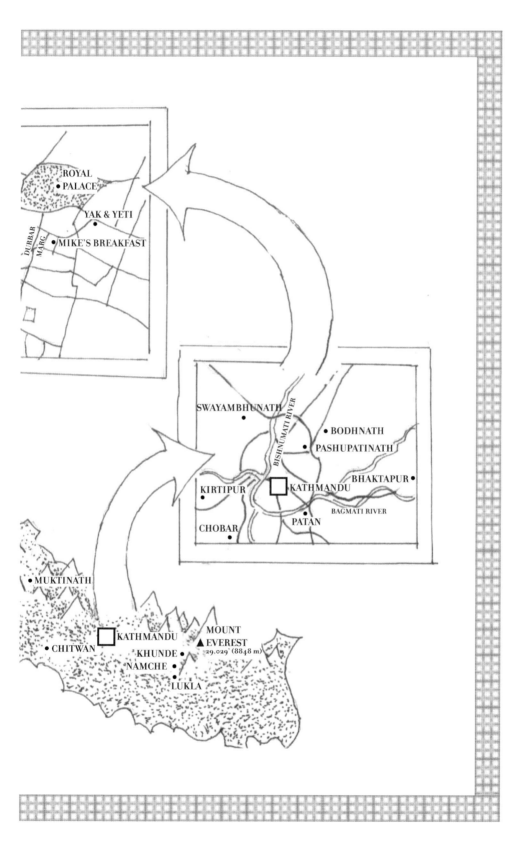

Prologue

How one begins a journey,
defines a journey.

—Lei

I HAVE NO CHOICE. I have to go. Something has to change. *I have* to change.

My duffel is packed. With an empty heart, but an adventurous spirit, I happily leave my life behind. As the plane lifts off the tarmac at Los Angeles International Airport, I depart with no defined goals and only the first two months of my journey scheduled. I am open to serendipity. I desire risk. I long to feel fear, anger, passion, and all those grand operatic emotions that have been leveled out of me until I parallel the horizontal landscape of the Los Angeles basin. I seek an epiphany. I need the world to point me in a direction—for if truth be told, I feel lost.

In the second week of March 1991, I arrive in Hong Kong. I have planned a week of transition from an American metropolis to an Asian one before I take on the Third World in Nepal. For several hectic days, I maneuver the city and absorb its architecturally significant high-rise buildings as well as its more colorful shops, markets, ferries, food, and gardens. After five days, my exhaustion catches up with me. I desire quiet, and trees.

I board a ferry to go to the mountaintop monastery of Po Lin on Lantau Island in the South China Sea, only to find myself surrounded by hordes of boisterous children with their families in tow. At the island, I disembark and queue up behind hundreds of people waiting for the bus to the temple. Sensing my frustration, a middle-aged Chinese woman explains that today is a school holiday. She tells me her name is Lei and introduces her husband and two children. Surprised to learn I am traveling alone, she insists I join her family for the day.

"How one begins a journey, defines a journey," says Lei.

The bus climbs up steep, winding roads through the forests that cover the island. Lei, her family, and I follow the crowd along a wide trail, until it opens to a broad plaza dominated by an ornate Chinese temple. We each light a bundle of incense sticks to honor the spirits and place the sticks in a stone urn among hundreds of others. Together, we enter the temple through oversized red doors. Lei bows toward a goddess honored by chrysanthemums, fruit, and candles, then turns and approaches a monk.

The monk hands each of us a cylindrical container filled with slender bamboo sticks. They are fortune sticks, says Lei, as she kneels on a cushion before the altar. I do the same.

Will your fortune focus on family, friend, or yourself? asks Lei.

This journey is about redefining me. I shut my eyes and make a wish as I shake the container. One stick inches forward and falls to the ground. Lei picks it up.

Number forty-one, says Lei as she gives it to the monk. Family, friend, or yourself?

Myself.

Married or unmarried? asks Lei.

Unmarried, I say. Lei translates for the monk, who looks at me for some time, and then speaks to Lei in Chinese.

Not real good. Not real bad, Lei tells me. You will be alone for a time, but you must take courage. To find a suitable husband for you will be difficult.

In the monastery garden among shade trees and chrysanthemums, Lei's family and I share a vegetarian lunch of noodle soup with mushrooms and greens, made by the monks. Lei's family wants to emigrate to New Zealand before 1997, when the British lease of Hong Kong will expire and the territory returns to China. Lei does not want to move and leave behind her family, her home, her memories, and yet she is afraid to remain and face an uncertain future. Today at Po Lin, she and her husband seek guidance.

After lunch, Lei hands out slips of paper and tells us to write a wish. I am pleased to be given a second chance. At a tree covered in paper bows in the corner of the courtyard, Lei demonstrates how to accordion-fold our wishes and tie them on.

Like butterflies! exclaims her young daughter.

I rise up on my tiptoes and tie mine to a branch. As a breeze fills the courtyard, our butterfly wishes lift on the wind. I wonder where mine will land.

As I take the ferry back to Kowloon on the mainland, across Victoria Harbor from the island of Hong Kong, I think of the uncertainty that lies ahead of me. My travels will take me into uncharted territory: first, the exotic cultures of Nepal and Bhutan and into the remote Himalaya; next, to Eastern Europe, so recently opened and democratized; then on to the urban delights of Paris; and ending with a tour of Scandinavia, including a week at a seaside cottage in the far-north Lofoten Islands above the Arctic Circle. It is there that I hope to have time to look back over my journey. I want to come home with answers, a new direction to my life, and a commitment to follow it through.

How did an ordinary woman like me end up on this extraordinary journey around the world—alone? I close my eyes, lean back on the wood-slat bench, and listen. We round the island of Peng Chau, waves slap at the boat as it cuts through rough water, and I remember—

The wonders of the natural world came to me early, but only during summer, for come winter in Michigan, my universe lay buried in deep snow. During my nursery school years, my family took summer vacation at my grandparents' cottage in Hampton Beach, New Hampshire, where I buried my little brother Tom up to his neck in sand and sunburned my nose while the ice cream–cold ocean froze my toes. I learned that the burn of saltwater on a clamshell cut felt like the sting of a jellyfish. As nature could be vicious, I liked that the boardwalk ran close behind our beach umbrella, in case civilization had to be re-entered quickly.

Nature first nurtured me within the shadowy enclosures of our overgrown garden. Between rows of asparagus gone to seed, I waltzed in my gown of delicate green lace with a prince. Under the crab apple, where my mother grew trillium and bleeding hearts, I imagined my own secret garden. On sultry days, I pillowed my head on moss and daydreamed summer away in the shade.

When my family bought a cottage on North Lake in Michigan, Mother Nature hugged me. My siblings, friends, and I explored distant lands, or traipsed across fields of bachelor's buttons and Queen Anne's lace to catch butterflies, or walked down to the lake to watch jewel-toned dragonflies copulate, or waded into the back bay where we counted our riches in tadpoles while smoking cattail cigars. Midsummer, we ravished wild blackberries and war-painted our bodies to ready us for a fight with its thorns. Only if our expedition numbered large would we disappear into dark woods.

At fourteen, my imagination blossomed with my love of reading. That summer, I babysat the two Farnsworth children, and together we explored every inch of the wild woods behind their house. We took safaris to Africa, where we fended off crocodiles (salamanders), orangutans (squirrels), and vultures (crows), while fearing encounters with the vicious wildebeest (their dog). The next day, I pirated us through the South Seas. Or we put our survival skills to use and lived like the Swiss Family Robinson. On days the humidity dripped off the sun, the children rested under a cathedral of oaks, while I took dance lessons from Daddy-long-legs, whose sultry tango aroused languid Lady-long-legs. The freedom I found in the Farnsworths' woods was not to be forgotten.

After high school, I went to college. There, I relished the opportunities and freedom that introduced me to new people and new ideas, as my world opened up to possibilities never before imagined. I studied Spanish in Mexico and French in France. I loved travel, although in the early 1970s, it still seemed a luxury. I wanted the world, but then came the fire.

In August 1972, university senior Shane and college sophomore I were drawn together by a night sky ablaze. We met while watching a farmer's barn burn, our passion fueled by freshly harvested hay. Two years later, we got married. Shane had been conditioned to expect the 1950s model of a wife. Somehow, he missed that I wanted my own career. His plans were for me to work with him in his future veterinarian practice. That was his dream, not mine.

His restless nature became my nightmare. While Shane studied pre-veterinarian medicine, I worked toward a degree in interior design. After three years of marriage, he said it was the longest he had ever lived in one place. I soon came to understand his restlessness. I worked full time and completed my degree, while doing our shopping, cleaning, and cooking. Shane worked a job for a few months, but decided it took him away from his studies. He did find time to gamble our money with a bookie, rejoicing at his contribution when he won, and hiding his losses when he did not. After three years of marriage, he began an affair with a woman at the school. Just before his graduation, just before he became a doctor, just before he would begin to make a financial contribution to our livelihood, I found out about their affair. When I confronted Shane, he did not deny it, and he expressed no interest in salvaging our marriage. That year, we both got new titles for a price. Shane became "Doctor." It had hardly cost him a dime. For twenty-five dollars, I became "divorcée." In 1976, divorce had to be handled delicately. Divorce was dirty. Divorce carried a stigma. I could no longer check "single" or "married," or even "widowed." I had to check "divorced." My life as I had planned it was over. I had failed. I was twenty-four.

To prove my resilience to myself, I moved out and moved on. In Chicago, I rented an apartment off North Lake Shore Drive near Belmont Harbor. I walked to the rock retaining walls along the shore of Lake Michigan to sit and look back toward my past. At first I bobbed like a boat at anchor, moving, but going nowhere. Some days I felt myself floating, and as I looked up at the sky, I imagined the waves washing me clean. Other days I struggled to remain afloat, and as the waves rose up toward shore, I felt battered as if I had been thrown onto the rocks. Some days I hurt that much. And then, more often than not, I began to feel myself sail. And I did learn to sail. Soon I could catch the wind, navigate the waves, and control my direction. I stopped coming to the rocks, turned my back on the east, and began to look west.

Hints about my future began a year after my move to Chicago; I just couldn't see the signs. My friends from Chicago drove five hours north to Door County, Wisconsin, to go bicycle touring, a sport that was new to me. The encouraging words of my friend George propelled me to endure sixty miles of the most physically demanding activity I had ever undertaken. He believed in me, so I believed in myself. Trust transforms. In time, I changed into an athletic woman who cycled double centuries and rode the Rockies. After introducing me to cycling, George introduced me to Nepal. "Read these books, *The Last Step: The American Ascent of K2* and *Annapurna: A Woman's Place*," he told me as he handed them to me, "and the mountains, and the tenacity of those who climbed them, will inspire you." I read them. We named his new J/24 sailboat *Annapurna*. I designed the logo and made the A's all mountains. After that, Nepal nested in my subconscious for another ten years.

Skiing taught me to love the mountains. In southern Michigan where I grew up, highway overpasses produced the most epic vistas. Drama came not from the landscape, but from the weather: blizzards, ice storms, tornadoes, and humidity so thick you could hang laundry on it. After I learned to ski in junior high school, I learned to love altitude—first on the icy slopes of Mount Brighton or Mount Holly, where I would rope tow up and hurtle down in less than a minute, and then on my first ski trip to Colorado. In Aspen, my desires changed. For ten more years, west I came and up I went.

I could become passionate about a landscape with mountains. I liked the emotions it drew out in me. I liked the letting go. I liked learning to confront my fears head on, as I raced down a mountain face, facing danger, facing a fall, and doing it anyway just for the thrill of it, invigorated as I slid to a stop, shouted, "Single," then jumped forward in the lift line to go up and race down all over again. My life was flat, so I sought out altitude with attitude, and the faster, the better. The Alps of Europe added new thrills: ungroomed trails, high-mountain huts serving exquisite cuisine, and après-ski dancing with European men. I wanted more. After traveling east to ski the Alps, I traveled west to California, in search of ever more demanding experiences. In 1984 I moved to Los Angeles, a city cradled between the mountains and the ocean. It seemed a natural progression.

The wilds of California first brought me into contact with the monumental topography of untamed lands. I felt exalted by the sheer cliffs of Yosemite Valley; I sang a joyful hosanna to the Joshua trees whose arms reached heavenward; I felt maternal hugging the girth of a sequoia with friends; I admired the palette of lichen that softened a ragged ridge of the Sierras; and I cursed the steep pitch of the mountains that rose up from the sea at Big Sur as I cycled south toward home along Highway 101. My world grew bigger and bolder in California. I had reached the edge of America, and still I desired more.

Having just relocated to Los Angeles and with no new friends to share weekend trips cycling and skiing, my career began to dominate my activities, and I saw less of the natural world as my priorities shifted. It was easy to lose myself in Los Angeles. I worked overtime and weekends. I drove miles to shop at trendy boutiques. I dined late with friends at restaurants recently reviewed. For a time, I soared, relishing the newness of Los Angeles and the quality of the architectural interiors work I could do there. And then came the recession.

On October 19, 1987, or Black Monday, the U.S. stock market crashed almost 25 percent, upsetting financial markets worldwide. Hundreds of overleveraged savings and loan associations failed, which forced government bailouts, huge budget deficits, and a downturn in real estate transactions. In 1990, the country plunged into a recession. Layoffs went deep. Corporate growth stalled. New architectural projects came to a halt.

My project died a slower death. Employed by a large architectural firm, I had managed our team's efforts for the design of a lavish new corporate headquarters for the previous three years. As we completed our work and readied the client's new offices for occupancy, the exuberance of the eighties ended. Now, there were signs that the corporation would not move into all the floors of its new headquarters, and even those staff who did move would not reside there for long. The client's executives should have seen it coming. The mood of the country had shifted with the economy. Our completed project, which had looked like an award winner, now appeared wasteful and extravagant to everyone. Our efforts were downplayed, then hidden from view, and soon became meaningless.

Our project team had given extra hours and sleepless nights to achieve perfection. The entire project was connected by reveals that delineated materials. Reveals crossed floors of honed French limestone, porcelain Japanese tile, and English woven-wool carpets; turned up walls of hammered French limestone, sandblasted American glass, and African and English wood veneers dyed in France, sliced in Italy, and fabricated into millwork in Houston and San Francisco before being installed in Los Angeles. The reveals continued, delineating ceilings of Thai silk panels, painted plaster, and custom linear air bars made in America. Reveals circled space, embracing its perfection, joining materials together to create a sumptuous, balanced environment for the corporation. I thought perfection mattered. It did not. Not anymore.

Cheap was the new chic. "We're a dynamic company" became the corporate jargon for "temporary" or "downsized," no, make that "right-sized," or even "obsolete." The sumptuous design of our project was out of balance with the times. I felt obsolete. My entire career had led me to this incredible opportunity, a project that challenged all I knew, but the stunning results were insignificant to the effort, as the project team willed it from an idea to a two-dimensional concept into a three-dimensional space. Now the corporation was embarrassed by what we had designed, they had approved, and the contractor had built, and fearful of criticism of their lavishly designed headquarters. The transient nature of my work lay before me. I felt worn out, disheartened, and as empty as the building shell we had started with.

Understated events celebrated the corporation's partial move to their new headquarters. Some staff moved elsewhere, and their floors were never occupied. Accolades were tempered by shock at the luxury of their new offices. Our years of work and sacrifice would soon prove to be a waste of resources, time, and energy.

Now what? After spending the last three years in high gear, I felt an urgent desire to get away and enjoy life. I would travel. I sought a location for physical adventure—without significant corporate influence; where communication with the office would be impossible; where I would be away from triggers of memories; and where I could erase my past. I decided on the Himalaya. For that, the project provided a catalyst.

My boyfriend, Marco, and I dated a year and then, certain our relationship would work, bought a house together. However, after two years with Marco, and six months before I left for Nepal, I climbed out of a dark crevasse that had become our relationship. Marco was attractive in a Mediterranean sort of way, dark olive with sheen. He was a neighbor, and kind when I needed a friend. I refused his advances at first. I should have stayed true to myself, but I was lonely, and bored. I moved in with Marco and committed to a relationship with a younger man at the start of his career. In other words, Marco did not make much money. Dutch dates were okay, but soon I was buying most of the groceries, and if it was my idea to go to a concert, the theatre, or a movie, I bought the tickets. Not that I minded. I saw it as an investment in our relationship. Besides, he never offered, and I wasn't cheap. Physical activities kept us busy. Energetic and eager to explore, Marco and I traveled beyond Los Angeles to the desert to hike or the mountains to cross-country ski. We cycled along the coast up into the hills of Palos Verdes Estates or took long walks along the Strand that fronts Manhattan Beach, Hermosa Beach, and Redondo Beach. Physical pleasures kept us together.

Trust makes a relationship. I trusted. I was wrong. After a year of cohabitating, real estate inflation drove us to invest as partners in a house in Redondo Beach. A commitment this big sent Marco to look around. I was too busy to notice. When I sensed him pulling away, I committed more. He took more. Finally, I began to see the inequity of our partnership, so although this sounds silly, I gave him a test. Would he split the cost of a new sofa with me? It was not a vanity purchase. We needed one. I wanted him to prove that we made decisions and invested as partners. He said no. I bought the sofa. He sat on it. I made plans. I told him I wanted to end our relationship. He wanted a marriage. Too late, I said. I was leaving to trek the Himalaya and travel around the world. He could stay in the house until I returned. Then we would sell it.

I had only one focus: my journey. That fall, I took an apartment on the beach for six months and moved in what I needed. I continued my job, but discouraged by my project's demise, I did only what I had to. As the recession took hold, my one-month journey expanded to a five-month around-the-world tour. I wanted to immerse myself in locations I had never visited. Daunted by the thought of trekking in the Himalaya, the world's tallest mountains, getting into tip-top shape became my obsession. I had committed to do the Annapurna Circuit, which crossed the 17,769-foot (5,416 m) pass at Thorung La.

As an avid downhill skier, I knew mountains up to 10,000 feet (3,048 m), where ski lifts brought me up and gravity pulled me down, but on this trip, I would have to rely on myself. I worked out on my NordicTrack, practiced yoga for flexibility, and hiked to the highest elevations I could attain in the San Bernardino, San Gorgonio, or San Jacinto Mountains outside of Los Angeles. Or I walked the beach and climbed the bluffs to the Malaga Cove Plaza Library in Palos Verdes Estates, where I looked out across the Pacific Ocean and envisaged my adventure taking me past villages and fields, forests and alpine tundra, then on to bare rock and up over the snowy pass. I kept on my feet as much as I could. After eight years in Los Angeles, eight years in my car, my body had to learn to carry a load again—me. I grew limber, strong, agile. At thirty-eight going on thirty-nine, I was in my best physical condition ever. Nonwork activities were my priority. I only saw friends who would hike with me. I planned days to shop for gear, get shots and pick up medications, pack and repack my duffel. In the evening, I read everything I could on Nepal. The day I checked off the last item on my list, I skipped a workout and celebrated with a bottle of wine.

My friends, family, colleagues, and clients responded with disbelief when I told them I was taking five months off work to travel around the world. Friends said two weeks, like everyone else, should be long enough. My family expressed concern that I would not be working. Colleagues told me that I was being favored to be allowed so much time off, although no one else had ever asked. The corporation worried about whom to call if a question came up, even though the project was complete. I had been in charge of projects, but I had not been in charge of my life. It was my time to go.

The most universal response I heard was, "I could never do that. I could never take the time." Yes, you can, I'd say. It's easy. First, you make plans, and then you go. I felt driven by a passion to seek change and release the me that I used to be when my imagination ran free, when landscapes offered possibilities, when each day allowed me to meld both into a magical experience. I was often asked if I was afraid, but I never answered that question. I was more afraid not to go.

Now in Hong Kong Harbor, as the ferry turns toward Kowloon, I feel my apprehension about traveling to a Third World country. Alone? the skeptics had asked, as if it was an acceptable excuse not to go. It's the best way to meet people and learn a culture, I had responded, pretending great confidence. Asia will be new territory for me. In Europe, I can speak some Spanish and French, and I understand their Western culture. Asia will be exotic, with strange alphabets and customs I know nothing about.

At the thought of needing help, I feel panic. And yet—

I have to go. I must go. And so, my journey begins.

fire

March – July 1991

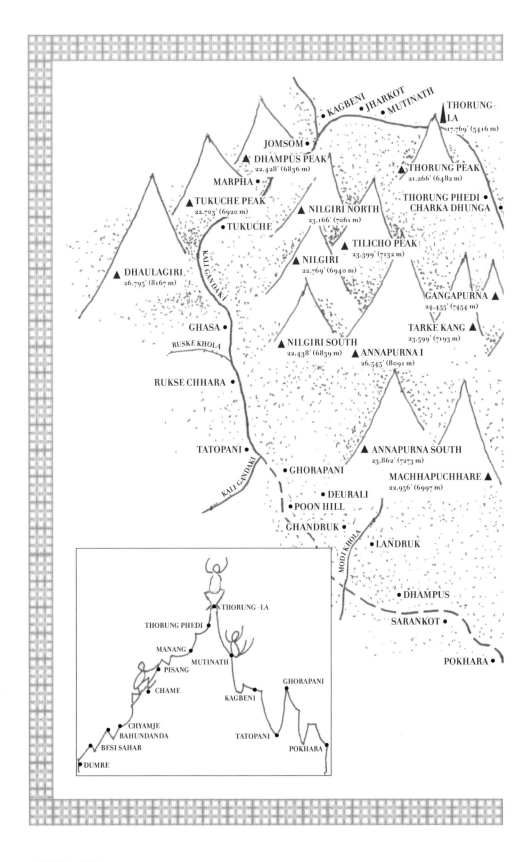

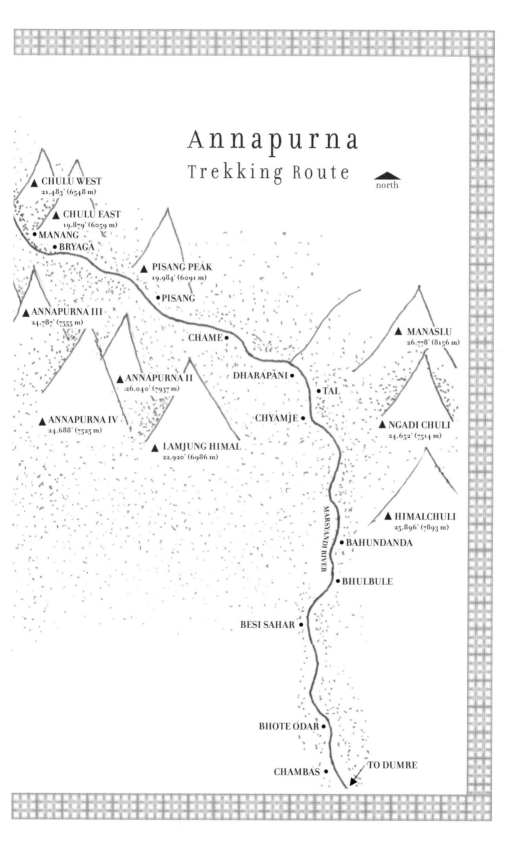

> *Namaste* means "the spirit in me
> salutes the spirit in you."
>
> —*Montego*

T HE HARVEST IS WOMEN'S WORK. At the end of our first day of trekking, I stand before low platforms raised off the ground. Sheaves of wheat fall away from center poles, creating a field of golden breasts. In front of me, women bend over to cut the wheat with a *khukuri*, a curved knife. In a single, rapid movement, each gathers a sheaf of wheat, ties the bundle with stalks, and then fills the outstretched arms of a child, who delivers the bundle to another woman to pass under a haystack. An old woman notices my interest and motions for me to come closer. As I near, sounds of laughter from below the haystack surprise me. I crouch to see five young women sitting cross-legged before large flat stones in a room formed out of their harvest. They motion for me to join them and slide over to make me a place. Both curious and honored, I enter.

Work done as a community brings joy. In the late afternoon, the wheat surrounding us glows golden. The air dusted by chaff focuses the sun's rays; long light falls as through a cathedral window in winter. Through hand gestures, I learn how to hold a sheaf, beat it five times on the stone before me, and then toss the expended sheaf to the old woman outside, who throws it up onto the haystack. I watch as two women create a rhythm of alternating beats on the same stone. I only get in the way of my partner.

The work is hard, dusty, and hot. I prickle from the chaff. As the sheaves slide up and down in my hands, my palms burn. My grip lessens as I tire, and my palms burn more. The grain piles up before us. These women ignore the physical discomfort. They laugh and joke and tease each other, but mostly, they laugh at me, not to mock, but gently and without insult. So, I laugh at them laughing at me. Our merriment makes us forget our work. Wheat grains pile up on the stones.

Desirous of their respect, I work hard. I grab. I beat. I toss. I grab. I beat. I toss. I grab. I beat. I beat. I beat—my arms grow tired. I soon need extra beats to release the grains, and I exhaust myself. I last twenty minutes. At home, I buy machine-ground flour already bagged. Does this flour taste different? Might I honor food more if I had to work so hard for it? They stop work and motion for me to stay. I smile and take my leave, a bit worried I might be missed at camp. As I stand up outside, their laughter resumes, and their beating. The old woman nods and the children watch me in wonder. I am exotic here and I like it.

As I walk back to our camp outside Bhote Odar, I realize that on our first day trekking, we gained only 361 feet (110 m) in elevation. I struggled in the heat and humidity. Another 15,965 feet (4,866 m) remains to be climbed, not to mention all the valleys and hills and mountains in between. Can I do this?

I think back on my short time in Nepal and am filled with more questions than answers. Four days ago, when the plane dropped into the Kathmandu Valley, I watched from the window as green hills pierced through the haze, followed by red-brick buildings. Our plane landed at quaint Tribhuvan International Airport to the jubilant shouts of the passengers, who were either trekkers ready for an adventure, or Nepalese returning home. I liked that Kathmandu was clearly not a destination for business travelers.

With my backpack hanging off my shoulder, I stepped out onto the stairs and into an oppressive wall of heat. The latitude of Kathmandu is 27.5 degrees north of the equator. I had just left Los Angeles, which is 34 degrees north, and warm and dry in summer. Kathmandu, with its summer monsoon rains and twelve hours of light, felt equatorial, even at 4,368 feet (1,331 m) above sea level.

I entered the chaos of Kathmandu. With no baggage conveyor to route our belongings to us inside the airport, luggage was hand-carried from the cargo hold and randomly presented to the passengers, who stumbled over duffel bags, suitcases, and boxes tied with colorful rope in search of their own. A boy grabbed at a duffel before me, lifted it into the air with ease and asked, This one? Taxi? No, I told him. This one? Taxi? I shook my head. This one? Taxi? No. This one? THIS ONE?

At the sight of a bearlike man holding a Malla Trek sign, I signaled, and he came to my rescue. Montego introduced himself as my trip leader, welcomed me to Nepal, and then directed two boys to take my large duffel through customs. After a wave of the officious security man's hand, we followed our driver to the van.

Montego came from Mexico, he told me as we drove into the city, and mountain climbing was his passion. He blended in here with his black hair, laughing eyes, and brown skin. Montego wore a T-shirt, jeans, sandals, and a single turquoise bead on a string around his neck. His laugh was loud and his hands danced as he talked and pointed out sights en route to our hotel. He told me he lived part time in Kathmandu, part time in Mexico City. Looking for common ground, I mentioned that I spent a summer in Tlaquepaque, Jalisco, in 1971. I'd studied pottery from native artisans, the pre-Columbian pyramids in Teotihuacán, and the machismo of Mexican men. He laughed and broke into Spanish. After twenty years, my Spanish had turned rusty. Here, I hoped to learn Nepali.

I arrived at the Malla Hotel in Kathmandu exhausted by several years of intense work managing an architectural design project for a corporate client's new headquarters, which they never fully moved into and would soon vacate entirely. I felt that my efforts the last three years had been meaningless. My adrenaline, which had held out in Hong Kong, was depleted. I refused dinner. I slept for sixteen hours. I ate breakfast alone. I slept again until late afternoon. I did not meet up with our trekking group until just before dinner.

I am curious to meet our trekking group. Sharon, in her early twenties, has all the characteristics of a young woman brought up in a good Southern California family of old money and blue-blood values. Oozing self-confidence, she is charming, vivacious, smart, witty, and kind. Her sandy curls fall to her shoulders. Her face is lightly freckled, lips a full pout, and eyes a pale blue. Sharon's physique is lean and trim, for good reason. Her boyfriend, Harry, is on his way to Everest Base Camp with plans to summit. Sharon intends to climb to Base Camp 1 or 2 with him. Our trek is to be her warm-up.

Being a Midwesterner, I feel a connection to Saul and Prudy, a couple in their early fifties, who hail from Michigan. Saul, a psychologist, is professorial in his demeanor, tall and rail thin with bookish glasses rakishly covered by disheveled sandy hair. He is quiet, but when he does talk, it is to relay a story about one of their numerous world adventures: African safaris, journeys to exotic locales in pursuit of a solar eclipse, and their recent excursion up the Baltoro Glacier of K2 in Pakistan. Prudy, who assisted her husband for many years with his work, has high cheekbones and short-cropped dark hair. They both dress as if they have just come off safari: white shirts, khaki pants, and hats with an extra-long bill and flaps that hang to their shoulders to protect their necks from the sun.

Paul, the youngest of the group, is stocky, in a baby-pudgy kind of way. His thick black hair and glasses define dark, intense eyes that look at the world with wonder and curiosity. Last year, he completed a degree in chemistry, and he still hopes to work in Silicon Valley. Jobs are leaving the valley however, and are hard to come by. Although Paul is tired of the university life, he considers graduate school an alternate plan. His parents, both doctors and immigrants from Thailand, have high expectations for their progeny. Paul has come to Nepal to find answers. This trek will be his first experience of camping, hiking in high mountains, and traveling to a foreign land. I wonder what he is getting himself into. I only hope that his youthful exuberance will be enough to push him over the 17,769-foot (5,416 m) pass at Thorung La.

Our group spends our first two days in Kathmandu sightseeing and acclimatizing to the exotic cultures of Nepal. In the ancient Newari town of Bhaktapur, we wander cobbled streets to piazzas with pagoda temples guarded by Garudas and Hanumans, mystical beasts of the Hindu pantheon. Along the Bagmati River, we watch pilgrims bathe upriver of the burning funeral pyres of Pashupatinath, Nepal's most sacred Hindu site. Nearby, in peaceful coexistence, is Nepal's most sacred Buddhist site, Bodhnath, where we circumambulate clockwise around its *chörten*, or shrine. As we circle, we turn prayer wheels and wish for a successful climb over Thorung La. Satisfied that the gods are now with us, we retire to the upper terrace of the Stupa View Restaurant. Montego orders us *ch'ah*, or milk tea, also known as *chai*. As we drink it, he explains that the domed structure before us is called *stūpa* in Nepali and *chörten* in Tibetan and Sherpa.

Below us, the town encircles the *chörten*, with farmland and new Buddhist temples beyond. A circle in the landscape looks natural, unlike our grids of streets and blocks of buildings. The architecture here is of the land—sun-dried brick the color of earth, or hand-hewn stone—unless it is painted, like the gleaming white *chörten*. Montego explains how a *chörten*, built to house sacred relics of Tibetan Buddhist teachers or the Buddha, take different forms in different countries. In Nepal, they typically consist of a stone plinth (square), a dome (round), a spire (triangular) topped by a moon (crescent) and a sun (drop shaped), to symbolize the elements of earth, water, fire, air, aether, and as a symbol for the Buddha. A *chörten*'s proportions matches those of the seated Buddha. From its cupola above the dome, a pair of eyes looks out in each of the four cardinal directions. Monks in crimson robes, pilgrims in layers of soiled clothes, and businesspeople in suits walk the stone-paved circuit around the *chörten* and turn the one hundred and eight prayer wheels set into its plinth with an intensity that suggests responsibility for turning the earth on its axis.

I want to understand their passion, absorb their spirit, and discover faith. I am tired of circling without purpose, of being an outside observer, a wanderer. I want to anchor myself. Before leaving Los Angeles, my project was completed. My two-year relationship ended. I felt a rumble of hunger. I came to Nepal to seek substance. I shiver as a breeze lifts blessings from hundreds of prayer flags draped out from the spire or on the poles that surround the *chörten*. I am an empty vessel, ready to be filled.

All morning we travel by van over paved roads to Dumre, which serves traders, trekkers, and porters at the crossroads to Gorkha and the valleys of Marsyandi and Manang. It is here we meet our trekking crew. Montego tells us our group of five trekkers is smaller than usual, due to cancellations caused by the political instability in the Persian Gulf. The Gulf War ended a month earlier; people's fears have not. Operation Desert Storm meant less work for Sherpas, due to the reduced bookings, and many have no other livelihood. I am shocked to learn that even a country as remote and peaceful as Nepal can be affected economically by U.S. actions, and U.S. wars.

Before Montego introduces us to our staff, he explains that Nepal is made up of many different ethnic groups, Sherpas being one of them. Our guides are Sherpas from the Everest region. Our porters come from the lowlands of Nepal.

Seventeen paid staff members, including myself, will support you, says Montego.

Seventeen! I am amazed. We knew this would be a supported trek, but no one had anticipated what it would take to get five trekkers over the Thorung La. Seventeen! We repeat the number again, and again, as if repetition might lessen its magnitude. Dorje, the *sirdar*, or lead guide, is responsible for the staff. Laugh lines cover his face below a cap he wears tipped to shade one eye. Tsuldim, one of two guides, is a small, older man, built like a weight lifter and sun-weathered. Kami, the youngest and quietest of our guides, has a curl in his hair. Tashi, sporting a white cowboy hat, will be our cook, and shy Pema, the kitchen boy. The porters number eleven, including three young women and a small boy dressed in short shorts, flip-flops, and a polka-dot hooded shirt.

From Dumre at 1,444 feet (440 m), we travel by bus toward Chambas over dirt roads unfit for modern transportation. Our vehicle is soon mired in muck. Efforts to extract our bus are to no avail. Impatient to begin our trek, we step into ochre mud that tops our hiking boots and walk to Chambas, gaining just under 200 feet (60 m) in elevation. With so much to look at, I soon forgot our frustrating start. Above us, rice paddies terrace the hills, while below us, banana trees encircle adobe homes of ochre and thatch with their well-tended vegetable gardens. The lush land sustains the locals, but living off it is hard work. I watch a child on a veranda rock a baby in a cradle as their mother kneels before a grinding stone to make flour. Beyond the wood stiles and lintel of a door that rises from a foundation, I glimpse a man applying mortar atop a wall of hand-hewn stone.

Our trek begins in the Himalayan foothills. I enjoy the walk and my body in motion, but the heat and humidity at this low elevation make me irritable. Tashi, who walks with me, senses it. To turn my mood around, he offers to teach me simple words in Nepali and Sherpa. I find this difficult. The unique sounds of each language make them hard to remember. Nepali is Indo-Aryan, derived from Sanskrit, while Sherpa is based on Tibetan. Tashi starts simply. I learn that *pani* (Nepali) means "water" and *himal* (Nepali) or *khangri* (Sherpa) means "mountain," and *la* (Sherpa) means "mountain pass," as in Thorung La, our destination. Tashi is friendly, ruggedly handsome, and tall for a Nepalese at six feet (1.8 m). He speaks a mix of British English and American English picked up from trekkers. Tashi carries only a small backpack, which leads me to surmise that the size of the load one carries in the Himalaya designates status. Tashi and our Sherpa guides were high-class.

Tashi helps me forget about the humidity as he points out details: the hollowed logs that hang from roof eaves and oozed honey, or the braided line of leaves, flowers, and amulets that mark the entrance of a village. In a small Hindu temple of sculpted adobe, my eyes follow a spiral of white paint that drips across an ochre-colored floor and ends in a lotus pattern surrounding a stone *lingam* anointed with oil, pigments, and marigolds. I recognize this phallic symbol and know I have entered an ancient world.

We arrive at our first campsite in Bhote Odar by midafternoon. Hot and mud-covered from our trek, Sharon, Paul, and I decide to climb down to the Marsyandi River to soak our feet. The local children lead us; a barefoot girl in a faded turquoise sari takes my hand at a steep embankment. The wide river moves at a steady pace, except where the children kneel and pull "boats" caught by rock eddies along the shore. My young guide shows me her boat: a single leaf woven into form by pine needles. As she cradles the boat in the palm of her hand, I watch it rock, feather-like in the breeze. She kneels again and releases it into the river's current.

I too must let go of the land and travel on water untethered.

As we walk the shore, I spot scores of leaf boats caught among stones. In simple English, the children explain that the villagers made them for a festival. At nightfall, everyone gathered by the river to release the boats. Each boat ferried a lighted cinder. I envision a highway of lights, a Los Angeles freeway of the Annapurnas. I imagine traveling down from the hills with them, past women washing clothes on stones, men siphoning off water for their rice fields, and children wading toward danger. The river and these people respond to the topography with a grace I too hope to learn.

At the end of our first day trekking, I return to camp in the late afternoon, having spent an hour working with the women bringing in the harvest. I should feel content. I do not. With time to just sit, my stress returns. I pull my yo-yo out of my pocket and fling it to the ground. Balanced by speed, seduced by gravity, and in repose at the end of a string, the yo-yo returns to the palm of my hand—and to me—as I hover above it: in control, tightly wound, and focused to avoid failure. I clutch the blue plastic Duncan, smile, and survey my new surroundings. Mountains half enclose me: Himalchuli, Ngadi Chuli, Manaslu, Annapurna II and IV, and Lamjung Himal. Snowcapped, they appear to bite the sky high above our first night camp at Bhote Odar.

I toss my yo-yo toward the ground. It hovers for longer than normal in the Himalayan air, as if relishing the freshness, as if halted by its purity, as if no string were attached and it could spin off into the world like quiet prayers on the lips of a Buddhist monk. To live free and true, guided only by the laws of nature, or the laws of one's nature, I too hover. My whole body smiles, as I begin my search for balance to the speed of my life and to the strings I severed back in Los Angeles.

I came to the Himalaya in search of me. My yo-yo snaps back. I must change. The yo-yo feels good in my hand, round and true, like the sun hovering over the himals. I want my today self to be devoured by these mountains. I want to pass through them, climb over them, and come out on the other side renewed, able to begin again like the day.

I came to Nepal to trek the Annapurna Circuit, an arduous twenty-one-day journey. After only one day, I feel the freedom of childhood begin to seep back into me. I remember when nothing else mattered but sending my blue Duncan down with a snap, so it could come back up with barely a flick of my wrist. Steady and determined. I hope trekking will go at a steady pace. A snap of the hand. Down. A flick of the wrist. Up. Nepal will be good for me. I will relax here. My only scheduled activities are to get up each morning and enjoy life.

Earlier in the day, the children I met along the trail loved my yo-yo. Initially, they approached me with what I soon recognized as the children's anthem of Nepal, "Gimme a pen," pleaded with outstretched hands and soulful eyes. Handouts encourage begging, said the trekking agency. Better to bring something to share. I searched through my box of treasured childhood mementos and brought along my thirty-year-old yo-yo.

I know time and a change in venue will reshape workaholic me, just as the glaciers reshaped the Himalaya. I perch on a stone wall with legs dangling and re-remember yo-yo tricks with the exuberance of a child learning something new. I "Walk the Dog." I "Rock the Cradle." Among these mountains, who will teach me new tricks? Montego, our trekking guide? Tashi, the cook?

I am an observer here. As I yo-yo, I watch to learn. Pema sorts out the stainless steel kitchenware into an ordered pattern on a tarp. Our Sherpas tease each other as they reorganize supplies. The porters return from the river with water in plastic jugs balanced on their heads, put the jugs down near the cooking area, and disappear. Montego and Tashi sit on their haunches and talk. Suddenly, like a butterfly on the wind, the exuberant energy of a newly arrived Sherpa to our camp diverts everyone's attention.

"*Namaste*, Nima Gyalgen!" shouts Montego. Surprised by my yo-yo in action, the Sherpa stops to watch me. He smiles. I blush. My yo-yo stops in mid-spin. The Sherpa is radiant! What a confident, carefree god of the mountains. What joy!

Suddenly I remember my little-girl crush on Bill, camp counselor and my first vacation romance. I was eight and spending my first two terrifying weeks away from home ever. Tall, gangly Bill saved me with his smile and easy enjoyment of life, for he made me feel safe and brought me out of my shell.

Bill taught me to swim. He coaxed me to enter the water. He instructed me to relax and enjoy suspending myself in a liquid lake. He tried to teach me to let go. I remained afraid. I knew water could drown me, especially deep water. I kept to the edges. I waded. I splashed. I stayed where my toes touched stones. I only swam if Bill was beside me. I refused to swim in deep water. Bill smiled and cajoled and clasped my hand. Bill loved the water. He showed me how to be gleeful while surrounded by a black, terrifying lake. Sometimes he would disappear underneath for a long time. I would grow frightened. Bill, come back! He always did, exploding out of the water with laughter on his lips. Come on in. It's fun! You can do it.

That's it! His glee. His fearless ease. Nima reminds me of Bill.

As I grew up, I began to understand that the same kinds of people appear in my life, and then disappear, only to reappear. Sometimes I know who they remind me of. Sometimes I do not. Many taught me something, but as their presence was often transitory, I have had to learn to let go. However, for the lessons I never finished, or skipped out on, or stubbornly refused to learn, those teachers return in another guise. Only repetition embeds a new pattern for living.

Bill trusted me more than I trusted myself. I learned to enter the water, but I did not swim in deep water that summer. I fought for control. I remained afraid.

This Sherpa guide could be my "camp counselor." I have to cross a 17,769-foot (5,416 m) pass. I'm scared! Nima reminds me of Bill. I choose Nima. Besides, that Sherpa looks fun!

I stare at Nima as he drops his pack to bear-hug Montego, then shakes Tashi's hand. The three men squat beneath a banyan tree. I see only their animated gestures and hear their laughter. In silhouette before a pastel sky, a Rorschach inkblot unfolds before me; from a massive tree trunk, branches reach out in all directions to end in the blackness of thick leaves, and roots stretch out above ground only to bury themselves in the earth, while the three men rest half above the horizon and half below. What do I see in this inkblot against the sky, all within the banyan's embrace? Balance. Stillness. Simplicity. Friendship. Joy. From my position outside the reach of the canopy, I know I am seeking what they have.

As I rewind my yo-yo, Montego and the new Sherpa rise and walk toward me. The Sherpa looks young.

"Meet my friend, Nima," says Montego. "He has no work this trekking season, so I invited him to join our trek." I smile.

"*Namaste*," says Nima, as he looks straight at me with palms together and bows.

Never have I felt so honored by a man.

"*Namaste*," I respond in kind, but feel silly as I mimic their ways.

"*Namaste* means 'the spirit in me salutes the spirit in you,'" says Montego. *Namaste* recognizes the sacredness and interconnection of all things.

Nice spirit.

Curious about my yo-yo, Nima insists that I teach him tricks. Delighted, he learns how to send it spinning. He laughs at his follies and jumps with joy at his success. So infectious is his delight, I laugh with a freedom not felt for some time.

"Dinner, *Didi*," announces Pema, the kitchen boy.

"Who's *Didi*?" I ask.

"*Didi* means older sister," says Nima. "You are *Didi*. All one family."

"Dinner, *Didi*," calls Pema as he walks toward the dining tent with a steaming bowl of soup. I take my place on a folding chair before a wobbly table, where the other trekkers and Montego are seated. As Pema serves up soup, the smell of garlic overwhelms us. After someone suggests that garlic's medicinal properties may help to fight off stomach bugs and altitude sickness, we don't waste a drop. Dinner is less interesting: spaghetti with a coral-colored tomato sauce, a flat white bread, and canned fruit cocktail. Montego knew when to leave. Over dinner, we comment on the beauty of the land, the steep pitch of the hills, the humidity and the heat. We talk of our photographic interests; Sharon photographed the children, Paul, the mountains; Saul, the landscape; and I, the architecture of thatch and sun-dried-brick homes; while Prudy stopped to observe each scene we found fascinating. Through the tent opening, I watch Tashi dish up rice and curry for Montego and the staff, who squat around the fire. I hear Nepali, Sherpa, and laughter.

That is where I want to be.

I look around the table. Our conversation is forced, conscious, cautious, as we check each other out. Over tea, Paul and Saul find common ground and talk technical about cameras, lenses, and film. Sharon and Prudy share tales of the children seen on the way. I interject in both conversations only long enough to be polite. I sit back.

Why did I come to Nepal? Why this journey? Escape? Partially. My lifestyle is comfortable. Boredom? In spite of continual crises, repetition reigns. Eat. Work. Sleep. I am burnt out. I want to rest my mind and work my body. I do not want to think. I want to be. I crave physically demanding days and aching muscles. I need to learn my body again, so I can reconnect my body to my mind, and rediscover my spirit.

Montego asks who wants to join him tonight at the *gompa*, the Buddhist temple next to our campsite. Sharon and I accept his invitation. The *gompa* is a twelve-foot-square (3.7 m) stone building with a corrugated metal roof and a wooden finial at its apex. With anticipation, I duck to enter and follow Montego, Sharon, Tashi, and Pema. Nima follows me. We squeeze onto a deep bench on one side of the room. How different from the stark simplicity of the Protestant churches of my childhood with their sanctuaries of blond pews, blue songbooks, white walls, white lilies, white candles, and white people enclosed in white clapboard with only the brilliance of stained glass windows to occupy a bored child's imagination. Even this smallest of temples is a feast for my senses.

A bright polychrome Buddha resides in each framed opening along the back wall. Sweet, spicy incense perfumes the air. Butter lamps glimmer and light an offering of fruit and grain. A Buddhist monk sits near me, an old *lama* wrapped in crimson with one shoulder and arm bare. His shaved head glistens as he leans over to prepare a simple altar laid out with ritual objects. The lama unwraps a saffron cloth from a rectangular package before him. As he carefully turns the pages, I realize it is a book of individual leaves of paper filled with graceful script. Prayers? I like their unbound freedom.

Two men from the village sit cross-legged on the floor. The youngest looks Tibetan, with a round face, high cheekbones, and dark eyes. He wears a blue tunic and shorts that show off his muscular thighs. He picks up a white conch shell, puts it to his lips, and blows. The conch shell's deep, sonorous sound pierces skin, muscle, bone, marrow. He has our attention. The other man, dressed in a dark suit, glasses, and traditional Nepalese *topi* hat, uses a crooked drumstick to tap a round, hairy, hide-covered drum that hangs from the ceiling. As the drumbeat grows deafening, the monk rings the brass bell held in one hand, shakes an ornate metal object in his other hand, and begins to chant. The two men join in. How I like their hypnotic chant, the incessant beat of the drum, the warmth of the room, and the animated, sun-wrinkled faces of the old men. What a counterpoint to the youthful glow of our Sherpa guides. I focus on each of them, except Nima, who sits cross-legged behind me, out of view, but not forgotten. I sense his presence, his restlessness, and his warmth.

How lucky to be in this room on this day on this trip. Energy invades me here. Not forceful, but subtle and soft, like the lingering smoke of juniper as it swirls over each of us, uniting those who come as witness. Mesmerized, but without comprehension, I can only let it seep in and wait for its effect. I shut my eyes, not because I am tired, but because a calm has come over me, a slowing down after the madness of my job, the preparations for this trip, and the long overseas flights to get here. From the vibrations in this room, I feel a minute realignment. A shift away from the past.

"Time to go," says Montego. "Tomorrow's an early start." I do not want to leave. I want to stay until the end. The Sherpas stay. I want to stay with the Sherpas. I am too uncertain to ask. Sharon and I follow Montego out.

Stars and a sliver of a moon illuminate the night sky. Starlight. Star bright. First … Which one? There is no first star, rather a sky crowded with them. I choose a bright star overhead and wish for a glorious trip and a new direction to my life. I nod in thanks. I crawl into my tent, undress, slip into a clean T-shirt, and slide into my sleeping bag. The night is warm, the chanting from the *gompa*, a murmur. I lie on my back and stare up at the tent dome above.

I know something has got to change. I am not middle-aged. How can I be? The puzzle pieces of my life do not assemble into a nice, comfortable picture of bliss, but rather dynamic chaos. I used to like my life, but my affection is waning for my stormy whirl of friends, cities, apartments, projects, clients, events, adventures, travels, travails, and boyfriends. Without distractions, Nepal will be a good place for me to focus on the future.

I fall asleep to the gentle percussion of banyan leaves, accompanied by crickets and a distant wooden flute.

The Himalaya play havoc with your plans.

—*Brian*

As WE LEAVE BHOTE ODAR on the second day of our trek, at 1,804 feet (550 m), the heat and humidity of the lowlands remains oppressive. I want to walk alone. The porters move out ahead of everyone and soon disappear. Montego and Tashi lead the rest of us. I follow them and soon outpace the others, but I maintain enough distance to discourage Montego or Tashi from waiting for me. I forget to watch my back. Tsuldim, one of our guides, follows closely and matches my pace. Like my shadow, if I stop, he stops. I try to relax. He only wants to help.

Tsuldim asks to carry my pack. I can carry it, I tell him. I need to get conditioned with it on. My daypack holds two water bottles, my fleece jacket, a journal, sunscreen, my camera, lenses and film, ChapStick, trail mix, and daily diversions like my yo-yo. It will grow heavier with added clothes and gear as we climb higher, confronting cooler weather and dramatically changing conditions. Too hot, Tsuldim tells me, as he again offers to carry it for me. I assure him I'm okay.

I pause to look at the election graffiti painted on the sides of houses, rocks, trees. In less than two months, on May 12, 1991, Nepal will hold its first democratic elections. With high illiteracy among its citizens, childlike images of a sun or a tree promote a political party. Tsuldim is tenacious in his desire to help me. *Pani?* Water? Tsuldim does not give up. I shake my head.

Tsuldim asks me how to say *gompa* in English, as I photograph a small temple. Temple. I slow it down for him. Tem–ple. He tries it, but p's do not form easily on the lips of Sherpas. At a water break, he asks me what *extravagant* means. I suspect he heard one of us use the word. I explain in simple English. At the next rest stop, Tsuldim tells me his clients are extravagant. They bring too many silly things to the mountain. His intelligence is impressive, but I crave quiet. I am still stressed out. Do Sherpas have a word for *stress*?

I find the second day of trekking difficult. I should have worked out more. As our trekking group leaves the dirt road for a trail, we gasp in unison at the magnificence of a panoramic view of the Annapurna mountain range, a skyline of white peaks shimmering in the early morning light. With views of Ngadi Chuli at 24,652 feet (7,514 m) and Himalchuli at 25,896 feet (7,893 m), we begin our ascent up steep rock steps, chinked to level and well trodden. This is not Los Angeles. There is no elevator or air conditioning. I ache. I sweat. I like it.

All morning among magnificent gorges and breathtaking vistas, we climb up and down steep rock steps, across a river, then back up steep rock steps, only to go down steep rock steps, then back across the river, and so on. Where the rock meets the river, the force of rushing water carves basalt into organic forms that look like the picked-clean bones of Mesozoic-era dinosaurs. Danger is everywhere, from the yellow trumpet flowers of datura, a sometimes-deadly hallucinogen used by Hindu *sadhus* as mystical sacrament, to the bushes with long thorns that line the riverbanks. I desire danger. I walk to the river's edge and step out onto a boulder. Water splashes around me.

The Sherpas run toward me. *Jiwaa!* Danger! They offer me a hand. Danger? They climb mountains! They should understand risk. Danger makes us feel alive.

We take photographs of the landscape, those who live here, and how they live: fried doughnuts hanging on a metal rod in a window, tempting a boy in blue; women in saris desirous of patterned fabrics held up by a traveling salesman for their consideration; and caravans of goats transporting goods in colorful leather bags. The people in this region are Brahmans, high-class Hindus who do not necessarily have wealth, and Kami, low-class blacksmiths, who are always poor. The Brahmans speak Nepali as their first language, unlike most other ethnic groups in Nepal. Many follow the concept of *jutho* and believe that the presence of a non-Brahman will pollute their home or food. Among both Brahmans and Kami, possessions are limited to basic needs, or less. All ages work. Without our photographs, we could never describe scenes so outside our imagination to others. Our cameras help us to see, and yet even with a wide-angle lens, our viewpoint is narrow.

I like the way a banyan tree hosts a village. At a dusty hilltop town of unpainted pine buildings with corrugated metal roofs, our group stops to rest in the shade of a banyan just as travelers have for centuries. A low wall encircles the base of the tree, so porters may back up to it and rest their loads without dropping their packs. Children play on the roots whose web entangles them, the rocks, and the earth. Old men crouch on top of the wall clad in shorts, shirts, and vests of light cotton, with rubber thongs on their feet and short cigarettes pinched between dirty fingers as they gossip. Under their community tree, I relish a moment out of the sun, which grows more intense as we climb higher.

The banyan and *peepul* trees are partners, married in wedding celebrations held by the villagers. It was under a *peepul*, or bodhi tree, in Bodh-gayā that the Buddha reached enlightenment, after meditating for forty-nine days. The banyan is the bodhi tree's male counterpart. As I sit below this banyan, the cool air improves my spirits. I relax and allow the rest of the day to flow over me like water over rocks.

Come afternoon, I find myself walking with the new Sherpa guide, Nima. He speaks in simple English often punctuated by Sherpa or Nepali or both when words stump him. Proud of his heritage, he tells me how the Sherpa, a mountain tribe from Mongolia, migrated to Kham, a historical region in eastern Tibet. *Sherpa*, or *Sharwa* in the Sherpa language, means "people of the East." After crossing the Himalaya, the Sherpa first settled in the Everest area, known today as the Solukhumbu district of Nepal, and so by proximity and acclimatization (my words), they became the guides and high-altitude porters of the first mountain expeditions, a tradition that continues today (my synopsis).

Nima fascinates me. His smile is eager and engaging. His luminous black eyes spill over with joy, and his button nose widens in proportion with his broad grin. His high cheekbones provide a welcome angle to his otherwise round face. His smooth, bronze complexion is flawless, but for the ridiculous tease of facial hair dusting his upper lip, as if to announce that he is no longer a boy, but a man. I want to tell him to shave it off, but do not. Instead, I wonder, How old is he?

I like to walk with Nima. I sense he wants to walk with me, for when Paul comes up and starts a conversation with him, he doesn't show the same desire to understand or speak English. Frustrated, Paul walks on, although it could have been that he noticed Sharon up ahead. I want to learn about Sherpas, but don't know what to ask. No doubt Nima is sick of the question, Have you climbed Everest? And how can I talk to him with my lungs bursting, my body overheating, and no visible end to these stairs? He'll just get impatient at my pace and race on ahead.

"Ugh! This heat. The humidity!" My sudden outburst surprises Nima. "Slow down."

I fall in behind Nima, who slows to pace me. It helps.

Men and this land have shaped each other over centuries. Whole mountainsides are terraced and planted with a spring-green carpet of rice. Locals navigate the edges of rice fields along footpaths that hold in water sent from rivers above to irrigate the paddies. Families must feel bound to a land they sculpted over generations. These people don't need to return to nature. They never left it. Primitive. Beautiful. Difficult. Subsistence living. They work the land, store what they need, and trade their surplus. I see no other opportunities in these foothills.

I ask Nima if we can stop to rest. Except for Sharon and Paul, the others are behind us. The sun's heat exhausts me, burns me. Unlike in Southern California, there is no marine layer to soften the sun's glare and lessen its heat. I seek shade. Nima and I stand out of the sun below a pine denuded of its lower branches. Mmmm—nice. I do not cool.

Nima stands tall for a Sherpa, taller than my five feet eight inches (1.7 m). His clothes hang off his narrow shoulders like wet laundry on a line. He could use a good tailor, even though his lean physique forgives his clothes. I like that word, *lean*. Lean looks. Lean toward. Lean on. A man should conjure up the word *lean*. Funny how Nima leans. He never stands fully upright. Instead, his long torso tilts forward over his short legs, whether he is on steep hills or flat land, load or no load. Nima looks like he is either continuously burdened by a load, or diving headfirst into the future.

As we descend single file from a village, we are caught behind a caravan of horses. The steep mountainside makes progress slow. Nima's crude English makes conversation exhausting, but I try my best. He wants to know if I come from a big family. I do. Four sisters. Two brothers. Two parents. Nine. I count them off on my fingers, oldest to youngest. Father. Mother. Me. Caryn, my twin sister. Tom. Jeanne. Gary. Cinda. Alison. He acts surprised.

And your family, Nima?

Four sisters, he begins, plus three brothers and two parents. Ten. Nima names them as he counts them off on his finger joints. Pala. Mama. Ang Chokpa, Mingma Futi, his two half-sisters. Tshiring Tendi. Nima himself. Pasang Gyalgen. Nima Nuru. His two younger sisters, Fumu and Kandu.

Another Nima? I ask. Nima tells me how the Sherpa name their children after the *za*, the day of the week that they are born on.

We were both born on Sunday, says Nima. *Nyima* means "sun."

I ask Nima-number-one his age. Twenty-eight, he tells me. Year of the Rabbit. You? he asks. Thirty-eight. Nima counts his finger joints again. Ah. Year of the Dragon. Eleven years difference.

I correct him: Ten years.

No, Nima tells me. Different than Westerners. We count from the beginning.

His questions continue. Where do I live? In Redondo Beach, California. He approves. He's seen the movies. Do I like Nepal? I tell him it is a beautiful country with friendly people. Like America? he asks. Nepal has big mountains; America has big cities.

"All my life I dreamed of going to your wonderful country of America," says Nima. I want to know why. "I want a more interesting life."

I think he has the most interesting life I have ever known. He tells me that the king is Vishnu, the snake god, and that Nepal is a Hindu country. Few opportunities are provided for its Buddhist citizens, such as the Sherpas. Nima has applied for a visa to the United States. He expects to hear soon.

Nima radiates happiness, and hope. I feel his warmth. I wonder: What is it with this man? Can his endless contentment be real?

"Nima, you smile constantly. Why?"

"Why be sad? You make people smile, good *karma*. Make angry, bad *karma*. That is the Sherpa way." When I tell Nima that I can help him learn English, if he helps me practice good karma, I get a reaction bordering on disdain.

"No practice! Only good or bad. Be good." I nod, embarrassed.

Once the trail widens, I fall back to walk next to Nima to make conversation easier, only to have him fall back behind me. I drop back. He falls behind. I am confused. Does he do this in deference to me, or out of habit from traveling on narrow trails? Shadow or guide is the only choices he gives me, never side by side, as companions.

The others in our group have gone on. Nima and I do not hurry to catch up. As we climb higher, the rice paddies disappear, the forest thickens, and the trail becomes more obscure. Nima steps ahead to lead me through a slide of boulders. At a narrow pass, he shouts to Pema, and I watch them leap off the ridge in a straight-down fury of a race toward a house far below. Spirited Pema, unfairly burdened by his *doko* of cooking supplies, stumbles more than once, while Nima, with his partially filled backpack, soars over rocks and foliage sure as a hawk diving for prey.

It looks to me like Nima needs no trail to know where he is going.

I wish I were as sure of my way. When I arrive at the bottom of the hill, Pema has gone on. Nima has not.

Do you climb mountains? I ask, sure that he must, after his last display of agility. Many peaks, he tells me. Everest? I have to ask. Yes, but not to the top. Their summit team reached the top, he says. The next day, when he went up, he climbed past the last camp, but a blizzard forced them down. I ask Nima when he is going back to Everest. He doesn't answer. Instead, he tells me about a well-funded five-month Japanese expedition up K2 from the China side in 1990. Nima worked as a high-altitude porter. Before heading to the north base camp of K2 in a remote part of Xinjiang province in China, the Sherpa guides and porters toured Hong Kong, Beijing, and Urumchi. Nima wants to know how these cities compare to those in the United States. I explain how New York City has tall buildings, like Hong Kong, but with no night market, or street closures on Sundays so Filipino maids may picnic, or old men who walk caged birds.

"Birds should not be in cages," says Nima. I agree, and then ask him to tell me more about K2.

This was a new route from the China side, says Nima. As they were readying the summit ascent, an avalanche swept through the high camp and injured many team members. Luckily, Nima had gone down to base camp earlier that day, so he missed getting caught in it. He woke up that night to such frightful thunder that he thought the world had ended. The avalanche did not hit the lower camp, so everyone there searched in the dark for their teammates. They found the first summit team blown far out of the path of the avalanche by its advance winds and dug them out. Many people were injured, but no one died. Their first summit team did reach the top several weeks later, but as part of the second summit team, Nima was forced to descend just short of the summit when another storm hit.

I want to live a long life, Nima tells me. After K2, he gave up climbing, forfeiting his position on an upcoming Everest climb to his cousin Dawa. Now Nima wishes he had gone instead. Dawa died in an avalanche on that climb. He left a wife and a son. Nima tells me all this with a smile. I am perplexed. Is his smile a mask?

"I am responsible," says Nima. "I should have gone."

Nima squats and gathers stones. I wait and I watch him place one rock on top of the next. With focused intention, he finds their balance. As his cupped hands release the last stone, his lips move. The wind takes his words. Nima rejoins me and says the cairn, or *theu*, is for Dawa, his cousin. I thought rock cairns along the path were only trail markers. His stones lay a foundation for prayer.

Concerned for his cousin's son, Nima wants to send the boy to school in Kathmandu. It would be a nice thing to do in Dawa's memory, I tell him, but Dawa's death is not your fault. Knowing I cannot relieve his guilt or ease his sadness, I encourage his kindness.

"If I can do one good thing for the boy," says Nima, "my heart will feel so proud." He stops. "Life changed. Everything about Sherpa life changed once foreigners came to the Solukhumbu." The edge in his voice surprises me. "We work for tourists. For mountain climbers. But Sherpas die! Too many Sherpas die in the mountains." Awkwardness comes over us as we walk. Does he resent me?

Nima and I do not hurry. We follow a ridgeline trail with views of the Annapurnas. I catch a distant view of our campsite on the other side of the river. I see Paul with his red pack cross the bridge. Our tents have been erected. No doubt Tashi and Pema have set up the kitchen and prepared tea. Nima tells me how, after the climb up K2, his expedition team came out by way of Pakistan along the Afghanistan border. I mention that I am on a trip around the world. Bhutan is next, and then my sister Jeanne's wedding in Prague, followed by the Alps and Scandinavia.

"I'm coming to the United States to visit my friend Jules in Portland," says Nima. "Then, to California to visit you." I flinch. He only wants a free place to stay.

Nima walks behind me along a well-worn trail as we near Besi Sahar and our campsite. He counts in English to demonstrate his prowess with the language. I hear sixteen, then seventeen. I stop and turn to speak to Nima—

I will marry a Sherpa. I will marry Nima Gyalgen Sherpa.

fire: The Himalaya play havoc with your plans.

I know this with a certainty like none I have ever experienced. It burns. Find my center. Touch it. Yes, right there. Feel how hot it is? Ouch! It burns. Twelve hours ago, we met. We walked together for two hours. What just happened? Must be the thin air. I cannot breathe. I am at only 2,690 feet (820 m) and I cannot breathe!

From the core of my being, my heart chakra, I feel him burn into me. *I will marry you.* Marry a Sherpa. A mountain-climbing guide. My whole being radiates warmth and I wallow in it for what feels like eons, yet exists but for a second.

No. No. No. No. No. Brain, where are you? That did not happen. I did not think that. I did not feel that. I cannot imagine that. Not that. Not him. Not ever!

This is unimaginable. One, he's Sherpa. Two, he's geographically undesirable. Three, he barely speaks English. Four, just look at him, so dirty and disheveled. Five, he's impossibly poor. That can't be the thunderbolt they talk about. Food poisoning? Himalayan juju? An aphrodisiac? Nima and me? A Sherpa and a city woman? Ha!

Breathe deep. Breathe. Breathe. Breathe. Damn it! This is ridiculous. Funny though, you have to admit. Outrageously funny. Sitcom funny. Roll 'em.

Scene opens with Caryl's personal Sherpa carrying her shopping bags down Rodeo Drive. Cut! They would never let him in the stores. Snobs. They barely let me in.

Scene opens with Caryl's Sherpa setting up her beach chair and umbrella. Cut! He's probably never seen the ocean, and is afraid of water and water nymphs in bikinis.

Scene opens with Caryl's Sherpa carrying her backpack while they hike Joshua Tree. Keep rolling. I like that. He finds the cactus weird, but so did I at first. You have to grow up with a thing, or live with it awhile, to accept it.

I have to admit, Nima is the most sanguine man I have ever met. Radiant when he smiles, and even when he does not. He reminds me of an acorn, with brown skin capped by thick black hair. Even has the sagacity of an old oak. And his strength. It does a middle-aged woman good to watch that mountain man work.

But—how would he fit into my life in Los Angeles? Or could I give up the comforts of my life to live in Nepal? Trade my kitchen for a wood-burning stove, no refrigeration, and a vegetable garden? Imagine, no car! Only goatherds or yak packs to jam up traffic. No medical insurance. No doctors. Only shamans. It's downright primitive. So Third World. The income of one top movie star exceeds the GNP of Nepal! Poverty prevails. My gasoline bill for one month equals a family's average annual income! I work with executives of Fortune 500 companies. Attorneys. Studio people. I do lunch! At The Ivy.

This could never work.

What would my friends say? My family would never believe it. I don't believe it. No. No. No. No. No. Impossible. Unworkable. I'm a project manager, for heaven's sake. I know the risks one can take and those one should not. I strategize. I plan. I guide. I execute. Execute this—this—this—whatever it is. This absurdity! Kill it!

I never needed a mountain to climb more. Great! A good sweat is coming up. I'll sweat him out. Make him disappear. Finally.

Where did he go? Funny how he got so quiet right after I felt that—that—whatever that was. This is all too fast! Too foreign! Too impossible!

This climb helps. Exhale it out. Stomp it out. Rise above it. Conquer it.

There he is. What grace.

Everything has changed. I feel unsteady. While I can barely lift my feet, Nima passes me as we approach the village of Besi Sahar near our camp. I look straight ahead and wait for my brain to catch up with my heart. I slip on the trail. I catch myself. I resent my emotional lapse. I am perplexed by my thoughts of that Sherpa. So powerful. Strange, really. I am drained, exhausted by the day and my emotions. I need to pay attention. I focus on my destination. I fell too far today already, and now, I have no one to save me.

Our campsite is open, exposed, and vulnerable, like me. I head straight for my tent. I want to forget, so busy myself arranging my belongings for the night. After Pema brings me a large aluminum bowl of warm water, I scrub hard to wash away those crazy thoughts of Nima. I put on clean clothes. I try to nap. Marry a Sherpa? It was only a dream. Nothing more. I never remember my dreams.

To avoid my thoughts, I get up and go out. I am lucky; the campsite is crowded. After I meet Brian and his friends from Boston, all trekkers, they invite me to join them for drinks in town back at Besi Sahar. At café tables below Cinzano umbrellas outside a restaurant that caters to passing foreigners, we order Star beers. In Dumre, a Coke cost four rupees, I comment, but here they charge fifteen. Brian reminds me that porters in flip-flops carry bottled soda and beer in stacked wood crates six or seven high on their back up these mountains. Near the pass, they charge thirty-five.

Brian's group just came down from Thorung La, not because they are doing the Annapurna Circuit in reverse, but because snow had closed the pass. They waited several days, a trekker named Jennifer tells me, but the snow never stopped. Another man, Ray, adds that the snow cleared up the day after they came back down. I look up at the mountains ahead. The weather today is clear. I pray we will get across.

"The Himalaya play havoc with your plans," says Brian, who suggests I get used to it. Take it one day at a time, says Brian, and the journey will be fascinating no matter what. The villages, the people, and the landscape are why he travels. Brian sounds like a Sherpa. Is it catching? My new friends wish me luck. Thorung La or bust! We click our brown bottles and down warm beer with an apple pie chaser.

After spoiling my dinner at the café, I eat little and retire early to write in my journal. It is an effort to record all I see and experience each day in a land as exotic as Nepal. Tonight I write about my second day of trekking, the diversity of the villages, the people, my trekking group, the landscape, the flowers, the stones, my new friends from Boston, and the food, until I tire and turn off my headlamp. I lie there and listen to the river. And then I hear the quiet conversation of the Sherpas.

Nima. He never came to mind while I wrote. How could I have forgotten him? One moment, thunderstruck, and a few hours later, forgotten. Strange, like a dream. Powerful, like an obsession. Lustful, like a longing. Apparitions of a husband? No way!

We all ignore warning. I lie still, assessing Nima. Attractive. Kind. Happy. I review my own feelings. Never have I felt such an emotional certainty. A *fait accompli*. A curse. A fate. A destiny. A path. A way. A mountain. A dream. A cause. An effect. A reaction. A hopelessness. And a hope.

I did not allow my feelings for Nima to surface in black and white on the page. However, like black and white, we are counterpoints. A compass and a magnet. One seeks direction. One guides the way. I did not write a word about him. I did not even write his name. Tonight, my subconscious action was to take no action. Tomorrow, the pull of the inevitable may be harder to resist.

Om Mani Padme Hum.

—Tibetan mantra

AFTER BREAKFAST, MONTEGO TELLS US that Nima will be working with the porters, who need to stay near us, for they carry our tents and duffels. Most porters reside in the lowlands; they do not like altitude, and climb mountains only to support their families. I look across the campsite to see Nima arrange a load on a porter girl. I feel jealous.

Our porter girls are Tamang, from a clan that migrated from western Tibet to the Kathmandu Valley. I can tell them apart by the way they dress, each in a green, a red, or a blue sari. All wear flip-flops on their feet and scarves over their braided hair. Shy, they avert their eyes when Sharon tries to photograph them. Their loads are carried from a tumpline on their forehead. Two-thirds of her height, the load tips a diminutive five-foot (1.5 m) girl backward. I notice they lean forward to compensate for their load. Red, who protects her back with a blanket, carries a four-foot (1.2 m) metal cage of thirty dozen stacked eggs. Green and Blue each carry two duffels bound together and stuffed into a *doko*, a triangular bamboo basket. Each carries a small bag of *tsampa*, or roasted barley flour, on top.

Our group moves in different configurations as we seek out those who fit our moods. Saul and Prudy walk on ahead with each other, their pants tucked into their socks to avoid leeches that reach out from leaves when they sense body heat, and then attach to you. The Sherpas tell me that they sprinkle the leeches with salt or hot pepper to remove them. Paul, infatuated with Sharon, follows her sprightly step, but struggles to keep up. I walk with our *sirdar*, Dorje, a middle-aged man who likes to tell stories. Montego moves back and forth between us.

As we climb higher, the houses are made of stone. Between laundry hung to dry, a sign before a lodge reads, *"Welcome for All, Hotel Snow and Lodge, Nice Food Available, Please let me know, What can I help For You."* Just off the trail before a cluster of houses, a tailor seated at his sewing machine repairs a pair of pants. At the next village, a balance scale large enough to weigh a man hangs from a log frame. A passing mule train raises dust. Porters pass us with steel I beams, mountainous blocks of foam, and fresh-cut lumber planks so heavy I cannot lift one. As we walk, Dorje sings a happy song. It's about a butterfly, he tells me. I remember the wish-fulfilling tree in Hong Kong and wonder—Did mine land in Nepal?

At our lunch stop above a stream, we sit on sun-warmed rocks. The guides and porters are there, and so is Nima. He ignores me. I am glad. I wander off to admire the lush greenery of this glade, where a waterfall drops to a river bordered by moss-covered rocks that shimmer in the sunlight and fields of upturned soil ready for spring planting. Away from the others, I hear only water, bees, and my breath.

At the top of a long climb, our group crests a hilltop, although any-where else, I would have called it a mountain. Perched on the summit at 4,298 feet (1,310 m), the village of Bahundanda, or "Brahman Hill," is a sprinkling of ramshackle shops and homes, often one and the same. Our group slides onto benches that line the wood deck of a tea shop, whose half-open Dutch door serves as the café counter. Beyond the interior's dim light, a woman stands before a shelf that displays her meager wares: a dozen cans of soda pop, scores of cigarettes, six wrapped rolls of coconut cookies, three pocket packs of tissue, one unwrapped roll of pink toilet paper, and two Lux soaps, plus a partial box of Tiger Balm ointment tins on the counter. Entrepreneurs like this woman make up a majority of

Nepal's economy. Her children, who speak English, take our orders. The proprietress's husband serves.

Up here, the thick humid air of the low hills veils the Annapurna Range. I can only imagine the grandeur of the view on a clear day. After a few complaints about the heat, everyone is silent. Although I look forward to the mountains and cooler temperatures, I cannot envisage climbing in thin air. Here, the air is thick, and I struggle.

Suddenly I see, rising like the sun, spoons, ladles, graters, wire strainers, aluminum pots, pans, colanders, and copper vessels appear above the edge of the hill. A net captures the four-foot-high (1.2 m) overflow of metal dishware in the *doko*. Finally, the *topi*-topped head of a traveling salesman appears, then his face, his torso, his legs, and his flip-flopped feet, all in the slow motion of one who carries the kitchenware for an entire village on his back, and so measures each step.

The salesman stops in the center of town, which is nothing more than a dusty patch of dirt. After setting down his *doko*, the young man unties the net, removes a calico cloth, and spreads it on the ground. With languid precision, he lays out his wares, "stocking" himself into the center. The town gathers. The bartering begins. Like America's Fuller Brush men to the stay-at-home women of the fifties, this salesman diverts the villagers from their mundane tasks with stories, gossip, and goods. I fall for him like everyone else in the village.

Do you think he has small tea strainers? I ask Nima, who stands with the porter girls and looks over the salesman's wares. Nima talks to the young man, who hands me two. I select one and Nima negotiates the purchase. Twenty-five rupees is a good price, I tell him. I think forty cents is a steal. Nima tells me I paid too much. He shakes his head and leaves with the girls. I put the tea strainer in my pack and follow. I slow down to enjoy the view and increase the distance between us. I want to forget about Nima. Yesterday was an illusion.

Vistas expand a person. I feel myself open to match the landscape that extends out before me, as hills rise up in their struggle to become mountains. I am a hill in training. I stretch to heights never before imagined. There is an energy here that fills me, and takes over body and mind. I like the challenge, but give myself over to exhaustion. Montego was right. The third day is the hardest.

A chill overcomes the day as we drop far below Bahundanda. Our wilderness campsite lies in shadow next to a river that has cut its way through rock. The sun disappears long before we arrive. Dinner passes almost without conversation. We retire early. So do the Sherpas. In spite of the cold, I like evenings in my tent. My large duffel supports my back as I sit up to write in my journal, warm in my fleece jacket and sleeping bag. The headlamp reflects off the pale blue dome of my tent. I hear the river. I hear my pen scratch paper. I hear my mind. I start to listen.

I wake up before the dawn and walk to the river in the diminishing darkness. I splash cold water on my face. I bathe as best as I can with clothes on. The water is cold. The morning is warm. My body moderates them.

I am restless. I want to move, be in motion, go somewhere. I want to learn, discover, uncover. I move. I leap from boulder to boulder. I travel over the water. The water moves. Never still, always changing, destination bound. Like water that quenches parched lips or baptizes a baby, I seek a purpose. I want to learn how to slip past boulders without worry, how to stay the course, how to never look back. I want to be like water.

I am restless. I sit on a stone cross-legged and take in slow breaths, out, in, out, in. I hold. Hold. Out. In. Hold. Out. In. Hold. I sit.

Mind. Stone quiet. Body. Stone still. Spirit. Like water.

The river embraces my stone and me. Stone rises. I float. Stone floats. I have no foundation. Stone is mind, body, and I. I give over. Water, my spirit, is guide.

I seek freedom. Freedom to be me, so I may travel like water and find my way. I am afraid. I have no control. I hang on tight and pray, as my stone and I spin into currents toward the unknown.

Today I walk with Tashi, our cook, who speaks good English. I tell him how exotic I find the food of Nepal. He asks about food in America. At a rest stop, he shows me the powders and seeds he uses, but we are unable to translate their names; many remain a mystery. As we climb up from the river in a light rain, a landscape of bamboo-covered hillsides with trees hiding orchids gives way to forests of fir among rhododendrons in bloom. Each step requires constant vigilance. I dodge cow pies, yak pies, horse pies, goat pies, dog pies, pies enough to open a bakery, but here where wood is scarce, the locals bake with these pies instead! Before us, a mother and her children fill a *doko* of dung. They will take it home and hand-splat each patty onto a sun-facing stone wall to dry. *Voila!* Organic fuel. No fuss. No muss. Just peel off, pop in the oven, and bring to full flame. We don't cook with dung in America, I tell Tashi.

At these higher elevations, the locals are either Gurungs, an ancient clan from Tibet; recently settled Tibetan refugees; or Brahmans. Pine forests and deep gorges shade the trail. The stone houses have shake roofs held in place by river rocks. Strings of prayer flags, or *lungdar*, are printed with a wind-horse that carries the prayers and are strung between trees in lines of blue, white, red, green, and yellow. Other prayer flags fly from tall poles. Montego makes sure we pass with the small white *chörten* on our right. Square at the base, a round dome rests above, and a square turret and spire finish it off. *Mani* stones are rocks of all sizes carved with prayers and set to rest at the base of the *chörten* so they may emanate blessings to all who pass. I like the generous spirit of the Nepalese, I tell Sharon. I feel welcome here.

All afternoon, we follow the trail high above the river. I watch clouds play hide-and-seek with the mountains. Near the village of Chyamje at 4,692 feet (1,430 m), we camp along the Marsyandi River, crowded with other groups from around the world. Foreigners double the population of a village each evening during spring and fall trekking seasons. The Sherpas, who all know each other, gather at the smoke-filled cookhouse to catch up on the news. Nima is not among them. No matter. I am distracted by a group of Italian men who bathe at the central water tap, stripped to their skivvies or less, oblivious to local customs of modesty. After the heat and road dust of the day, I too desire a bath. The swift river is not safe; the aluminum bowl of water Pema brings is too small. I have seen local

47

women bathe discreetly at the village's central water spigot. Can I?

After the Italians leave, I make my way to the village's water source that runs constantly. I am dressed in a T-shirt, skirt, and flip-flops. I place my soap and shampoo on a stone ledge. I cup my hands and splash my face with cold water. I plunge my head under the tap. I hear laughter. I shampoo with eyes closed and rinse in bone chilling water. I wet and soap a bandana. I slide my hand up under my T-shirt to wash breasts, back, torso. A shudder brings goose bumps and the realization that I have gained a physical confidence. With this bath, I celebrate my body. I wash shoulders, arms, feet. I reach under my skirt to wash stomach, thighs, knees. I feel refreshed, purified by water that pours forth. I turn back to face a group of smiling Italians. I bow. Perhaps the tall one could help me forget about Nima.

Like water, the best trails respect the topography and find the path of least resistance. Each day as we gain altitude, I notice a change in the vegetation, architecture, and people. Each elevation range tells a new story, like the mountain's layers of rock. The topography of Nepal outrivals anywhere else for diversity—a new chapter every 500 feet (152 m) or less—and follows the way of water as it falls 29,029 feet (8,848 m) from the top of Mount Everest to India at sea level. In between, there are frequent diversions. I read the river backward as we trek up toward the source of Asia's water.

I am thankful for the companionship of others as we climb. Conversation helps me forget my discomforts, and Nima, who is again with the porters. Although my legs have become stronger, my lungs still ache as I climb. I slow down to allow Paul to catch up with me. As a new college graduate, Paul can go anywhere, do anything, be anybody. But who? He talks to discover the answer. Chemical engineer? Paul wants to invent something and get rich like many in Silicon Valley. The next Galen Rowell? Paul wants to photograph the world. He loves cameras, has his eye on a Hasselblad. I say nothing to discourage his dreams.

After hiking this morning through canyons and forests in the shade, our group appreciates the sun's warmth when we reach the sunlit meadow at Tal. The chicken that Pema bought this morning clucks as we near. Orange tarps have been laid out to sit on. Pema and Tashi cook lunch. After a hot meal, our group naps with our backpacks as pillows; Sherpas sleep in the meadow; porters curl up on warm rocks; ravens rest in trees. When the sun dips into afternoon, we move on. No one passes us on the trail as we continue up. The water doesn't rest, but it doesn't hurry here either. Neither do the insects who gather our crumbs. Otherwise, we are alone in this monumental landscape, and I am living a dream.

We hike a ridge above the river all afternoon, and then descend and cross to our camp on the west bank, far away from any village or other trekking group campsite. Before us, the broad face of Annapurna II stands tall at 26,040 feet (7,937 m), only emphasizing the distance we have yet to travel. Enlivened by higher altitude, our Sherpas build a bonfire after dinner. Dorje begins to sing. Sherpa voices gather and rise like the flames, until they echo off the mountains that surround us. More like a chant, their repetitious songs have more beat than melody. I am mesmerized. Swayed by the music, one by one the Sherpas begin to dance, arm in arm behind the fire as they stomp their feet in a pattern that I think I have figured out, just as they change it. As a log explodes, I follow the rise of sparks. The moon is not yet up. In the darkness, I see the Milky Way. I remember skies like this as a child, when I felt safe in darkness. Living in the city, I have forgotten what the night sky looks like.

Go dance, says Montego. With the livelier beat of their next song, joy shines on the faces of the Sherpas. I cannot resist. Neither can Sharon. Their dance line breaks, and we hook arms in unity. Linked together, we move as one, stomping out percussive rhythms as the Sherpas chant their song. I watch their feet and try to follow. I fail and fake it. No one cares. We dance before the fire. Everyone joins in but the porters, who do not know Sherpa dances, and Montego, Saul, and Prudy, who prefer to watch. Paul lumbers forward, back, and steps on toes. I move back when the line moves forward. Sharon dances with grace. At the end of the line is Nima, more self-conscious than the other Sherpas. As if forecasting our group's successful summit, the moon appears to cast our shadows up to the mountain's snowy peak. Thorung La or bust! I hope the days ahead are as easy.

Early the next morning, our group reaches Dharapani at 6,201 feet (1,890 m). We enter the village through a square stone arch, or *kani*, topped by three towers painted red, white, and black: a *kani* both marks the entrance to a village and reminds those who pass of their spirituality. Tibetans reside in this area. A whitewashed stone wall at shoulder height leads toward the *gompa*. Travelers going our way walk to the left of it, while those coming down the mountain walk on the right. A Tibetan ahead of me reaches out to the wall and flicks his right hand to spin prayer wheels, while his left hand snaps a stick to keep his three *zopkyok* moving forward. A *zopkyok* is a cross between a cow or bull and a yak or *nak*, and cannot reproduce. Stocky, with a thick brown coat and small horns, they adapt well to the mid elevations. The prayer wall holds copper wheels with prayers in raised relief, and an occasional replacement wheel fashioned from a vegetable oil can. To maximize one's effort, a paper roll printed with thousands of prayers is placed within each wheel. Blessings fly out as the Tibetan spins them. I am not a Buddhist. If I turn these wheels, do I too release prayers?

At a small building adjacent to the *gompa*, we squeeze in around a prayer wheel that almost fills the room. Does its size affect the power of its prayer? We line up behind Montego, grab the hip-high wood rail of the wheel, and walk clockwise three times in a communal spin for the planet. Between faded images of a curtain and lotus petals, the chromatic Tibetan script encircling the wheel is the same mantra or prayer that the old people say as they finger their prayer beads, Montego tells us above the squeak of the wheel's gears. *Om Mani Padme Hum. Om Mani Padme Hum. Om Mani Padme Hum.*

The stone *gompa* is a larger building than the cozy chapel of Bhote Odar. A cupola, with eyes looking out in all four directions, tops the metal roof above ornately carved wood-frame windows and doors. A wall of small niches holds prayer books, wrapped in red cloth. The altar is comprised of ornately painted niches, and centered within sits a blue-haired gold Buddha swaddled like a mummy with his riches. Did the Buddha ever dress in silk brocades after he left the luxury of his kingdom behind? Who are all these gods? So fierce. Others kind. Some women! I like this religion.

A balance of effort and reward keeps us moving deeper into the valley. After following a wide mule track down, we cross a ridge and turn west toward the upper region of the Marsyandi River valley, known here as the Manang Valley. As the rock-strewn path narrows, it becomes difficult to walk. The fir forests beyond the trail look impenetrable. The way becomes steeper. Halfway up, where red rhododendrons spill out of tin cans before a simple wood teahouse, we stop. The pine building, enclosed on three sides, opens to the trailside. In the center of the dirt floor, before a firepit, a young Tibetan couple warms chai and fries potatoes for our crew, who squat at the fire. Nima is among them. Our eyes connect. I look away. I seek safety among my fellow trekkers outside on the bench. We order black tea. Prudy comments how this teahouse is a pleasant surprise. Sharon wishes that there were more of them. I wish that I had not met Nima.

It rains on and off, but dressed in my rainproof pants, coat, and hat, I am lucky. Many people we see along the way are Tibetan refugees who have settled in Nepal or are working their way through. The local families are Buddhist and share what they have with the Tibetans, until they move on to Kathmandu or to Dharamsala in India or stay where they were first welcomed. I cannot imagine their hardships.

As I crest a ridge, the wide upper Manang Valley opens up before me. Snow-covered peaks fill the horizon. I am surrounded by mountains: Annapurna II, III, and IV, Gangapurna, Tilicho Peak, Tarke Kang, Chulu West, Chulu East, and Pisang Peak, to name but a few. I love the freedom in these wide-open spaces, where nothing grows tall, and vistas take me into distant lands. The clear air intoxicates me. The altitude makes me giddy. I laugh at everything. The Sherpas love it! The pine forests disappear as we trek toward the arid lands of the Himalaya rain shadow near Tibet. Across a broad valley lies the pass at Thorung La. I pray for clear skies and no snow. I am closing in on the Himalaya, the cool air invigorates me, and I feel strong.

I stop to watch two young Tibetan girls comb tangles from each other's long black hair. They part it, plait it, and add red barrettes at the ends. I stand beside the stone wall that marks their yard, but they take no notice of me. Pride. Shame. Shyness. I cannot tell. Each carries a toddler wrapped in a fabric sling on her back. While their tattered, unmatched clothes emphasize their poverty, their neatness suggests a pride.

Our group enters Chame late in the day, soaked by an afternoon downpour. Montego has procured rooms at a lodge, so we can dry our clothes and get a good night's sleep. We are grateful. Over dinner, Sharon asks how the 8,600-foot (2,621 m) altitude affects everyone physically. I have to drink more water to avoid headaches, I say. The dry air sucks all moisture from my skin, Prudy comments. Bronze-toned Paul likes the increased heat from the sun, but fair-skinned Saul has to slather on more sunscreen. None of us like the rain.

I am relearning to honor the night. While the lodge has electricity, it works for only a couple of hours a day, and the light is too feeble to read by. The darkness is absolute. As no wind can reach us, the air is as still as ice, and as cold, when it seeps between cracks. After dinner, I go to bed, happy to crawl into my sleeping bag. I lie with eyes open and see only blackness. Black is peace. A restful lack of color. No wonder we wear it to funerals. Rest in peace. Rest in black. In blackness.

After dinner, Pema filled my two water bottles with hot water. I snuggle close to warm Nalgene, one on my back, the other against my chest. I feel lonely. As much as I delight in this journey alone, sometimes I'd like a companion.

By morning, snow frosts the dark canyon walls above Chame, but we walk toward bright skies and snow-covered peaks. It's our seventh day on the trek, and the mountains before us have grown as we approached them. I stop to photograph craggy-faced Gangapurna, at 24,455 feet (7,454 m), its sharp peak pierces a passing cloud. Winds pull the cloud shape long, until it breaks free and begins to bunch up again in blue sky, readying itself to play with another peak.

The altitude is more noticeable today. My chest aches as we climb. The forests are sparse from both altitude and deforestation, since wood is cut for cooking and heating at a rate no longer sustainable. I look down to the river—boulders from high up the mountains have traveled on the force of water from snowmelt and summer monsoons to rest along the riverbed. In the rain shadow of the Himalaya, the land is rocky and harsh, like the life of those who live here. In the serenity of this landscape, I want to walk alone. I have almost forgotten Los Angeles: the traffic, the millions of people, the disappointment of my project and my relationships. In these mountains, my past fades to a dull memory. I like the loss.

Across the broad valley, orchards of apple and cherry trees in bloom explode from a landscape of gray stones, as a testament to the locals' inge- nuity and hard work. Orange tarps are laid out for our lunch break. Pema cooks. Porters nap. Sherpas sit in a circle and talk. The trekking compa- nies encourage a separation between trekkers and staff, and I don't like it. What I do like is our nomadic life on trek. I find it exciting to stop in a different place every day for lunch, and to camp. The Manangi people who live here are partially nomadic, working as traders between Tibet, Nepal, and India. Our Sherpa guides trek for weeks at a time with new people to new places, or sometimes with repeat clients to familiar places, always moving. Everyone in Nepal follows the water. I am curious how the Sherpas, who are gone for long periods of time on treks and climbs, maintain community. What kind of relationships do they have with their spouses, children, and relations who do not travel with them? I sense a restless nature in our Sherpas, as if nomad is in their blood. While I love to travel, I like the sedentary comfort of my home. Could a Sherpa? Dorje, whom I walk with the rest of the day, provides insight. Does he like to go on trek or be home? I like to be home, he says, just not too long. He goes home for festivals, during the summer monsoon, and when he has no work. He laughs and says he prefers to go places, be with friends.

The Manangis who populate this region are successful traders and herders who practice Tibetan Buddhism. We pass *chörtens* built of stone and painted white, ochre, and burnt sienna, topped with prayer flags, and surrounded by *mani* stones. We stop to rest at one. My finger traces a prayer to acknowledge the effort made to create this blessing. Generations of rain and wind have removed the stones' sharp edges. A patina of gray-green or rust-colored lichen accents other prayers. In these wide-open lands, power lines from a hydroelectric station and a prayer wheel wall lead to the vanishing point of Pisang and our campsite. A study in grays, Pisang is a village of stone houses set among glacial rocks. In spite of the austerity of the landscape, this must be a wealthy town, for each prayer wheel niche is unique, carved in wood and painted with clouds, leaves, and sacred geometries. I take no chance and turn all one hundred and eight copper wheels. *Om Mani Padme Hum.*

Montego leads us from our camp in lower Pisang at 10,466 feet (3,190 m) to upper Pisang and the *gompa* that rises out of rock. An elderly caretaker unlocks and opens the entry door. We gasp in unison. Illuminated by the dying light of day, two skulls and an angry red face watch us enter. Two white skull masks grin wide to show us big teeth and red gums below black nose holes and sunken, bloodshot eyes. Eyes bulge out below thick eyebrows on the center, red-faced figure with fangs bared above a black beard. Take heed. Not everyone who enters does.

As two English men follow us in, one of them comments on the items he'd like to acquire. These religious objects of veneration are not for sale. To these men, I sense they are collectibles, or bounty. While I tour the rest of the temple, I watch them. So does Montego. And they watch us. As they examine the artifacts, they whisper to each other. They do not hurry. I look at the same artifacts with a different intention. I focus on the interiors of the *gompa* in the fading light. The ornate ceiling rises up in multiple layers of carved wood painted like a *mandala*. Prayer books line one wall in red niches. *Thangkas* hang from beams, the religious paintings covered by silk and framed by faded brocade panels. I don't peek at the paintings like the two men do, even though I want to. *Thangkas* are sacred, created by monks according to Tibetan Buddhist teachings. A large drum painted with clouds hangs near an altar crowded with statues of the Buddha and *bodhisattvas* in niches. With the sun down, the temple interior grows dark, and the caretaker motions for us to exit. The two men approach the caretaker in an attempt to negotiate. The tall treasure hunter leans over the old caretaker, who refuses all offers. They leave empty handed, but on their way out, I hear them mention *thangkas*. The treasures of village temples are being sold off out of greed or necessity, or objects are simply stolen, along with trust.

From the monastery terrace, we watch dark storm clouds cover the mountains. They move with an anger that makes me nervous about our trek tomorrow. Montego tells us not to worry, for the high Himalaya make their own weather. We will remain below it. A light rain will keep the dust down. I want to believe him.

Goods for sale are found in unlikely places in Nepal. The following day, on the windswept plain of the upper Manang Valley beyond Pisang, an old Manangi and his wife sell trinkets and treasures. He wears his *chhuba* with the sleeves tied around his waist, and a turquoise sweater. The fur of his Tibetan hat hides his eyes and offsets his long nose. A scarf wraps around his wife's hair, and a jacket covers her *engi*, the traditional jumper-like dress of the mountain women. The couple's weathered faces remain stoic, as they spin their handheld prayer wheels, while Sharon and I look over two tables crowded with all things Tibetan: prayer wheels and beads, jewelry, tea bowls, and bells whose chimes echo off the mountains, all arranged among bottles of Coke and Fanta. I pick up a *dorje*, the ornate metal object used by the monk the first night of our trek. *Dorje* means "thunderbolt," according to Dorje. Sharon and I search for the authentic. The pious old man smiles so kindly, we trust him.

All our Sherpa advisors pass us and enter the lodge up ahead. Sharon and I, left to barter on our own, knowingly overpay for an old wood tea bowl lined in silver for Montego and his bride, a braided yak-hair rope for Sharon's ranch in Montana, and a lump of turquoise of questionable authenticity flanked by two coral beads on a black string. I like this old man, who chants like a monk as we finalize the deal. I put the necklace on. The old man smiles and pockets my rupees into the fold of his *chhuba*. When Dorje and Tashi notice my necklace, they smile and make no comment. A Sherpa never speaks to disappoint.

Geology, not botany, defines the arid landscape in the Himalayan rain shadow at elevations over 11,000 feet (3,353 m). Like sentinels, the rocky foothills must be crossed before you get to snow-covered mountains. The pale line of a trail meanders over the land. Trees are nonexistent; bushes and ground cover struggle to grow. Only ravens and insects keep us company. A single flower catches my eye. A diamond-like pebble glimmers in the sun. I bend down to pick it up. The clear crystal of quartz allows me to see into its center. I want to see into my center. Here, it is possible.

Just before the village of Manang at 11,598 feet (3,535 m), the valley floor rises up as far as I can see. With no level land, the Sherpas have pitched our tents on the earthen rooftop of a large stone house built into the mountainside. We climb up a series of notched log ladders to get to our tents. Below us lie the village and farmlands; beyond, a canyon drops toward the Marsyandi River; on the opposite side of the river, Gangapurna rises, epic in its immensity.

As I look at Gangapurna, with its massive base clinging tightly to earth, I know that my climb up must come down—back to my life in Los Angeles, where I will have to face what I want, where I want to go, and what I want to do. The joyride up is easy when everything remains possible, but the thrill of dropping down, down into a narrow canyon where I could lose control terrifies me. And my skis will be no help in the Himalaya. No help at all. Change may be inevitable, but it sure is hell to deal with.

It's the husband-and-wife Buddha in *yab-yum*.

—*Monk at Muktinath*

AS I STEP OUT OF MY ROOFTOP TENT, I am greeted by predawn stars fading into a turquoise sky as the gold sun rises behind the eastern mountains and colors the face of Gangapurna coral. Pearl-like above it all, the silver moon bejewels the day. *Rinpoche*, I have learned, means "jewel" or "precious one" in Tibetan Buddhism and is a title bestowed on incarnate lamas who manifest an enlightened nature and embody the Three Jewels: *Buddha*, the ultimate nature; *dharma*, the true path or teachings; and *sangha*, the spiritual community. This morning I feel rich and bejeweled. Someone is looking in on me.

My morning in Manang vibrates with life. Crows caw. Dogs bark. A rooster crows. A yak bell thuds. A baby cries. Tympani ring out when a copper pot fills with water. Herders shout. Goats clatter along stone streets. A conch shell bellows. A drum beats. Monks chant. I am glad to be awake, blessed by a sunrise that lights up the face of Gangapurna, the moon, and Venus.

I remember my mornings in Los Angeles. The calming voice of Bob Edwards would wake me, and I'd lie and listen to NPR until the last minute, then jump out of bed, shower, dress, do my makeup and hair, skip breakfast, seldom make the bed, drive to work, park below our building, stop for tea on the way to my desk, rummage my file drawer for a granola bar, and eat it while multitasking voicemail, my schedule of the day, and the urgency of the documents left on my chair by colleagues the night before, or while addressing whoever approached me first thing with a problem. I would seldom notice the sun rise or feel the crisp air of morning on my cheeks. Here in Nepal, I remember how precious mornings are and vow to celebrate them all.

Good morning, says Nima. I turn to see him perched on the edge of the roof.

Namaste, Nima.

Beautiful sunrise.

You saw the sunrise? I ask. How long have you been here?

I saw you get out of your tent.

Someone was looking in on me.

Today is a rest day in Manang, so we can acclimatize before our climb over the pass. In search of solitude after a week surrounded by our trek-kers and the ever-attentive Sherpas, I sneak off after breakfast alone. I walk back down the trail to Bryaga, an ancient town set into a lunar-like land-scape of rock pillars. High above the village, electrical cables from a nearby hydroelectric dam crisscross an ancient *gompa*. The intrusion of modern technology disturbs me. As a visitor, I want time to stand still here. I scold myself for such thoughts—the villagers deserve heat and the warm glow of a lamp—but I continue to detest the wires that ruin my photographs.

Over the centuries, the villagers carved prayers into stone and offered these *mani* to the gods by placing them on the long wall dividing the trail outside of Bryaga. Before me, stacks of *mani* surround slate panels etched with images of the Buddha, Rinpoches, bodhisattvas, and sacred objects. I lay a sheet of drawing paper against a deeply incised prayer. Starting at the upper corner and working my way down, I rub my pencil across the Tibetan *mantra, Om Mani Padme Hum*, to transfer the blessing. Hail to the Jewel in the Lotus. I want to take it home.

The book on Buddhism I brought with me explains the mantra's

fire: It's the husband-and-wife Buddha in *yab-yum*.

meaning. The seed-symbols, *Om* and *Hum*, refer to the "infinite" and the "infinite within the finite." *Mani Padme*, the mantra between them, translates as "the jewel in the lotus." A metaphor for the Buddha, or the enlightened mind: it arises from human consciousness like a lotus flower emerges from mud. This oldest of Tibetan Buddhist mantras is made to Chenrezi, the bodhisattva of compassion, and is repeated to benefit others, and to help a devotee reach an exalted state. *Om Mani Padme Hum.* I whisper it as I work.

By my action, the dark graphite left by my pencil reveals the prayer. Yet it is the negative spaces, the pure white paper, that speaks the prayer, as if *Om Mani Padme Hum* had always existed on the page. I only had to find a way to see it. As the morning warms, the wind picks up, and my pages snap in the wind like the prayer flags that surround me. As I transfer-rub a finely etched relief of the Buddha onto my paper, the locals stop and watch me. Nervously, I show them my work. I am afraid that they may not approve, and may accuse me of stealing the Buddha. Surprised to find me here, the locals leave with a nod and a smile.

What is it about Nepal that awakens my spiritual nature? I have never before made a rubbing in a cathedral or temple, nor had any inclination to do so. Here, it feels so natural, perhaps because the Nepalese, no matter which religion they practice, incorporate spirituality into their daily life. Most perform a morning *pūjā*, at shrines found on street corners or hilltops, or in courtyards or shrine rooms within their homes. Many who pass by pause to honor the deities with a nod, a prayer and incense, a dash of pigment, a garland of marigolds, or rice held ready in a pocket for offerings. Monks, *babas*, and *sadhus* mix with the businessmen, who stop to give tribute. Women sit before temples and for a few rupees dot *tikas* of red pigment on the foreheads of devotees. Prayer flags identify a Buddhist's home. The strong spirits who live here have caught me up in their celebration.

Above Manang, where the trail crosses the locals' fields, I stop and look back. Smoke from morning cooking fires blankets the town, while the bright sun silhouettes the square houses and prayer flag poles that step down the mountainside. Sunlit Gangapurna, Annapurna II, and Annapurna IV dominate the landscape. Ahead of us, Chulu West is visible, and for the first time, the white tip of Thorung Peak. Against the barren landscape, Prudy thinks the peak shines like a beacon. Saul stops to photograph it. Paul tells me he now knows he can make it over. Sharon thinks it looks near. Montego tells us we are three days away. I cannot wait to see it up close.

As we climb, only low shrubs of tiny leaves and flowers cover the hillsides. I reach for a branch. Ouch! Thorns protect it, as if the plant understands how hard it is to survive at this altitude. Nima, who suddenly appears behind me, approaches the plant with care and picks tiny leaves with his fingers until his cupped hand fills. He lifts it to my face. Incense. I am transported to the *gompa* that first night in Bhote Odar. Nima drops half into my hand. We both pocket our share. I finger the leaves to let them perfume my hand, and see Nima do the same as he walks ahead of me. He travels fast at this altitude. I cannot keep up, and he soon pulls far ahead. Since Besi Sahar, my focus has been on my journey, not Nima. And yet each time I see him, I am happy.

On the sloped pasture of Charka Dhunga, our campsite, I struggle to sleep at an altitude of 12,598 feet (3,840 m). My heart races erratically. I am cold. I sleep lightly. I wake to tremors in the earth. Earthquake? I sit up alert. After living in California, my body is attuned to the warning signs. Next to my head, a yak snorts, bellows, and tears into the grass with a mighty chomp. I freeze. Only ripstop nylon separates me from the yak's horns. The yak chews, and I imagine his mouth open, as he slurps up grass and drool. Fully awake, my senses heightened by fear, I am afraid to move. What if I startle him? If I don't move, will his long, twisted horns gouge my head as he dives for a tasty morsel peeking out from below my tent? I hear the wind in between his chomping. I hear his hooves crush all below them. I feel him shudder, as if he too is chilled, in spite of his thick coat. Suddenly, I shiver. My nylon bag rasps. The yak stops eating. Does he hear me? I hold my breath. I imagine the yak's ears perked up. I hear the wind.

fire: It's the husband-and-wife Buddha in *yab-yum*.

I remain still. I long for breath. I must breathe. I must—I gasp.

Horns. I'll be gouged!

The earth shakes, followed by aftershocks. The yak lumbers across the field. I close my eyes, but do not sleep. Soon, the tremors return.

By the time I get up, the yaks are gone. Did I only imagine them? Over breakfast, everyone's stories and the dark circles under their eyes confirm I did not. We are glad today will be a short trek to Thorung Phedi.

The trail is now composed of rocks in varying sizes that make walking difficult. Each step requires care, and we soon exhaust ourselves. When I stop to look up, the immensity of the landscape is unfathomable. At 13,000 feet (3,662 m), tiny spring flowers fight to bloom. Beyond, Thorung Peak glistens white in this otherwise gray-brown landscape. The valley falls away as we climb, and the mountain face that we must traverse becomes steeper as the canyon narrows. We trek close together, less apprehensive with others nearby. Nervous laughter ripples down the line as Saul steps onto rock scree and sends a footfall of rocks cascading down into a now distant valley. A Sherpa is there to grab him. Montego tells him to stop. The trail up ahead crosses a large slide of gray rock that falls deep into a canyon. One slip and—Bill!

I again remember my camp counselor, even with no water in sight. You'd be proud of me, Bill, I think. I have practiced fearlessness a lot since summer camp. I've learned to enjoy it—most of the time. Right now, I'm scared, Bill. Take my hand. Actually, make that Nima. Think Nima. He may still be with the porters up ahead, but he's much closer than Bill. Focus on Nima. Hold his hand. Do not be afraid.

To cross a loose slide of rock requires technique. This rockslide begins far above us and tumbles toward a river far below. Those who came before us wore down a trail across the slide, their weight shifting stones until they settled into a downward-tilted path that is better than no path at all. Dorje crosses it first to make sure it is safe. I watch him, how he leans into the mountainside, walks swiftly, and focuses on where he is going. Not until he arrives safely on the other side does he turn and wave for us to continue. Sharon, who is lighter than me, goes first. Sharon has become a good trekker, light on her feet, assured and steady. She makes it look easy. When she reaches Dorje, she stops next to him, turns, and waves. I want to go before the larger men. I lean in toward the mountainside and walk fast, watchful of every step. I look down, but not all the way down, for just as in driving, we tend to follow our gaze. I look three steps ahead. I am only midway when I hear a rock cascading down above me.

"Don't look!" shouts Dorje. "Keep moving!" A frantic Dorje waves me forward.

On unstable ground, the body senses danger if it rests, if it allows the loose rock scree to take one's full weight. I must become lightness at this moment. At the sight of terra firma, I race forward to be sure I am free of the slide. My legs shake, and a breathless laugh releases tension. I gasp for air. I bend over to send blood back to my head. Bronze lichen spots the rock. Water puddles in concave stones. Small brown grass sprouts from a crack. An anemic spider dives into a dark refuge. All living things struggle here. As I watch the others cross, I cannot help but think about tomorrow. I look up. From Thorung Phedi—*phedi* means "foot of the hill"—we still have over 3,200 feet (975 m) to climb to reach the pass at Thorung La. The snow line is visible above us. Camp is not far beyond. All I can think of are the treacherous, snowy, cliffside trails, icy ledges, hungry crevasses, and slippery slopes. Do I anger the mountain goddess as I tromp over her? And how does she decide whom to punish? Will she punish me? Maybe, like the rest of us, all she wants is a little respect.

Sheltered by walls of rock, our campsite at Thorung Phedi is a welcome sight. The smallest of creeks runs past the kitchen fire, and a layer of ice spreads out from the water's edge to capture pebbles in a freeze play. A light dusting of snow covers the tents, the earth, and the dark hair of our staff, who arrange and rearrange our gear. Montego recommends we do the same. Our departure tomorrow will be three o'clock in the morning.

Nothing comes easy at this altitude. I repack my duffel, write in my journal, and try to rest. I can't nap. My heart races and sometimes misses a beat to reset its rhythm. I lie in my tent bundled up in my rated –20 degree Fahrenheit sleeping bag with all my clothes on—underwear, long underwear, pants, fleece pants, turtleneck, fleece jacket, down jacket, wool scarf, gloves, and hat—and I am still cold. I focus on all the terrible things that could go wrong tomorrow, until I catch myself. I get up and go outside. It is dusk. The snow has stopped.

I turn around full circle to survey our campsite. Below cloud cover, rock walls surround me, close enough for me to read their detail. This is the end of the line, where we must cross the pass or go back the way we came—or fall. The exposed geological forces here are like a class on the formation of mountains: uplifts, clefts, schisms, and swirling layers of eons-old rock. I loved the study of geology in college. In time, we all arrive where we should be.

"*Didi. Didi,*" says Pema. I open my eyes to darkness. "Good morning. *Ch'ah.*" I sit up and fumble with the tent zipper. The light of the flashlight held between Pema's knees grazes his cheek and the upturned corner of his mouth as he pours tea. I appreciate the warmth of the cup in my hands and thank Pema, who holds back the tent flap.

Snow! I shiver. As I drop two teaspoons of sugar into my tea, someone passes by with a kerosene lantern and exposes the ferocity of the blizzard. I ask Pema for the Sherpa word for snow.

"*Khaa, Didi.*" Their word for snow has a cold dullness to the sound. Fortunately, "*Didi,*" his "older sister" term of endearment and his *ch'ah* bring me warmth—but not for long. Montego shouts, Get up! We must hurry. Thorung La may become impassable.

I step outside and look up at the mountains. Their peaks are invisible. How will we find our way? None of us came this far to fail, so we scurry to prepare for our departure. The porters, who know the danger, only want to get over the mountains. Last night, Dorje gave them wool socks and green Chinese tennis shoes. If he gives them out too early, the porters sell them off and cross the pass in flip-flops.

A half hour later, our group assembles and Montego assigns each of us a climbing partner. He warns us to stay close together, for if we stray, no one will find us in the snowy darkness. Headlamps worn over our face masks will light our way. Single file, Sharon, and then I, follow Tashi. Nima, who carries the oxygen bottle, treks with Saul and Prudy. Montego is with Paul. The other Sherpas go with the porters to ensure they cross the pass.

The near-vertical trail ascends a wall of steps cut into the snow last evening by our Sherpa guides. Overnight, the worst of my fears left me. As the nervousness of anticipation dissipates, adrenaline takes over. My breath is labored. I know the air is bone dry by the dull crunch of snow as I step. I taste metal, cold like iron on the tongue. I smell ice, the scent of stillness. I feel wet wool, musty from my breath. My other senses become keener when I cannot see the way. I grab tight to my hiking pole as it stabs at the next step and I hoist myself up. We move at a perfectly acceptable glacial pace as we climb against gravity. Through the snow, I focus on vague forms that appear, then fade like a mirage, or change shape like kaleidoscopic visions during a migraine, or disappear altogether, so I become disoriented like a sailor with no horizon.

I like Tashi, but today I want to walk with Nima. I thought I had put Nima out of my mind and stopped these irrational thoughts. Since Besi Sahar, Nima has been with the porters. I've barely seen him. Out of sight, out of mind worked, sort of. Then last night when I passed him on the way to the dining tent, he smiled—just smiled. I wish Nima could guide me over the pass. Strange. I sense him with me, even when he is not.

In the blizzard, the mountains have been leveled out. The eerie silver light of dawn mimics a palladium print with shades of old-world grays. Our danger no longer comes from altitude, but disappearance: a fall into a crevasse, separation from others, or a slip into oblivion. Tashi leads, and Sharon and I follow closely, content to not make our own way today. I feel strong. Thorung La or bust! Each step requires precision. My body remains tense, muscles alert, ready to respond should I slip. The feet of those before us have iced the trail. With fresh snow on top, the ice is as invisible and treacherous as the black ice on roadways. Take it slow. Attention. Test. Focus. Balance. Whoa! Where's Nima? Sharon, Tashi, and I pull far ahead of everyone else, except the porters, whose hazy figures

fire: It's the husband-and-wife Buddha in *yab-yum*.

wander past us like ghosts coming in and out of the spirit world. I should be exhausted, unable to lift a leg, but instead move at a steady pace. Giddy from lack of oxygen, I cannot stop laughing. A power with a sense of humor resides here.

"I love Nepal. I want to live here," I tell Tashi. Perhaps it is the protective veil of snow that allows me to speak my fantasy. My rational mind knows the sameness of my life will resume once I return home, and yet, while I am in Nepal, I refuse to believe it. I have experienced another way. On the wind, I hear Tashi. Come to Nepal! The mirage hovers momentarily, and then vanishes. Nepal has no need for a manager of corporate architectural interiors projects, I tell him, knowing Tashi has no understanding of what I do for a living, and if he did, he would find it extravagant. I am stuck in America.

"You could be my assistant," says Tashi. "Only problem is getting a visa." I mock disappointment. Tashi has a solution. "Marry a Nepali!"

At 17,769 feet (5,416 m), the ridiculous becomes sublime.

Reaching one's goal can be anticlimactic. At Thorung La, Sharon and I act like conquerors: we puff out our chests and plant Tashi's ice axe. Click. Tashi captures our summit. Except for the lack of oxygen, I could be anywhere in a whiteout. Unable to see the lands I now claim, I have no choice but to forget the prize and love the journey. From here, it is all downhill. As we descend, the snowfall lessens and reveals black rock-slides and dry brown mountains, reminding us that we are still in the rain shadow. My body senses the change in direction: the pressure of my own weight and that of my backpack on kneecaps, the mash of toes in the front of my boots, and the backward lean into the mountainside.

"Let's race," shouts Tashi, as we stand atop an endless blanket of rock scree. Given we are going down and follow the natural trajection of the scree, we agree that this looks safer than traversing it as we did before Thorung Phedi. Besides, one gains fearlessness—and foolishness—upon reaching one's goal.

Tashi leaps into the scree like a boy into a sandbox. Sharon and I see no reason to linger. Sharon jumps with the grace of the musk deer. I follow. The tension of crossing the pass dissipates. I leap long. I feel free. I am unbound. Going straight down proves easier than traversing a slide. I chase after Tashi and Sharon through black scree in quick pursuit. I lean back and leap and slide as rocks roll around me and under me and I roll with them, at one with the earth. Together, we keep moving. We travel in trust: the earth, Tashi, Sharon, and I. I laugh and shout and sing as a richer mix of oxygen enters my brain. I am high. This is fun! I love Nepal!

After a climb of 3,268 feet (996 m) and a drop of 5,302 feet (1,616 m), we arrive at the village of Muktinath by noon, tired, hungry, and proud. Tashi tells us that today is the fastest he has ever crossed the pass. We believe him. Prudy and Saul join us a couple hours later, without Nima, who stayed behind to help Montego with Paul. The three of them arrive late in the day. An exhausted Paul beams with pride at his accomplishment. Nima congratulates him on crossing the Himalaya. Montego hopes that since we are now headed for home, we will all be faster. I am in no hurry. I could linger in Nepal for a long time.

For our reward, Sharon and I each splurge on a ten-rupee bowl of water warmed by the sun in the lodge owners' rooftop solar tank and made hot in the kettle over their dung-fired stove. An old woman brings the two bowls to us on the sunny upper terrace of her run-down lodge. I lean over the aluminum bowl and pour water over my head. The air is cool on bare arms, the sun warm on my back, and the lather heavenly on my head. I squeeze my hair in my fist to wring out the dust. After Sharon and I comb out our tangles, we sit with our backs against a stone wall to sun dry our hair; more blonde, her hair looks radiant; less blonde, my highlights shine; both fresh and renewed, we relax.

Inner recesses, once in shadow, grow light. Between the direct heat from the sun and its energy stored in the stone wall, I am warmed to the core. Awake, I am anxious to live, ready for—*Marry a Nepali.* What a funny thing for Tashi to say. He knows nothing of my thoughts about Nima. Funny? I guess a relationship with a foreigner is easier for them to imagine than for us. And yet, I can imagine Nima.

fire: It's the husband-and-wife Buddha in *yab-yum*.

The next morning, Nima rejoins our group of trekkers. Now that the porters are headed for home, they need less supervision. I am excited when Nima positions himself beside me to lead us up the trail toward the temple complex at Muktinath.

Usually he works as a *sirdar* or trek leader, or as a high-altitude guide on expeditions, Nima informs me, as if to impress, not just as a guide or a porter. Lowland people work as porters now, not Sherpas.

Curious, I ask him if the Sherpa have moved up in the world. I only confuse Nima. Moved up? We live high already. What I mean, I tell him, is that Sherpas are more important. He thinks not. Everyone's important. Lowland people. Mountain people. Same. Nima smiles. I clarify. I mean, Sherpas have jobs with more responsibility. Nima nods and tells me it's because Sherpas speak many languages and are good with clients. I want to know how many languages he speaks. Nima lists them. Sherpa. Tibetan. Nepali. Hindi. English. As he counts them on his fingers, I am shocked to see him move to his other hand. French. Japanese. His clients talk. Nima listens.

Do words resonate with more clarity in the quiet of the mountains? Our conversation ends abruptly when someone else demands his attention. I am disappointed. I like Nima. Within moments, Nima reappears at my side. I am glad. We pass through the temple gate into the complex of Muktinath—together.

"Today is a new beginning," says Nima. "I've decided to give up smoking." In a strange way, I think he wants me to be aware of this, as if he is doing it for me. I tell him I support his decision, but go for the fear factor, hoping to keep him true to his word. Smoking kills. Alarmed, he assures me that he never smoked much. He prefers chewing tobacco. I wince. On seeing my reaction, he makes another declaration. From now, no more tobacco. Nima has made his commitment on sacred ground.

From a high vantage point at the back of the complex, I scan the horizon. On this clear day, I can look beyond the golden spires of pagoda temples and shrines, and past the barren brown hills, to see myself encircled by snowcapped mountains awash in the soft light of morning. I have this strange sensation of being held in the palm of the land's hand, complete with a French manicure. What a ridiculous metaphor! I've got to get out of Los Angeles! Engaged in their own discoveries, none of my traveling companions takes notice when Nima leads me to the Vishnu Mandir Temple and away from the others. I am overcome with the sensation that he specifically wants to be here with me. I like that Nima will give me the alternative perspective I seek.

I am confused. I see Buddhist and Hindu people here. Why both? Nima explains that people of both religions, as well as Jain from India and Bönpo from Tibet and the Kingdom of Mustang, make pilgrimages to Muktinath. All share the same sacred site? I ask. He looks surprised by my question. They do, says Nima. In Nepal, anyone can visit a Buddhist temple, but only Hindus and Nepalese, regardless of their religion, can enter a Hindu temple.

Can I enter a Buddhist temple?

Nima laughs.

Yes. No difference.

Nima wants to know about my religion. I was raised a Christian, I tell him, although right now, I'm not sure what religion I am. I believe in a spirit, and I believe in myself. As my words spill off my tongue, I realize how self-centered and shallow they sound. Nima only knows of Christians from a porter's story, and he interrupts the telling with his laughter. The missionaries gave the porter books and food and talked to him of their god. He thought them generous. One day, the porter had a headache, so a missionary gave him two aspirin, then hit the porter's head with a Bible and told him the words of their god had cured him.

The Nepalese government used to not let missionaries in, says Nima. Now, they do.

Nima is passionate. It's not right to force new gods on people, to steal their religion, or say bad things about their beliefs, he says. Why do foreigners think what they have is best?

They only want people to know there is another god, I tell him.

Nima objects. Another god? Nepal has plenty of gods. When they rob people's gods and give them a new one, they steal people from their

fire: It's the husband-and-wife Buddha in *yab-yum*.

family, their country. Why do foreigners always have to own things? Own all those crazy junk things they sell in Thamel. Own people after they make them Christian. Own mountains after they climb them by giving them names, when they already have names. Chomolungma is Chomolungma. Not Mount Everest!

I empathize, but respond more strongly than I intend. I suppose Sherpas are perfect, I tell him. All smiles. No problems. You wear a mask like your monks when they dance. Sherpas are actors.

I am not an actor, he says. I am Nima. Nima Gyalgen Sherpa. Not so perfect. But why make others unhappy? Why be sad?

Nima, I say. I like you. I like the Sherpas. I love Nepal.

He smiles, and my previous words melt off his face.

I am sorry, I say.

Stupid word, *sorry*, says Nima. What is said is said. No *sorry*. Only karma.

We both pause to quiet our emotions as we look at the early light on Dhaulagiri. Nima suggests we go visit the *sadhu*, the wise man, by the temple to get a *tika*. I remind him that I am not Hindu. Neither is he. He laughs. No matter. This is Nepal.

A *tika* is a Hindu blessing for the start of a new day. Outside the temple, I bend down toward a scantily dressed, ash-smeared *sadhu*. He dips his fingers into a bowl of red pigment mixed with rice, places a *tika* on my forehead, and chants a blessing. Nima looks at me as I stand up and brushes a stray grain of vermilion-colored rice off my cheek. I feel beautiful. Nima squats to receive his *tika*, then stands and looks at me.

Never underestimate the power of hallowed ground, a holy man, and vermilion. A seismic shift alters our relationship from this point forward. I catch myself feeling overjoyed at wandering the ancient temple complex of Muktinath with Nima. At the far end, where a stone wall holds back the mountainside, one hundred and eight brass cow-head spouts flow with sacred waters. Nima cups his hands at each to fill them with water eons old, the melt from ancient ice glaciers. After Nima douses his head, he anoints mine. Even in the cool morning air, the spirit of Muktinath feels warm as it washes down my face. I look up at Nima, my vision blurred by water, and know that through this holy water he has found his way in.

Fire burns on water. I burn.

At the ancient Tibetan-style Jwala Mai Temple, Nima asks the caretaker monk to open the small door below the altar in the temple's main room. We witness the sacred, the auspicious coming together of the elements: fire, earth, water—us. I am skeptical. I see a flame, a puddle, and darkness. I tell Nima it is a trick. He assures me that here above the earth, fire burns on water. I tell him it is a gas pilot light. He assures me fire burns on water. He points. I question. How is the unimaginable possible in the Himalaya? I only have to believe, he says. Can anything be so simple? Nima doesn't answer me. His silence tells me yes. Nima watches fire burn on water. Nima believes. For me, everything requires an explanation. There has to be gas. They enshrined it, knowing believers would walk for miles to worship burning water and give alms. I cannot fathom possessing such faith, but Nima's is rock solid, so I drop it.

The temple interiors delight me. I did not expect to find such fine examples of Buddhist art at over 12,000 feet (3,658 m). Every wall of the temple interior is painted. I wander away from Nima to enjoy the fluidity of lines drawn by artists' hands and the boisterous use of color. Delicately drawn, these strange landscapes convey stories, rich with symbolism, but silent to me. I am the unbeliever. I like the calm within this temple, and the quiet, as no one else is here but the old monk who guards the flame, Nima, and me. I must admit that even when we disagree, I still like Nima.

Mapped out in two dimensions, this world is at peace. I am invited into the world of the Buddhas and gods, who float amid green hills, waterfalls, snowcapped mountains, snow lions, curly clouds, and rainbows. My world is upside-down with no map for where I am going, but when Nima stops beside me, global warming begins.

Nima laughs at a monkey. Enchanted, I point out a flower by a river and ask if it is a lotus. Nima nods as he traces a water buffalo and in a scholarly voice tells me that you'd never see them so high in the mountains. I note the sensual qualities of the hand gestures. *Mudrās*, Nima tells me. He directs my gaze to a snow leopard hiding high in the mountains. In the dim light, I strain to see it. Nima guides my vision. Snow lions are difficult to see, even in real mountains, he tells me. He has seen them only once. A mother and two babies playing in the snow. So cute. I want to know what it is with him and animals. He tells me he just likes them. And the gods? Gods are gods. Nima likes the animals.

In the cold temple interior, I feel the heat from Nima's body radiating out toward me. I fight an urge to lean back against him, so he can wrap his arms around me and keep me warm. Stop it, I tell myself. Look at the Buddha. Look! Buddha is doing what I was thinking. The Buddha? I stare at a sensual rendition of a blue Buddha in a sexual embrace with a white consort. Both are unclothed. Does Nima see me as a white consort, I wonder? Imagine if this were Jesus and Mary Magdalene. In a Christian church, this image would be pornography! I am confused and ask Nima to explain. As embarrassed Nima asks the monk about the image, all I can ask myself is: Has Nima ever had sex? Then I remember I am in a sacred place of worship. I look at Nima and know I could worship him. I try to focus on the Buddha, not Nima. The Buddha. The blue Buddha with his white consort. I focus. All I see is blue Nima with white me.

"It's the husband-and-wife Buddha in *yab-yum*," translates Nima for the caretaker monk. Before I can ask Nima any more questions, he turns and walks out. Only later do I read that *yab-yum* means to be in union, inseparable. As a yogi visualizes the cosmos, the Divine Father is the energizing aspect, and the Divine Mother, the intellectual aspect, and together they represent the Buddhist concept of non-duality. *Yab-yum* assists practitioners in fusing the masculine and feminine energies within themselves on their way to enlightenment.

From Muktinath, the dusty trail drops through Jharkot, a village of mud houses with precious bundles of twigs stored at the edge of flat roofs. Mustangi and Thakali people of Tibetan origin live amid the arid landscape, where sand-colored fingers of rock line the valley. At the village center, we stop to watch the villagers break rocks with hand tools to repair their road. The men break up boulders; the women shatter them into rocks; the children hammer them to coarse gravel. A few years ago, an international relief organization taught the locals how to build outhouses to improve sanitation and lessen disease, Montego tells us, and how to build a chimney to vent smoke from their homes. Change comes slowly in these isolated areas. We travel in a time warp.

As we walk down a wide, dusty canyon towards Kagbeni, I am self-conscious of my explosive feelings for Nima, but do not sense anyone notices. Sharon walks with Dorje. Paul talks to Montego. Saul and Prudy talk to each other. Far down the trail, our guides, Tashi, Pema, and the porters, race ahead to find a campsite, as once they set up, they can relax. The pass was hard, everyone is tired, and they know what lies ahead. While I am no longer oblivious, I take each day as it comes.

At a small roadside *chörten* buried in *mani* stones, a ram's horn crowns the *chörten*, and the bone attached to the horn is carved with prayers. I like that a simple arrangement of rocks, horn, and sky is a prayer. Always curious, Nima wants to know how we display our prayers in America. Prayers are private, kept within a church, and often silent, I tell him. I spare him an explanation of our displays: gravestones, crosses bearing plastic flower wreaths to mark a highway accident, crucifixes that honor Jesus—and Christmas decorations that do not.

Chörtens and *mani* stones mark a sacred place, according to Nima. These granite *mani* were incised with patient tenacity, and allow their makers to share prayers with the world. Often carved to honor a person, *mani* may be carved to better their creators' karma and improve their future lives. *Mani* stones, once shared, become a communal prayer. As I stand on hallowed ground with Nima, I am grateful to receive its blessing.

I am confused by Tibetan Buddhism, which is complicated by its many gods, sacred symbols, and ritual objects, not to mention the rituals themselves. My head spins. When I ask Nima about them, he doesn't have an answer. He assures me that only the monks need to know all those things. Monks meditate, not the people. The Sherpas honor the monks and support them with money, vegetables, and rice. The monks care for the Sherpas. Sometimes, a monk visits a Sherpa home to bless a new house or a new child, but mostly they reside at their monastery or in the mountains. Why the mountains?

Mountains are our mothers, says Nima. His family spent their summers in the high pastures of Lumding, a valley west of his family farm that begins at the foot of Khatang glacier. They lived in a simple one-room dwelling of stone surrounded by high peaks, waterfalls, and mountainsides of azaleas and rhododendrons. His father's brother, Uncle Lama Zepa, meditates there in season, but otherwise lives in a rock cave above Nima's parents' home. Nima tells it matter-of-factly, as if a cave dwelling is a common place to reside. A cave? I want to understand. Someone has to control the spirits, says Nima. Someone powerful like Uncle Lama Zepa, or a Rinpoche. A Rinpoche is born again and again, like His Holiness the Dalai Lama, who has had fourteen births. I am curious. Do you ever seek guidance from a monk? I ask. Nima reminds me that he, not the monks, is the guide. I haven't been to church for years, I tell Nima. He looks displeased.

"Then it is good you came to Nepal, and to Muktinath."

"And saw the blue Buddha." Nima blushes and runs ahead.

I see our campsite beyond a blossoming apple orchard, an oasis in this arid landscape of rock and dust. Before Dhaulagiri, the ochre façade of a *gompa* rises above the confluence of the Jhong Khola and the Kali Gandaki. Where rivers meet, Buddhists build their temples. We camp on hallowed ground.

The mood of our group has shifted. At our campsite in Kagbeni the next morning, everyone is jubilant. We share tales of our crossing, the hardships encountered, and end with accolades all around. Talk about our future plans weaves into our conversation as we dine on pancakes with peanut butter and honey, hard-boiled eggs, and chai. Paul remains undecided, considering graduate school or a job to gain experience. Saul and Prudy have patients who wait for their return. Sharon talks of her upcoming wedding. I still have four more months of travel, I tell them.

I'm taking it one day at a time. Montego tells me I must be learning from the Sherpas.

From Kagbeni, we walk the dry rock riverbed of the Kali Gandaki River and enter the world's deepest gorge. Divided by the peaks of the Annapurna Range and Dhaulagiri, glacial waters from the Tibetan plateau carved out this immense riverbed that rests up to 19,000 feet (5,791 m) below them. We follow the water's route past caravans of goats carrying salt in decorated leather saddlebags and trains of horses, festooned in red yarn pom-poms and Tibetan carpets, that transport cheap Chinese goods down to Pokhara. In this gorge where we all look like ants, I can't help but question my significance.

As the vertical faces of mountains extend high about me, I feel trapped, with no shore, no easy way out. Ages ago, water shaped this land, mapped its relief, its outlets. Now these mountains and valleys shape me. I am leaner, more spiritual, and more attached to these mountain people, to Nima. I am like this land, alive, impatient, yet resistant, both cautious of change and desirous of development. Together, we continue to evolve and adapt to seismic shifts in our landscape.

Nima seeks a *shaligram*. I watch him pick up a stone and smash it on a boulder to crack it in two. Shaligrams are prehistoric ammonites. When split open, they reveal the embodiment of the Hindu god Vishnu—or a 130 million-year-old marine creature fossilized in sediment. You decide. While a shaligram is frozen in time, Nima changes before my eyes, or more exactly, in my mind's eye. I enjoy watching his lean, agile body as he squats to sort stones, then rises and leaps toward me in an explosion of joy when he finds one full of possibility. Nima shows me that this one, so black and round, must be a shaligram. He raises his arm and tosses the stone against a boulder with a fury. The stone fractures into shards. Try again. The next one bounces off a boulder without breaking, even after several attempts, its secrets not ready to be revealed. Like a shaligram split open to expose its true nature, Nima's childlike sense of wonder comes packaged in a strong and confident man. *Oh my*—Nima is as rare and precious as the shaligrams he hunts for.

fire: It's the husband-and-wife Buddha in *yab-yum*.

Since Kagbeni, Nima and I have hiked with each other. I sense that Montego and our Sherpa guides wonder about our relationship. No doubt the trekkers find our relationship inconceivable. I do. As I struggle to cage my feelings for Nima, they escape at the sight of him. My only cure is to leave Nepal. But what if he comes to America? What then?

Nima struggles with English, and I with comprehending him. At times, we walk in silence, but Nima, always curious, cannot keep quiet for long. He used to have a girlfriend, he tells me, as if to let me know he has experience. They broke up a year ago. I mention that I had a boyfriend and we broke up six months ago. His roommate married a Japanese girl and hoped to live in Japan, but she wanted to live in Nepal, so they live in Kathmandu. Nima prefers American girls, he tells me. I propose a hypothetical: If he married an American girl, and she wanted to live in Nepal, would that decision be okay? He keeps his options open. Okay Nepal. Okay America. I mention Tashi's solution—marry a Nepali. He looks pleased.

"I'd like to cook a real Nepalese dinner for you," says Nima, as we leave the Himalaya rain shadow behind. "Will you come to my house in Kathmandu?"

"I'd be delighted!"

As if swept off his feet by my acceptance, Nima slips over the ridge and disappears so abruptly that I wonder if he ever really asked.

I stop to look up at the Annapurnas. I seek guidance from their goddesses. Should I encourage Nima? I listen. The wind carries the thunder of an approaching yak caravan. A boulder cascades down the mountain. The singing of river stones calms me like a gentle rain. And then, I hear it—the joyful laughter of Sherpas. I trek down the trail with my words on the wind chasing after Nima.

Nothing impedes Nima's progress on trails in Nepal. He leaps long and stretches his stride to match the tilt of the mountain as he cuts off switchbacks on a straight-down course. I stay on the trail, only to find Nima waiting for me at the bottom. Together, we begin to climb. Nima is most happy when gaining altitude, burdened by his backpack, and sporting a smile that charms the birds.

Wealth returns to both landscape and villages as we descend from barren, windswept plains to lush pine forests and fertile fields of barley lit by the afternoon sun. At Marpha, the gorge narrows to a more human scale. The town is wedged between sandstone cliffs and terraced fields of fruit trees that drop down to the river. Over a small creek, a water-turned prayer wheel emits continuous blessings for the village of Marpha. The villagers are primarily Thakali, a Tibetan and Nepalese mix, who have built a pleasant town of stone-paved streets with underground gutters and running water, which offers our group an evening of urban comfort. The village's riches come from trade along the Kali Gandaki route between Tibet and India. The sophisticated two-story homes have slate roofs and carved-wood windows. Prayer wheels positioned on both sides of each front door offer a doubled opportunity for a blessing.

Once exposed to a touch of civilization, I slip back into it and relish my cold shower in Marpha. Refreshed, Sharon and I walk into town with Montego and Nima. At the restaurant, Nima recommends the vegetarian egg cheese pizza. We order two, plus three warm beers, and a soda for Nima. I like dining out. I like Nima even more. I sense he watches me, and wonder if the others notice. Montego gives me a mischievous look, but says nothing. While Sharon and Montego talk of their upcoming weddings, Nima describes his farm in the Solukhumbu district in the Everest region. As if to tantalize, Nima tells me how his village, high above a river, is more beautiful than Marpha, for his home looks out over fields of potatoes, buckwheat, and cabbage, and across the valley to mountains.

"Will you ever move back?" I ask Nima, who resides in Kathmandu.

"I'm going to America."

The noncommittal skies of morning give our group hope for sunshine. By midmorning, the trees provide little shelter against a relentless wind and rain. I stop to put on rain gear. Everyone else's remains packed in their duffels, safe and dry with the porters, wherever they are. Two Nepalese locals on the trail put up umbrellas. The Sherpas ignore the rain. As we drop in altitude and the depth of the Kali Gandaki gorge lessens, the lushness of the landscape returns. Fog plays hide-and-seek with Dhaulagiri and Niligiri. We follow the river all morning, as if on a forced march, with few photo stops and little conversation. I find it more pleasant to walk alone and create my own mood. Unlike the others, I am dry and warm in rain gear.

Every moment shows me something new. I see far. I see near. I do not yet see within, but I draw closer. Rain intensifies the forest's vibrant colors as we climb up toward our camp at Ghatte Khola. I stop often to photograph, and I fall behind the others, who are anxious for shelter. My insular mood, encouraged by rain and fog, leads me to look at the details of the landscape. I kneel to better see mushrooms nestled in loam. Fern fronds pattern the middle ground. Nuthatches crowd in bushes to wait out the rain. Gray langur monkeys leap playfully between trees.

I follow a low stone wall across a meadow toward the sound of Sherpa voices. Upon reaching our camp high above the Ghatte Khola, two tarps tied between trees provide the only shelter: one for the Sherpas and the cook fire, and one for the trekkers, until the porters arrive with our tents. Rocks rolled under our tarp roof provide cold seats. As I take mine, the conversation is in full swing. Each person ups the other's complaint, be it soreness, stiff joints, exhaustion, rain, chills, sunburn, humidity, heat, homesickness, altitude sickness, the runs, or the delinquency of our porters. With a long list of maladies to voice, each person hopes for sympathy, or at least empathy, or at the very least, notice.

Dressed in pants, two shirts, and a gray wool cap, Pema serves tea with a smile. Tsuldim, who wears cotton khakis, a thin black sweater, and a T-shirt, chants as he runs through the downpour to bring us popcorn. Montego, in his yellow-and-black ski-school jacket and wool cap, brings biscuits and promises our tents will arrive soon. No one appreciates their efforts. Even when obscured by rain, the Himalaya reduce you to size. Right now, everyone is cold, tired, and ornery after being caught unprepared for the weather. At first, I thought that a chance for the group to unload would be cathartic, but I now imagine that this conversation will continue through dinner. Normally, I would engage in a group rant, but

I don't want to be miserable today. What a contrast to the rain-soaked, smiling Sherpas. How can we be so different? The Sherpas still have tents to erect, tea to serve, dinner to cook, dishes to wash, while dressed in clothes not as warm or waterproof as ours, and with no way to dry their rain-soaked garments. Too comfortable in our luxury, even with our staff to wait on us, we are miserable. I don't want to be like the rest of us.

I get up and invite myself into the world of the Sherpas. Montego is there. So is Nima. I squat before their fire and notice potatoes roasting among coals. Pema hands me a cup of sweetened milk tea. The Sherpas extract roasted potatoes from hot ash with their bare hands, toss them from hand to hand to cool, then squeeze off the peels and pop the potatoes into their mouths. Scores are devoured this way, and in between his takings, Nima peels and hands me one.

I taste fire, earth, rain. I swallow joy.

> Mountains change a person.
> —*Sharon*

WITH THE STEADY RHYTHM OF RAIN on our tents, a good night's sleep does wonders for the mood of our group. So does the sun as it washes the face of the mountains before us while we eat breakfast outside. Montego points out Dhaulagiri, Niligiri, Niligiri North and South, and Annapurna I. From the massive face of Dhaulagiri with its icefall, high winds blow snow from the 26,795-foot (8,167 m) peak. The light plays tricks, and a mountain casts a shadow on the blowing snow.

After the pass, today is a well-deserved rest day, and a day for chores. The meadow becomes a laundry: tree limbs hold jackets and sleeping bags; bushes hold shirts and pants; sturdy grasses hold underwear and socks. Boots breathe fresh air. Men lather and shave. All of us wash from bowls of hot water provided by Pema. The sun lights the meadow and dries our blue tents. Some people nap. Others play cards. The porter girls braid each other's hair. Pema gathers firewood. Saul and Prudy read. Paul sets up his minitripod to photograph Dhaulagiri. The chill and evil spirits of yesterday are gone.

Enlivened by sunshine, Sharon and I climb up above our camp, tempted by a herd of longhaired goats and perspective. Petite purple irises carpet the upper meadow. White rhododendrons are visible above. Every scene is a picture for our cameras. Suddenly, from out of nowhere, a bedraggled Tibetan charges toward us with arms waving wildly, like the goddess, Kali. Sharon and I stop, unsure what to do. We thought we were alone here. The Tibetan halts before us. We should have brought a Sherpa. The man's sudden grin disarms us, as best as two women can be in the company of a man who smells like rancid butter and wood smoke. His fleece-lined coat appears never to have been washed; a raven may nest in his hair; and dirt cakes in the fissures of his forehead. He gestures for us to follow him. We look at each other. Should we go? Sensing our discomfort, he smiles, revealing brown teeth. He leads us up past thickets of brambles toward his black yak-hair tent. We question his intentions. Only after we pass the tent do we relax. Sharon and I continue to follow him as he climbs, rounds a stand of bushes, and stops. The shepherd turns toward us with a grin. Behind him is a brilliant stand of red rhododendrons. He points at our cameras. What a scout! We bow in gratitude. Before we can take his picture, the Tibetan has returned to his goats.

Higher up the ridgeline, Sharon and I look back up the Kali Gandaki to take note of where we have been, then south toward where we are going. The sunlight on the water casts shimmering ribbons of light on the mountainsides. A golden eagle plays in the updrafts, diving and rising on the wind. I am jealous of the eagle, the shepherd, and Sharon. The eagle soars without a care. The shepherd finds joy in a flower. Sharon has her future as planned out as her wedding. Up ahead I see only mountains.

The Kali Gandaki River no longer runs as a thread within a broad, flat river basin between Dhaulagiri and the Annapurna mountains, as it waits for the next snowmelt or monsoon rains to fill it. Here, the river forces its way through a narrower gorge between lesser mountains. This river, a source of water and of life, is named after the Hindu goddess, Kali, who is associated with death. I ponder the irony.

On my second day in Kathmandu, I was introduced to powerful Kali at her open shrine in Durbar Square. Her image burned into my psyche, so fascinated was I that such a wrathful deity could be a woman. Her power over the Nepalese, who worship her with animal sacrifices, is of a magnitude incomprehensible to a Westerner. Death is not an end, but a time of transformation. Kali, whose name means "the black one," is both the act and agent of transformation. She is one of the best-known manifestations of Maha Devi, a *shakti* or wife of Shiva known for her dominating and sexually active ways. Kali, dressed in a necklace of human heads, stands triumphant on a human body, and dominant woman that she is, sometimes even stands on the body of Lord Shiva himself. Her black color represents the immeasurable depth of time, which she alone keeps moving forward, and is suggested by her flying hair and flailing four arms that spread power in all directions. She exudes a primordial energy. She holds the divine sword of supreme knowledge in one hand and a human head in the other, together a symbol of transformation to the Hindu's supreme reality. For balance, her other two arms reach out in gestures of giving and protection toward her devotees, who make animal sacrifices to her to free their own spirits: water buffalo for anger, goat for lust, sheep for stupidity, duck for apathy, and chicken for timidity. Compassionate with the poor, she'll accept raw eggs in place of a chicken.

I too am formed by what I come in contact with in Nepal. Like the river, I am in an act of transformation. I seek experiences. I look for challenges. I test fate. I succeed. I fail. I transform. After Thorung La, I gained a strength. I can do anything if I put my mind and my heart to it. I only have to figure out what I want. With a growing certainty, I know Nima is in that equation.

In the Himalaya, I have come to learn that it is easier going up than going down. Going up wears less on the body, if I pace myself. Going down destroys my knees. Going down, I could fall. Following our rest day, we leave the rain shadow behind, as we descend and again follow the Kali Gandaki. Broadleaf trees push out the pines as the canyon narrows to a chasm that will plunge over 3,200 feet (975 m) to Tatopani. Wet granite steps littered with leaves cut through a forest of evergreen oaks and ferns. Light filters through the leaf canopy and dances from one verdant plant to another. Clouds and forests now hide the mountaintops of Tukuche Peak,

Dhaulagiri, and the Annapurnas that were visible this morning.

For a time, I trek with Paul. He talks to me like he might a big sister— if he had one—of girls, school, girls, parents, girls, authority figures, girls. I learn more than I want to know. I listen and laugh and console when appropriate, but selfishly, I want to enjoy the quiet of the woods unencumbered by his problems.

Comfortable with my body and steady on my feet, I pick up the pace. Soon, I am alone. I don't slow down. I like to feel the fall of the mountainside as I descend, and trust my muscles to keep me aloft. Rain filters through the tree canopy, barely reaching me. I keep moving. I dance down rock steps. Long. Short. Short. Longer. Taller. Short. I adjust. The rain falls harder. I hear it hit leaves. Rain puddles on stones. Head wet. Shoulders wet. I don't care. The rain is warm. Purifying. I want to live outdoors. I like weather, rather than the captured, manipulated, blown, chilled, heated, filtered air of our buildings. I feel so free—

Nima is there to catch me. With a vise grip to my elbow, he lifts me back onto the trail. During my mind meanderings, I slipped, a little too sure of myself for the conditions. He knew it was coming and had perfectly positioned himself just behind me. I stand and rest to catch my breath. In a sudden deluge, nothing will keep us dry. Within minutes, we are soaked, but neither of us moves. Instead, we look up at the thick waxen leaves that hide the sky and let rain wash over us. Nima still holds my elbow.

I know a teahouse not far from here, says Nima. We'll stop there.

I proceed with caution. Nima follows. There has been no lodge for some time, so when we arrive, the teahouse is crowded with guides, trekkers, and porters who encircle the fire. Steam rises from their wet clothes and their teacups. I squeeze onto a bench beside the lodge owner's young daughter, who looks to be all of three. Needing no encouragement, she crawls onto my lap and nestles in, as if we had known each other in a past life. I bounce and coo and sing to her. She smiles. I name herAnnapurna. The Sherpas emote empathy as they watch us. In Sherpa culture, a thirty-eight-year-old single woman with no children is unfortunate, and with no husband, downright tragic.

When the rain stops, "Annapurna" takes my hand and leads me outside to the patio. Dressed in a pink robe, she looks flowerlike, so I pick her a nearby rhododendron and fasten it onto her collar. The music of a *mondal* moves her to dance. She takes my hand and tugs. Unable to resist this beguiling goddess, I rise. Fluid and rapturous, she sways to the music; hand on one hip, the other to the sky, her hand folds and unfolds in a coquettish gesture of innocence. I watch and mimic her, my teacher. We dance alone. No one wants to leave the fire or miss another round of tea, except Nima, who sits down to watch. We dance on, my teacher and I. I lose myself to her charms, and the moment, as I sway to the *mondal's* rhythm. I am a goddess, anointed by a child, baptized by rain, brightened by the sun.

Only when everyone readies to leave the teahouse do we stop. Annapurna holds my hand tight. I want to take her with me, but instead present her with my yo-yo. I bow to this goddess child and feel a deep loneliness as I take my leave.

By the time we reach Ghasa, at 6,562 feet (2,000 m), a village of wood homes among forests and ferns, the rain falls steadily. We thank Montego, who has booked rooms at a lodge. Dry, cozy, and crowded, we are happy to mingle with international guests around a wood-burning stove. I enjoy the change in company. A couple from New Zealand talks with Paul. Others, from France and Spain, speak among themselves. The group of Italians, the ones who watched me bathe at Chyamje, nod to me, and I blush. On a bench that lines the wall, a Polish woman sits reading in one corner, Sharon in the other. Most are traveling without Sherpas. They prefer to carry their own gear, and stay and dine in lodges. As Pema comes in from the kitchen with tea and popcorn, I am grateful for the camaraderie of the Sherpas.

The next day, I decide to walk alone and try to understand the changes that have come over me. I think of Nima. I think of Nepal. My changes reflect the surroundings. In this infinite landscape, I feel free. More open. Happy. Strong. Never have I been so aware of the impact of place on my outlook. What am I doing in Los Angeles? I never chose to live there; it just happened. The firm I worked for in Chicago decided to open an office in Los Angeles, and I wanted to leave the Midwest, where I grew up. Now I feel stuck. I need to take control, be more aware of my needs, and set my course.

As we drop another 2,000 feet (610 m), the forest opens up to bamboo and poinsettias taller than I am. The Buddhist Thakali live in this area, as do the Magar, who practice both Hinduism and Buddhism. Terraced fields become more frequent, with high-altitude crops of barley and potatoes giving way to rice and millet. Women dressed in color-ful saris stand calf deep in water and bend over to plant rice. Through the genius of local engineering, water has been diverted from creeks to flood rice paddies in a controlled flow. At times, we walk along the edge of a paddy. As I watch water stair-step down a mountainside to irrigate fields that feed the villagers who reside at the foot of Annapurna South, I marvel at their ingenuity.

The architectural vernacular, dependent on local materials, changes with altitude. As in the lowlands we began in, the thatched-roof houses are red-and-white adobe made from a combination of dung for adhe-sion and clay for color. I see a woman refresh the entry of her home by slathering a mix of ochre-colored clay and dung over its front stoop. As a counterpoint to these ancient construction practices, solar panels and water tanks provide electricity and hot water to the more fortunate, while others live as they have for generations in huts of woven bamboo with rice-stalk mats for floors. I stop to watch a family on their verandah; a grandmother sleeps, a young child dresses a baby, and a mother peels potatoes for supper, and sings. Beyond, the father plows the fields behind yoked water buffalo, a group of older men squat near the trail to smoke, and a young boy perched in a tree cuts firewood with his *khukuri*. This is a different kind of busy than in Los Angeles; subsistence living gives purpose, and days spent in nature give pleasure.

Just before Tatopani, election signs reappear. Many are in Nepali, but one stone along the trail reads "Long Live CPN United (M.L.)." Nima is pleased Nepal will hold its first-ever democratic elections for national leadership, but is not certain anything will change. He does not trust the politicians, although voting—the opportunity to politically express oneself—excites him. He dreams that one day, the Sherpa, the Gurung, and other Buddhist ethnic groups in Nepal will have elected officials with influence.

"My dream," says Nima. "Everyone equal."

The hot springs of Tatopani, at 3,871 feet (1,180 m), is a popular destination with trekkers. *Tato* means "hot"; *pani* means "water." My dream, I tell him. His hype made me anticipate more than the two shallow, stone-lined pools, one murky, the other almost empty of water. A wood hut sells limited "spa services" and sodas. There are no towels, robes, or good-looking masseurs for a rubdown afterward. I look at Nima. He would do, but I don't ask. The rest of our group sits along the edge of a steamy hot tub, soaking their feet. I untie my boots and step in. *Ahhhhh.* Even I, the skeptic, linger.

The climb today is brutal, as the trail rises 5,233 feet (1,595 m) in elevation from Tatopani to Ghorapani. We begin our ascent in oak forests on steps of well-crafted stone towards Ghorapani. According to Nima, the villagers maintain the trails in their neighborhood, for these trails are their highways. The footsteps of generations of travelers have worn each stone step concave. Paul and I walk one behind the other and switch places every so often. He is proud of the progress he has made on this trek. I tell him he should be, and compliment him on how fit and trim he looks. He tells me that climbing got easier once he learned that a steady pace is better than sprints until exhaustion. Be the tortoise, not the hare.

Hypothetically, Paul wants to know what I think about the viability of a relationship between two different cultures? I tell him it depends on the two people. I ask Paul if there is someone that he's interested in. He's not. Could I ever marry someone from an Asian culture? he asks. It would be fascinating, I tell him. Paul makes his point: How about a Sherpa? He knows. I pretend to ignore him. I like Nima a lot, Paul tells me, and I know Nima likes you.

As in any repetitive act, climbing these stone steps becomes a meditation. After an hour, conversation becomes infrequent. The group grows quiet, reflective. Like these rocks, we are trampled on, and like earth under pressure, we become strong. We now carry ourselves up to our goal with grace. All morning, we climb steps of all sizes: short and tall, broad and narrow, flat slabs and boulders, and where the land flattens out for a short distance, dirt and pebbles. I follow Nima when the others fall behind. Are we there yet? Nima smiles. Nepal has taught me that there are many false peaks that promise, only to disappoint. Celebrate only after you have arrived.

"Are you testing me to see if I'd make a good Nepalese woman?" I tease Nima. He grins.

"You'd make a good Sherpani."

At the edge of a dense rhododendron forest, Montego warns us to stay together, as a woman recently disappeared here. At the last teahouse, I had seen a photo of a British woman on a "Missing Person" poster. I had felt safe in Nepal until then. Each of us walks with a guide. Through an arch of pink rhododendron trees at least seventy feet (21 m) high, Nima leads us into darkness, for the rhododendrons' thick leaves block out most light. Cool, moist air wraps around me like the moss on the trees. Gnarled tree roots reach out for me like the arthritic hands of an old witch, ancient with evil.

"Watch it!" yells Nima, who grasps my arm as I slip. "Here, take my hand." I do, as he points out slippery roots to avoid. He holds my hand tight with his elbow locked to keep me close. I am fully supported by his body as he guides me in dim light over twisted bronze roots bedazzled by ruby-red petals. It's hot in here. His strength courses down his arm and into my hand. As I connect physically to this powerful man of gentle nature, a surge of energy fills me.

We walk on through a mist that fogs our perception. First, I see, or think I see, a child, barefoot and disheveled, who suddenly disappears like an apparition. Soon after, a thin woman in black eerily fades into, then out of, the mist between trees. I hear a siren's call. I want to follow her into an ancient fairy tale. Once forests like this covered the earth. As long as we feared the forests, their mysteries remained secure, but unable to resist their intrigue, we cut away at the forests' edges, generation after generation, until little is now left to fear. Or is it? Emboldened, we now use forests like these for our pleasure or our gain. We think we can win the upper hand. In these primal forests, I feel forced to confront what we have done to the land. We invented houses and locks, not to keep ourselves in, but to keep our fears and all that lives in the forest out. Today, our homes shelter us from the memory of trees.

I am unfamiliar with nature this primal. I feel afraid and stay close to Nima. We walk in sight of each other, our group's energy taut like a rope in tension. Roots rise and fall to create traps for toes; trunks too wide to see around harbor the unknown; with no wind, waxen leaves rustle only when touched; and I hear the leaves. The forest ignites my imagination. I think of J. R. R. Tolkien who wrote his experiences in similar forests into *The Hobbit*.

Fear dances on the edge of passion. As we near the edge of the forest, Nima stops before a rhododendron bush graced with light from above. He inspects several blooms and selects one. I hear the snap of a branch. He presents the red blossom to me, cradled in the palms of his outstretched hands.

Fear dances on the edge of passion. I clip the flower in my hair. Nima smiles. Framed by the pink and red blossoms around us, we are prince and princess in a fairy tale.

Fear dances on the edge of passion. Once out of the woods, and not wanting to lose my prince, I race down the mountainside after Nima, who runs in playful pursuit of three porters, who sprint toward a teahouse far below. I dance down the hillside between towering trees among a sun-dappled, spring-green fantasia of waist-high jack-in-the-pulpits, conscious of their phallic spadices. I focus on Nima ahead of me; there is no trail; the foliage hides what lies below. Nima taught me that when racing downhill, you must never hesitate. I trust Nima, and he trusts me, so I trust myself.

I arrive at the teahouse not far behind Nima and the three burdened porters. I did not hesitate. I know he'll be proud. I walk up to Nima, who sits in the sun and drinks tea at a table of Nepalese. He continues his conversation and ignores me. I enter the teahouse confused by his desire to be with me, then not. For ten minutes, I sit alone and question everything I have felt the last eighteen days. What do I want? What does he want?

Sharon, Paul, Saul, and Prudy join me. Paul asks what is bothering me. I slap on a smile and talk about the child and woman I saw in the forest. No one else saw anything. Perhaps they were not looking, or not searching. Myths, fairy tales, stories. Because all of these help one stimulate the imagination, search for identity, learn how to handle emotions, and explore the meaning of life, children love these tales. Am I such a child? My imagination runs wild here. Who I am is in question. My emotions reach highs and lows as great as the Himalaya. And I know less about life and where I am going than ever. I need answers, not tall tales. I order a Fanta, regret it comes with no ice, and drink it from the bottle. I eat the Indian version of snack food with a crunch. I desire sugar and salt, in a kind of *yab-yum* diet. My cravings may be satiated. My hunger is not.

At the end of a long day and a tough climb, we reach the village of Ghorapani at 9,104 feet (2,775 m). To accommodate the many tourists who visit, a profusion of lodges hang off the hillside among trees whose lower branches have been cut for fuel. To stay true to tradition, our group gathers with others to watch the sunset over the rhododendron forests and distant himals. As boisterous red and pink blossoms fade to black against a sky the color of rhododendrons, I stare at Nima in profile. This man has recolored my world.

We hike higher toward the skies. It is early morning. Thin cool dawn. A peak sparkles white between clouds below a moon colored coral like a bead that the eons have aged. The skies brighten. Day moves in.

Montego, Nima, and Tsuldim lead us up Poon Hill, 1,372 feet (418 m) above Ghorapani. No one brings backpacks, except Nima, who never feels right without one. Nima wears a long-sleeved T-shirt in pink with a white stripe down each arm. Two pink rhododendrons stick out from his pack frame at ear level. Sharon compliments him on his fashion choice. Paul tells him pink is a girl's color. Nima thinks he looks like the *zopkyok*, those colorfully decorated pack animals. "Nima *zopkyok*," we call him. He loves it.

From the grassy summit of Poon Hill, we look out over forests of rhododendrons in bloom. I watch a soft mist lift off the valley and a brightening light struggle to pull color out of the land. Below the hilltop, we face east and watch the sun rise. Colors grow more intense, from a silhouette without color into grays that suggest color to an explosion of white, pink, and red among green that stretches across the valley and up the mountainsides beyond. I will not be able to describe a rhododendron forest any better than I can the Himalaya. To know, one must travel at sunrise and bear witness.

After our descent from Poon Hill, we climb again to Deurali Pass at 9,941 feet (3,030 m). After an ascent to Poon Hill, the descent, and an even steeper ascent to the pass, we are tired of the ubiquitous roller coaster of Nepal's topography. As we crest the ridge, the views of Annapurna South and virginal Machhapuchhare, or "Fish Tail Mountain," help us forget our exhaustion. Montego tells us that the Nepalese will not issue climbing permits for anyone to summit the 22,956-foot (6,997 m) Machhapuchhare. Although some have tried without a permit, none have succeeded. From here, the village of Ghandruk far below appears to hang from a mountainside. Fertile terraces of ripening grain cover the slopes. The air is hot and humid, similar to our first day on trek, but now in tune with my environment, I take no notice.

In this part of Nepal, generations of families have tamed the land. The Gurung people, who are Buddhists, populate this area, and many Sherpas have friends and relatives here. As we drop down toward Ghandruk at only 6,365 feet (1,940 m), where we'll camp tonight, everything looks orderly. Terraces have been sculpted up and down every visible mountain-side from hilltop to the river in hundreds of steps, like a giant's stairway to heaven. Without the benefit of machinery, the Gurung have reshaped this monumental valley. As I sit on a stone wall and watch the moon come up over the valley, I find the immensity of their effort hard to fathom. I long to be back up in the high mountains where the natural world has barely been touched by man, and at least stands a chance of recovery. This highly manufactured landscape is the Los Angeles of Nepal.

After twenty days of trekking, our bodies are in tune with the environment. With extra oxygen in our blood, our pace is fast. We move along the edge of fields as we leave Ghandruk, then down steps toward the Modi Khola river far below. Even in the early morning, I feel the sun's heat, so I welcome the cool air of the deep valley as we descend into shadow. Part of the trade route, a well-constructed bridge crosses the wide river. Even in Nepal, commerce attracts infrastructure improvements.

After a climb up from the river, we reach Landruk by midmorning, a charming town of thatched-roof adobe houses decorated with simple symbols. On the stone plaza that marks the center of town, we sit at tables before the Shangri-La Guest House and Restaurant and order drinks. Nima, on his knees, balances green Sprite bottles vertically end to end. Now, at four, he tries for five. Focused, he holds the next bottle over the others. Two fingers hold the top of the bottle, while his other hand cups around its base, but without touching, as if to protect it, like a just-lit match, from a breeze. We hold our breath as he slowly lowers the bottle. Slowly. Pause. Slowly. Pause. Slow. Ly. Hold. His fingers release their hold. Five! A porter shouts Nima's new record. Five! For a moment, the world rests on its axis. Five, I whisper to Sharon. Laughter. Nima restarts the world. As bottles roll across the plaza, I like that Nima knows how to play.

From Landruk, we descend and follow a ridge past industrious Gurung villages and farms to our lunch stop. After a large meal, everyone spreads out across a broad terrace of grass. Most doze in the sun. Three Sherpas play cards. Sharon reads. From the edge of our mountainside terrace, I look down on a farmhouse and watch a woman work with a length of cloth. On her back, she carries an infant in a cloth slung over her shoulder; she squats to pick vegetables that disappear into folds of fabric that cradle her child. I wish her a crib. The young woman reappears on the roof without the child; she gathers ears of corn from under the eaves and places them into the cloth that hangs as a bag. I wish her a basket. After a time, she spreads out the cloth in the farmyard; she stone-grinds the corn and gathers up her flour with the cloth. I wish her a funnel. She gives the cloth a shake; she wraps it around her hips and inserts her *khukuri*. I wish her a scabbard. The young woman disappears into the forest; she returns with a bundle of fodder and the cloth protecting her back. I wish her a *doko*. She unpacks her bundle; she wipes her forehead with the cloth and entwines it turban-like around her head. I wish her a hat. She disappears below the terrace with a plastic jug; she reappears with the water jug balanced on the folded cloth on her head and swings her arms to her song. I wish for a magic cloth.

The Australian Camp above Dhampus, at 5,183 feet (1,580 m), is the most beautiful camp on the trek, Nima tells me, as we walk together after lunch. As we near, Nima points out a green meadow far below dotted with blue tents. Beyond are the shimmering waters of Lake Phewa. Around us rise Annapurna I, Annapurna South, Machhapuchhare, Annapurna IV, and Lamjung Himal, their snowy peaks delineated by grass and sky. Nima grins as if to say "I told you so" and races down the last hill toward camp. After lunch, Sharon and I pull out our sleeping pads and lie in the sun and talk. She confides that while she's ready for Everest, misses Harry, and is excited to see him again, she's worried. Mountains change a person.

I know what she means. I do not want our trek to end. I like to live day by day, each filled with the new, the unexpected. I like my fellow trekkers, and that we have found common ground. I like to laugh with the Sherpas. I like to live outdoors; watch the sun rise with a cup of chai in hand; and experience nature—a river for a bath, trees as umbrellas, and mountains to test me. I am fascinated to observe how I respond as I adapt to the topography of land, life, and Nima.

As if in acknowledgement, I squint up at the peaks that surround me. I may have begun as water, but at this moment, I feel more like rock, hard and fit. The baggage I brought from Los Angeles is gone. I am ready to take on—

At the sound of joy, I sit up. Nima tosses his keys high in the air and catches them in his held-open pant pocket. He rarely misses. He acts like a boy. As Nima chases after flying keys, the rest of us race after his laughter.

After so many clear mornings, today's is a disappointment. Haze flattens the view as the sun rises and clouds cut across Machhapuchhare's center, like a knife severing a fishtail. The pewter skies resemble fish scales as they give over to the last shimmer of life. I too feel resigned to fate, and I don't like it.

I don't want to return to the way I was. I have changed. I fear I will lose this tender new freedom. Vulnerable to influences, criticisms, and the familiar, I must remain vigilant. I must hold on to the spirit that got me over the pass, the mind-set that opened me up to Nepal. I like the new me. I want to keep it.

I miss the meandering trails of the mountains and resent the encroaching signs of civilization. Today, we hike a red dirt road built by the Chinese. Populated by Brahmans and Chhetris, the villages we pass through on our way to Pokhara are like "the strip" of American cities, for this highway attracts commerce in its worst manifestation. Dirty, dusty shops sell cheap Chinese and Indian imports—hung below roof eaves, displayed along porch railings, and cascading down steps toward the street. Signs advertise cigarettes, like Yak and Everest, or Bengali chew. Tata buses or trucks from India, fancifully decorated with Hindu gods and goddesses, travel loaded beyond capacity with people, goats, and chickens.

Our final night in the mountains is at Sarankot, a destitute town with relentless child beggars. No one is happy to see our campsite, adjacent to a dusty road, but our tents are set up and tea has been set out. Tashi tries to make up for the dirtiness of our campsite with a dinner of garlic soup, fried noodles with eggs, steamed vegetables with cheese sauce, *momos* with tomato relish, "buff" burgers (water buffalo), and a frosted cake. The cake prompts Paul to ask who is getting married. Both Sharon and Montego respond affirmatively. Paul warns me to be careful. It could be catching. Montego tells me I can no longer use altitude as an excuse. Earlier today, he told me about a friend's relationship with a Sherpa that did not work out. Too many differences. Montego knows.

I do not want the camaraderie I shared with the Sherpas to end. After dinner, as they crowd around the cook's fire, Nima asks me to join them for three-card poker. I agree on the condition that he be my coach, and follow him to the fire. At each hand, Nima leans toward me, points to a card, and whispers a move. Pick up the Jack of Clubs. Play the Eight of Spades. Keep the Queen of Hearts. I follow his lead. When it is my turn to deal, coach Nima moves from squatting behind me to sitting next to me. With a ruthless grin, Nima shuffles the deck like the best in Vegas, and before I can pick up my cards, he takes them. For all his playfulness, I now witness Nima's competitive side. The game is his. I am his financier. I succumb to the magic of *rakshi*, firelight, and Nima.

I am in the circle, and not. Language is a barrier. They talk Sherpa or Nepali. Nima, caught up in the card game, pays me no attention. I stare at the fire and track a flame down to its hottest point, its origination, to blue. Ironic. Blue is a cool color. I feel blue, like fire. Blue and hot. Slighted. Ignored. How could I ever think I was anything more than a client to Nima? And that he was anything but a vacation fantasy! Besides, I could never go back to Los Angeles with a Sherpa. No way! What is so natural in the Himalaya would be so impossible at home. Just picture everyone's reaction when I tell them about my new boyfriend. The difficulties it will bring to me, and to him. I should not care, but I do. Somewhere in those flames, I can envision a relationship with Nima. I watch the fire burn. No way could a relationship ever work. I'd be coal, a by-product of fire and pressure. Toxic. Toxic heat. Leave it buried, even if you only have to strip-mine to find what lies just below the surface.

A coal seam catches fire. Nima's arm ignites mine. I thaw. So smooth. I don't want him to move away. Body talk. Electric. Lean closer. Closer still. Spontaneous combustion engulfs us. Desirous, my body burns. Flames leap out from me, like from the gods on temple walls. My multiple arms brandish objects of obsession, pieces of memories of Nima and our trek around the Annapurnas. A curl of smoke lifts me onto a mountaintop. As the air clears, blue Nima floats on a cloud.

"Caryl. Caryl?" He nudges me. "Caryl, our turn. I need more money." Nima leans closer to count rupees laid out on the ground before us. We are engulfed. I burn. We burn. I know he burns. I know. I know him. I know Nima.

Nima extends his arm behind my back and I lean back. Lean back. Lean toward. Lean on. I touch him. Nima does not move his arm. As the crescent moon thirstily gulps snow from the mountain, I drink down the last of my *rakshi* and feel myself melt around Nima.

Pema and Montego take home most of the winnings. I get lucky and win big, only to lose big. Three times this happens, before I lose it all. Suddenly I hear my mother's voice—Lucky in cards, unlucky in love. Unlucky in cards, lucky in love. Tonight I go to bed feeling lucky. Although I have let my feelings for Nima go only skin deep, I sense a forthcoming gamble where we will both have to show our cards.

Given the altitude we reached, the end of our trek is anticlimactic. I never thought our trek would end like this. After two hours of trekking, we reach Pokhara. All anyone can think of is the life they have to get back to. The Sherpas have their families and friends. Nima has disappeared without a word. Sharon and Montego have their fiancés. Paul has his adult life ahead of him. Saul and Prudy are at home with each other, wherever they are. As I sit with Sharon before our lakeside bungalow at the Fish Tail Lodge in Pokhara, I think only of Nima and don't say a word. I am suspended. I am not going home. Just going. Alone.

> Death is the hunter. Don't be shy.
>
> —*Montego*

EVERYONE'S ARMOR HAS RETURNED, snapped into place for reentry into the civilized world. As we walk back together to the hotel through the dark cobbled streets of Kathmandu after our group's final dinner at the Yak & Yeti, I realize we acted as self-conscious as at our first dinner together before the trek. We remain strangers, although Sharon and I may get together in Los Angeles, and I may stay in touch with Paul, who needs a friend right now and told me he would call. With Nima out of the picture, it is easy to let go. Right now, I want no attachments. I want to move like water, steady and persistent with the ability to overcome obstacles. I want to delight in eddies, dance down waterfalls, and meander toward home. I convince myself that I am glad to have heard nothing from Nima. A relationship would dam my way.

On my third day in Kathmandu, as I walk east from the Thamel along Tridevi Marg, a taxi stops at the corner of the Royal Palace and blocks traffic. A man dashes toward me, dodging Range Rovers, Land Cruisers, buses, rickshaws, and *tuk-tuks*.

It's Nima!

"*Namaste*," says Nima. "I never got your address in California." He hands me a notebook. As I write, I wonder if I am doing the right thing.

Nima wants more.

"I'd like to visit you in America," says Nima.

"Not in Kathmandu? Not here?" I pause, confused. "I'll be at the Kathmandu Guest House after Chitwan." I describe for him the three-day elephant safari I have planned to the Royal Chitwan National Park along Nepal's border with India.

"I'm very busy," says Nima.

Forget him!

After breakfast, Montego, Sharon, and I take a taxi from Kathmandu southwest to Kirtipur to meet a professor from Tribhuvan University. The professor, who is helping Montego organize his wedding, is tall and lean, with darting eyes that take in each of us. He wears the traditional narrow pants, long shirt, and black vest, and sports a *topi* hat atop his graying hair. Everything in Nepal has significance, the professor later tells me, even the *topi*. Part of formal attire, like a tie to Westerners, the *topi* is worn when visiting government offices, by businessmen and on special occasions. Worn to one side, its asymmetrical shape represents Mount Kailas in Tibet, the most sacred mountain to Buddhists and Hindus.

In Nepal, the religions mix. The professor is Hindu. The wedding location for Montego's ceremony is a glimmering gold Buddhist temple with commanding views of the valley. The professor knows enough about Buddhism to make the arrangements. After a temple tour and Montego's approval, the professor introduces Montego to the musician who will play at his wedding. In spite of the musician's shyness, the professor insists that he play a tune for us. The middle-aged musician's face looks worn from worry and the sun. His orange-and-black *topi* is cocked toward his left eyebrow, and his head tilts in the same direction as he tucks a small fiddle or *saranghi* under his chin. As he raises the bow and begins to play, all I want to do is dance. We clap and shower him with accolades. The musician carved this *saranghi*, says the professor. The musician turns it over to show us the elephant god, Ganesh, whose trunk winds up the neck of the instrument. A hide stretches over the bowl on the face below four wire strings played by a bamboo bow. We all express delight with the craftsmanship. After encouraging the musician to sell his *saranghi*, the professor acts as middleman and begins to barter.

New beginnings and luck are manifest in Ganesh. Shiva's consort Parvati, who is also known as Annapurna, the goddess of abundance, bore the child Ganesh. When his head was accidentally severed, an elephant's head was grafted onto his neck. Ganesh has one tusk and a fat, white-skinned belly; rides a shrew; and loves food offerings, especially on the propitious days of Tuesday and Saturday. His four arms hold a discus, a mace, a conch, and a lotus. With godlike powers, Ganesh decides who succeeds and fails, who places obstacles, and who removes them. I like Ganesh. I offer a fair price and buy the ten-inch fiddle. The musician looks relieved. Pleased with the progress of his wedding plans, Montego returns with Sharon to Kathmandu. I remain with the professor, who has offered to give me a tour of Kirtipur and beyond.

As we walk the narrow streets between sun-baked brick homes with carved-wood windows, the professor reminisces about old Nepal and remembers a time with no cars, no crime, and no trekkers, as his country was closed to most outsiders. The Nepalese lived a simple village life; they grew their own food and raised animals; they socialized with their extended families who lived nearby. We were a happy country, the professor tells me, as he describes how the women wore ankle bells and danced in the streets. He misses the sound of their bells. In the past, he says, men were home, not on trek or traveling abroad or in Kathmandu running a business, like today.

Families were closer then. Wistful, he grows quiet. I think of my own family. My parents left home when they went to college and never moved back. I did the same. While we never danced in the streets or wore bells, my family ate dinner together, knew our neighbors, went to church, and felt part of a community. Now I live in Los Angeles, one of the most-populated places on the planet. No wonder I feel lost.

"You live in America. You are fortunate," says the professor, as he motions toward his motor scooter. "Come. Let's go."

After a short scooter ride, the professor and I dismount at the birthplace of the Kathmandu Valley. Traditional ways dissipate like the smoke that belches from factories at Chobar Gorge, cast off for the benefit of material progress. According to both geologists and myth, eons ago, the Kathmandu Valley was a lake. Each religion practiced here tells a different story about the valley's birth. The Buddhists tell of a turquoise lake and a lotus flower that floated in its middle. As a manifestation of the primordial Buddha, Ādi-Buddha or Svayambhū, the lotus emanated a blue light. This sacred flame drew devotees from distant lands to its shores. The professor points out a deep divide in the rocky hillside. That is where the Wisdom Buddha, Mañjushrī, used his flaming sword of wisdom to cut through the mountain that held back the water, thus draining the Kathmandu Valley, says the professor. On the valley floor where the lotus settled, they built the great *stūpa* of Swayambhunath.

I follow the professor toward the sounds of sitar and flute to an open gazebo adjacent to a Hindu temple. We sit down on cushions to listen. The Nepalese audience pays us no mind, as if we were expected. I close my eyes. In spite of his disappearance at Pokhara, all I envision is Nima. I am sitar. Nima is flute. I am enchanted. We play well together, as counterpoints, one sonorous and philosophical, and the other light and playful. Our song is long. I like that. I pray for a harmonious future together, for guidance, and to give thanks. *Sitar and flute.* Ancient. Intertwined. Bound. At the rustle of silk and the jingle of bangles, I open my eyes. The woman next to me moves over to let the professor stand. The professor extends his hand and I rise. Our song is not over; the coupling of sitar and flute continues.

The professor stops next at a small temple near the river. He takes my hand, walks me under the eaves, and cranes his head back to look up. I do the same. Holy sex! Copulating couples are carved into the wood roof eaves. Each strut demonstrates a different sexual position. Considering the shyness of the Nepalese, I am surprised to find the sex act honored and celebrated on their temples. A well-endowed man enters a woman from behind and clasps her hourglass waist, while her melon-shaped breasts pop out toward us. In the next one, two men and one woman form a sandwich of bodies as they alternate which end is up. In the next, he mounts a woman, his cannon ready to shoot. Each woman is the same; her face serene, her hair crowned with jewels, and her figure iconic. Is this to teach? Are the monks not as celibate as I thought? I am too embarrassed to ask the professor, even though he tries hard to engage in conversation about their positions.

At the village of Chobar, the professor suggests a leisurely climb up stone steps to a temple high above us. He stops often to point out sites of interest. It's good to rest, he tells me. Midway up, he pauses yet again, faces me, and takes both of my hands in a way that makes me wonder where this is going. He smiles enigmatically as he tells me how I must have done many good deeds in the past to be rewarded with this pilgrimage. Now it is my turn to smile.

"Karma good," says the professor. He squeezes my hands and takes one. I want to believe he's the nice grandfatherly type, and let him get away with this intimacy.

At the top of the hill is the towering pagoda of Adinath Lokeswar Temple, whose façade lies buried beneath a celebration of kitchen utensils: water vessels, pots, pans, colanders, ladles, and more. As a bold public symbol of domesticity, Hindu newlyweds make offerings to ensure the prosperity of their household. Marriages are arranged in Nepal, as they last longer if families are compatible, according to the professor. He's been married for decades. He explains the well-defined roles of their ancient civilization: the husband works; the woman takes care of the home, the children, her husband, and his extended family if she is blessed. And she will bear him many sons, if he is blessed. Parents know what is best for their children.

Dun. Dun. Dun. An aluminum ladle moves slightly in the wind, gently sounding a brass plate. Nima told me that Sherpa women were independent. What if they are not? Would he expect me to cook for him every night? Be at home? Have lots of children? The professor is Hindu. The Sherpa are Buddhist. I want to ask the professor about the cultural differences of their relationships, but I don't want to explain why I ask.

At the professor's home, I get a glimpse of marital bliss. While his wife cooks us a lunch of *daal bhaat*, the professor and I sit on the floor beyond the kitchen curtain and talk of Hindu customs. I meet his wife when she serves us, but she never joins us for lunch, and will eat only after her husband and his guests are satisfied. Before the professor begins to eat, he pinches a few grains of rice from his plate and throws them over his shoulder while chanting a prayer. The Nepalese honor the effort the rice made to grow, he tells me, and they celebrate the sustenance they derive from it. The professor eats with his hands. I eat with a spoon. When I ask a question, he tells me that to talk and eat is not good for digestion. I refrain. I hear the sound of my spoon hit the stainless steel plate. I hear the flies overhead. I hear silence. Our silence honors the rice.

After lunch, life in Nepal slows down for an hour. When the professor's wife takes our dishes, I thank her. She nods and disappears behind the curtain. The professor excuses himself and returns dressed in a light white cotton shirt and pants. It is time for my nap, he tells me. He points me to a daybed bright with sunlight, then goes to lie down on a rug in the kitchen. I doubt I can sleep here, but I do. Thirty minutes later, I wake up refreshed, with the sun on my back and a desire for Nima.

My day with the professor continues to be one of premonitions. That afternoon back in Kathmandu at the home of his French friends, the professor presents me with his book on Nepalese marriage customs. Marry a Nepali, he tells me. A Nepali will make you a good husband. He pats my hand. Good husband. His friends nod in agreement. I let him know that he is not the first person to tell me that. As he chatters on about his wedding years ago, I open to the table of contents. There it is. I can leave now.

Back in my hotel room, I open the book and read the chapter entitled "Sherpas."

Kathmandu is a gentle city, but there is much to explore throughout the surrounding Kathmandu Valley. I walk the main boulevards out of the city center and head south toward the ancient royal city of Patan. My map is worthless in its haphazard maze of pedestrian streets and alleyways, as fire: Death is the hunter. Don't be shy.

I search for the Golden Temple. Hopelessly lost, I hire Savendra, a young man who has been trailing me, as my guide. We walk through a labyrinth of courtyards and rooms, each unveiling itself as we pass through one opening after another, until I lose all orientation.

Some relationships crescendo more quickly than others. Savendra chats as we walk, curious to know where I am from, how long I have been in Nepal, and what I am doing here. He stops. Do I like the Nepalese? He looks into my eyes and asks this with great seriousness. I laugh and tell him I do. I like their kindness. In between his questions, Savendra points out historic or religious sites as we pass them. He's a nice young man, and I respond kindly to his interest and curiosity. As we enter the interior courtyard of the Kwa Bahal or Golden Temple, I notice we are alone. The original Buddhist monastery was built at this location in the fourteenth century CE or earlier, says Savendra. The afternoon sun flashes off metal roofs of gilded copper, a contrast to the intricately carved wood windows and brick façades. He motions for me to follow him to a dark corner. I listen as he explains a wall painting about the wheel of life that illustrates the stages from birth to death, from Eden-like landscapes to hell. As I move in closer to see more detail, Savendra moves closer to me. We almost touch. In simple English, he whispers to me how beautiful I am, how rich Americans are, and then he says what I now realize he intended to say to me from the beginning: "I love you. Love me?"

"No!" I jump away. Savendra is not deterred. He wants marriage, children, and America. Now. Does he think an American girl traveling alone is more desperate than he is? I laugh. He can't be serious. You don't even know me, I tell him.

Savendra insists he does. He knows our love will be beautiful. As soon as I saw you, I knew, he tells me. His brown eyes look at me, through me, and all the way to our American shores.

What a line! He's not a guide. He only wants to get to America. Love me? He doesn't even know my name. This man is a joke. A con. And Nima? Nima is not a joke. Nima is not a con. Nima is NOT a—Now doubt lingers over Nima like smog over Kathmandu. My chest aches. I

101

feel dizzy from too much happening so fast. I shove a handful of rupees at Savendra and walk away with the hope that I will not need another guide to find my way home.

Nepal is a land of contrasts, and I love that it is so different from my home. As I leave Patan, I walk back to Kathmandu along the polluted Bagmati River, whose banks are home to destitute children who play in its mud, women who wash clothes in its waters, and men who squat in the nearest shade to smoke. Back home, my homogeneous existence allows me to easily ignore the poor, who are relegated to neighborhoods the more affluent never have to enter. I know they exist, feel empathy for them, give money to charities that support them, but otherwise, I live my life with little thought about their existence. It is easier that way. Driving in Los Angeles traffic is stressful enough. I don't need to try to save the world. Here the poor are part of the tapestry of a community, woven into society, rather than cut out and set aside. I am fascinated by this different paradigm.

Back at the hotel, I take a cool shower and read for an hour. I dress for dinner and walk to the nearby La Dolce Vita restaurant, where I order manicotti and a salad. I eat alone. Not wanting to return to my room, I write postcards. I talk to a German couple seated next to me who have just come from an ashram in India. I envy their companionship. If I go back to my hotel, I will only feel disappointed that I have heard nothing from Nima. I order another glass of red wine and sit back to listen to the music. *Sitar and flute.*

When Montego comes in with friends, I am glad I decided to stay. He thought I was in Chitwan. I thought he had returned home to Mexico.

"Good luck on your trip. Be careful." He hugs me. "Oh, and happy marriage." He laughs.

"And what do you mean by that, Montego?"

"Death is the hunter. Don't be shy." Montego winks and rejoins his friends.

What did Nima tell him? I am not on a 'round-the-world husband hunt. A relationship is the last thing I need right now. One is easier. No conflict or confusion. Except the minute I think I am back in control—Boom! I am starting to think I should fear contentment more than turmoil. Contentment is transitory. Turmoil is not.

I want to talk to Nima. After I return from Chitwan, I will have only four days left in Kathmandu. I need to know how he feels; and even more, what do I feel?

I take out a pen, flatten my napkin, and draw two columns. "Pro" heads the left column. "Con" heads the right.

Pro	Con
Good–looking	Bad clothes
Sex appeal	STD?
Joyful	Constant smile (believable?)
Kind	Dark side not known
Wise	3rd grade education
Funny	Bad slapstick jokes
Big family	Family issues?
Speaks seven languages	Limited English
Walks 3x faster than me	Doesn't drive
Extremely strong	Doesn't look strong
Hard worker	Hard gambler?
Does not drink	Used to smoke & chew
Climbing/trekking guide	Non-transferable skills
Rich in spirit	Poor

I've never used the word *wise* to describe anyone I've dated before. Interesting word choice. He must be smart to speak so many languages, although his limited education is where our differences will show the most, where others will judge him. I may accept him, but will my family and friends? What about his lack of civilized acumen? Does he own a suit, know manners, understand wines? Has he read Shakespeare?

J. D. Salinger? Wendell Berry? At least Hermann Hesse's *Siddhartha*? Can he even read?

In America, I will be the guide. Do I want that? Do I really know him? Know his culture? Poor is problematic. Does that matter? Poor. If it is true love—Poor will matter. Love and no money. Failure from the start. In Los Angeles, he will not find work as a climbing/trekking guide, so what can he do? Some minimum-wage job, so I have to support us both? Not my partner! Not again. Poor matters. Poor matters a lot.

Life is exhausting enough, and here I am wearing out my brain imagining something that is not going to happen. Nima has not called. I am going to Chitwan early tomorrow. When I get back, I will have only four days left. How much can happen in four days? And back in the States, without the exoticism of Asia, I cannot fathom starting a relationship with Nima. Marry a Sherpa? Impossible!

I decide to forget about Nima and focus my desires on sighting a Bengal tiger. Heading southwest from Kathmandu, I travel by car to the Terai region, which borders India, to spend three days at the Royal Chitwan National Park. Royal Chitwan, in the Rapti Valley at just 492 feet (150 m) above sea level, was once the private hunting grounds for Nepal's royalty. Today, these choice lands of floodplain jungles and elephant grass are nature preserves to protect the Asian elephant, one-horned rhinoceros, Bengal tiger, and all life of these lowlands.

Nestled among a forest of towering *sal* trees, the Chitwan Jungle Lodge is a cluster of bungalows that surrounds a thatched circular dining room among gardens that lead out to the elephant mounting station and pens. In the lowlands near the Indian border, heat settles on the day like an anvil. I am happy to flow from one planned activity to another, as languid as the Rapti River we float down in our wooden canoe. I have expended too much time and imagination on the impossible. I no longer want to think. I drift. The spirits will determine my harbor.

Over dinner my first evening at the resort, I make friends with a Belgian couple who take me into their care during our three-day safari.

Their closeness only makes me miss Nima. Richard, tall and rail thin, has blue eyes that provide a much-needed contrast to his khaki coloring and clothes. Although Emma looks matronly by comparison, and plump in her lace-collared blouses, she is surprisingly open to everything. Together, we three share an elephant with his *mahout*, or trainer. The mahout sits just behind the elephant's head with his feet under her earflaps to steer, while we sit in opposite corners straddling the bamboo frame on the elephant's back with our feet in leather slings. We track a tiger; chase a one-horned rhinoceros as he crashes through the forest; wonder at the novelty of the tropical flora and fauna; and one day, catch a glimpse of paradise.

"Un Ange!" shouts Emma from her seat opposite me on the elephant, as we tromp through the jungle's understory. Our mahout abruptly stops our elephant. No one moves. We fall silent in disbelief. Between the trees flies an angelic white bird with twenty-foot (6.1 m) tail streamers that arch gracefully behind. For a moment, our dreams materialize on the wings of this mystical vision. Back at the lodge, our safari guide tells us we are blessed, for the paradise flycatcher is the most spectacular bird in the Terai, and as rare a sight as the Bengal tiger.

Come evening, the throb of drums and a fire call everyone to the dance circle. Only I am alone. I stare into the flames and think of Nima, who sat close to me on that last night of our trek before a fire. I feel the burn. I wish him here. Neither moonlight nor starlight permeates the jungle canopy. Blackness engulfs us, except for the firelight that glows brighter as it catches more logs. I look for him in the fire. I stare. The drums. I focus. The drums. I see blue. I see blue Nima with white me.

With a crash of percussion instruments, I look up to see people from an ancient tribe of the Terai, the Tharu, gather around the fire. Each man is dressed in a short white shift belted with a hip-height red sash and holds a thick bamboo pole. As the beat changes, the men begin to dance. Battles are re-enacted through a series of bold rhythms with bodies, sticks, and drums in crescendo. Stick to stick, stick to shoulder, twirl, stick to stick, lunge back, jump up, stick to stick, twirl, all in a ferocious demonstration of athletic prowess. And always the throbbing drums. The Tharu men prowl around and eye each other, pacing like tigers. As drums explode, the battle begins. Stick to stick, in rapid exchange, they beat off their opponents, as each jumps and lunges at the other. Some leap over the fire to crash sticks with another alone on the other side. Others twirl and whirl, while sticks bash and crash in a communal frenzy.

Enthralled, I watch their imaginary night battle, so ferociously fought by these sons of ancient warriors. What is it they battle? The night? Their fears? Their brothers? The intrusion of outsiders into their homeland? This is more than a dance; they are obsessed. Suddenly, in one unanimous leap, their sticks meet in a crushing blow above the fire. When bare feet rest again on dry earth, there is silence.

I breathe deep the steamy jungle air to quiet my inner stirring, aroused by the fervor of their movements and thoughts of a Sherpa. A dark, handsome Tharu man approaches, grasps my hand, and leads me to the dance circle. Others have similarly been summoned to dance. We place our hands on the shoulders of the person before us, until we are one. Sweaty from exertion, the heat of my partner's hands melts through my T-shirt. My body burns. Nima holds me. I do not turn around. I do not want to be disappointed. Nima. Nima. Nima. The drums pound his name deeper into my psyche.

A jungle rhythm interrupts my reverie. As feet pound the earth, bodies begin to move in unison, and an international circle of pulsating bodies dances around the flames, up and down, forward and back, side to side, commanded by strong hands on the taut skin of drums, pounding, tapping, and beating out sounds fit for a sweltering tropical night. Primordial spirits awake in me as I share this dance of endurance and mystery with unknown men and women, for together we are bound, physically by our touch and spiritually in our dance, as burning embers fade, and yet on and on we dance to exhaustion, for no one wants to stop, or be released, so we circle around, and strong shoulders steady me, and my tired feet barely lift themselves from the earth, for our togetherness maintains my strength, and only much later is desire danced out of me, when a communal peace fills the void as drums erupt into silence and the Tharus release the bond, and at that instant, we leap in unison in one climactic gesture to the spirits, arms flung skyward as we shout our release to—night!

I am "un" bound.

This is not Los Angeles. The drive back to Kathmandu from Chitwan follows thousands of hairpin turns over a sometimes-paved road. I focus on the horizon line to fight off nausea. We climb to over 4,500 feet (1,372 m) on a ribbon of road, traverse steep and at times almost-vertical hillsides, ride their crest, then drop down to cross a river, and do it all again. As I look down, I notice how the rugged terrain of the area has been domesticated into terraced fields of wheat, rice, and vegetables, the fields dotted with houses that match the color and texture of the land. Unlike the geometrically plotted subdivisions in the States, or randomly shaped organic ones, the Nepalese live in harmony with the land and respond to its topography.

I see the relationship of farm to house to village. Even the footpaths are visible, where they connect community and country. Footpaths bind Nepal, not the roads, and not a single freeway. These ancient footpaths, used for centuries to transport people, animals, and goods, are still used today by necessity, as roads access only a small percentage of the villages and an even smaller number of homes. I am surprised how few people have cars, but then again, few places can be visited by automobile. Instead, Nepal is a country of personal connections. Pedestrians, an endangered species in Los Angeles, converse with each other here, stop for tea, offer help, or walk together. I was never lonely on the trails. Children asked, Gimme a pen? Goats with their herders jostled me as they passed. Lodge owners beckoned me in for tea. Trekkers shared stories and countries. Sherpas made me laugh.

Any messages? I ask the desk clerk, who checks and shakes his head. I have three and one-half days left. How could a Sherpa make me feel so miserable?

I nap fitfully for an hour, until a knock on my door startles me. Yes? I freeze. A Nepalese in the hall announces that someone is in the lobby to see me. I don't respond. Madame? I smile. Madame? He knocks. I fly off the bed. Thank you, I shout at the door. I'll be down.

It's Nima!

Where're my jeans? Damn it! And my T-shirt. It's wrinkled. And my hair hasn't dried. It may not be Nima. And if it is, he's already seen me on trek without a proper bath for days. And my earrings. How come every time I'm in a hurry I drop one? Damn. And what if it isn't Nima? Then what is all the fuss about?

The throw of the bolt echoes down the stairs. Locked. My door has closed.

Now walk. Down. Why do I have to be on the third floor? This is harder than descending the pass. Down. Down those wide, white marble stairs. The late afternoon light floods the stairwell. Intuition says Nima. I feel his energy. I am shaking. I feel like that junior high ingénue when popular Mick asked me to dance and held me awkwardly as we slow-danced across the gym floor to the Everly Brothers, and I tripped over his feet and grew red with shame, sure he'd never ask me to dance again. And he didn't. What if my meeting with Nima goes like that?

At the second-floor landing, I pause at a table that holds a pitcher of purified water. Pour. Steady. Drink. Cool. Pour. Stop stalling. I want to delay what feels increasingly inevitable. I stall to keep life, as I know it, in place. Sip. I stall to avoid a collision with the future. Sip. Cool. Better. Resistance is no longer possible. Steady. Make it a memorable entrance. Floatdown this grand stair. Be free. Be regal. Walk with the fate-is-inevitable-chin-up pride of the queens of Henry VIII. You may lose your head, but no one is going to see you flinch over it.

Somehow, the power of my conviction gets me down the stairs. I enter the lobby and the desk clerks smirk as they nod toward my guest. My precarious balance falters. I blush. They whisper as I cross the lobby. If our rendezvous feels difficult here, I cannot imagine surviving people's smirks and judgments at home.

Nima. It is you.

Namaste. Nima's smile is radiant. His trekking clothes have been abandoned for a shirt, jeans, and flip-flops. In the background, a young man watches us. Nima introduces Purba, who only smiles when I ask him a question, just like Nima smiles when he doesn't comprehend.

Kathmandu is undiscovered territory for us. Nima suggests we go for coffee. I suggest we go for beer. We silently dart between the cacophonous crowds of tourists, locals, shopkeepers, dogs, and *tuk-tuks* that fill the streets of a Thamel neighborhood in the late afternoon. Nima acts awkward and self-conscious. Where is the Sherpa confidence that attracted me to him in the mountains? Hardly a fortuitous start. I must be crazy to continue. Beside a street-level shop, we climb a flight of stairs to a pub. There is a sunny outside terrace, but Nima leads us back to a dark corner, out of discretion, or embarrassment. We order our drinks. Nima keeps an eye on the door and says nothing. I drink half my beer, nervous in his silence. Purba watches me. To break the ice, I chatter on about Chitwan, the jungle, and how I rode my elephant through tall grass toward the river in pursuit of a one-horned rhinoceros. Although Nima has never been on an elephant safari, he acts uninterested and keeps glancing at his watch. How can a Sherpa be so busy?

I took a bath in the river, I say, with my mahout—I pause for dramatic effect, hoping to get Nima's attention—and his elephant. Purba laughs. I continue.

It was so easy. When the elephant leaned forward, I grabbed her ears and climbed up her trunk, onto her back and then sat behind the mahout. Once in the river, the elephant showered us with water from her trunk.

Nima laughs, which makes me glad to know he is listening.

Then the elephant shivered and began to lay down in the water, I say. Did he crush you? Nima looks alarmed.

Almost, but I swam off. It's tough work to wash caked-on mud off an elephant's skin. I think her coarse hair scrubbed my hand more than my soft palm washed her bristly back. She just lay there, like a princess at a—

I realize neither of them will understand the word *spa* or its hot-stone massages, seaweed wraps, aromatherapy, manicures, pedicures, and facials, so I end the story by lingering over the word to suggest the experience—Spa-a-a-a-a.

Nima laughs. He wishes he could have seen me bathe the elephant. You will, I say. My Belgian friend, Richard, photographed the entire event.

Nima looks concerned. I thought you went alone?

I did.

Then who is the Belgian?

I describe Richard, an ethnologist and anthropologist, who spent over twenty years in the Congo. Do you want to join us at Mike's Breakfast tomorrow morning? Nima declines. He looks jealous, so I leave out the part about how I wore the Belgian man's clothes after mine got wet, first in the river, and later during a hailstorm; how we'd agreed to meet in Europe; how I'd spent three days with him and his wife; and how in all that time we never exchanged names until we went to say good-bye and exchanged addresses. Dancing with the native Tharus would have been too much. I do not want to lose Nima.

Richard's wife, Emma, is coming to breakfast too, I say. Please come.

I'm too busy, insists Nima.

Too busy! To think that I thought he was interested. Sure read that wrong. Bet he doesn't even know where Belgium is. Or the Congo. Too busy? I have three days left in Nepal. Forget about him! I sip my beer, watch him squirm, and let our pregnant pause go to full term.

Come to dinner, he says. Tomorrow at my house. Nima guides me back from the edge. I'll pick you up at the hotel at five. He confirms before I can compose an answer.

Tourists, trekkers, and those who work with them come to Mike's Breakfast to escape the chaos of Kathmandu. The next morning, only Emma joins me for brunch. Richard is ill. We travel by rickshaw, bumping along side streets to Durbar Marg, and then turn off and stop before Mike's, hidden behind stucco walls in a canopy of trees. Located in the courtyard of an old estate of the former ruling elite, the once opulent and now decaying home is a backdrop to the new Nepal that caters to foreigners, rather than banning them. We sit at a table beneath bottlebrush, banana palms, trees and bamboo, order *crêpes* with fresh yogurt and tropical fruits, and share a pot of tea. The songbirds above us will dine off our crumbs.

fire: Death is the hunter. Don't be shy.

Emma loved living in a foreign country, she tells me. She and Richard have been married over twenty-five years, and they lived together in the Congo much of that time. She raised their children, kept a home, and worked with him in Africa. Emma loved the daily newness of the place and the unexpected. She learned the local customs from those she worked with and those who worked for her. She preferred the Congo's weather to Belgium's weather. Emma enjoyed having Richard all to herself, as family was far away and never came to visit. She had friends, but most expats came and went, so she never got too close or too tired of them. She liked the cost of things, except the imported goods. She appreciated the informality compared to her country, although at times, the locals had to be taught proper manners. She also enjoyed helping Richard with his work, being part of his team, and receiving respect for her work, in spite of her lack of formal training. But mostly, Emma liked the freedom.

I too would like the freedom, so—Could I live in Nepal, live with someone who is gone much of the year on trek, and make a cross-cultural relationship work? And could Nima commit his life to a wife?

I wanted America my whole life.
This is my dream!

—*Nima*

NIMA PICKS ME UP FOR DINNER at the Kathmandu Guest House thirty minutes late. In Nepal, there is a phenomenon known as Nepalese time. Locals, who give appointment times a wide berth, consider it normal to be late, or early. The Nepalese do not understand why we Americans never have time, complain of it, are frustrated by it. No rush. No worry. There is always tomorrow. Whoever first said the proverb "Never put off until tomorrow what you can do today" doomed Americans to a life of toil. It is insidious the way such ideas seep into a population. I constantly seek efficiencies and rush to squeeze in one more activity. I go to bed exhausted and can't sleep for thoughts about tomorrow or yesterday. Thanks to Nepalese time, I am now at least aware of the pressure I put on myself.

When I enter the hotel lobby, Nima looks out of his element. He stands close to the exit and twists a finger around his hair, which he's had trimmed since yesterday. He wears jeans and a T-shirt under his black, pink, and turquoise jacket with the embroidered Buddha Vairochana eyes on its back. He loves that jacket and wears it with confidence. The jacket was made in France, Nima told me while on trek, adding that the French wear the brightest colors of all the trekkers. I wonder if he identifies with them, or just likes their style. American men would have thought it feminine.

I greet Nima with a *Namaste* under the ever-watchful eyes of the desk clerks. He looks embarrassed and walks out into the courtyard without holding the door. I exit behind him, lost in my own thoughts about where this is going. I have no doubt that many foreign women have had dalliances with the locals, and then never saw them again. Am I to be just another one?

As if inspired by the red hibiscus blooming in the hotel courtyard, Nima can no longer contain his excitement. "I got my visa!" he beams. Nima says that in the morning he received a six-month visa, and he will leave for Seattle in ten days, so come afternoon, he called his friend Jules in Portland to tell him, bought his plane ticket, and packed. I squeeze his arm.

"I'm so happy for you, Nima." A relationship could really be possible. *I can do this. I must do this.*

In that moment, I decide my future and tip toward Nima. Unable to communicate my feelings at this moment, I express surprise that he is packed already. I tell him it took me months to plan and pack for my five-month trip.

"I'm not rich like you," says Nima. "Not so many things."

I work hard to forgive his poverty. I must if this relationship is to work. I question whether I have it in me to support another man. I had told myself I would not. The United States is in recession, and even minimum-wage jobs had dried up before I left. Will he want to live in there with me? I love Nepal, but could I give up everything I've worked so hard for? I could never let go that much. As we walk toward his house in the Lazimpat neighborhood, I worry. Nima, on the other hand, details for me the contents of his luggage, the arrangements he has made for his apartment and possessions in Kathmandu, and his plans for his arrival in America.

"I wanted America my whole life," says Nima. "This is my dream!" Caught up in his euphoria, I mirror his excitement. Nima is only just getting started. "And I can visit you in Los Angeles!" He twirls in the street like a dervish.

fire: I wanted America my whole life. This is my dream!

Nima in Los Angeles? What then? My excitement shatters. I am stranded, like a polar bear on an iceberg, unable to comprehend my fate. No one will be there to help. No one, but Nima. As we walk, Nima chatters on about his travel plans. I am not listening. How will his visit work? I wonder. My job demands too much of my time. He doesn't drive. Barely speaks English. And those clothes! Where can we go and feel comfortable? What if someone sees us together?

Nima senses my anxiety attack and inquires if it is okay for him to come to Los Angeles to see me. He wants to come see me. I push back. You're not coming to see me. You only want a tour guide and a free place to stay. Scared, I allow a mean edge to creep into my voice. You're not coming to see me.

Nima looks crushed. Yes, I am, he says. He speaks simply. You are my friend. I have fun with you.

I soften and half smile. He continues. I want to see you, and see all the things you told me about on trek. Do you want me to come? he asks.

I apologize for my harshness. Nima asks again. Do you want me to come? Nima sees the possibilities. I see the reality. Nima in America? With me? Of course, I want you to come, I say. I remind him how I gave him my address. I assure him, and myself, of the wonderful times that we'll have.

Nima in America—with me.

Nima brims over with questions. Is Seattle a big city? Bigger than Kathmandu, I tell him. Do I live near Seattle? Los Angeles is over three hours away by plane. Nima asks if I live on the other side of the country. I assure him I do not and inform him that he'll need five hours or more to fly across the United States. Five hours? Wow! Does my family live in my village? No, and Los Angeles is not a village, but a sprawling metropolis, a huge city, with over twenty million people. I am impressed by the power of the unconscious mind when I realize how often I say things to him in multiple ways, like "metropolis" and "huge city," as if to help him improve his English and comprehend new words in preparation for his future in America. Twenty million people? Wow! His village of Chhuserma has thirty-eight. I'm not sure who experiences more culture shock, him or me.

Nima wants to know where I'll go next, and if I am traveling with anyone after I leave Nepal. I explain that I'm joining my family in Prague and meeting friends in Switzerland and Sweden. Nima looks concerned. I assure him that I have no one. He'll arrive in America three months before I return, he realizes. While Nima expresses disappointment, I am relieved. Nima will have time to ease his rough edges before I see him in the United States.

"I received a six-month tourist visa," says Nima. "Three months with Jules. Three months with you." Nima's decision to move in with me has been made.

Nima's apartment in Lazimpat, near several national embassies, is in a nice neighborhood with tree-lined streets and newer buildings. However, in the humidity of Kathmandu, even new buildings look old in a matter of months, as the concrete façades stain easily from mold, water, and smog. His enclosed courtyard garden holds guava, mango, and banana trees, flowering red hibiscus, orange bird-of-paradise, and vines of peas and beans that tangle themselves around everything, including a few stalks of corn. As I pass by his garden, I am entranced. His ground-floor apartment is off a narrow side street populated by pedestrians and motorcycles, thus keeping the frenetic traffic noise at a distance.

My disappointment, when I find out there will be more than the two of us for dinner, surprises me. In the kitchen, the cooks stop long enough for Nima to introduce me to his sister Kandu, and his brother Nima Nuru, who, but for the curl in his hair, looks like a younger version of Nima. I'm from a big family too, I tell them, looking for acceptance. Four sisters. Two brothers. I hold up my fingers on one hand while pointing to first a female, then a male with the other, unsure who knows English. Nima's family makes me the center of their attention as they clear a place for me to sit and offer me chai. Although Nima has disappeared, his family dotes on me. Only later do I realize that this night was my introduction to typical Sherpa hospitality. Lesson one: You are seldom alone. Lesson two: Family is everything. Lesson three: All friends are family.

fire: I wanted America my whole life. This is my dream!

As I settle in, Zangbu, a Sherpa friend, arrives with his American wife, Beth. Zangbu is young, shy, and awkward when addressed in English, but certain of his forthcoming success in America. My first impression of Beth, although older than Zangbu, is young-at-heart and fun-loving, for her eyes laugh as much as she does. She loves the Sherpa, adores Zangbu, and tells me how proud she is to be part of their culture. She wears an *engi*, the typical Sherpani dress. Curious, I want to learn of her experience, but she disappears into the kitchen with the others.

While I sit alone and wait for the others to return, I look around the apartment. The sparse living room furnishings consist of a daybed, a bookcase, a tape player, a map of America, and competing posters of His Holiness the Dalai Lama and Sly Stallone, with Sly up by one. Colorful Tibetan rugs cover all horizontal surfaces. Four sagging iron beds are squeezed into two bedrooms, and in one, a curtain on a wire forms a closet to hide trekking equipment. The kitchen holds a propane stove, a tin sink, a table, and a stool. Bare bulbs light the rooms, and candles sit around for use during power blackouts, which happen on a rolling basis in Kathmandu, as demand for electricity surpasses supply.

When Nima returns, he hands me a pink album with a floral cover without a tinge of embarrassment and tells me that these are his photographs from his K2 expedition. Is that you on the camel? I ask. In rough, inhospitable desert terrain surrounded by earthen mountains, there is brown Nima, as if camouflaged to blend in with his camel and the landscape. Nima tells me how his expedition rode camels for seven days from Urumchi across the Tarim Basin, skirting the Taklamakan Desert and passing through Kashgar before crossing the Shagskam River to get to the north base camp of K2 in China. Besides the camels that carried the expedition members and their supplies, an additional seventeen camels carried liquor. I listen with disbelief as Nima describes his Japanese clients and their parties and pursuits on the mountain. Their expedition forged a new route, partially up the Northwest Face of K2 and crossing a portion of the North Ridge as well. K2 is the most difficult mountain to climb of the all the 8,000-meter (26,247-foot) peaks, says Nima. His voice drops to a whisper. I gave up climbing after that, he says. Then, my cousin Dawa died in an avalanche. I must take care of his wife and son.

Nima, you cannot blame yourself, I say. It was an unfortunate accident.

But if I had gone to Everest, he wouldn't have died.

Why does he tell me this story again tonight? It is too easy to fall for a man seeking empathy.

Kandu, his younger sister, reaches out with both hands to present me with the "Family Album," so identified by the gold script on its black cover. I open it with great anticipation, for I have not trekked the Sherpa regions of Nepal. Nima points out his parents and grandparents. The women wear plain jumpers with striped aprons. Most of the men wear Western clothes. I want to understand a woman's role in their culture and ask why the women wear traditional dress and the men do not. Nima tells me it's because most Sherpanis feel more comfortable in an *engi*. I sense that is a man's perspective, and suggest how hot and hard it must be to hike in a long wool skirt. He assures me that they are used to it. Kandu remains silent. According to Nima, Kandu likes to defy tradition and dress in pants. Tonight, she wears an *engi,* no doubt pressured by her older brothers. Only married women wear the apron, which according to Kandu can function as a pot holder, a carrier for wood or potatoes or beans, a towel to wipe one's hands, and a lap blanket to keep one warm.

Our fashions are far more frivolous, I tell them.

"Fffffribolous?" Nima wants to know what it means. Frivolous. Not having any real value or use, I tell him. Like high-heeled shoes. For style. He doesn't understand high heels and comments about how difficult they must be on trails. Too frivolous, he says, and looks to me for a reaction. You're smart, Nima, I say. He beams.

Memory is a muscle. While on trek, Nima had tried to teach me Sherpa, but we personified the cliché: my mind was a sieve, and his, a steel trap. He grew frustrated with repeating words to me, only to start all over the next day.

I thought Americans were smart, he told me one day, exasperated with my ineptitude.

fire: I wanted America my whole life. This is my dream!

We know a lot, I had answered, we just don't remember. We have books and libraries and computers. In the Solukhumbu, paper and pencils are a luxury, so Nima has had to remember things like accounting for the money he spent on treks when he was *sirdar*—thousands of dollars and thousands of calculations that he performed and retained in his head.

Do you remember everything I ever said to you? I ask.

Yes. He smiles. I think it fortunate that he does not always understand.

Nima goes back to the photo album. Only the older men sport the traditional tunic, or *chhuba*, tied on the side and worn over pants. His grandfather was a trader who traveled to India and Tibet. He planted a willow tree from China next to their old house. His grandfather either walked or rode a horse, and took pack animals with him. Yaks were used when going over the mountains, and horses when going south. When Nima was a boy, many villagers kept horses, but they ate too much, and as the vegetation thinned out, it became too much effort to climb high for fodder to feed them. Few travel by horse any more, Nima says. Yaks still cross the mountains with the Tibetans, but now, with limited ability to trade with Tibet, Sherpas walk to Lukla and take an airplane to pick up supplies in Kathmandu. Although their way of life has changed, I struggle with how I could ever fit into it. Nothing, absolutely nothing, is familiar to me until he says "airplane."

I'm not sure I'll ever get back to Nepal to see your village, I tell Nima. It's a long way to come. Like a salesman hot on a prospect, Nima ignores me and launches into more tales, pulling me in with his photos of Sherpa Shangri-La. He points out his house, a simple two-story stone structure nestled into a hillside with a high bluff beyond. I had envisioned it before. As a young girl, I used to dream of living in a simple two-story stone house with a symmetrical pattern of windows and a centered door, like the Pennsylvania Dutch homes of Lancaster County that we passed on our way to visit my grandparents in Philadelphia. In my mind's eye, I added a horseshoe-shaped driveway lined with lilacs to welcome my guests, and stacked stone walls to define the property. In Nima's photos, stone walls define their fields, and a footpath and an outhouse replace the lilac-lined driveway, but otherwise the similarity is uncanny.

The animals live on the first floor, says Nima, and the family above.

The barn animals live in your house?

Animals are family too.

Nima explains the efficiency of this arrangement: the animals heat the house; the family has to build only one building; it's safer for the animals. His relationship with animals is just as pragmatic, for to Nima, *zopkyok* are like sons who plow the fields. A *zom* is like the mother who earns money, as *zom* milk and butter can be sold at market. I express concern over the animals' smell. Everyone laughs. Nima explains the value of dung to fertilize fields, make plaster and mortar in buildings, and burn as fuel at altitude. I am not convinced. I ask him about the interior rooms. We live in one room, everyone together, he says. As if reading my mind, Nima blushes. No problem, he assures me. Everyone is used to it.

I stand my ground. "Well, I could never live over yaks."

"*Zopkyok* and *zom*," corrects Nima. It's too warm for yaks where his family lives, he tells me. But, everything is changing. These days, the Sherpa build lodges and teahouses for foreigners, not animals.

Nima and I have much to learn about each other. His family farms barley, wheat, potatoes, and vegetables. His mother and sisters used to spin wool to weave into carpets. Now his two older sisters run their own lodges in Lukla. His mother milks their *zom* and sells butter at the weekly market in Lukla, a two-hour walk down below their home. Could I really live there? I wonder. As children, Nima and his older brother Tshiring Tendi took their *zopkyok* and *zom* each summer to Lumding, the high pasture on the other side of the mountain to graze. He tells me of picnics at glacial lakes high above a valley, of waterfalls and hillsides of flowers.

"You must see it one day," says Nima, his face bright with memory. "See the other side of the mountain."

When I ask if he had a happy childhood, his smile shrinks to a line. He pauses and tells me how his father thought little of school. He needed the boys to care for the animals. And his father was mean. Nima ran away from home for good at fourteen. He had tried a year earlier, but his father brought him home. I could never have left home at that age, I tell him. Growing up, I was taught to be fearful of unknown places and people. My community was like milk, homogenized and white. I grew up among Christians of the Protestant religion. Catholics were different. Jews were exotic. I did not know anything about Buddhists or Hindus or Muslims. Blacks lived on one edge of town, Mexicans on the other.

"People are the same," states Nima. "Inside the same. The rest is like clothes. Like North Face person, or REI person, or Patagonia person. Otherwise, the same."

I wish I had photographs of my "village" to share with Nima.

I learn that Nima has never been to the ocean, although he flew over one once on his way to China. To look down on an ocean is one perspective. To wade into its water is another: the push of waves, the pull of kelp, the grace of gulls, the disgrace of flotsam, salt on lips, sand on oil, sun on water. I cannot explain an ocean any better than I can describe the United States, with our cities and suburbs, megamalls and minimalls, freeways and tollways, corporate farms and patio pots, First World luxuries and Third World–made mass commodities. These Sherpas cannot imagine my world. I visit from another planet.

After helping in the kitchen, Nima's friends Zangbu and Beth join us. She sits beside me and asks about my relationship with Nima. I tell her how we met and comment on how adventurous she was to marry a Sherpa. Beth points out that living with a Sherpa comes with both challenges and rewards. She tells me I'll like it. I assure her I have not committed to any such thing. I barely know Nima; he will be in Portland, not Los Angeles; Southern California is too different from Nepal, and he won't like it; it would be such a lifestyle change; it—She smiles and interrupts me. She thought like that too, her first trip to Nepal when she met Zangbu, she says, but she kept thinking about him, came back, and made the commitment. Beth is convinced that it will be much easier for me with Nima in the United States. You're lucky, Beth tells me. Sherpas are irresistible. Don't fight it.

I ask how Beth and Zangbu met. Like us. He was her guide. They have known each other two years (if you count the length of time since they met) or forty days (if you count their time together). I want to know how she made the decision to marry him. Intuition, she tells me, and she wanted his child.

I'm not sure I want children. Irresistible. Intuition. Those I can comprehend. Beth seems happy, positive about their future. I feel less crazy knowing another American woman who married a Sherpa.

Tonight, Nima's family makes me feel at home. I am their honored guest with the best seat, the first plate of food, and wine (expensive in Kathmandu) that gets topped off after every sip, so I lose track of how much I drink. But I don't care, for I am having the most wonderful time. How simply they live, and yet, they treat me like a princess. To be uniquely special is new to me, for I was born a twin, part of a mismatched set of girls, fraternal sisters, and the oldest. Even as a fraternal twin, I was always only the other or "which one are you," even though we were not identical and shared only a family resemblance—and all our toys, clothes, friends, activities, and a bedroom with twin beds. We distinguished ourselves through our interests and talents. When Caryn asked for ballet lessons, I demanded tap; as teenagers, Caryn went for boys, so I went for books; as adults, when I went for men, Caryn went for kids. I lived my younger years in identity crisis, so I appreciate it when these Sherpas, who have no idea I am a half, treat me like a whole, like royalty, and allow me to reign over their spartan apartment in Lazimpat.

"We like to eat with our hands," says Nima, as dinner is served. "The food tastes better. No metal in the mouth." I watch them artfully scoop up rice, dal, goat curry, and yogurt, with their fingers, and then lick them. No way is Nima eating like this if he comes to visit! I appreciate that I am given a fork.

Following the meal, I enter the kitchen to help clean up, but am escorted back to the living room by Kandu. No problem for me. Sit down. No problem for me.

I'm not anyone special, I say to Beth, who clarifies. To Sherpas, everyone is special.

fire: I wanted America my whole life. This is my dream!

Nima walks me back toward the hotel along the pedestrian walkway. I am pleased to hear his family liked me, were surprised I was so kind and friendly toward them. Nima grasps my hand as he talks, and I let him hold it. I like them too, I tell him. They are kind. Nima Nuru is a great cook. Is Kandu always so shy? Sherpanis are typically shy. Kandu has a big heart, he says. I assure him that I like Kandu. I like everyone. Nima squeezes my hand. I like Nima even more.

Just before the lights of the avenue, he pulls me close. I no longer have a reason to resist. The evening confirmed what I already knew. Nima is a good man. He kisses me. So, I kiss back. In fact, I kiss back for a long time. It just seems the right thing to do. As soon as we stop, Nima admits he's never kissed before. I don't believe him. He explains that they don't kiss in their culture. This is his first time. I laugh and compliment him.

He says they don't hold hands either. Nima still holds mine. He pulls me close. I rest there for a moment, and then put space between us without letting go of his hand. I am curious to know how Sherpas ever have a relationship, with the men in the mountains and the women left at home to run their lodges. Nima points out that there is an off-season, without treks and climbs. I guess I do not look convinced. He blushes and confides that they still manage to have big families.

"You are like fantasy dreaming," says Nima, as he pulls me to him. He points up at the moon rising over the trees along the avenue. Large bats, that hang sleeping in the trees by day, swoop around overhead. Keep them away from me! I duck my head into his shoulder.

While fearful of bats, I am more afraid of Nima. I have just kissed a Sherpa. I just kissed a Sherpa, and I liked it. I want to kiss him again. This cannot be happening. With bats flying overhead, perhaps it would be best if his next kiss were a bite on my neck, so I might end this dilemma. I would swoon in his arms and fall to the ground. I would not have to get up and decide what to do with a Sherpa lover who is coming to see me in Los Angeles. I would be happy to settle for a B-movie release.

As Nima leans down to kiss me again, I pull away. He looks surprised. I see Nima. Nima smiles. I fall under the spell of a virgin kisser.

How big is your room? he asks. And I thought him shy.

Big enough for two, I tell him. I ignore the shouts in my head to stop. Tonight we are equals. Our differences only increase the exoticism of our coupling. I revel in the joy of teaching Nima variations on the kiss. He has innocence without the ignorance or awkwardness of encounters at a younger age. We begin with our lips, then the face, the ears, and slowly our bodies. His skin is silk, and I relish his luxuriousness. He is not crass or primitive or crude. Under his tender caress, I am porcelain being molded, tickled into form, rising up with his fingers. He is clay, sienna-colored, of the earth, natural and strong, rising with a power I can hardly control. I think I am shaping him, but he is shaping me. Lean and fine and precious. I am bejeweled and painted in dazzling colors. He is rough and incised with a folklike whimsy. *Porcelain and clay.* Out of nature. Being with this Sherpa is the most natural relationship I have ever known. Easy. Artful. Pure joy.

"I love you. I want to marry you," whispers Nima. His words silence my body. It is too fast. Why does he want to ruin it? Don't look at me like that. I cannot answer you. My chest aches. It is too soon. Too soon.

"Nima, I'm eleven years older than you. You need to find a young Sherpani."

"You're my Sherpani. I knew it the first day when we trekked together." He smiles. "Ever since Besi Sahar."

I am suspended. My body refuses oxygen. My heart is a hovering hummingbird, its wings beating fast. That is where I knew! My brain goes numb. Thoughts no longer matter. That is where I knew. That is where my heart knew. My heart knew!

"At Besi Sahar, I knew I was going to marry you," repeats Nima, as if to be sure I heard his declaration. He tells me how he just had this feeling and knew. Then he seldom saw me until Manang on the roof one morning, and he still knew. When I danced with the little girl, Annapurna, he knew. And on the street in Kathmandu, our chemistry was so hot. "I knew we had to be together. I've known since Besi Sahar."

This cannot be happening. How could he have known? At Besi Sahar,

fire: I wanted America my whole life. This is my dream!

I was struck with that thought—*I will marry a Sherpa.* I did not believe it then. I do not believe it now. What a terrifying prospect. It would be fun. Hello everyone, meet my fiancé, Nima Sherpa. Priceless to see their reaction. No. Penniless! This is too sudden. Too absolute. This is no longer "fantasy dreaming." I need the clear light of morning, and distance.

I need time. I tell Nima nothing about my feelings at Besi Sahar. Besides, Nima believes in mystical occurrences and will insist it is auspicious, us both feeling the same thing in the same place. An auspicious conjunction. I cannot argue his point, but I see the future. An auspicious conjunction with consequences. It's the consequences that I fear. I need to see Nima in Los Angeles. I need to know how he fits in there, how I feel about him there, and who I am when I return.

"I like you, Nima," I say. "Let's see how it goes after you get to the States."

"You and me. No problem," he says. "So easy. We were husband and wife in a past life." Nima makes his statement with conviction. Nima tells me it must have been a while since we last saw each other, because we are so hot.

I touch my chest. Ouch! It burns. What a reunion! Does Nima understand the weight of his words? Love and marriage are strong words that require an extreme commitment. Beyond his words, what action, what value is implied? I know little about the cultural traditions of the Sherpa. And with no guide, I can only follow my intuition, like Nima.

In spite of my conflicted emotions, I sleep well next to Nima. I wake up beside this strong but gentle man and remember the pleasures of yesterday, while Nima's smile radiates sunshine like the day. He suggests a visit to Bodhnath. I am honored. Bodhnath is the most sacred site in the Kathmandu Valley for a Buddhist. No man has ever taken me to a holy site following a night of lovemaking.

The sky is blue and filled with cumulus clouds. From the golden spire above the white, domed *chörten*, the all-seeing eyes of Buddha Vairochana, the Great Illuminator, look out over Bodhnath as we walk around the *chörten* three times and turn its prayer wheels. Blessings spin from the wheels and join those being blown by the wind off prayer flags that rim the *chörten*. Nima comes several times a week when he's in Kathmandu, he tells me, and walks the *kora* at least three times to show proper respect. I respect a man who can make that kind of commitment.

The hot day feels humid and heavy, like my mind, clouded by too many thoughts, questions, and concerns about the future. I turn the prayer wheels with an irritable frustration. Each spin represents a new scenario, a question that has to be answered about our relationship. Spin. Will this work? Spin. Who will I introduce him to first? Spin. How will I tell my family? Spin. Spin. Spin. Nima brings me back to the moment.

"I love you, my Sherpani," says Nima. "I know you will say yes."

"I'm not a Sherpani, Nima."

"My Sherpani."

His heart shines clear, adamantine in his conviction that I will be his wife. He points to the morning star. Venus, I tell him. Goddess of love. The planet Venus circles around the sun, like we do around Bodhnath. Nima is surprised to learn it is not a star, but more like the earth. I explain how the earth is a planet and circles the sun. *Nima* means "sun." Warmth radiates from him, like his namesake.

"Caryl, my Venus," he whispers, as he draws me into his galaxy.

Time is not our friend. We drop everything else for each other. For the next two days and nights, Nima and I are inseparable. We fill them with lovemaking. He makes me forget the past and the future. I exist for him, and he exists for me.

The second night, Nima insists we make love with the lights on. Our bodies reveal our history, as we lie naked on our pushed-together beds in the Kathmandu Guest House. He begins by comparing our skin tones, the whiteness of my breasts, the pink of their nipples, and the darkness of pigmentation spots that match his skin coloring. My finger traces a half-moon scar on his head that grows no hair. Nima tells me that he and his brother Tshiring Tendi were play fighting with their *khukuri*. And this. He points to his thigh. All Sherpa boys played with *khukuri*. And this. I shake my head. I ask about his ankle and foot. His toes are deformed and curl under, while his ankle is wrapped in scars, a map marking many incisions. Nima changes the subject. He asks about the seven-inch scar on my arm and if someone hurt me. Car accident, I tell him. I ask if he slept on a bed of nails?

Not nails. Nettles. Nima tells me that when he was a boy, he was responsible for keeping the goats out of their fields, but there were so many, he could never get them all to leave at once. He'd chase some out, only to have others go in. His father, furious at the loss, sent Nima to pick a *doko* full of stinging nettles.

We lie in silence.

Nettles in Nepal have big long needles, he says, like thorns. Nima measures off the first two knuckles of his middle finger with his thumb. He says his father would stuff him into the *doko*, then tied it across the top so he couldn't get out. He learned it hurt less if he pushed the thorns into his back, rather than fight to avoid them. He tried hard not to move until morning. Nettles are like nails, he says, only you don't bleed so much.

We are learning each other. I look again at his back and see polka dots of darkness. I rub them with the hope I can erase his stigmata, still raw and exposed long after they have healed. Nima notices my smile scar below the belly. A "bikini cut," the doctor told me, after he removed an ovarian cyst. Nima looks concerned and asks if it will be a problem to have children. No problem, I assure him. He kisses my scar. Enough has been exposed for one night. I turn off the light. We hold each other.

"I love you, Nima." I have to say it. It is true. For someone not given to extreme passions, I feel immense conviction. I am energized. I radiate heat like a sun-warmed rock, passive energy stored for the cold days to come, and renewed by the warmth from my "sun." The rest of the night, I live a waking dream. Mountains of emotions overwhelm me as our bodies communicate our feelings for each other. We merge together like two rivers at a confluence, at that sacred place where Buddhists build their temples.

In the lessening darkness, Nima tells me he wants to have children. I remind him that I am almost thirty-nine and too old. I used to want children. Not now. As the oldest of seven, with the last sibling nine-teen years younger, I feel I have raised a family. Nima assures me I am not too old. Must I choose between Kathmandu or children, Paris or motherhood, Aspen or nursery school? A life without children suits me fine.

Nima, I say, I like my lifestyle. I don't want to change.

As I listen to myself talk, I wonder. What do I think marriage to a Sherpa is going to do? Keep me in the same social circles? Set me up for a promotion? Get me introduced to "important people"? I think not!

But we must, says Nima. Otherwise, who will care for us in our old age? Sherpas must have children, or people think something is wrong.

If I were to have children, it would be with this man. I am not. But at this moment, I do not want to disappoint. I learned that from the Sherpas. I want a daughter, I tell him. We'll name her Annapurna. Nima thinks mixed children are beautiful. I agree. Like porcelain and clay. She will be delicate and strong. He wonders whom she'll look like.

Porcelain and clay. Are our properties compatible?

Today marks an end, and a beginning. At the airport, Nima presents me with a *khata*, a white-silk blessing scarf. Our last kiss tastes bittersweet. I am off to Bhutan for three weeks. He leaves for America in a few days. I will not see him for three months. Then we will have a couple of months before his visa runs out.

"I'll wait for you," he says. "Will you wait for me?" I confirm.

I am engaged. Engaged to marry a Sherpa.

We lean against a column and cuddle close to extend the moment. To avoid my own thoughts, I imagine the circuitous journey Nima took to have ever crossed paths with me. He grew up in a small village in the mountains that was accessible only by walking. It was community in its truest sense, where everyone knew everyone, and helped every-one, and knew everyone's business, and everyone's name, and everyone walked through unlocked doors unannounced, and were always welcome for supper, and everyone looked after each other's children, and shared great-grandparents, and lived simply among their own kind with their

fire: I wanted America my whole life. This is my dream!

animals on tilted mountainsides among fields with a river far below and mountains above and gods that looked after them all.

And yet, Nima yearned for more. He was curious and tried hard to converse with tourists who came to visit, and he learned their languages and about their countries and the world beyond his mountain home. He desired travel and adventures, as did the tourists (although he laughed to think that they came to his country for adventures that he experienced every day), but he was tired. Everything was hard in Kathmandu, with electrical blackouts, few cars, and limits to modern conveniences or the bounty found in stores like those he'd visited in Hong Kong. He was tired of walking, shopping daily for food, working twenty-four hours a day on trek and then having no work the rest of the year. He was tired of hanging out with friends and dreaming big dreams and knowing they were dreams. Nima decided he needed an adventure. The Himalaya offered him none, so—Nima is coming to the United States of America.

"I love you," says Nima. He kisses me. Will Nima disappear from my heart once the scenery changes? Will he fade like my favorite coral T-shirt, worn out after too many washings on river rocks so that I never wear it again, but place it at the bottom of my dresser, a keepsake of my adventure? I see the future. Nima will go into my photo album, and just as he showed me his past adventures that first night before dinner in Lazimpat, I will show my future boyfriend photographs of Nepal and point out the Sherpa guide who was kind to me and cooked me dinner, and I'll leave out the rest. My boyfriend will never believe it anyway. Men never do, when the drama of your exploits exceeds theirs.

I touch my center. Ouch! It still burns. Nima will not disappear.

The airport security checkpoint is my border between Nepal and the rest of the world. As I let the world swallow me up, I feel I have never been so full, or so empty. I need space, quiet, solace more than ever. I am exhausted. I need to get myself out of Kathmandu and far away from Nima.

It's another hour before my plane leaves. I need air. I stand by the window. Breathe. Remember. Breathe. Wonder. Breathe. Imagine. The fog begins to lift.

We are cheering for you both.

—Henry

DUE TO THE LIMITED FLIGHTS to Bhutan, I arrive several days ahead of the group I am to trek with through the Bumthang Valley. I spend two days of sightseeing in the capital city of Thimphu, a village by First World standards. I want to return to the mountains; I desire a landscape that will trigger memories; I want to remember Nima.

As the sun rises behind me, I hike up the valley from the Motithang Hotel toward a forested mountainside, in search of the trailhead. With each step, my hiking boots knock droplet after droplet of lustrous dew from blades of grass. I now understand what the desk clerk meant, when he told me that Motithang means "meadow of pearls." He suggested I hike to a Buddhist monastery high up above Thimphu.

I travel light and alone. The cool morning awakens me. I follow the trail across meadows full of grazing oxen and into a forest. The mountain rises steeply before me, with few switchbacks to break my ascent. I stop often to catch my breath in the thin air and cool down, as the sun's warmth penetrates even this dense forest of fir and rhododendron trees. Bhutan is known for its botanical offerings, the desk clerk told me. The ancient Tibetans gave Bhutan the name Lho Jong Men Jong, "The Southern Valleys of Medicinal Herbs." He had smiled and assured me that I would return from this trek healed.

An ease returns to my step as I walk. After twenty-four days in the Himalaya, I walk with a grace not experienced since childhood. The path follows a steeply pitched hillside covered in loam and wild strawberries. Only an occasional tree root provides a surer step. In moments of frustration, I slip backward as loam falls away, or slide on berries slick under my feet as I cross this carpet of red, green, and white strawberry plants in fruit and flower. This bright berry, my nemesis, is also my reward. As I rest in the shade of tall firs, the strawberries, sweet and full flavored, taste as their creator intended them to taste. Tiny as peas, but plentiful, the delicious treat fills my cupped hand and stains my fingers and lips red.

Red is my temptress. Thornbushes, her revenge. Desire is punished. Desire brings great suffering. Desire is bondage. We are free only when we give up all desire. As I fight the thornbushes, I remember the rhododendron blossom Nima picked for me before Ghorapani. It was red, the color of passion. I snap a rhododendron stem and clip the flower in my barrette. Passion red, for Nima.

When the trail disappears, I stop. Silence surrounds me, except for the rustle of rhododendron leaves in the breeze. As I absorb the stillness of the forest, I notice a small group of prayer flags high in a ravine. A raven overhead caws out its sacred sounds, *Ah! Ah! Ah!* In Bhutan, to kill a raven is the same as killing one thousand monks. The monastery must be somewhere above the prayer flags. I push toward the ravine and fight my way free of the underbrush to another trail. Or is it the same trail? I no longer know. Sharp switchbacks lead me up. I wish for a guide, and yet, feel safe without one.

Three-quarters of the way up, I stop before a log bench that rests in a rock fissure below the prayer flags, certain a monk chose this shadowy resting place. I sit. Lustrous from centuries of monks in meditation, the log bench welcomes me. My hand slides over its heart, across its veins, and over the edge to the papery skin on its underside. A rhododendron tree in its past life, it now provides a respite to all who caress it.

A life force cannot hide itself forever. Water gurgles up from deep within the earth and spills out from a rock fissure onto a path at my feet, like the blood from a wound on the earth. Invigorated by its release, the water dives off the trail to free-fall some distance before it gives life to the white-flowering daphne bushes below. I sip the water. It tastes fresh and earthy. Alive. Unlike the embalmed waters of cities like Los Angeles. I could grow and flourish here, through simple daily acts like cupping my hands to catch the earth's life force and drinking it down so that it mingles with my own.

Once in this place of contemplation, after the strenuous hike up the mountain, my heavy breathing quiets and my pounding heart subsides. The forest's density prevents me from seeing far. From this meditative seat, perhaps I see all I need to see—the forest, the rocks, the water, and myself—and all that matters is this moment. The monk who placed this bench expected its user to be present. I sit still. I rest. I breathe. My body relaxes. My mind does not.

What about my future? Our future? Three days ago, I left Nepal happy, sad, jubilant, and traumatized knowing Nima wants to marry me. The Himalaya aligned our destinies, like a giant magnetic force. It pulled me to Nepal, and pushed Nima to the United States. Next week, he'll be in Oregon. In three months, I'll be there too, so we can spend two weeks together before I return to Los Angeles. I promised him that.

Nima and I fused in Besi Sahar like a fulgurite, like lightning meeting sand. Think about it: The Buddhists monks use a *dorje*, which means "thunderbolt." Bhutan, or *Druk yul*, means "the Land of the Thunder Dragon." Do the spirits in these mountains determine our destiny? In Los Angeles, spirits come only with ice cubes or film credits.

Nima and I are opposites. My mind directs my actions. Nima's intuition directs his. I am educated and read directions. Nima is street-smart and possesses great survival skills. I am smart. Nima is wise. We do share similarities: curiosity, desire for adventure, courage to explore the unknown, and a passion for each other. But marry a Sherpa?

Reflection does not bring me answers. Instead, the stillness gives me time to think, and my thoughts only stress me out. Montego once told Sharon and I not to overthink relationships. Just experience them, he said.

Montego's axiom was easy to follow when I was with Nima, but now it's impossible.

Although time has stood still here for centuries, I cannot be in the moment without my tranquility being trampled by demons in all their manifestations. I think of the demons that the Bhutanese paint on the walls of local temples, with their angry eyes, six flailing arms, and a heavy foot crushing a body beneath. The demons of Tibetan Buddhists represent one's internal struggles, and in this spiritual land, I sense they know mine. I try to sit still. Be present. Relax. No deadlines. No schedule. No answers. The future will come quick enough. Yes? No? Maybe? I don't know! Monks retreat to mountaintops in search of answers. Onward and upward! So will I. The vigorous climb up the last steep pitch relaxes me. My restless demons depart as I walk, the faster and harder, the better.

As I pass from forest to meadow, a stand of prayer flags greets me. Mottled sunlight illuminates the white gauze prayer flags, hand-printed from woodblocks by local monks. Some flags stand tall on poles. Others are square and strung on a cord between trees. I feel welcomed and warmed as the wind's breath blows through each flag to cast its prayers. I pass among the flags and continue toward a typical Bhutanese temple, no bigger than a large house. Of fine proportions, its whitewashed walls angle in toward the top. Deep, overhanging eaves shadow a painted red sienna band. Few windows pierce the temple's thick façade. For lack of fasteners, strategically located river rocks hold the wood roof shingles in place.

My arrival surprises a Bhutanese couple. A fairy tale caricature of an old woman hunches under a load of faggots carried from a tumpline on her forehead. She stares at me as I approach, while she rests on her stave in conversation with a man. The old man's eyes squint in sunlight that brightens his wrinkled face. Gray tufts of hair sprout below his nose and lower lips. A dirty brown wool cap with a yarn ball at the top sits jauntily on the man's head. Under his black *go* he wears a plaid flannel shirt and too-short brown pants that show bare ankles and tennis shoes. The woman's thick salt-and-pepper hair is cropped straight to frame her lined bronze face and plump cheeks. Over her faded magenta blouse, the old woman wears a patched *kira*, the traditional woven woman's dress, belted by a yak-hair rope.

"*Kousouzangpo la*," I say in my guidebook Dzongkha, the language of Bhutan, as I nod their way. The old man and woman smile and show missing teeth. The woman moves her leathery hand to her mouth. She wants food. I motion for them to sit on the slate entry steps of the temple and watch their eyes brighten as I open my pack. "Let's eat," I announce with an air of celebration.

Gnarled hands reach for everything with excited curiosity. Their interest turns to reverence when the old man pulls out a paperback book whose bright red cover displays a golden Buddha. Staring at the Buddha, the man begins to chant. He gently touches the Buddha image to his forehead, then the old woman's. The man reaches toward me with the book. I bow to the Buddha and touch my forehead to the sacred image that up until that moment had been only a paperback that I treated poorly. With the holy book clasped mindfully between his dirty hands, the old man bestows his blessing with the reverence, dignity, and grace of the highest of lamas. I am charmed.

Is Pala, Nima's father, like this man? Softened with age and now wise? Or will he be rough around the edges and still mean in his patched-together clothes?

My Ziploc bags packed with lunch are a miracle of Western technology to this mountain couple. Entranced by how they open and shut, the woman extracts treasures one by one, opening and closing the bags: crackers, Bumthang Valley cheese, a Swiss chocolate bar, and my home-made trail mix. I break the crackers and pass pieces to the couple. In spite of their own hunger, they share their food in a delightful communion with a white hen, a scrawny rooster, a gray kitten, and a puppy. The spirit of the encounter carries the conversation. The couple and I talk throughout lunch, although neither of us comprehends the other.

Saathi, the woman says, and repeats the word, slower each time until I understand.

Saathi. Friend, I tell her, as I take her worn hands in mine. I give her the leftover food. She gathers up the Ziploc bags in her apron and beckons for me to follow.

Will Nima's mother be as friendly toward a daughter-in-law who is a foreigner? What if she doesn't accept me? Or thinks I am not good enough to marry her son?

Ch'ah, says the old man, as he cups his hands and pretends to drink.

Kadrinche la, I thank him. I pause at the threshold for my eyes to adjust to the darkness of their one-room dwelling, attached to the temple. I slip off my hiking boots. Years of wood smoke have blackened the walls and ceiling, which now absorbs all light.

Does Nima's family live in such darkness?

Across the room, the old woman slides open a low wood panel. A shaft of sunlight illuminates their furnishings: an earthen stove, cooking pots, utensils, dishes, and a wooden trunk, which the woman opens. She rummages around, removes a square woolen mat decorated with a diamond motif, lays it on the pine floor by the window, and motions for me to sit.

The man stokes the fire. From a tin canister, the old woman takes a handful of tea and throws it into the pot. I look out over the valley through a trefoil-shaped opening toward the mountains. The forests are dense here, in contrast to Nepal, where trekkers and population pressures have denuded the hillsides. The couple remains silent; here, conversation is not necessary during a meal or its preparation, as partaking of the fruits of the earth demand a mindfulness.

Could I live without dinner conversation?

As the tea brews, the man disappears and returns with a painted china bowl that he hands to the woman. She fills the china cup and two wooden bowls with tea. Still on her haunches, the woman crosses the room, cradling the china bowl with shaking hands. She bows her head and offers me tea. I bow my head and take the cup. I sip her sweet, creamy tea and imagine a wise lama once drank from this same cup. I smile and nod. She grins. Five times the old woman fills my tea bowl, until I remember that as their guest, I must be satisfied before they eat. I refuse more. The old man mixes his tea with *tsampa*, a finely ground barley flour. She takes out two crackers from her Ziploc bag and softens them in her tea to make them easier to eat. When they finish their meal, I stand up to leave. Warmed by their kindness, I clasp their hands in both of mine. *Saathi.* Friends.

At the forest's edge, the old man points out a frequently traveled trail back to town. The skies have turned stormy. I catch a glimpse of Thimphu in the distance. For a moment, I sense Nima. I see my future. Unpredictable as it is, I feel ready to face it. The gracious spirit of these mountain people makes me certain. I feel sure his family will be similar. All I offered them was a simple lunch. They shared with me the best of what they had. And a blessing.

A Sherpa is a blessing.

Erosion has taken a heavy toll on the hillside, laid bare by foot traffic. I climb in, out, and over deep gullies cut into the red-brown earth by the rushing waters of seasonal snowmelts and monsoon rains. I pass through a forest that gives way to an open slope planted with scores of poles bearing long gauze panels of prayers and topped by swords of victory, or *gyalzen*, thrust into the clouds. White flags dominate the sky, occasionally interrupted by a yellow, green, red, or blue one. I walk among them. I look toward the sun. The thin open weave of their fabric allows me to see through one prayer and beyond to the next, and the next. In the wind, prayers race off the flags with an urgency. The late-afternoon sun shouts from behind darkening storm clouds. I drop my pack. I stand tall like the prayer flags. I let the wind take me. I feel prayers wrap around me in an embrace.

Give me courage. Steel my conviction. Keep me free.

My prayers mount the wind-horse and ride a gale born in the turbulent Bay of Bengal that now blows over gentle Bhutan, toward the high Himalaya, and into mystical China beyond.

I arrive in Prague, Czechoslovakia, in May 1991, only eighteen months after the Velvet Revolution, a citizen uprising that replaced the Communist government with a democracy. As I consider a relationship with Nima, I too feel like a revolutionary. I turn away from expectations. I desire change, seek renewal, and demand fearlessness. I want to seek the "truthful life" that Václav Havel referred to in his 1978 essay "The Power of the Powerless." He suggests that the future may already be here. We just don't always see it. He did. I do too. Only, my revolution is alone.

My sister Jeanne, who came to Prague to teach English at the International School, met Ken, who worked in the Foreign Service at the American embassy in Prague, and they fell in love. My parents, my sister, Cinda, with her husband, and the groom's family have all flown in from the United States. At the elegant rococo Ambassador's Residence in Prague, our host Ambassador Shirley Temple Black receives us. Excited to meet Shirley Temple, the mother of the bride asks to have her picture taken beside the ambassador. My mother tells the ambassador how she admired her movies, and how she adored her Shirley Temple doll with its curls, clothes, and glass eyes that followed you, and—the ambassador makes a diplomatic excuse and backs away with a bow. Caught up in her past, my mother holds my father and I captive among her memories.

Following the wedding service, Jeanne, Ken, and the ambassador greet the guests in the embassy's grand hall as silver trays of champagne are circulated. As lovely as Jeanne's event is, the sumptuous elegance leaves me hollow. In Sherpa fashion, I drape two white-silk wedding *khata* from Bhutan around the neck of each newlywed. I bow with hands together. I utter a prayer. I tell them nothing of my engagement to Nima.

Missing the spirituality I felt in Nepal, I retreat to sacred places. At the eighteenth-century CE Saint Nicholas Church on Old Town Square, I light one candle for Nima, one for myself, and one between us to acknowledge our fire. At the Old Jewish Cemetery, where layers of souls lie buried one on top of another for lack of land allowed the Jews, I walk between rows of moss-covered gravestones lined up like dominos between trees whose roots mingle with the dead. Everywhere, papers peek out below small stone cairns. Like the small roadside *chörten* crowned by a ram's horn carved with prayers that I saw as I trekked with Nima from Muktinath to Kagbeni, each memorializes the dead, or the living. Faith, and its practice, is more universal than we want to acknowledge.

I am drawn to a headstone. The incised name has weathered, along with the age of the deceased and the epitaph, but here, in the absence of memory, I connect. I tear a corner off my used train ticket, write a prayer, and position it below three stones next to another similar cairn on the headstone. Am I drawn to this place by the power of the dead? Or a call from the living? Or both? I close my eyes and channel my prayer toward Nima.

Back at Jeanne's apartment, I call Nima in Portland and connect with an old lady who does not understand me, so I hang up. I decide that a new city will help me forget about Nima.

The formality of Vienna, Austria, is a culture shock. I came for classical music, Vienna Moderne, and Sacher torte, only to learn I am not ready for the Western world. Or for my parents, who have joined me and are driving me crazy. Travel mellows me. Travel gives them an edge. We part ways. I travel alone.

On my first day in Budapest, Hungary, I place a call to Nima and wake up his friends at four in the morning. Nima is river rafting with his friend Jules. *Nima is in America.* I walk Budapest and see only Nepal.

I met Lars ten years ago while skiing at Bad Gastein in the Austrian Alps. He was Swedish, young, and fun to be with. We skied well together. Lars and I reunite on an island off the coast of Göttskar, Sweden, under a blazing sky as luminous as a woman's silk sari. The night is ripe for romance, but I am not the least bit interested in Lars or his tall, buff Swedish scuba diver friends. What is it with that Sherpa? Around a bonfire on a night that gets as dark as dusk, we talk and drink and sing. I feel welcome, but alone. I walk to an ancient labyrinth marked by stones and travel its sacred circle toward the center. I remember the moonlight that illuminated Annapurna II, the heat of the fire, and how I danced among Sherpas. I reach the center and turn back. There I found freedom and joy. As I leave the labyrinth, I know I will find it again.

In Lars's apartment in Göteborg, I set my alarm for three in the morning. I call Nima. No answer. I leave a message. Sleep is impossible. I drink a shot of Glenlivet from the duty-free bottle I brought Lars. The phone rings. It's Nima!

"I dream of you all the days," says Nima. He feels so right. I am crazy, but maybe crazy is what I want. Trample convention. Toss out predictability. No man has ever showed himself to me like Nima. Conversation is difficult, so we end the call after discussing plans for our reunion in Portland.

From Göteborg, I take the train to Stockholm and rendezvous with my girlfriend Tracy, who works in London. The beauty of Stockholm, a city of islands and bridges, is a surprise, and so is our hotel on a boat. As we bob on the waves over dinner, I tell Tracy how the boat's unsteadiness is so apropos, and proceed to tell her about Nima. My flood of memories almost capsizes our boat. This might be real, she tells me, as she points out the glow emanating from me when I talk about Nima—and even when I do not. She noticed it as soon as she saw me.

From Stockholm, Tracy and I catch the overnight ferry to Helsinki, a city of bold and brawny architecture bisected by wide boulevards that anticipate a parade. Helsinki leaves us cold. Only within the rock-hewn chapel walls of Temppeliaukio Kirkko, which is carved into bedrock, do we find warmth as morning light filters in from above and washes the altar. Behind the altar, water seeps from cracks in stone; each trickle is carried by near-perfect acoustics, reminding me of the glacier it was shaped by, and of Thorung La. Within this rock womb, I am silenced, stilled by the raw power of the natural world as adapted with kindness by man. I sit and meditate. I pray for clarity. I light a candle to our future. I am warmed.

As Tracy is an architect and I am a designer, we both look forward to our architectural pilgrimage to the Hvitträsk home and studio of Eliel Saarinen, his two friends, and their partners. Built on a forested ridge above Lake Vitträsk, grand wood-shingled houses with clay-tile roofs dominate the idyllic setting. As we linger in the garden among wild roses and honeysuckle, I read for Tracy a letter written by Alma Mahler (herself married to four famous men) about her hosts at Hvitträsk, who believed that life without variety was mere existence. I agree, I tell Tracy. Except they exchanged partners. I only want to share cultures.

fire: We are cheering for you both.

Serendipitous events continue to make up my journey. Tracy and I arrive in Norway in time for a historic event. Thirty-four years since the last coronation, and seven centuries since the last Norway-born king was crowned, Harald V rides toward the twelfth-century CE Nidaros Cathedral in his coronation parade somewhere up ahead. Tracy and I view the end of the parade from the curb as citizens in traditional costume march by us in step with their national anthem. In Trondheim, the capital of Norway until 1217, every house window wears red geraniums for the occasion. From a native, we learn that during World War II, young Prince Harald lived in Washington DC, where the United States must have freed his thinking, because he married a commoner, who will become Queen Sonja. Many criticized him for not marrying a royal, but most Norwegians believe that mixed blood strengthens a family line.

Sitar and flute. I am inspired.

From Trondheim, Tracy and I travel by coastal steamer past Norway's fjords to Stamsund on the Lofoten Islands. I have all day to dream of Nima—literally all day. It is midsummer and the sun touches the horizon for only a moment in the predawn hours before it begins to rise. Shortly after sunrise, we cross the Arctic Circle. For a week, we live in a red clapboard fishing shanty built on a rock outcropping along the shore. After six days, Tracy teases me about how there was only one time that I did not use Nima's name in a sentence: As she was cleaning a twelve-pound codfish given to us by a fisherman, the dead fish surprised us with a flop. "Oh, shit!" we exclaimed in unison.

The Lofoten's magical isles offer promise for sailors and seekers. From the plane on my return to the mainland, I see the islands rise out of the water, brilliant green in sunlight, only to disappear in a mischievous fog in an instant. Like the surreal Himalaya, I wonder if they ever existed. Do I? Does Nima?

Back in Göteborg, I decide to call Nima. Nima is rafting the Snake River with Jules, says the voice on the phone, who introduces himself as Henry, a friend of Jules. Nima has told me so much about you. He'll be sorry he missed you. Nima told me to tell you that he will keep his calendar open whenever you get to Oregon. All I can think is how irony has no cultural bounds.

"Everyone adores Nima here," says Henry. "We are cheering for you both."

For not talking to Nima, I feel great.

In the Alps above Interlaken, Switzerland, I exit the gondola and begin a short hike to a high pass. Before I begin my descent, I stop to build a *theu* for Nima. My hands grow cold from stones extracted from snow. I place a rough, dark stone on a rock outcropping where views down the valley are wide and long. On top, I rest a smooth pebble of white quartz. *Porcelain and clay.* Three men, who had thought they were first on the trail, ask how I got here. On the back of a tiger, I tell them, by way of the Himalaya. Surprised I am hiking alone, they insist on escorting me the remainder of the circuit. I entertain them with tales of my adventures. I tell them nothing of Nima.

In Paris, Jeanne and Ken are kind enough to share their honeymoon apartment in the sixteenth *arrondissement* with me for a few days. I decide to live local. I pick up my paper at the corner *tabac*, take *le petit déjeuner* at a café a block beyond, and wander the hilly tree-lined streets of the Passy neighborhood near the Bois de Boulogne. The writer of *La Comédie Humaine*, Honoré de Balzac, once lived in this neighborhood and introduced realism into his novels by creating characters that were neither good nor bad, but human. At the Maison de Balzac, I linger over the details of his life and his words. I know Balzac understood how I could love someone like Nima. His words are simple: "We love because we love."

I decide that for my last European excursion, I must seek inspiration from another literary figure as revolutionary as Honoré de Balzac and Václav Havel. Riding the train north from Copenhagen, Denmark, I make the pilgrimage to Rungstedlund, the ancestral home of a writer known as Karen Blixen, as Baroness von Blixen-Finecke, or, by her pen name, as Isak Dinesen. Karen wrote tales of destiny and courage, including her autobiographical book *Out of Africa*. On the vast and sometimes harsh Kenyan plains, Karen surmised that the round shape of the earth was so one "could not look too far down the road." Even after circling the globe, I cannot see my future any better than she saw hers in Africa. I walk through the fields behind her home and out to her grave, below a tree that lived longer than she. I breathe deep to absorb her independent spirit, her courage of conviction. I know I will need it. In two days, I will be back in America—and in less than a week, with Nima.

Nima, it's July 18. I just sent you my final postcard.

earth

July 1991 – March 1994

Caryl caught the bouquet!

—Alison

IN NEPAL, NIMA AND I HAD FEW opportunities to look at each other face to face. He either walked behind me or led the way, or we were in the dark. I last saw him last three months ago. We had agreed to rendezvous in Portland, Oregon, in July, before I returned to Los Angeles. I am now at the Portland airport, and I cannot conjure up his image.

What if I don't recognize him? Or he doesn't remember me? That's not him. Too heavy. No, too light skinned. Maybe? That young man sure looks like Nima. Is he? He looks so skinny, all of sixteen, and scared to death. Should I leave while I still can?

"Caryl!" shouts a tall, older man. Nima had shown his friend Jules my photograph. That boy is Nima? Yes. I shake all over as Jules, a youthful-looking man in his late sixties, tries to break the ice and talks about Nepal. I hear, but do not comprehend. I look at Nima. He appears nervous, but happy to see me.

Hello, Nima, I say. We kiss awkwardly. Nima steps back, self-conscious. Jules appears excited to see us together. I blush and wonder what he thinks of our union. Nima has told me so much about you, says Jules. I thank him for hosting Nima. It's easy, he tells me. Nima is a joy to be around.

How do you like America, Nima? I ask. What have you been doing? I talk to keep myself from feeling like all this is a mistake. And yet, I feel happy.

I love it here, Nima beams. Especially now. He takes my hand. Jules and I rafted the Snake and Salmon Rivers, and went through Hells Canyon. I flew a plane. I climbed Mount Hood—so many things to do in America. I went—

I remind him he has ten days to tell me everything. Jules laughs and tells me how Nima has made many friends.

Friends? Women? A minute ago, I wanted to run. What is it about this Sherpa?

Nima and I made love day and night during our five days in Portland and Seattle. On the sixth day, we drive to Bellingham to see my brother Tom. While we were growing up, I could get Tom, who was two years younger, to do anything. Tom has the family blue eyes and reddish hair, which he wore in a crew cut as a boy but now wears long as a man. What else he's done as he matured I never ask, and he doesn't tell. All I know is that he traveled around Central America, moved to Washington State, lived in a commune, got a degree in horticulture, and somehow managed to buy a farm near the foothills of the Cascade Mountains.

Tom knows of Nepal and Sherpas, as he's known mountains and climbers. Nima and I stay with him, his wife, and his two daughters for two days. Tom's house is small, so we sleep in the barn, pee in the fields, and make hay until the sun shines. In the foothills, when we hike, Nima is bored and I am happy. At the water park, when we waterslide into shallow pools with my nieces, Nima is in heaven and I am bored. Tom finds Nima simple and delightful, joyful and young, but too young and too simple for his sister. It's your decision, he tells me. His children understand Nima; they shower him with hugs the morning we leave for Vancouver, Canada.

Enamored with the new, Nima wants it all. He seeks to experience everything, so in one afternoon we photograph each other as we window-shop on Robson Street, with me before a window of fashion shoes and Nima before a window of sport shoes; and then we walk to Queens

Bay and sit on rocks along the shore to watch a man balance stones to create sculptures of impermanence, and I photograph Nima beside them; and then I insist on driving him to Stanley Park where we can walk and enjoy the woods, but he tells me it is too much like Nepal, so we do not stop until we reach the Vancouver Aquarium and he tells me why we should go in, even though we can't really afford it: he does not know much about fish, because Nepal's lakes are too high and its rivers too turbulent; and he finds the fish fascinating and races from tank to tank and asks where they all come from and how they got here and why we keep them in tanks and where they sleep and how could we eat those with shells or pincers or teeth and why would we eat those with beautiful colors, until he grows bored and we move on and as I drive, he points out rhododendrons and firs and pines from Nepal—the center of the world according to Nima—and then he sees the totem poles and asks to stop. He laughs at the animals and calls out the ones he recognizes and asks about those he does not and even disagrees with the interpretation of others which I tell him is how the Indians saw them, and he insists that Indians didn't make these totems as he has never seen the Hindus make such a thing in Nepal and he doesn't recognize any gods, and I have to explain that they were made by Native American Indians not India Indians, and he asks me to photograph him in front of a totem and next in front of English Bay with the city of Vancouver beyond; and then he photographs me and says it is time to go to Chinatown; and we get lost and he does not mind for he gets to see more tall buildings and he wonders how they build them; before I can answer, the sidewalks grow crowded with people and he tells me which country they came from and is specific about the Asians—Korean, Vietnamese, Thai, Indonesian, no, Filipino, Tibetan, Chinese, Japanese, Chinese, Chinese, Chinese—and he announces that we must be in Chinatown, so I park under a neon sign forming Chinese characters before a vegetable market that flows out onto the street; and we walk along narrow sidewalks and he relaxes and becomes the tour guide and compares Vancouver's Chinatown to Beijing and Shanghai and Urumchi as he tells me again about the trip he and seven other Sherpa were sent on and how they crossed the Taklamakan Desert in far Western China before they got to the north base camp of K2; and now in China-town he points out the region in China that people came from and notes their distinctive features or dress to impress me with what he knows about the world since much of the day has been spent on what he does not know; and I listen and he smiles and takes my hand and leads me along streets and alleys that he does not know, and yet he does, for they remind him of Kathmandu and he tells me how at home he feels here; he stops and asks if this is okay and I nod and he lifts back the door curtain that keeps out flies and leads me into a restaurant where he orders jasmine tea and dumplings and steamed rice and we eat with chopsticks as he did as a boy, and then he tells me he is happy here with me and I tell him I am happy too—and exhausted.

As we sit in the restaurant, Nima talks about his employment ventures in Portland. He cooked rice at a large wedding for a Jewish bride and an Iranian Muslim, who are friends of Jules, and he is proud that everyone loved his rice. Another time, he was a sandwich. When I cock my head in question, he clarifies. A sign. For a travel agency. Some friend of Jules's. Nima thinks Americans do silly things to get business. He laughs. His most recent job was the back half of a dancing camel. Another Sherpa was the front. Children kept petting them. All for some restaurant guy who is a friend of Jules.

Jules certainly has lots of friends! I exclaim.

Jules is just like a Sherpa, Nima says.

Later that night, Nima calls Jules. He misses him. Jules tells Nima that if he can get to Newcomerstown, Ohio, he can work for two months on Jules's friend Daniel's farm. I encourage him to go. Nima wants to earn money. He feels himself a burden to others. I offer him a frequent-flier ticket. I tell him that before I return to Los Angeles, I have to fly back to Michigan to attend my sister Cinda's wedding. I suggest we fly together.

"Perfect. Then I can meet your family and go to my sister-in-law's wedding."

"Nima. She is not your sister-in-law. And we are not married!"

"Almost. Besides, Michigan is on the way to Ohio. Jules told me."

I am not ready for Nima to meet my family. And I am not a friend of Jules.

On our last night in Vancouver, I splurge on tickets to *The Phantom of the Opera*, only to learn that Nima cannot sit still. He wiggles and scratches his head and talks to me and gets up to go to the bathroom three times during the performance. I hold his hand tight, in an attempt to control him, but it is hopeless. Shhhhhh, they scold. Control him, they demand. You need to reimburse us for our tickets, they hiss. Animal! My ears ring.

What a disastrous dry run. Is this what my life will be like? I cannot be with him among people I know. Or family. And certainly not in Los Angeles!

Following our Pacific Northwest reunion, Nima and I fly to Michigan to attend my sister Cinda's wedding to Lance. It will be held at my parents' home at North Lake on the tenth of August. After I introduce Nima to my parents, I step back to watch them figure each other out. Nima smiles his charming smile and takes my father's hand between both of his. My father looks uncomfortable. My mother smiles and welcomes him into her home. I catch a questioning glance between my parents.

My mother Alice is fair and gentle, a woman of compromise and compassion. Her delicate, pale skin and soft blue eyes hide a strength evidenced by the way her children respond to her and the way she reacts to her husband. Passionate about New England, where she grew up, my mother put her children to sleep with stories about family, Hampton Beach summers, and the Bow girls. Those who know her appreciate her generosity. She taught me to cook and sew and ice-skate. She loves to nurture, both people and plants. Being the oldest of seven, I learned from her how to raise a child, which is why I lost interest by the time I could have my own.

My mother is a counterpoint to my father, Robert, who goes by Bob. His voice is loud and deep and excitable. As children, we tried to avoid him, but he sought us out to play, unaware of his gruffness. He taught me to waltz and swim and drive. He loves to tease, but his sarcasm scratches at my self-confidence. He tries to express emotion, but just doesn't know how. My father is tall at six foot four (1.9 m), and although once slender, he has filled out in middle age, which makes him intimidating, in spite of physical limitations from polio contracted while a serviceman in the Philippines during World War II. Without a back brace, a lack of back and thigh muscles causes him to bend forward and limits his mobility, except in water. While he uses his voice to keep up with his family, he never complains about his disability. From my father, I learned that persistence, tenacity, and great faith conquer adversity.

My parents ask too many questions. I don't want to answer those addressed to me, and Nima does not understand half of those asked of him. Instead, Nima fakes it. He nods or answers, even though his answers don't always match the question. I am glad my parents often don't understand Nima's English. Everyone feigns politeness. What a charade!

My father asks Nima where he went to school. I blush. Why must he embarrass us both? Nima never got past third grade. Dad's questions are relentless. How big is your family? What does your father do? What religion are you? I had wanted to come to Cinda and Lance's wedding alone. Nima had insisted that he join me. Family is everything, he told me. Questions. Too many questions. Too few answers. My shoulders ache from shrugging. Nima takes no notice. Nima is happy to be with family.

Out on the lawn, I watch Nima play games with the children and amaze my brothers with feats of physical strength. What a boy! Last night, he had my siblings and cousins gathered around him while he told stories of mountaineering. I imagine what they are saying: Nice guy, but what is the possible attraction? Worse, Why is my daughter/sister/aunt/cousin/ friend shacked up with this guy? Sex with a virile younger man? No other plausible reason. It won't last. I cannot stop imagining what they are thinking. I was glad when my parents had us stay with the neighbors our first night, and then later at a cabin in the woods at the end of a long dirt road.

While I try to be invisible, Nima thrives at being the center of attention. When the wedding photographs are taken, Nima happily centers himself among a garden of girls in floral dresses. My disappearing act works until my youngest sister, Alison, tracks me down. Alison is big boned, like our grandmother, but has the face of a porcelain doll. She loves to tease her older siblings, who for years had the upper hand. Alison pulls me into a crowd of young women who stand ready to catch the bouquet. Excited by the opportunity and promise of marriage, Cinda's bridesmaids position themselves up front. I relax until Cinda looks over her shoulder and targets me for the toss.

With thirteen years between us, Cinda and I were never close growing up, until she entered Northwestern University in Evanston north of Chicago. She would visit me in Chicago or call when she needed an older sister to talk to. Following college, Cinda, a Spanish speaker, traveled alone throughout South America to chase dreams, knowledge, and experience. I admired her for that. We relocated to California within a year of each other. I moved to Los Angeles, alone. Cinda migrated to Berkeley and moved in with Lance, whom she had met on the beach in Acapulco, Mexico.

Cinda, who rowed for her university crew team, moves with the muscled stiffness of a weight lifter but is changing. She has grown her blonde hair long, lost weight and muscle mass, and begun to wear the tighter clothes of a Californian. Today, Cinda wears a flowery dress that falls off her shoulders, with her hair up and makeup on, but her arms still work like an athlete's. Cinda's toss is spot-on.

"Caryl caught the bouquet!" shouts Alison, pleased by the success of her scheme. Alison likes Nima. I blush. I try to act like marriage is the farthest thing from my mind, but I am a terrible actress. While the younger set teases, and guests ask if Nima and I have any future plans, none of the adults in my family mentions marriage. Our union seems implausible, but I know better, and Nima knows for sure.

> Nothing changed here. You did.
> —*Simon*

IN EARLY AUGUST, MY JOURNEY ENDS, and our adventure begins. After our trip to Michigan for Cinda's wedding, I leave Nima at the Detroit airport with a friend of Daniel's who has agreed to drive him to Daniel's farm in Ohio. I return alone to Los Angeles to sort out my messy relationship with Marco and buy out his share of our house in Redondo Beach. I will need a home, and although I sometimes question Nima's intentions—wonder if my feelings for him will change now that I am back in Los Angeles; feel uncertain about the future with a Sherpa and the difficulties it will bring both of us; wonder if I have the strength to withstand the opinions of others who may not be as open to him as I am; ponder if this is just vacation lust that will not last; and recognize with a rare certainty that it must—I know Nima will need a home too. Landing at the Los Angeles International Airport, I feel blown off the mountain. Rarified air has turned to smog, polluted with innuendos, insults, and incriminations.

Marco thinks I want him back. I do not. I made clear when I left that there was little chance of reconciliation. We all hear what we want to. No, you cannot be mad at me about my money that I spent on my trip. Yes, my credit cards are maxed out and my bank account is empty. So what! It was worth it. Why? Are you kidding? I just circumnavigated the globe. I paid my own way. Worth it? Absolutely!

We argue over our shared affairs, which is only the house as I own everything else, and yet Marco has the audacity to ask me how he is going to live with nothing to move into the condo he just bought. Grow up!

The value of real estate went sky-high while I was gone, so after I buy him out and refinance the house, I still owe him money. He gives me a year to pay him off. Okay. Nice guy. I allow him to remain in the house until his condo is available. Okay. Nice gal. I tell Nima that he will have to wait. I decide to tell Marco nothing about Nima. Marco and I have to continue to live together, after all.

My cousin Walt and his wife, Madeline, stop for a few days on their way home to Denver from Hawaii. I consider them my mentors. When Madeline found out she was pregnant with their first child, Walt quit his job at the post office, Madeline took a sabbatical from teaching, and they drove from Colorado to New York City, sold their car, and boarded a plane to fulfill a dream—to circumnavigate the globe. While they traveled, Madeline saw doctors in whatever country they were in. Their daughter, who was nurtured in the womb while Madeline floated on Southeast Asian seas, is serene. I am glad to have Walt and Madeline visit for a few days, for they understand the need to realize a dream and also the difficulties of transition after being gone six months. They were fortunate; they had each other. I have no one—and I have a secret.

On Saturday, Madeline and I walk the beach under overcast skies, with visibility limited to the length of the Manhattan Beach pier. No one knows the complete truth about Nima except Tracy in London. I need to be assured that what is about to happen should happen; I want to be convinced that I have the strength and conviction to make a relationship with Nima succeed; and I need to know that I have support. Madeline is well traveled and open-minded, and she takes chances. She understands a spirit like Nima. She married my cousin, Walt, after all.

Walt looks like Santa Claus going bald, with hair and beard still gray. Walt lifts your spirits, so family, friends, and strangers all welcome him.

Walt tells stories longer and more linear than a Sherpa's, converses with a laugh in his voice, and loves to eat. People take him in for his company, feed him for his stories, and give him drink for his laughter. While Walt explodes with delight, Madeline's strong spirit nurtures. She is soft and round with golden curls, gentle eyes, and a voice that strokes words as she listens and asks questions. Her actions are directed toward results. Walt is like a tumbling river rock, not inclined to land for long. Madeline is like the river that eases his edges and provides a harbor. Together, they balance out their journey.

Madeline and I walk barefoot along the shore and scatter sandpipers. When the tide recedes, I feel the ocean pull me toward Nepal. A sign? I smile. Madeline wants to know why. She asks if something happened on my trip. I blush.

I knew it, she tells me. I feel the heat.

How can I tell her? What do I say?

You're glowing. Who is he? Madeline asks.

An ice dam gives way. I tell her about Nima. I tell her about our auspicious conjunction with consequences at Besi Sahar. My story delights Madeline. She likes that he is Sherpa; supports passions of the heart; but tells me that it will be difficult. She convinces me that if we believe in our union, others will follow.

Water shapes rocks. Love shapes people.

I knew my return to my job in Santa Monica in mid-August would be difficult. I did not expect it to start at my bedroom closet. After living out of a duffel bag for five months, a large closet space, a dresser, and seasonal clothes in the guestroom overwhelm me. On a train ride from Prague to Budapest, I had talked about the responsibility of freedom with a young man from eastern Czechoslovakia, where Communist rule had recently ended. He found the freedom of choice he gained felt like a burden. He was inexperienced at making his own decisions, having relied on the state his whole life. His wish for freedom was now reality, and he wasn't sure he could handle it. This morning, having too many clothes seems a funny way to empathize with the young Slovak's burden of free choice.

Going back to work proves a challenge as the economy has not improved much since I left. After the good times when work was plentiful and real estate prices high, everyone now is waiting for the country to come out of recession following the stock market crash and the bailout of the savings and loan institutions. The office bustles with activity as my colleagues attempt to create work to keep their jobs. There were layoffs while I was gone. Although I was given permission to take five months off, it was with the understanding that I was an at-will employee and might not have a job when I return. I took a gamble. Could I lose my job? Curious colleagues ask about my trip, but few ask for details. I am disappointed. I cannot let go. I want to hold it, turn it over, poke it, dig deep into it, cherish it, and never forget it. The movie in my mind plays constantly.

I find my architectural design firm has recently won a project to renovate and expand the Beverly Hills Hotel and Bungalows, now owned by the sultan of Brunei, the wealthiest man in the world. I am to manage the project. The demands are significant: learn the project's intricacies, coordinate activities, develop a strategy, bring the team to consensus, and regain the hotel's five-star status. I find focus difficult. As I battle my uncertainty about my job and my certainty about Nima, I reel from the pressure.

As I fill my coffee cup, my colleague Simon asks me about my trip. It was full of surprises, I tell him, unsure where to begin. Simon, who recently returned from a year in Europe at our London office, thinks even five months is a long time to be gone. He found it hard to come back, and wonders if I do.

A rush of emotions crashes over me. I explain how my adjustment to work is far more difficult than I could ever have imagined. I stop. Simon waits for me to continue. In a flash, I silently recall my return to the States and my time with Nima, my struggle to reconcile my old life with the new, and my fear that I have made a mistake—and will fail.

"It's so difficult." My voice cracks like quiet thunder. "Everything has changed."

"Nothing changed here. You did." Simon leaves me alone to sort it all out.

A few weeks after my return to Los Angeles, Linda, a work consultant and friend, calls to schedule lunch. Linda had joined me on hikes while I trained for my trip. She's anxious to hear of my adventures. Thin, with short, dark hair and a long face, Linda laughs easily, shows great curiosity, and is genuinely interested in others. She grew up in Redlands with the San Bernardino Mountains as her backyard, so she loves to hike. Her positive, game-for-anything attitude is just what I need.

Over lunch, I talk about my trip. Nepal intrigues Linda the most. She wants to know about the mountains, the dangers, the Sherpa—and what happened. I ask her to be more specific. You are so obvious, she tells me. Look at you bubbling over with secrets and the joy that only comes from the right relationship. How did she know?

I tell her about Nima. A Sherpa? Yes, I tell her, and describe his kindness, his wisdom, his joy. As I recall our cosmic happening and Muktinath and the Kali Gandaki and Kathmandu, she climbs through Nepal with me, interested in the details of our unfathomable romance.

By the end of lunch, Linda, with the conviction of a convert, says, "Go for it!"

Nima writes me from Newcomerstown, Ohio. "This land is like Nepal. More simple and less machines. People travel by horse! I like it. I bought you a straw hat to wear in your garden. Nima Yoder"

Nima, I learn, adopts personalities quickly. The name Yoder in Ohio Amish country is like Sherpa in the Solukhumbu. During his Amish phase, Nima transplants flats of frisée, watercress, and purple mustard in Daniel's hydroponics greenhouse. Nima works harder than anyone, Daniel tells people, but he's not perfect. Nima won't kill harmful bugs.

The Amish farm life makes Nima homesick. I want to go home to Nepal, says Nima on the phone. Not so much benefit here. Not so much to do.

I encourage him to stay and tell him that if he goes back, I may never see him again. Nima misses his family and Nepal. He is disappointed that Ohio has no mountains. He also misses me. Nima, who spent all his money to come to America, now realizes how expensive things are here compared to Asia and worries about having enough work.

In America, no money, no nothing. No good English. No school. I want to go home. I want Nima to come to our home. His frustration only reinforces my resolve. I write him a letter and tell him how it hurts me to hear him sound so sad. I tell him how much I love him and need him to stay. I explain how I am buying the house and once final, Marco will move out. I remind Nima that in Kathmandu, we promised ourselves to each other. I plead with him not to lose faith and let go of our dream.

Nima is so despondent in Ohio, I bring him to Los Angeles for a week in mid-September. The first weekend, we go camping at Joshua Tree National Monument with my friends Jack and Mary. During the week, since Marco has not moved out, we move into the only place I can afford, a sleazy motel near the ocean and the oil depot. All week thick fog obscures our ocean view. I am in a fog, humbled by this hotel, yet happy. While I am at work, Nima explores Manhattan Beach by himself, but cannot get his bearings in the fog and stays close to the hotel. He begs me to come home early, but I cannot. We eat dinner out each evening and Nima experiences his first artichoke, avocado, and Mexican meal. Nima wants to explore Los Angeles. I only want to explore Nima. It is a wonderful and disappointing week for us both. On Sunday, I drive Nima to the airport to fly back to Ohio. When I kiss him good-bye, I empty all over again.

While we were camping at Joshua Tree, Mary asked if I would be interested in a class on Buddhism at UCLA. With a Buddhist in my future, I agree to join her. Mary, a work colleague, was envious of my journey to Nepal, and is fascinated by the Sherpa I brought home. The language of Buddhism is new to me. While I believed in reincarnation, I had no serious interest in Buddhism before my journey. Now, I am curious. As I take notes on the teachings, I begin on the path.

earth: Nothing changed here. You did.

I am a mirroring container. I reflect my past and my future. Action, and mental volition or karma, has inertia that carries me forward. I must change the sense of what it is to be a person, to let go of my sense of self. There are Four Noble Truths and Three Gates of Deliverance. My mind is luminous, but defiled by obscurements. The best way to learn non-attachment is to help others. There is no soul in Buddhism; there is action, but no actor. The purpose of practice is not to improve one's level of concentration, but to gain access to various states of mind. Aggression and passion, the male and female duality, are the pulse of life and part of the spiritual process. Wisdom is to be cognizant of the universal flux. To understand Buddhism, I must let go of Buddhism itself.

After our first class, my mind overflows. In the next classes, we learn the history of Buddhism's spread throughout Asia and why its different schools developed. At the end of October, the lecture on Tibetan Buddhism is lead by a teacher/monk who dresses in crimson and saffron robes. He tells us that Tibetans believe that the bodhisattva of compassion, Chenrezi or Avalokiteshvara, chose to reside in Tibet because Tibetans were the chosen people to carry Buddhism forward. As a large portion of the Tibetan population was made up of impoverished nomads in touch with the land, they had the proper psyche to absorb the Buddhist teachings, once the great monks mystically blended the nomads' long-held beliefs in animistic spirits with Buddhism. For these highly spirited people, compassion was expressed as a warrior, a benevolent vitality within each of us, and this is known as the Mahāyāna tradition.

The Mahāyāna tradition recognizes that we exist with others, and so must learn how to be in the world while we progress on our path. According to our teacher at UCLA, the first step for any Buddhist practioner is to obtain a luminous mind through a path of meditation, concentration, wisdom, and compassion. Before we start on the path, we are instructed to answer three questions. I find it interesting that the first question addresses my current cause of suffering—change. Our teacher called this Buddha's question: What drives me to want to change and grow at this time in my life? I went on my journey in search of change. If

161

I had answered this question before I left, I might have been more directed. Now there is Nima. Nima is synonymous with change. He needs to be part of my answer.

The second question: Do I have the capacity to be with others in a truthful and loving way? Since I met Nima, I know I have the capacity for great love. But, the professor explained that this question is more about what we do with our feelings, our capacities, and the like. I know I am not in control of my emotions.

The third question: Can I accept all aspects of life, whatever the realities and circumstances, as an integral part of myself? This is where I fall flat on my face. I cannot accept things as they are. I want them to be the way I think they should be. I tilt at too many windmills.

I have work to do before I begin on the inner path. Living with a Buddhist raised on these teachings will help.

My relationship with Nima began with an unconscious motivation that surfaced as we watched TV together in our sad hotel on the beach during his visit from Ohio. On the TV screen rose a mushroom cloud that Nima said looked taller than Mount Everest. What is that cloud mountain? Nima asked. Suddenly blasted by the revelation, I told him that the bomb was what brought us together.

The decade before I was born, the United States dropped the atom bomb on Japan. During grade school, the Cold War dominated foreign policy, and Russia was in Cuba. During Civil Defense drills, as the sirens screeched, our class would be ushered to the school basement, where we would crouch on cold linoleum and shelter our heads with our hands. With eyes closed, I dreamed about a man who would one day make me feel safe.

One night, from the shelter of my bedroom, I heard both the TV and my parents whisper of war. I huddled under blankets and worried that my parents had not built a bomb shelter in our backyard or stocked provisions. I felt unprotected. At age eight, I was cognizant of our atomic future. I pledged that my husband would be a rugged survivalist who knew how to live in the wilderness. I had it all planned out. When the bomb dropped, my husband and I would be packed, ready to make our way into the wilds of Canada. He would know what to do, how to take care of me, and together, we would repopulate the earth. I never anticipated the consequences of this deep-seated childhood fear, for in less than a week, a rugged survivalist will be living with me!

In mid-October, Nima returns from Ohio to Los Angeles within days of Marco moving out. It is always paradise with you, Nima tells me that first night together in our Redondo Beach home. Nima loves his new house and wanders from room to room and opens every door, drawer, and cupboard. He removes dishes or clothes or whatever to examine. He asks what this is or how that is used or why those are necessary. I too go through closets, to find clothes for Nima. I throw out most of what he brought with him, which leaves him with my hand-me-downs, two pairs of jeans, and a black leather jacket he bartered for at the Islamabad bazaar on his way back from K2. With the last of his own money, Nima wants to buy a television. At the store, he picks out the biggest one he can afford. I'll learn English faster, he tells me. I expect he will learn far more.

"Cloud bread was a mystery," says Nima, as he passes me a basket of Italian bread. "We ate only flat bread in my village." When he was little, someone gave him a loaf of soft bread. He thought if he ate it, he would float, so he ate the whole thing. "Cloud bread was just bread. Just different, like people."

Any sweets? I ask, still unfamiliar with Sherpa cuisine.

Foreigners brought us candy, says Nima. He tells me how the Swiss and French gave them chocolate, the Italians shared dried fruit, the Belgians handed out a chewy white candy, and Japanese treats were like colored rubber.

I share with him how my grandmother sent figs, dates, and kumquats from Florida at Christmas. Nima is not impressed and tells me how he and his brother Tshiring Tendi stole the thick cream at the top of the churn by the handful, when their mother wasn't looking. I cannot compete, so I stand to take my plate to the kitchen.

"Clean your plate," says Nima. "The food knows. Food has karma too. Haven't you ever heard a noise in your stomach?" I laugh. "For each bite you leave on your plate," he says, "you'll hear a hungry child cry."

Nima, who prefers his own cuisine, often cooks. I call his favorite dinner "the white meal": a heaping plate of white rice (poor people eat brown rice, according to Nima), potato-and-cauliflower curry, yellow lentils, and salt. After Nima moved in, I gained weight so fast that I thought I was pregnant. I took a test. False alarm. Only a carbo-belly. I now insist on less salt, more color on the plate, and I serve myself.

"Salt was like gold to the Sherpa," begins Nima. A long time ago, the yak was asked to cross the Himalaya to fetch salt from Tibet. He asked his brother, the water buffalo, if he could borrow his coat to keep warm, as he knew he'd encounter deep snow in the mountains. In exchange, the yak lent the water buffalo most of his horns. When the yak left, he wore his own coat and his brother's. The yak found the mountains populated by people who needed his expertise, so he decided to make the high Himalaya his home. That is why the water buffalo has no hair and long horns, while the short-horned shaggy yak can keep himself warm in extreme conditions. Nima finds it sad that the brothers can no longer visit, for if they do, one of them always gets sick.

According to Nima's Uncle Lama Zepa, when the yak went up into the Himalaya, he carried Buddhism between his horns. When I question the possibility of animals spreading Buddhism, Nima laughs and tells me it is true. Guru Rinpoche flew to Bhutan on the back of a tigress, a manifestation of one of his consorts, so she could assist him. He meditated there for three days. Later, a monastery called Taktsang, or "Tiger's Lair" was built on the side of the mountains where he landed. A great teacher, Guru Rinpoche also built Samye, the first Buddhist temple in Tibet. When the Tibetans first began to build it, spirits destroyed their work, so Guru Rinpoche chanted mantras to tame the spirits. Soon men built by day and the spirits by night, until the temple was completed. According to Nima, huge columns hold up its roof, which surprises him, as there is no wood for hundreds of miles. The spirits built many things earth: Nothing changed here. You did.

back then, Nima says, but now there are too many people and not enough land, so the spirits have gone into hiding, some underground, others in the mountains, many in the sky.

"One day, the spirits will return to help us," predicts Nima.

"Great story, Nima, but I can't wait. I've got too many things to do." I clean the kitchen, and then the refrigerator, which overflows with an abundance of foam cartons and plastic containers.

"Don't throw that out!" shouts Nima. I remind him it is stinky, week-old spinach. Nima tells me that he'll eat it. In the village, they store rotten vegetables in wood tubs to make a stew when they can't get fresh ones, and boil them to get rid of the rotten smell. Nima gets up from the table. We can get fresh produce all year in America, I tell Nima. I switch on the garbage disposal and knowingly grind up food karma.

Our first blissful weeks in November turn to apprehension as Nima watches the calendar. Immigration said he could stay in the country until they make a determination about his visa extension, but his visa expired in mid-October. We feel uncomfortable with his status. If Nima returns to Nepal—the distance feels insurmountable. How can our relationship have a future?

"Somehow we'll make it work." I try to assure us both.

Nima suggests we live in Nepal. I have changed enough to accept a Sherpa, but not enough to move to his country. I cannot let go. I expect a steady income. I do not trust him to care for me there. A simpler life appeals to me, but to give up my lifestyle is another thing altogether.

"I can't do that, Nima. It is too much of a change."

"What about me coming to America?" he argues. I point out that right now I am the one with a job, money, and a house. "Then marry me, Sherpani."

Marriage? This is too fast. Too rushed. Nima and I have talked about marriage, but I have not yet agreed. And if I do, our wedding will be in the spring.

"Nima, we need to live together longer."

"Why not now, Sherpani?" he pleads. "I love you. You love me. Simple."

"It is not simple, Nima." Failure is not an option. Not this time. I cannot explain my reasons, my past relationships, or my fears. "We have to wait."

"Then I'm going home!" Nima stands defiant.

Think, Caryl. You think you're scared? What about him? He only wants to feel safe. If he leaves, it's over. That may be the easiest outcome, but you went to Nepal to seek a redirection of energy toward something more meaningful.

"Caryl?" Nima's voice startles me. "Is everything alright?"

"I'm thinking." I think so hard that my head hurts. I rationalize. I love Nima. Making our marriage work may be easier than dealing with the immigration system. And if things don't work out—well, nothing is forever.

"Sherpani, I want to stay with you forever." Nima doesn't plead. His declaration is convincing, simple, and I know life will be like that, with Nima.

"If that is a marriage proposal, Nima, then I accept."

Nima wants to set a wedding date. All I can commit to is "soon." No family, I tell him. Just us. Maybe a few friends. I don't want anyone to rain on our parade. Parade? Nima thought we were talking about our wedding. I laugh. Joyful Nima hugs me, smothers me in kisses, and pulls me onto the Tibetan carpet he brought me from Nepal as if in anticipation of this moment, when we would lie together and honor our vows.

With the responsibilities of a soon-to-be husband on his mind, Nima happily goes out to look for a job. He knows life to be easy in America. As the week goes by, I see his self-confidence diminish, but he refuses to talk about it. I had expected job hunting to be difficult in this economy. On Friday night, after we watch *Dragon: The Bruce Lee Story*, Nima tells me how he identifies with Bruce Lee, another Asian who struggled in America. Bruce Lee immigrated to the United States, married a white woman, and experienced the prejudices of the fifties and sixties. Although Bruce Lee was the most accomplished martial arts master, a Caucasian was cast in the first kung fu movie.

"Living in America is like that," states Nima. "Unfair for Asians."

"Unfair for Asians? I don't think so, Nima."

"What do you know? You're white."

Concerned for Nima, I ask friends if they know of anyone he could work for. I explain his skills: mountaineering, sheepherding, and farming. He's strong, I assure them, even if skinny Nima doesn't look it. As I call in favors, a couple of friends come through.

Nima begins his career in America with odd jobs that brush him up against celebrities. Nima's first job is with Randy, a friend's handyman who is also a Buddhist. One day, they chop down two trees. Another day, they work four hours moving heavy furniture for a movie star, who serves them pizza for lunch and pays them each one hundred dollars. Once home, Nima cannot stop dancing.

"She was nice. So pretty. Who's Rae Dawn Chong?"

Nima next works with Case, another friend's friend, who cleans carpets. Today, they work at a beachfront house in Malibu owned by a rock star.

"He has three or four houses! Funny name. Who's Sting?"

Next, Nima works for Jim, who owns a window-washing business. Nima doesn't particularly like the work, but he loves to see how the well-heeled live in America, and is shocked when Jim has to pay four dollars to get into Rolling Hills Estates. Four dollars supports a family in Nepal for a week. The amenities of the rich amaze Nima—swimming pools, Jacuzzis, tennis courts, big gardens, huge houses—even horses!

The first week in December, Nima's pick-up jobs run out. With his experience and newfound confidence, he bicycles from restaurant to restaurant in the Manhattan Beach, Hermosa Beach, and Redondo Beach to look for work. In spite of the economy, I try to remain positive to keep his spirits up. I assure him that America is full of opportunity and tell him how immigrants built this country. Nima does not find that immigrants are welcomed and announces that from now on, he's only going to Asian or Indian restaurants. I am surprised, but say nothing.

My return to work is difficult. I want to be with Nima and help him transition. I want to write in my journal and record his delightful ways of seeing the world. I want to relive my journey and try to work out where I go from here. My priorities and my work obligations are out of sync, which is a pressure I put on myself and do not reconcile. One night I come home and crash. I fear for my job. The recession continues. Jobs are scarce. Our project's city review submittal package for the hotel renovation is nearly ready. Fortunately, the city of Beverly Hills' approval process will allow our work to ramp up at a steady pace, and a busy team is a happy team. On the other hand, the viability of the entire project is in question. If we don't get city approval, the project will be canceled. I can barely move.

I feel deluged by Nima's requests for help as he settles in, and apprehensive about our pending marriage. Adjusting to each other is more work than I anticipated. Some days I worry that the novelty of a Sherpa in my life may wear off, but most days I feel certain about Nima. My pride and sense of self is in transition. The confidence that I once had now wavers. Los Angeles respects position and image. How does a Sherpani fit in? Since my return from Nepal, I am uncertain of who I am, what I am, and where I am going. To merge my community with Nima feels impossible. I withdraw. I shut down and shut out everything. Nima has never seen me so quiet. Or so still. I stare ahead, not processing what I see. But I do see. I see how others look at me; I hear what they say; I smell their judgments; I taste their reactions; I feel their response to Nima. Or do I imagine them? An anxiety attack in a person who normally demonstrates self-control shocks the witness. On this day I shatter before Nima.

"Talk to me," whispers Nima. I am silent. "Talk to me." I can't talk. "Talk, please, Sherpani?" I sense fear. More fear than my own. I break open. I talk.

I talk about work. I talk about my client, my colleagues, and the general contractor who shook his fist in my face as he backed me into a dark office while screaming at me about the notes I diligently kept on our meetings. I talk to Nima about my job and how I could lose it. I talk about our lack of money. Our debt. I talk about alternatives. I talk about us, how we don't have time for each other; then I talk about me, and how

I don't know who I am anymore or where I fit.

"I am lost, Nima."

I cry. He holds me.

"You must be patient. Not such a big problem. You didn't lose a child or parent or brother. You only lost yourself." Nima smiles, triumphant. "And then, I found you!"

His simple love calms me. He rocks me, strokes my hair, and chants quietly. I do not sleep. I remember the growing pains my twin sister, Caryn, had in her tenth year. I would lie in bed and listen to her cry herself to sleep. In my youth, I never had growing pains. I rarely cried. I do now. Quietly, so as not to awaken Nima.

In early December, Nima makes his debut at my office Christmas party being held at the Beverly Hills Hotel. At the end of the month it will close for a two-year renovation, and I'll be busier than ever. Nima looks handsome in black slacks, a vintage tie, and a blue-black shantung silk dinner jacket we bought for three dollars at the annual Palos Verdes Estates garage sale. Although Nima has been in America eight months and has developed some social grace, he is a fish out of water here. He looks this way and that as he takes in the hotel's faded five-star ambience. I am glad that Nima's smile and mastery of English disarm many of my curious colleagues, who recognize his unique nature and pull me aside. Interesting to talk to. So handsome. Such a gentle man. Lovely smile. I thank them. I am proud. This may not be so hard after all. The champagne makes me happy and I float through the evening with Nima by my side. For those who shoot glances our way and whisper, I want to tell them his story—

Because he was born at home at dawn; because he played in the natural world; because he cared for animals from age five and drove them up over high hills to summer pastures by age eight, alone; because he knew silence there among waterfalls; because he slept on beds of moss near the creek and heard stones sing and insects scurry; because he cried when he got lost in the wild; because he discovered the kindness of strangers; because his father and mother could not show their love; because his two older half sisters could love him; because his older brother was his best friend; because he had other younger brothers and sisters to love when they hurt; because Tibetans escaping torture and death found refuge in his family's home; because he heard the refugees' stories of escape; because he heard his grandfather's stories of distant lands; because the villagers knew each other and cared for each other; because the *gompa* was part of his community; because the monks blessed them; because his family fed and cared for the monks; because he refused to kill anything; because he spoke the truth; because he was generous; because the Buddha blesses the compassionate; because he lived off the land and understood it required care; because his hands knew plants and animals and rocks he could grow and nurture and build; because he lived below the goddess, Chomolungma, whom the West renamed Mount Everest; because people came to climb the mountain; because he learned geography, languages, cultures, and an appreciation for diversity from strangers; because he worked on the mountain, first as a kitchen boy, then cook, then guide; because he crossed ladders over crevasses; because he scaled vertical ice walls multiple times a day with eighty pounds on his back while gravity pulled at him and mocked his prowess; because he carved out new trails in ice on land never stepped on by man; because he roped himself to inexperienced climbers; because he led; because he scaled mountains in darkness; because he neared summits in blizzards and made the decision to go on or turn back; because he knew the ethereal nature of things, the futility of desires, the exhaustion of work with little reward; because he saw avalanches and dug out the injured; because he took risks; because he faced death; Nima grew wise.

Few will listen to his story. Most will not believe. I must be patient. Nima is a gift. In time, those deserving of Nima will unwrap him.

Ahhhhh. So good to meet you. So good.

—*Lama Geshe*

O**N OUR FLIGHT FROM LOS ANGELES** to San Francisco on December twentieth, clear skies and an almost-full moon light our way up the coast. The night mirrors my clarity. After we made the decision to marry four weeks ago, I have told no one about our wedding tomorrow beyond our five guests. While armed with emotional conviction, I remain intellectually fragile, and so avoid any communications that would upset my balance. I don't want to explain my actions. I want to follow my heart. No one else can know what Nima means to me, the pull from the center of me to the center of him. We turn inside out for each other and envelop the other. Our love is profound, prophetic, pure. Only believers will witness our union.

I called my younger sister Cinda, who lives in Berkeley, California, to ask if we could get married outside in her backyard. The twenty-first of December will be the eve of the winter solstice, I told her. Cinda loved the idea of hosting our wedding. Cinda likes Nima. Cinda also met her husband, Lance, under exotic circumstances—on a beach in Acapulco, Mexico. Sometimes you just know, Cinda told me. But Lance was American, not Nepalese, and a lawyer, not a mountain climber. Cinda tells me I'll have my own mountains to climb, but she is supportive. My choice for a husband fascinates her. Cinda and Lance first met Nima when he and I flew back to Michigan to attend their wedding. They look forward to our visit.

The next morning is a rush of preparations for our afternoon wedding. Lance and Nima lay sod in the yard to complete a home improvement project that needed a deadline. Lance, a few years older than Cinda, is tall and broad, and a mentor to Cinda. He exudes experience, and she wants to learn. Cinda and I clean the house. While she orders our wedding feast from her favorite neighborhood Greek restaurant, I pick flowers along their fencerow and arrange them. When the bell rings, I open the door to greet our reverend. Cinda found her in the Yellow Pages, talked to her, and decided she would be perfect.

"I lived in Tibet in a past life," says our mail-order-ministry reverend, who tells me she feels blessed to be administering our vows. The reverend is an elderly woman with beauty parlor gray hair, ashen skin, with a blush of rose at her cheeks, a small mouth, and wire-rim glasses that frame pale eyes. Soon after her arrival, she dons a silver robe and places a burgundy sash around her neck. She looks ministerial. In a soothing voice, she tells us how she always makes it her duty to know her clients before she performs the service. The reverend asks us a few questions, and then requests the rings.

"We don't have rings," I inform her. The reverend believes that we should have rings; they are an ancient symbol of eternity, of endless love. I tell her that Nima and I do not need a symbol. What about others? A ring announces your love to others.

The reverend is right, I tell Nima. We need rings.

As we drive toward downtown Berkeley, Cinda suggests the street vendors who sell inexpensive handmade jewelry along Telegraph Avenue. With little time to make such a significant purchase, Cinda, Nima, and I dash from stall to stall. At a booth festooned with strings of prayer flags or *lungdar*, we stop. Their jewelry is well-made. Nima chooses a trapezoid of blue turquoise on a wide band for me. I select an oval of green turquoise on a narrow band for Nima. I pay sixty-seven dollars and forty-nine cents for our two symbols of eternal love. Darn cheap, when I consider that in three hours Nima will slip the ring on my finger and our lives will change forever. The clarity of what I am about to commit to surprises me; my certainty springs from my heart—and my past.

We were husband and wife in a past life.

At the bakery, Nima stares in fascination at decorated cakes whose heights compete with mountains and whose frilly frosting suggests snow. I choose two petite single-layer cakes, one chocolate and one cheesecake, simple and unadorned. All I need is to lick the chocolate off Nima's lips to celebrate, I tell Cinda. Nima is disappointed with my choice and points to an artistry in sugar. I shake my head. Disappointed, he promises that in five years he'll be rich and will buy me a big wedding cake for our anniversary.

At Kathmandu Imports, Cinda and I select cedar incense and a tape of flute music. Excited to converse with a fellow countryman, Nima talks to the owner in Nepali. I still have to shower and dress. Nima, I interrupt, we must go. The Nepalese talk on.

"Nima, please. Our guests will arrive in an hour!" No movement.

"Nima! Let's go!" Nima listens to Cinda.

Back at Cinda's home, Nima and I dress for the wedding. Cinda admires our untraditional wedding attire as she hands me a bouquet of orchids to accent the fuchsia, sapphire, and emerald Thai silk suit I had made for me in Bangkok. Nima looks like a million dollars in vintage chic, the same outfit he wore to my office Christmas party.

As our guests arrive, I realize how glad I am to have friends in attendance who support us. Mark, a colleague, lives in Venice, California, and plans to spend Christmas with his family in the Bay Area. Fascinated by Sherpas and mountains, he joined us in Joshua Tree on Nima's first trip to California. Once Nima became the focus of an informal hiking club, Mark became its staunchest member. Mark is slender, with dark hair and an energy like Nima's, always in motion. Gentle, yet savvy in a street-smart kind of way, Mark understands Nima.

My friend Robin and her husband, Tony, are on their way to visit his family in San Francisco. Robin, a bicycling buddy, met Tony when she moved to the Bay Area. They now live in Santa Barbara. Their marriage is proof that online dating works. Robin is a lover of birds and has a personality to match—chirpy, chatty, and flighty, she is everywhere at once, interested in me, curious about Nima, his family, and his country. A speech therapist, she works with Nima on his b's, p's and v's, which all sound the same to his ear. Nima likes the attention he receives from Robin.

After thousands of miles together on our bicycles, Robin and I have roots. Although I attended Tony and Robin's wedding in Chicago, and visited them in San Francisco, I barely know Tony. He is quiet, unless the conversation veers toward bicycles or computers. He repairs bikes by day, studies to be a computer technician by night, and gives Robin the companionship she longed for.

Nima and my wedding is simple. The reverend nods. I begin.

"Both in our cultures and in our lives, this evening before the winter solstice symbolizes an end and a beginning; of days of darkness becoming days of light—together we will create this light."

The reverend leads Nima and me through our vows. Together we light a unity candle and exchange rings. Nima reaches for a white wedding *khata*, lays it across his forearms, places his palms together to form a lotus bud, and bows toward me. *Namaste.* The spirit in me salutes the spirit in you. I do the same. He then reaches over my bent head and lays the long white scarf on my neck. I repeat the blessing for Nima. In a small shop in Bhutan, when the woman behind the counter told me these finely made *khata* of silk were used specifically for weddings, I bought six of them: one each for my sisters Jeanne and Cinda and their husbands, who I knew were getting married, and one each for Nima and me. Somehow, you just know.

"And now I pronounce you husband and wife," says the reverend. Nima and I kiss.

"Caryl Sherpa." Nima grabs my hand and refuses to let go. "My Sherpani. Mine."

Nima's afraid of losing you, Lance tells me. Nima is special, says Cinda.

earth: Ahhhhh. So good to meet you. So good.

Thank you for believing in us, I tell them. It means a lot.

"Let's call your parents," says Nima. "They will be so excited!"

Cinda and I exchange glances, not so sure. Although my parents have met Nima and know we live together, I am certain our relationship befuddles them. Nima dials. I tell him I need to talk to them first. The phone rings.

"Nima!" He hands me the phone. I am nervous. My mother answers.

"Hi, Mom. I'm married. Married to Nima." Her only response— That's nice. With nothing more to say to her, or for her to say to me, I hand the phone to Nima.

"Hi, Mom. This is your son-in-law, Nima." His grin is as wide as the Himalaya range is long. "Okay." Nima pauses. "Hi, Dad!"

Cinda cannot stop giggling. Mother must be speechless, she says. She gave the phone to Dad. We listen and imagine their words. Up until now, Nima had called them Bob and Alice. Now it is Mom and Dad. To mask the rush of emotions I feel at this moment, I laugh and imagine my father and mother faint with hysteria on the other end of the line. I tell my sister how glad I am to be an older, experienced adult. Cinda says she wishes she could see their faces. Jubilant Nima only wants to share his joy— with family.

On the second day of our honeymoon, we drive the Pacific Coast Highway north to Mendocino to have dinner with Nima's Nepalese friends David and Sita. We spent our wedding night in San Francisco at a hotel off Union Square. Unfortunately, the champagne, the king-size canopied bed, and the bride were all lost on Nima, who hollered from a toothache. I drowned my disappointment in champagne.

After our disappointing first night as a married couple, we are surprised when David and Sita tell us that their wedding gift to us is one night in the Bridal Suite of a local roadside motel. We had expected to sleep on their sofa. As Sita unlocks the room to show it off, she tells us how she looked at all the motels in the area and this was by far the best. Our spacious accommodations blossom pink and white on walls, floor, and furniture. Festooned in lace, eyelet, and organdy, the king-size

175

canopied bed lies buried under heart-shaped pillows. Nima thinks it's pretty. I think the room looks like the closeout counter of a bridal shop. We both thank them for their generosity. On the second and last night of our honeymoon, I lie awake and again listen to my husband moan about his toothache. I am disillusioned. Since when does marriage make you celibate?

Back in the Santa Monica office, the news of our marriage comes as a shock to friends and colleagues. Reactions span from joy to confusion to disdain: I thought he was just your stud muffin. Are you crazy? A Sherpa? Nice name though. Well, you two will have an interesting life. No work for a Sherpa in LA. Are you moving to Nepal? Good luck. It won't be easy. Do you have altitude sickness? Such a gentle man. At least you have someone to carry your luggage. No way!

I confirm I married a Sherpa.

Awesome!

"My family and I would like to give you and Nima a wedding reception," says Mahnoosh, a colleague from Iran. Mahnoosh, an architect, is a model-thin Persian beauty with eyes that flash with passion. I am surprised by her offer. Our relationship has been respectful colleagues, not close friends. Her family would like to follow a few of their Persian customs, she says. We'd be honored, I tell her. Mahnoosh explains that when her mother heard Nima had no family, no clan in Los Angeles, she wanted her family to fill in. As immigrants themselves, her mother appreciates the importance of family and tradition on such occasions. Her family talked and everyone wants to help.

"But we don't even know your family." I am embarrassed by her generous offer.

"My mother will be disappointed if you don't accept."

I accept. We set a date in mid-January. Nima is thrilled—and then not. After we returned from our honeymoon, I took Nima to the dentist, who pulled his two top front teeth. Forced to wait for false teeth to fill the gap, and unable to fund a temporary, Nima refuses to attend our wedding party without a full set of teeth. I call the dentist daily. I worry. Nima frets. I call. It is the day before the party. We both have to be there, I insist. Nima is too embarrassed to go. A cancellation. The dentist calls. We are lucky. By late afternoon, Nima's smile is restored.

Nima and I arrive early to our wedding party, which Mahnoosh is hosting in her Pasadena condo. We are curious to meet our hosts. Mahnoosh introduces us to her parents, her siblings, and their husbands and wives. Mahnoosh's mother, Mrs. Bahar, is a vivacious woman whom Nima takes to immediately. She pulls him aside to talk. You speak good English, she tells him. That's important. After living fifteen years in the States, my husband still won't speak it.

Mr. Bahar nods to Nima. As Mrs. Bahar shares with Nima her family's struggles upon their arrival in America, Nima opens up and shares with her his frustrations with learning English and with his job hunt. She encourages him to be patient. Not everything comes at once. He has a nice wife. Now, he must go to school. Education is important in America, she concludes. Nima assures her that he will. Mrs. Bahar pats his hand, smiles, and gets up to set out the meal.

"White flowers are a traditional Persian wedding blessing," says Mahnoosh, when I express delight over the profusion of flowers. One of the women tells me that Mahnoosh got up at four o'clock in the morning to go to the downtown flower market. Surprised, I thank her. Mahnoosh tells me it was nothing. Her mother took two days off work to cook us a traditional Persian feast: saffron rice cake, shish kabobs, a wedding *polow* with orange peel, eggplant braise, a pasta meat dish, and salad with mint yogurt dressing. Sounds delicious, I tell them, and I love the baskets of radish rosettes and scallion flowers. They look difficult to make.

"It's tradition," says Mrs. Bahar. "We must."

"We still can't believe you did all this for us," I tell Mahnoosh and her mother. "We're strangers. And not even Persian."

"All the same world, Caryl. No one strange." Nima bows toward them. "*Namaste* to my wonderful family."

After dinner, we sip tea from tiny copper cups with Mahnoosh's family and our guests, who are work colleagues and their partners. Inspired by the traditional music of Iran, the Persian women of the family begin to dance, and soon we all join in. I enjoy the hypnotic music and fluid movements of supple bodies as they gracefully sculpt air. Nima, no longer shy, asks me to dance. He moves like the Persians, with catlike grace, spinning stories with his hands. I move to the beat, and jerk like stop-and-go traffic. Everyone dances for a time, only to drift back to the sofas in exhaustion and soon depart for their long drives home. In the end, Nima is the only male among stunning Persian beauties. They smile and flirt. I am jealous. I wish I were dark like them. As if held captive by his charisma and enraptured by his smile, the women dance and dance and dance around Nima.

"That was the best party yet!" says Nima as we drive off down the Pasadena Freeway to live happily ever after, for better or for worse.

On my way to work, I drop Nima off at the high school near our home, where he can register at the start of winter quarter for an English as a Second Language class.

Level four! shouts Nima, when I return home. I am smart, Caryl. I placed high!

I am proud.

His ESL class meets five mornings and two evenings a week. Nima fails his first test in class, then gets a 90 percent on the same chapters. Nima calls me at work to tell me his score and to promise that he is "studying himself very hard." He can't believe how much there is to learn. He asks for my help. We work on his ESL homework in the evening. Nima enjoys reading, especially about compassionate historical figures, like Abraham Lincoln or Florence Nightingale. Other lessons offer practical knowledge like what to expect when you go to the doctor, or how to get a green card, or what to do at the bank, or how to protect against AIDS. His grammar exercises prove too abstract for him; Nima resists rules. Smart Nima, however, excels at vocabulary.

Nepal is a cocktail country, he says to me one evening. I ask if they are teaching him to become a bartender. He laughs. No, silly. About people.

earth: Ahhhhh. So good to meet you. So good.

Different kinds of people? A variety of people? I ask. He nods. I now say things multiple ways to ensure better comprehension. Nepal is a *diverse* country, I tell him. *Cocktail* means a mixed alcoholic drink, but it's an interesting metaphor. Nima asks for the meaning of *metaphor.*

We talk in circles. How do I explain *metaphor* to the linear mind of a Sherpa? I must think hard about the meaning of words, how to use them in sentences, act them out, or find their synonyms. I explain why words like *live* and *stock* mean something else when combined into *livestock,* or how *stock* has multiple meanings. I clarify the difference between *nip* and *pinch.* An animal nips. A person pinches. One is playful, the other more menacing. One makes you smile, the other, frown, and both may make you slap the "animal" that nips or pinches you. One night in bed, Nima tells me his foot-fingers are cold. My feet reach over to warm his, but I do not correct him. I like *foot-fingers.*

Being around Nima alters my perspective. One night as I lie on the sofa and Nima studies on the floor, I place my foot on his shoulder. He lifts it off. Never put the bottom of your foot on anyone's head or shoulders. The gods enter a person there. Nima places his palms together, bows three times, and taps his head and shoulders to assure the gods I meant no disrespect. To make double sure, I mimic Nima.

Our home begins to welcome the world. Nima tells me that he understands the Asian students when they speak English, but not the Hispanics. As Nima is a natural linguist, I suggest he learn Spanish. When I arrive home from work a few days later, he greets me with "*Como estás?*" then introduces me to his Peruvian classmate. A few days later, he comes home elated and jumps around as he tells me about the poster of Bodhnath at his school. There is an American-Nepal Society in Los Angeles, and maybe more Sherpas! Nima calls the number listed, and talks and talks in Nepali. I cannot understand his conversation, so Nima gives me the summary. There are two hundred fifty Nepalese in Los Angeles, but only one Sherpa. A Nepalese family named Govinda lives only six blocks away. He calls the Govindas and talks and talks.

What a good day, says Nima. Their son, Hari, and his sister will be in

179

ESL too! Both Nima and Hari have been in America less than a year, so their struggles are similar. Hari's features are Aryan, more angular, unlike the round Mongoloid face of the Sherpas. With his coarse black hair, dark eyes, and bronze complexion, he is often mistaken for a Hispanic. Although class and ethnic differences exist in Nepal, in America, their shared experiences and common heritage bind Nima and Hari together. Hari often stays to have dinner with us, and in turn, the Govinda family invites us to family dinners, Nepalese holidays, and their daughter's Hindu wedding. With a connection back to Nepal, Nima finds America friendlier, and his dependency on me lessens.

One night when Nima is at class, I arrive home to find the table set and dinner on the stove. The stress of my day disappears. When Nima comes home, he tells me that he has too much time to think during the day and not enough to do. In addition to school, he wants to work. I work hard, he tells me, which is good karma for me, but not so good for him. His karma account has fallen behind. Only in a human rebirth can we forward the cycle of existence, or *samsāra*, as only when we are reborn as humans do we have the capability to overcome the three unwholesome roots—hatred, desire, and delusion.

"Karma is important," says Nima. "For example, first my parents made me, then my mother carried me for one year, and then it's pee and poop and feed me. I must pay them back."

In spite of what Nima thinks, he has good karma.

"My brother Pasang is coming to live in the States!" shouts Nima a few days later as he hangs up the phone. "Lee just called to tell me."

Several years ago, Pasang met Lee on trek in Nepal, says Nima. Two years ago, Lee sponsored Pasang's first visit to the United States. Pasang lived with Lee's family in Hawaii for six months and took ESL classes to improve his English, a skill critical for advancement in the American trekking business. Nima bubbles over with excitement. Lee said that his family is moving from Hawaii to Palos Verdes, just south of us. Pasang will be within easy driving distance. With Lee's sponsorship, says Nima, Pasang can pursue his dream: life in America, a high school diploma, and college.

earth: Ahhhhh. So good to meet you. So good.

Nima cannot stop dancing. He misses his brothers. Until then, the Govinda family, Jules, and I fill in.

Today is a big day, Caryl.

I know why, but ask Nima for an explanation just to hear the excitement in his voice. I get to meet a Sherpa! Sonam Sherpa! Remember? He invited us to his house the first Saturday in February.

As the door to the apartment in the Los Feliz neighborhood opens, Sonam's American wife, Becky, greets us. She motions for us to sit on the sofa and serves us chai tea while apologizing for her husband's absence.

Honey, come on out, Becky shouts to the bathroom door. Then to us, He's fixing his hair. She hands us a photo album of Sonam's recent trip to Nepal. Sonam, she says, please come meet your guests.

His album is a scrapbook of photos, tickets, matches, memos, and receipts, all collected during his return visit to his village of Rolwaling last year. Meticulous notes about the trip are written on Nepalese paper and pasted onto each page, as if floating over his memories. He misses Nepal as much as Nima does.

Honey, come on out! Becky shouts to the door, and then turns to us. We met in ESL. To the door: Sonam! To us: I was his teacher. Door: Honey! Us: He stood out among a room of dour-faced Koreans, like a ray of sunshine. Door: Honeeeeeeeeey!

I laugh. That was my first impression of Nima, I tell her. Sunshine.

Honeeeeeeeeey! The bathroom door opens. Sonam steps out. His thick hair is gelled upright by sweeps from a wide-toothed comb.

Conversing in Sherpa, Nima and Sonam first determine if they are related (both have the same clan name of Salakha), whom they both know, and what common experiences they have shared. Becky and I get only a partial translation. Sonam's village is close to Nima's home, but hard to visit, as access is over a treacherous, snowbound pass. On his last trip home, Sonam brought a video camera, video monitor, and battery pack, so he could show off his wife and his life in the United States to his family. They were shocked. No one had ever seen television. Sonam pops his videocassette into the player and introduces us to his family, his village, the wedding party, and then lets it play for the rest of our visit. I am mesmerized, curious to see how Sherpas live. Is this how Nima's family lives? Inside is always dark. Outside is always bright. Everyone always smiles. And everyone is poor.

Sonam and Becky are rich compared to his relations in Nepal. I look around their apartment. From my seat on the sofa, the living room, dining area, and kitchen are fully visible, as is the bathroom, bedroom, and entry door. Powder-blue carpet, a blue velvet sofa, mismatched lounge chairs, and a small, dark, oak table with two chairs fill the room. Two end tables hold large lamps, family photos, and a prayer wheel. Posters tacked high up the wall include Guru Rinpoche, various Himalaya mountains, and His Holiness the XIV Dalai Lama. The petite kitchen meets their needs. I hear footsteps above, children next door, and traffic below. I think of Sonam's family and the unspoiled mountain landscape that surrounds their home. Wealth comes in many forms.

After our hike up to the Hollywood sign above Sonam and Becky's apartment, Nima gives Sonam the nickname Hollywood. Nima and Hollywood speak in Sherpa, but I can tell it's about job hunting. Hollywood offers advice and encouragement. Life is hard for an immigrant, he tells us both, especially starting out. He encourages Nima to be patient. Nima had expected more from America. Frustrated and depressed, he knows we barely make ends meet and the recession has worsened. Hollywood promises to talk to the owner of an Indian restaurant nearby whom he knows. Hollywood gives us hope.

In Los Angeles, where connections make or break you, it is good to know a Sherpa.

Today, Nima is champagne with bubbles rising to the surface in anticipation of a celebration. I have promised to take him to Chinatown, just north of downtown Los Angeles, to shop for his most important holiday of the year, *Losar*, or Sherpa New Year. We have scheduled a party for early March. In the Solukhumbu, the villagers celebrate for days, according to

earth: Ahhhhh. So good to meet you. So good.

Nima. Our celebration will be at our home. The guest list keeps growing. At thirty-five, I tell Nima we have to stop. The house can hold no more. I am thankful our *Losar* will last only one evening.

The bazaar of small shops and stalls in Chinatown reminds us of Kathmandu. We select spinach, tomatoes, daikon radish, Japanese eggplants, and bitter gourd from crates that line the sidewalk. Inside the market, sellers in stall after stall hawk electronics, leather goods, toys, and clothes. I buy a gathered skirt in spring colors. From the butcher, Nima buys fresh chickens, slaughtered while we shop. At the grocery store, he purchases items not found at Ralph's or Safeway: rice noodles, dried Szechwan pepper, shrimp chips, basmati rice in a twenty-five-pound bag, a bamboo steamer for *momos*, and a huge aluminum teapot. Generosity shown to family and friends during the weeklong celebration is a tradition. Over the next few months, we will have to be even more frugal. We did not save enough.

While *Losar* preparations occupy our week, Nima informs me that he and Hari will cook their traditional food. I'm to set everything up and make the fruit plate. I am happy. For the first time since his arrival in America, Nima has taken charge.

In Nepal, Nima commanded respect among the men who worked with him. I could lean on him there. In America, Nima's confidence has disappeared. He can be shy and withdrawn with strangers. I get frustrated, as he is too willing to let me do or talk or answer for him. I don't want to. I try to hold back. I push him to respond, but people here don't make it easy. Everyone is in a hurry. No one wants to try to understand an immigrant, if there is an American around who can answer for him. Nima asks a question, and people look at me as they answer. Or they ask me a question that should be directed to Nima. What would *he* like for dinner? How old is *he*? Does *he* speak English? I want to challenge them, but I never do. I avoid confrontation. I resist making someone else uncomfortable, even when they are wrong. Fool that I am, I let them make me feel uncomfortable. Talk about a double standard that is not in my favor. What am I thinking? Worse, I allow them to put Nima down. I hate my politeness. No, make that inaction. I am embarrassed, but not enough to keep Nima from shrinking. I am glad today will be different.

The squeak of the rolling pins mixes with the chatter and laughter of Nima and Hari, who shape dough and seasoned meat into dumplings, or *momos*, to be eaten with sesame-seed chutney or tomato-chili sauce. The men cut vegetables and fruit, hand-grind spices, chop meat, and cook up the ingredients into curries of potato and cauliflower, chicken, pork and daikon, and garbanzo beans with vegetables—to be served with *daal* and rice pilaf. Finally, Hari blends yogurt, mangos, and bananas to create fruit *lassi*, a refreshing beverage. Yesterday, Nima twisted cookie dough into fanciful shapes and fried them to create the traditional *Losar* cookies. Now I arrange platters of tropical fruits to look like those that the vendors who wander the streets of Kathmandu balance on their heads, only to take down and place on three-legged collapsible stools to sell coconut, pineapple, mango, or papaya, fresh but for the dust of the day.

I know guests will ask why we are serving tropical fruit, when Nepal is covered in snow. I will inform them that Nepal rises from near sea level to the top of Mount Everest, at 29,029 feet (8,848 m), all within the width of the state of California. The Sierra Nevada mountains are less than half the height of Mount Everest. Because Kathmandu is closer to the equator than Los Angeles, even at over 4,000 feet (1,219 m) above sea level, it is still semitropical. They will comment on what an amazing country it must be. I will agree and tell them that Nepal has even more amazing people. They will nod, and I hope they will get to know Nima.

Although Nima has no statue of the Buddha, he creates a shrine without one. On the bookcase in the living room, he places lighted candles and incense, two small *mani* stones, a Shiva *lingam* we received as a wedding gift from my friend Mary, a wooden snake from Mexico, flowers, and a plate of *Losar* cookies, sweets, and dried fruit. Nima performs three prostrations, then chants prayers before his altar, then performs three prostrations. The Buddha is a state of being.

As I have no Sherpani *engi*, I dress Bhutanese for the occasion in a royal-blue silk blouse and a *kira*—a three-panel black fabric rectangle embellished with colorful silk threads woven in a geometric pattern—

that I wrap around me like a jumper, pin at the shoulders, and tie with an embroidered sash. Nima dresses in Sonam's green silk *chhuba*, belted at the waist like a big baggy bathrobe and worn over a raw-silk mandarin-collar shirt and black pants. His silk brocade hat with fur-trimmed earflaps suits his joy.

We greet our guests with palms together and a bow. *Namaste.* The spirit in me salutes the spirit in you. My, your life has changed, Caryl. What an international gathering. Interesting outfits. He's handsome. Your life could be a movie. With that smile, Nima could be a star. This is like a trip around the world.

Our guests are American, Nepalese, Filipino, Czechoslovakian, Cuban, Pakistani, Chinese, Peruvian, Indian, Iranian, and Mexican. Some are Nima's ESL classmates; others are my colleagues, clients, or friends. I catch snatches of conversations between people from faraway places—Here, the wisdom of elders is not respected. We met when I was overseas. Looks like a beautiful country. Beautiful women, too. Imagine. He grew up in California and still lives here! What an interesting life you climbed into!

After our last guest leaves and we climb into bed, Nima tells me that to prepare food for others is equal to preparing food for a shrine. If you feed others, you honor them. I snuggle in close to Nima, pleased we could share with others and happy our first *Losar* was a success.

Nima kisses my breasts and mounts me. To make love is the same, says Nima. Each of us is an altar.

One day when our differences collide, I tell Nima his universe is not the same as mine. He asks what *universe* means. I rent the video *The Right Stuff*. Nima's grasp of the concept of space is like my comprehension of Buddhism. We may mentally understand concepts, like the universe or karma or *samsāra*, the cyclic existence, but find they are difficult to accept when learned as an adult.

Outer space? asks Nima. Is that past the moon? I explain that outer space includes the moon and everything past it. Man has walked on the moon, but that's as far as we've gotten.

Wow! Man on the moon? Could I go there? asks Nima. I am shocked that Nima never knew. The first lunar landing happened over twenty years ago, and we have returned since. The summer before my senior year in high school, I gathered with friends at someone's lake cottage to watch the first moon walk, mankind's giant leap. I thought that the whole world had watched. Nima reminds me that he grew up in the mountains with no radio, TV, or newspapers. How could he know?

Nima ponders his new knowledge. We were born on earth in this life, he says. Shouldn't we stay?

I'd love to orbit the earth and look down on it, I tell him. What's an *orbit*? he asks. Conversations with Nima orbit. I try to put his questions into a context he understands, and explain that an orbit is like a *kora*, but instead of circling a *chörten*, you circle the earth. I watch Nima's eyes grow wide, as he considers the possibility for grace. I describe our solar system. I draw planets that circle the sun, moons that orbit the planets, and the phases of the moon. He asks what it's called when the sun goes black. An eclipse, I tell him. Nima explains how they happen. One day, a man borrowed food from the devil. The man never paid the devil back, so the devil made the eclipse to remind us to pay back our karmic debts. I wonder: Could our collective indiscretions someday extinguish the sun?

I select the movie *Star Trek* to provide an alternative vision. As a spaceship rockets past galaxies, Nima asks about all the little white spots. Those are stars, like small suns, only far, far out in the universe. I describe space and its infinite realm, but Nima is a concrete thinker. His vocabulary consists of active verbs and nouns he can see and touch, not concepts.

Is there a gate to get into space? asks Nima. It takes imagination to envision the universe.

In our youth, my peers and I developed a collective vision of space as we learned about the relationships of planets, moons, and constellations within the vastness of the universe. As children, we could stretch our imaginations to such lengths. What does Nima envision? Does he imagine space as a celestial realm above the world's cosmic diagram, the mandala, like the monks do? Does it have an end? A beginning? Could

earth: Ahhhhh. So good to meet you. So good.

he fall off? I want to know if he thinks other beings live in space. Or gods? I prod. While Nima wants to understand the Western vision of the universe, he has become aware of his educational gap and his distinctive worldview. He is not always cognizant of the innocence of his inquiries, but he knows when someone asks questions that point out his ignorance. Self-consciousness and silence settle over Nima like the haze that slinks into the Los Angeles basin.

Since meeting Nima, I too must reconsider the universe. So much has changed. I seek a new direction, a redefinition. It is not immediate, but a slow seep of actions that trigger reactions and cause evolution. I circle, and notice my orbit has been altered. I pull away from the earth. Gravity retains a lesser hold. As my adventure with Nima continues, I pass planets, move among moons, and shimmy closer to the stars.

A few weeks after our *Losar*, Dolma, a Tibetan friend who grew up in India, calls Nima and asks us to join her family for a New Year's celebration at the Tibetan Buddhist temple in Los Angeles. The date of *Losar*, based on the Tibetan calendar, changes annually and may even fall on a weekday. With everyone's busy schedules in the United States, *Losar* may not always be celebrated on its actual date. Always practical, the Tibetans and the Sherpas adapt to the environment and culture they live in.

Dolma is short and stocky with flawless skin and black hair worn in a ponytail. She is more comfortable dressed in the traditional *engi* than in Western styles. In contrast, Dolma's husband Grant is tall, lean, and pale. We met them at the first American-Nepal Society meeting we attended, and were inspired by the success of their cross-cultural relationship.

On the drive over, I envision a grand temple with golden roofs festooned with colorful prayer flags and banners. But Los Angeles is not Tibet. The temple off busy La Cienega Boulevard is a converted two-story apartment building with a single flight of stairs to an upper-level balcony that faces a parking lot filled with Tibetans and plastic-draped tables of food. While Dolma introduces Nima to her friends, he cannot stop smiling. As their conversations are in Tibetan, Grant and I stand to the side and talk about how different our lives are and how we'll always be outsiders. Although cultures cross-pollinate, our differences dissolve only at the intersection.

Nima interrupts me to make an introduction. "Caryl, this is Lama Geshe, who runs the temple," says Nima. "Caryl is my wife."

Lama Geshe fascinates me. His crimson and saffron robes set off a dark shaved head illuminated by dancing eyes. I sense wisdom with humor. A Geshe is both a scholar with a doctorate in traditional Buddhist studies and a spiritual teacher.

"Ahhhhh." He takes my hands between his palms and looks deep into my eyes. "So good to meet you. So good." I like his attention, but pull away, uncomfortable with his gentle intensity. He moves on to others. What did I lose?

I am lucky. A month later, I get another chance.

At the entry to the Beverly Wilshire Hotel in Beverly Hills, I stop our Honda hatchback between a limousine and a Porsche, get out of the car, and hand my keys to the valet attendant. Nima and I step toward lights and cameras, only to be ignored by all but the doorman, who holds the door open as he looks beyond us toward the next arrivals here for a fundraiser for Tibet. We enter an elegant world of beautiful people among mahogany, gold, precious jewels, silks, brocades, and palms. Nima wears his usual vintage garage sale. I wear a simple black cocktail dress that I think looks chic, until I pass Cindy Crawford in her satin gown and radiant jewels, on the arm of a handsome man. Nima can compete with any man's looks, but I am no match for Cindy.

There's Richard Blum. Nima points out a successful-looking man in a tuxedo, who, he explains, has been friends with Nate, Nima's former boss at the trekking agency, since they met in Nepal years ago. Richard is president of the American Himalayan Foundation, a sponsor of the event. Nima walks up and introduces himself. Richard offers his hand. Nima talks about Nepal and when they met. Richard nods at the appropriate points as he looks over Nima's shoulder to see who else has arrived, and I look over Richard's shoulder in search of celebrities. Richard graciously

earth: Ahhhhh. So good to meet you. So good.

excuses himself. Tonight, Nima's genuine desire to connect is out of step. Everyone Nima has ever known is his friend. Bye, Richard. Nima waves to his friend. Nima is a man with panache.

A thin, elegant Tibetan woman approaches us. *Tashi Delek*, she says. She bows toward Nima, and I watch her long black hair fall across her silk-brocade *engi*. *Tashi Delek*. Nima acknowledges her with a bow. I do not exist. The woman speaks to Nima in Tibetan for several minutes. She glances at me on occasion, well aware that I do not understand. Nima does not introduce me. Is she making a pass at him? Does he know her? She is gorgeous, and knows it. Nima speaks. She laughs, and her hair flies. He loves long hair. She speaks. He smiles. She speaks in a whisper. He fawns. A flush of envy rises up.

Tashi Delek, Nima-la. The lovely Tibetan squeezes his hands and moves on.

Nima-la? I ask, bothered by her term of endearment. Who is she?

The most famous singer in Tibet.

You never even introduced me, Nima. Do you know her? He does not, but recognized her from her albums. I push envy aside. Nima has taken my hand. He suggests we find Hollywood. Normally, I would assume Nima means his friend Sonam Sherpa. Tonight, I am not so sure.

The banquet hall is a sumptuous sea of tables set in crystal, china, and silver. Thousands of roses perfume the air. Celebrities, dressed to the nines in couture tuxedos and gowns, mill among them. There are celebrities I knew had an interest in Buddhism: Steven Seagal, looking Asian in his ponytail and mandarin silk shirt, actress Shirley MacLaine, and the avant-garde composer Philip Glass. I am surprised to see Sharon Stone. Harrison Ford and his wife, Melissa Mathison who wrote *Kundun,* are major patrons of the event.

I guess we are all searching, I tell Nima.

Anyone can be a Buddhist, says Nima. Even you.

Nima! Hollywood shouts. Nima. Over here. Hollywood Sherpa introduces us to the Tibetans at our table. We take our seats just as Nima's friend and master of ceremonies Richard Blum welcomes us. He introduces his wife, California senator Dianne Feinstein. Senator Feinstein talks about the importance of life. She talks about 1978 as if it were yesterday, and how she found Mayor Moscone after the former supervisor Dan White shot him. She felt his pulse and the warmth of his blood; she felt life leave a body. She immediately assumed the role of acting mayor of San Francisco and announced the assassinations of Mayor Moscone and Supervisor Milk. Each life is important, including those of all Tibetans, she says in closing. Her passionate stream of consciousness speech moves me to tears. My tablemates are restless; the senator is just the warm-up act.

Tenzin Gyatso, His Holiness the XIV Dalai Lama, walks to the microphone with a spring in his step. He waits for the thunderous applause to lessen. To my surprise, the Dalai Lama begins with a joke. In English. A Protestant minister would have begun with a prayer, but he knows his audience. His joke puts the crowd at ease. His message in English is about the plight of the Tibetan people, both those who remain in Tibet and those who struggle in exile. He has a gentle voice; the audience strains to hear his every word as he speaks of compassion, a nonviolent approach to solving problems, and the need for face-to-face conversation among world leaders. In straightforward words, he asks for our help.

Nima is starstruck. *Reverent* may be a better word. Never before have I seen him so still. The Tibetans are rapt with attention. His Holiness concludes. The audience rises and applauds. The Tibetans and Sherpas bow. The Dalai Lama places his palms together to honor his audience, smiles, and exits the stage. The room explodes with chatter and soon empties. Unlike the others, we stay to eat our dessert.

The next morning, we are back at the Beverly Wilshire Hotel. I feel like a regular. I never imagined it would be my Sherpa who would make it so. I sense an increased energy among the Tibetans compared to the previous night. The Dalai Lama is to perform a private prayer service for them and the Sherpas. Lama Geshe greets us in the lobby. This time, when he clasps my hand in his and looks directly at me, I am not so uncomfortable. I like Lama Geshe. I hope to learn from him.

An assistant to the Dalai Lama escorts us upstairs and opens the door to a small room. Except for a low dais at the back with a single chair, the rest of the room is empty of furniture. Tibetans sit cross-legged on the floor. Some whisper among themselves. Others sit quietly and finger their prayer beads. The room is nearly full. Nima and I find a seat, just as the door in the back opens. A flurry of smartly suited Tibetans sweeps into the room, followed by His Holiness the XIV Dalai Lama, whose crimson robe soars like a kite on a gusty day. Everyone rises and bows to ensure their heads are below that of His Holiness. Some drop to their knees, touch their foreheads to the ground, and place their palms together at the top of their heads. Unsure of protocols, I peek as the Dalai Lama walks toward the dais, and notice everyone's head remains bowed until he sits down in the room's only chair. He nods to friends. He adjusts his robes. He pushes up his glasses. He smiles. He speaks. Everyone laughs. I don't. Today, the Dalai Lama speaks in Tibetan.

While the audience looks enthralled, I am disappointed. No wisdom will be gained today. Without the Dalai Lama's teaching to focus on, I notice that my knees hurt and my buttocks have gone numb. I try to meditate, but the world around me intrudes. I hear a cough. I hear a murmured chant. I hear fabric rustle. I hear the back door open. I hear whispers in English. I am disturbed that they let someone in after His Holiness has begun. I want to turn and look, but do not. I keep my eyes shut and focus on the sound of His Holiness's voice. Suddenly, the empty space on the floor beside me is filled with an aura. The late guest? I peek. Bare feet. Male. Not Tibetan. My gaze tracks up thin, blue-jeaned legs over the back of a crisp white shirt with rolled-up sleeves to light-brown curly hair that drops past his starched shirt collar. Nice. He turns slightly. I catch his profile. Richard Gere!

As Richard bends to sit down on the floor next to me, I follow his every move. As his hand touches the carpet, a bangle slides from wrist to hand. He sits cross-legged with an ease reserved for dancers. He does not acknowledge me. I take solace in the fact that he doesn't acknowledge the Dalai Lama either, at least directly. Instead, he shuts his eyes, rests his wrists on his knees and is still. I follow his lead. Stillness is a virtue.

When the audience laughs, I open my eyes. His Holiness rises. Richard rises. Bodyguards surround the Dalai Lama. Nima stands, reaches for my hand, and pulls me up and along with him. We position ourselves near the aisle with palms together and heads bowed to receive a blessing as His Holiness walks through the crowd. As His Holiness reaches us, his hand rises in a final blessing before he flaps his crimson wrap wide and disappears behind black suits and double doors. I look back and search the audience. Richard Gere has gone.

"Wasn't he wonderful?" says Nima.

"Yes." I am wistful. "I feel blessed."

Why create a mountain
when there are real ones?

—Nima

O̲UR "FAMILY" CONTINUES TO GROW and develop roots. Nima and I both like to surround our lives with people. We both need the support.

Ed and Liz, our next door neighbors, adore Nima and enjoy helping him settle in. Ed works ground service for a major airline at Los Angeles International Airport. With his shock of golden curls, beard, jeans, and printed T-shirts, he looks like he still lives in the 1970s. Casual in both manner and appearance, Liz dresses like Ed, but wears her hair short. She is a freelance journalist who writes for drag-racing magazines. Ed and Liz have invited us to the circus.

On the drive over, Liz wants to know about the animals in Nepal. Nima describes migrating cranes who fly over the Himalaya, and the iridescent purple, green, and copper Himalayan Monal; he tells us of encounters with the wild mountain goats, musk oxen, and bears; he mimics a red panda eating bamboo; and he speaks with reverence about the snow leopard cubs he once saw. Nima's world is in sharp contrast to the captivity and staged fanfare of the circus.

The Circus Vargas Big Top has been set up in the parking lot of the Redondo Beach High School. I expect Nima to like the daredevil acts of the trapeze artists and acrobats. Instead, Nima finds the circus acts simple. He is no doubt jaded by the feats of endurance witnessed while on climbing expeditions. Nima's interest is the animals. He points out dogs that ride scooters, walk on their hind legs, and jump through hoops. He singles out a chimpanzee that claps both hands and feet together when an elephant lifts a scantily dressed woman up, by its tusks. I want to know why. Animals are less silly than people, he tells me, and more gentle—even the elephant.

It is still early when we get home. I putter around the house in an attempt to regain order. Nima follows me everywhere and asks questions like a relentless journalist in pursuit of the truth. Why? How? What does it mean? Where does it come from? When will you answer me? I respond with an edge in my voice: I don't know. When seeking knowledge, Nima's curiosity never falters. Why? Because. But, why not? Ahhhhh! I can't know everything.

Nima needs more family than me.

An ESL classmate of Nima's calls me to say that her brother-in-law and his wife, John and Dora, need someone to do a few days' work in their yard. They live in Manhattan Beach within walking distance of our house. Nima meets with them and gets the job. He tells me that John and Dora, both about seventy, emigrated from China when they were teenagers. They have three grown children: their daughter Theresa lives with them, their older son Thatcher lives in Seattle, and son Allan in the Bay Area.

After his first day of work, Nima comes home clutching a shoebox poked with holes. Dora thought he should have a pet to care for. She told me that everyone needs a friend to talk to, says Nima. He opens the box. A canary looks up. So cute, chirps Nima. Birds shouldn't be in cages, I cluck. Then, we buy one.

A week after Nima began his work for John, he comes home and announces that he is taking his Sherpani to dinner to an Asian restaurant recommended by Dora: he received his first week's pay. I put on a linen shirt to dress up my jeans. I redo my makeup. I clip in silver hoop

194

earrings. I want to look nice for my date. Nima slips on a shirt and slacks. He combs his hair. He checks the cash in his wallet and counts it out like he did that night in Sarankot when we played cards and lost—and won. Nima is starting to win.

I start the car. Nima reaches for my hand and pulls it to his chest. My heart, he tells me. I melt. We make out in the garage for so long I wonder if we should stay home. Nima has other plans. He pushes the garage door opener and lets in the world. I begin to back up. I focus on the rearview mirror. I focus on our driveway that slopes up to the street. I focus on the plants that crowd the drive. I don't focus on Nima. I don't see his arm move. I don't see his hand reach. I don't see him push the button.

Screams of ripping metal shout through the car roof. It might as well have ripped into me. I feel the gash, the burn, the pain. I see red. I smell blood. I taste anger. Too shocked to stop, I hit the accelerator to free my car, my Los Angeles legs, from this monster. Loss of limbs is not an option, not in Los Angeles.

The metal screeches as I continue to back up. I look at Nima. He freezes in time. A look of horror replaces his joy. I see fear. I feel no pity. Only anger. I scream. The garage door screams. I scream. The metal rips. I scream. Nima remains immobile. The garage door comes toward my front window. I push hard on the accelerator. My mind speeds ahead of knowledge. I desire daylight. Freedom. I want to drive away. Forget about money. I want to disappear. I want Nima to disappear. Once "free," I stop. I get out of the car. Nima remains immobile. I cry.

"Nima!" He sits. I speak firmly. "Nima." He opens his door. A deep gash runs the length of my Honda hatchback's roof. The paint is gone. Metal is exposed. Nothing is punctured, but my sanity cracks. I rage. I don't think Nima knows the meaning of my four-letter words, but my cries and fists that pound the roof help to translate their meaning. Through it all, Nima stands erect, with one hand in the pocket of his jeans while the other traces the crevasse in my car roof.

"Not so bad, Sherpani," says Nima. "No hole. No accident." I clarify that it was an accident and remind him how many times I have told him to keep his hand away from the garage door opener until the car is out of the garage. "I'm sorry, Sherpani."

"Stupid word, *sorry*. Remember, Nima? Why do you ruin everything? Do you think we are rich? I work hard to buy what we have. I take care of things. You destroy things—like Kali!" Nima's contrite, but proud expression only angers me more.

"It is only a car, Caryl. Not you. Not me."

"Yes, Nima, but it is our only car." My rage exhausts me.

Our neighbor Crissy runs over to ask what happened. I point out the ugly gash. Crissy, in her cheerful voice, notes that at least the car still works. Nima looks redeemed.

"Get in, Nima." I pull the car into the garage and shut the door. Nima and I sit in darkness. "We are not going out tonight, Nima. Get a job. The free ride is over!"

Nima punches the side of his head. "So stupid. So stupid."

Good. Normally, I would stop his self-inflicted abuse, tell him he is smart, and boost his confidence. Not this time. The pressure on me has been building. Our miniscule savings have dwindled. My credit cards are still maxed out. Our property taxes are due. My car is now wounded. So is Nima. So am I. So is our relationship.

We are lucky. Scars mark memories, but they let wounds heal. We have to get to the bottom before we can rise.

A few days later, Nima's friend Hollywood Sherpa takes Nima to a local Indian restaurant. Nima comes home victorious with a part-time busboy position at five dollars an hour. He can ride his bike to work, and complete his work for John. A weight begins to lift.

Soon after, Dora calls to ask us over for dinner. Dora exudes graciousness when she greets us at the door to her home. The Chinese décor has grown less formal over time, just as I imagine John and Dora have done the longer they've lived in the United States. Dora's short gray curls frame her bright eyes and understated smile. Her dress is casual: loose black pants, an overblouse, and terry slippers. She introduces us to Theresa, the youngest of their three children. Theresa greets us with a bold voice and a stare, although I notice, through her thick glasses, that one eye wanders. Although the day is warm, she wears a sweater over her cotton dress. John enters with the energy of a man half his age, shakes Nima's hand, and introduces himself to me. Dora tells me how much she likes Nima. John is amazed by Nima's strength and speed. Theresa smiles at Nima, as if to acknowledge his kindness. I am happy to see Nima's new family expand.

How's our bird? asks Theresa.

He sings every morning, I tell her. Nima takes good care of her. He named her Tweedy.

Mother thought Nima could give the bird a good home, Theresa says.

As teenagers, John and Dora left their families in China; each immigrated alone to America. They understand what Nima is experiencing. John, a retired aerospace engineer, teaches bridge. He also runs daily, often winning races in his over-sixty age group. Dora smiles and whispers that he's often the only one in that group. Dora used to teach Chinese cooking. As each course is passed around the table, my admiration for her culinary skills grows.

After dinner, while we sip jasmine tea, John shares photos of their travels, his desire to return home to China, and his dream to trek to Everest Base Camp. When he asks Nima about leading a trek, Nima jumps at the chance. John wants to go for his seventy-third birthday and bring his two sons. Dora shakes her head. Nima, the optimist, supports the idea. John wants to take the route up to 18,192 feet (5,545 m) at Kala Pattar near Everest Base Camp. Nima explains how the route would take them past Nima's family's village. As Nima and John discuss a trek, I dream of a Buddhist wedding in Nepal.

On the walk home, I share my idea with Nima. He is ecstatic. I suggest a wedding in his village in the Solukhumbu before the trek, but Nima tells me too many friends and relatives now live in Kathmandu, so the Sherpa community center in Bodhnath would be better. I like the idea of Bodhnath and orbiting the sacred *chörten* with "my sun." Nima corrects me. Not orbit. *Kora.*

Each spring, Nima and I return to Joshua Tree National Monument, for to see a desert in bloom is a blessing. The blue sky intensifies the red color of rock monoliths. In spring, the hills are green, unlike the dusty gray of other seasons. Explosions of purple and white flowers up close blend into the green with distance, unlike the hot pink, orange, and yellow cactus flowers that shout, Pick me!

A Joshua tree (*Yucca brevifolia*) looks like a shaggy beast with multiple arms and sprigs of white flowers that shoot out from its body. Only a painter like Frida Kahlo could ever have imagined one without seeing it first. These sensuously prehistoric trees once covered the area's high deserts. The local Cahuilla Indians made baskets and sandals from the leaves, and ate the trees' budding flowers and seeds. The Mormon settlers gave the Joshua tree its name. I admire the Joshua trees' silent exuberance as they raise their arms in prayer.

This Easter weekend, I am drawn toward a lone tree while Nima erects our tent. In the narrow shadow of the Joshua tree, I sit on a rock made smooth by ancient floods and incessant winds. In this spare land, I become aware. I feel the sun's warmth radiate from the rock. I taste salt on my lips. I hear a stone roll. I witness a hawk circle. I listen to the wind, my mind, and silence. I hear the echoes of ancestors from these trees. Over eons, the Joshua tree has changed little, remaining shallowly rooted in sand even as the world changes around it and pushes it toward extinction. Like the Joshua tree, I too hang on to shifting sands. When the world pushes in around me, I fight back; I adapt and remain open to evolution. I am lucky I have the ability to change venues, seek resources, escape threats. My roots are those of a nomad. The Joshua tree teaches me that to not change and adapt is to die off. I reject such a fate. I move on, and have Nima to guide me.

Linda, one of our first supporters; Hari, Nima's classmate; Mark, who attended our wedding; and Ryan, a colleague from work, arrive at camp soon after we do. Ryan has a stocky build and a laugh that draws you to him. I am pleased to see him drop his blue-suit persona for a relaxed, humorous one. This group knows how to leave work behind, enjoy the camaraderie, and relish the physical.

Nima, "the rabbit," as Linda calls him, cannot stop hopping around on the rocks that surround our campsite. With cold beers in hand, the rest of us sit back to watch him climb and leap and stretch over chasms toward bigger and bigger rocks: 100 million-year-old plutonic intrusions of granite weathered into organic-shaped monoliths that seem vaguely human. Nima jumps from boulder to boulder with no signs of slowing. Undeterred, he begins a free climb up a lone menhir that rises more than forty feet (12 m) above the desert. I sit up, attentive. Mark and Ryan are impressed. Hari is surprised. Linda laughs, but shares my concern. I begin to panic. I see nothing for him to hold on to as he stretches out, spiderlike, and reaches for a fingerhold, a toehold, then lifts himself up to the next fingerhold. His pace is steady and sure. Nima snakes over the top curve of rock with feet kicking, then stands and prances on the summit. He shouts and waves to us all. I decide to arrange my clothes inside the tent. I don't want to watch Nima come down.

At daybreak, we shuttle our cars and begin a long hike along the south to north route of Boy Scout Trail. We begin at the trailhead north of Hidden Cove in the high Mojave Desert, with plans to end our hike at Indian Cove in the low Mojave Desert where we left our cars. Our pace is rapid in the cool morning across terrain that changes little in elevation as we near the Wonderland of Rocks. When we enter the canyon, the landscape changes dramatically and so does the trail, which becomes hard to follow. Nima takes the lead and we drop 400 feet (122 m) in a short distance. The trail he tracks rises and falls over boulders. Within a canyon, we seek out alternate paths along its sides when the drop becomes too high or the rock face too smooth for our abilities. When there is no alternate path, Nima extends his hand to each of us to help us surmount the obstacle.

Within the canyon, we are of the earth. Rock formations surround us. The famous San Andreas Fault runs just beyond the park's western borders. Mark does not want to be here in an earthquake. Linda likes the cool air of the canyon, even in the noonday sun. I like the stillness. We move on, in and out of shadows, passing by layers of sculpted rock. The earth's mystery intensifies. How were these boulders sculpted? What lies beyond? How far down might we go? Below the level of the land, there is no horizon, no view. We become disoriented. Ryan suggests we have lost the trail and plants a seed of doubt. Mark suggests that Nima climb up to get our bearings. Above us on the canyon edge, Nima shouts down that footprints head off in another direction, and tells us to come up. He can't be right. I insist he come down. I want to linger within the earth, track the path of water, and remain submerged in silence. After I convince the others, we push on.

When we come upon a sign that reads "Willow Hole," we follow it toward the promise of willows and water. Canyon walls provide shelter. A spring cools us. Willows speak to our imagination. I teach Nima the word *oasis*. Here, one can comprehend the word. A rivulet of water pools among the willow's roots. We cup our hands and drip cool water over our bodies. We anoint our heads. We share the food we each have left. Indian Cove must be near. We drink our last gulps of water.

The hike exhilarates us, but after far more bouldering than we anticipated, we are exhausted. We left one car at the end of the trail, and then drove back up into the park, but as we come out of the wash, we are unable to orient ourselves. Without a map, we journey by instinct. The trail out of the canyon goes south. We should be heading north. So we do. We follow the wash as it fans out over the desert floor. We are certain that we are back on track after we pick up multiple footprints, grow concerned as they lessen, and panic when there are none. I notice the vegetation has changed, from Joshua trees and juniper at the higher elevations where we started, to desert scrub: creosote, paperbag bush, and cheesebush. And yet, there is sameness to a desert landscape of scrub and red rocks. We thought we'd recognize the giant monoliths that surround the parking lot, but our perspective is different. We do not. We only know that if we keep walking, we will hit the highway, which seemed much closer when we drove into the park. We grow tired and anxious to find our car before dark, and we walk; the day grows long and we burn from the day's exposure in the sun, and our thirst increases; we see a house and another and finally someone is home; we drink water from their hose and ask for the direction of the road, and they point; we walk on and our joy decreases along with the number of sacred Joshua trees as we drop in elevation, and chaparral scratches our bare legs; then a mirage of a lake appears and our thirst becomes insatiable and our pace picks up and finally our joy explodes as the mirage hovers and fades into a road.

To make up for our lack of water all afternoon, we down tequila shooters. Nima and I share with our friends our plans for a Buddhist wedding followed by a trek to Kala Pattar. We invite them to come. Everyone would like to. When the stars blur, we crawl into our tents and sleep until midmorning. We regret last night's indulgences over fried eggs and bacon. Nima, who doesn't drink, feels great. His infectious energy invades Linda, who offers to teach him to drive.

The desert roads are empty and safe for a beginner. I am skeptical as I watch confident Nima climb behind the wheel of Linda's red 928 Porsche. Linda sits in the passenger seat and instructs him on how a car works: pedals, buttons, turn lights, headlights, stick shift, steering wheel, brake. Nima nods in understanding. I question his comprehension, but keep silent. Linda instructs. Turn the car on, Nima. The engine rumbles. Shift into first and step on the gas. The car jerks to a start, wiggles, and moves forward erratically. Good, Nima! That is the last we hear, as Nima drives down the road and weaves into the sand and then back onto the road before disappearing behind boulders. Twenty minutes later, Nima returns with a grin brighter than a desert day.

"I'm saving my tips to buy a car like Linda's!"

One Sunday morning, when the Los Angeles roads are their quietest, I decide to continue Nima's driving lessons. After almost getting killed, I drive us both home. We are not a good combination on the road. I make Nima too nervous. He makes me too scared. I open the Yellow Pages to "Driving Instructors" and call. I register Nima for private lessons. He starts Monday. I am surprisingly jubilant, considering I just spent three hundred and fifty dollars that we do not have. I consider the price of life, liberty, and happiness, not to mention the safety of others, worth every penny. Within days, fearless Nima can drive.

Soon after, Nima knows only fear. We are three days into a civil disturbance that the media calls "the Rodney King riots." They were sparked by the April 29, 1992, acquittal of criminal charges against four policemen who beat Rodney King while arresting him, purportedly in an effort to control his violence. The arrest was videotaped and made national news. It now plays repeatedly, along with the recent helicopter news tape of the Reginald Denny beating at the intersection of Florence and Normandie, which is where the riots began. Civil unrest tears at the fragile façade of Los Angeles. A curfew for the entire Los Angeles area is in effect from 7:30 p.m. until 6:00 a.m. The news media tallies the crisis: death count at 40, injuries at 1,899, fires a whopping 3,367, and in spite of the 4,000 National Guard members on the streets and 4,000 army soldiers and marines in waiting, arrests total 4,393 with over 550 million dollars in damages. As Nima takes measure, the riots continue.

Although the riots are extensive, I understand their boundaries and what an uncommon event this is. The world Nima came from was simple and safe. The entire country of Nepal, similar in size to California, has less population than does Greater Los Angeles. Nima has no basis for calculating this destruction.

Death could happen today or tomorrow, says Nima as we climb into bed. I assume he wants to talk about the riots. He tells me that he must be prepared. His cousin was young, happy, and then, in a moment, gone. Nima waves his hand, simulating the avalanche on Everest. He wants to know what happens when someone dies in America. He's heard that people are placed in a box and dirt thrown over them. How can you find the way to your next life? Be reincarnated? Christians go to heaven or hell, I tell him. They are buried, not reincarnated.

But that's wrong! says Nima. Everyone is reincarnated. And everything. When Sherpas die, the family carries the body up into the mountains, prays for a good next life, and burns the body. One begins one's journey as smoke and ash on the wind.

Nima does not want to be buried. How can you get out? he asks. One's spirit has only forty-nine days to find another body, or you exist halfway between life and death for eternity.

After I assure him that he can choose to be buried or cremated, Nima's talk of death stops. Now I lie wide awake and ponder my options. Can I choose my fate by choosing my religion? One death is final, and I either rise in rapture, or sink into a demonic afterlife. One death is circular, and I repeat. I was brought up a Christian, and yet cremation and reincarnation offer an alternate, another chance. I too want my ashes to rise from a mountaintop. I want to refuse heaven and hell. I want to circle, and with each birth, learn and grow and reach for enlightenment. Am I a Buddhist?

Nima and I both sleep with devilish dreams. We wake up early, unrefreshed. Nima tells me he dreamed of running downhill. He must be careful today, as something bad may happen to him or his family. I hold him and we sleep again until sunshine brightens the bed quilt.

Over breakfast, Nima tells me how there is a reincarnated Buddhist monk who wrote a book about the future of the world. The monk predicted that after two hundred years, a powerful country would begin to fall. Nima and I look east and watch billows of smoke move closer and grow darker. We turn back to the TV to watch widespread riots continue for the fourth day. From the flash point in South Central Los Angeles, the riots spread into mid-Wilshire, Downtown, Hollywood, Pasadena, Compton, Hawthorne, and Long Beach. In the Beach Cities, we are surrounded on all sides, trapped, but for the ocean, and Nima cannot swim. Nima thinks the country that will fall is the United States. Too many guns, sex crimes, and acts of violence, says Nima. Nepal, at least in the Solukhumbu, does not have these things.

Perhaps they do, I tell him, but with no TV coverage to broadcast the events, the population remains unaware. Nima denies these things happen in Nepal. I doubt him, but drop it, for I can see how upset he is, how scared. Here, our television media favors bad news, I say. To assure him,

I explain how the United States and its citizens do many things to help people both here and around the world. He wants to believe me, but cannot reconcile the image he once held of the United States with what he now sees on TV.

The riots continue to rage and fires burn. I cannot afford to stay home from work without pay. Civil unrest is not covered in our leave policy. Fortunately, my drive to the office in Santa Monica follows the beach: far enough from trouble to be safe.

I do not get home until eight in the evening. Nima hugs me tight, relieved to know I am still alive, and refuses to let go. Nima tells me how he called the office out of concern about my safety, but I wasn't there, so he talked to Mark, who assured him I'd be okay. I told him how I tried all day to call him back, but the phones were overloaded and I could not get through. Nima, afraid to go out, sat home alone and watched the insanity taking over Los Angeles. Nima lightens his squeeze, but does not let go. I left work early, I say, only to sit in line for thirty minutes to get gas. Traffic was a nightmare. Only the beach route was safe, and everyone knew it. My thirty-minute commute took three hours. Nima finally releases me and points to the television screen.

"Look at them!" say Nima. "Those things don't happen in Nepal."

A family leaves an audio store with three shopping carts loaded with stolen merchandise, and a baby. People run out the front of a building as the back end burns. A woman falls and a man steals the boxed television she just stole. The police stand by their squad cars and watch, outnumbered and helpless in the mayhem, even as two men fight with garbage can lids just before the news station cuts to a break.

"I thought America was the best country in the world," says Nima. "Better than Nepal, Europe, everywhere! Not now. We would not do these things in my country." Last year during the democracy riots in Nepal, says Nima, the police shot people who did these things. They had few problems. "These people are crazy! They hurt each other. They burn innocent people's property. Such terrible, terrible, terrible people."

Never have I seen Nima so emotional. He is scared. So am I. And no one in the city is sure what will happen next. I ask how they punish criminals in Nepal.

Local justice, explains Nima. Once, a policeman accused a villager in Namche of a crime. The people in his village knew the man was innocent, so they gathered up dirty discarded shoes and strung them on a cord. Shoes are the most unclean things there are. The people placed the necklace of shoes around the policeman's neck and forced him to walk through the Namche Bazaar on market day. I laugh. Nima doesn't.

"My brother Pasang always talk, talk, talk about America this, America that," says Nima. "But he was in Hawaii."

"Hawaii is in America," I remind him.

"Hawaii is an island," Nima tells me. "Problems are far away, like in the mountains." He's had the day to sort this through.

"So what caused the riots?" I ask Nima.

"Iraq karma."

"The Gulf War?"

Nima radiates an unsettled energy that I sense from across the room. He asks if I remember the violent movie that we watched the other night. I nod. He had asked me to change the channel when two men dunked another man's head into a toilet to get him to confess.

"Life can be like that," whispers Nima, who tells me his father, Pala, would hold Nima's head under water until he almost stopped breathing. I hold my breath. "But that wasn't the worst. Pala would—" Nima puts his hands behind his back and pinches his shoulder blades. "What do you call this?"

"Handcuffed?"

"He'd sit me down at the base of our prayer flag pole, tie me to it, light a fire in front of me, and throw in hot chilies. I couldn't see from the burning. My throat would close up. He'd leave me there until the fire went out, sometimes overnight." I am speechless. The burn of hot chilies is intolerable, and I leave the kitchen when Nima cooks with them. I mention that at least he's used to it.

"You never get used to it!" We watch Los Angeles burn. Violence can rage, like these riots, or be quiet, like the pain inflicted within families. Some never escape violence. Others, like Nima, have better luck—and do.

"My father did bad things, cruel things, but I still love him. He's my father. At age six, I decided to leave home. Every day, I thought about leaving. And then one day, I did."

The skies have cleared and the riots subsided. Memories don't linger, for those who live in communities not destroyed by the fires. On his day off, Nima proposes a dinner out with his wife. When I express delight over a rare Saturday-night date with my husband, Nima reminds me—we date every day. I love this man.

After dinner, we walk to the theater in Hermosa Beach to see the movie *K2*. Nima hopes I might better understand his experiences, and the beauty of the Karakoram.

The movie begins with the Paramount logo. "That mountain is not K2," says Nima. I try to explain what a logo is, and the corporate concept of brand.

"Why create a mountain when there are real ones?"

The movie brings back memories for Nima, as his expedition came out of the Himalaya through Pakistan after their team's ascent. To show off, he translates the dialogue of background characters that the director included for authenticity. He makes sure I understand that the further the actors climb up K2, the faster reality diminishes.

You'd never do that on K2, he tells me. That's an unsafe move. Those are not experienced climbers. I hear a man behind us question Nima's knowledge to his friend. There's no support staff, Nima says. Impossible.

The actors summit without them. The camera pans the view from the "summit of K2."

"That's not the Karakoram!" shouts Nima. The entire audience turns toward us. No way are they on the summit of K2, he says.

It's Hollywood, Nima.

The movie credits suggest that Nima may be correct. The movie was shot in Pakistan and the Canadian Rockies of Whistler, BC. Nima believes they filmed the climbing scenes in the tamer peaks of the Rockies. That was not the Karakoram, says Nima.

Nima's intelligence continues to impress me. After Nima receives his learner's permit from the Department of Motor Vehicles office and we return home, he hands me a box.

Open it, says Nima. I open it.

Cash! Cash? I ask. I count. Eighteen hundred dollars!

I've been saving my extra money, says Nima. My first instinct is to be mad at him for squirreling away his tip money, while I have been pinching pennies, but then I realize his wisdom. He can't buy a Porsche, but it's enough to buy a 1985 Buick Skylark four-door automatic, plus a few months of insurance.

Nima's excuses for an excursion are endless, and I must go with him. Let's go to the store. I have to get the car washed. Hollywood is coming, so I need to get milk for tea. Do you want a ride to the beach? I need to get gas. Can't we go?

On a summer Sunday, I convince Nima to stay home and do chores around the house with me. While he weeds the yard, I paint the house trim. A Sherpa husband and wife spend little time together, says Nima. He likes this better. When Jules calls later that day and I share with him our conversation, Jules, unlike me, is not surprised at Nima's delight. For all the wonderful qualities of the Sherpa, Jules too finds it surprising that Sherpa men and women are not more involved with each other's lives. It's a mystery, says Jules with a laugh. He suggests that perhaps separation of the sexes is their key to happiness. Sherpa-like in his joyful love of life, single Jules would know.

Nima continues to look for excuses to take excursions in his new car. Although I will be driving, Nima insists we take his big Buick to the airport to pick up my parents. They are flying in from Florida, where they moved to escape Michigan winters. We'll spend the Fourth of July weekend and my birthday with them.

At least he's safe in this car, says Dad, as we exit the airport.

At the Zane Grey Pueblo Hotel overlooking Avalon Bay on Catalina Island, off the Southern California coast, blue water, white boats, and graceful eucalyptus lull me into a peaceful state. Although my parents have come for a visit, I am exhausted from long hours at work. I only want to relax, doze in the sun, and enjoy the pool on the upper patio, at least for one day. Despite Nima's Buddhist upbringing, stillness is not something he practices, so when he can't be active, he talks—What is a telescope? What does *negotiation* mean? Where does that road through the hills go? How long is the road around the island? How many people live here? What year was this hotel built? Who is Zane Grey?—Anything foreign is of interest to him. Whenever he shops for clothes, he looks to see where they were made—Taiwan, India, Bangladesh—often Asia, rarely the USA. He is proud Asia dresses America. My parents recognize my exhaustion and try to answer his endless questions. I sense their wonder at how elementary his questions are and their surprise at his youthful exuberance.

On our second morning, we drive our golf carts up a winding road to the botanical gardens. Touched by the tranquility of this hilltop retreat, I wander off alone. I muse over the Jerusalem thorn, green wattle, and the bronze-and-copper-colored stonecrop. I enjoy their names as much as their appearance.

Come look, Caryl, says Nima, who dances among trees. Himalayan pines! Just like home! He strokes their bark, fingers their needles, and pockets a cone. My mother, an avid gardener, asks Nima what kinds of plants grow in his country. With a wave of his hand, Nima tells her all these plants—from tropical to glacial—grow in Nepal. Nima is happy to have found an audience, and so is my mother, who teaches him plant names in English.

Back at the hotel, my father decides to take advantage of the pool and teach Nima how to swim. First, he must learn to float. Relax. Lie back on the water. Nima tries, but his head comes up, his legs and arms open wide, and his feet poke out of the water like a starfish drunk on sunshine. He sinks butt first to his own laughter and spits of water. My father pulls his head out from under the water. Just relax, my father tells him. Let's try again. Nervous Nima tries, but stiffens and sinks again, and again, and again. When Nima's reruns bore me, I leave to dress for dinner.

Once dressed, I lie down on the bed and close my eyes. I love Nima, but some days, I sink. No one knows how hard this relationship is, the effort it takes to meld two cultures, two diametrically opposed sets of experience. Carefree Nima is often oblivious to the demands on me to support us, deal with our affairs, file for his immigration, manage our money, and act as his teacher/coach/mentor. I resent how Nima manages to float through life, let go of worries, and live in the moment. I try to give him weight, but Nima is helium personified. I pull him down, but Nima always rises. I want to float like Nima. I want him to care for me, teach me, free me. Instead, I am exhausted by the pressure I put on myself, grounded and unable to rise.

When Nima bursts into the room, I refuse to open my eyes. He leans over me and shakes his head like a dog coming out of a pool. You animal! Go take a shower. I jump up, step into the hall, and slam the door. Silence. I luxuriate in the musty dark corridor, reminiscent of a Zane Grey Western. I imagine a life on a ranch nestled at the foothills of mountains where I could ride the range with—Stop. Stop being unfair. Relax. Learn to play. Give him a chance to teach you. I breathe deep and go back into our room. I sit on the bed and wait for Nima. I stop thinking. I stop feeling. I just am. Stillness is a virtue.

My parents, Nima, and I celebrate my fortieth birthday with wine, watermelon salad, pasta primavera, birthday cake, and conversation. Nima tells us he loves watermelon. In Nepal, they eat all of it, including the fruit, seeds, and rind, which is pickled to eat in winter. My mother tells him how she loves watermelon pickles. Should she make him some? He'd love her to. Score.

I show Nima the necklace and earrings my mother bought me for my birthday. I like their symbolism. Handcrafted in silver and bronze by a Hopi Indian woman, the spiral design represents migration, either the number of journeys a tribe has made to the four corners of the world, or a broadening of consciousness, the ultimate destination after any journey.

209

A migration means movement; a journey brings awareness.

"Handmade things last," says Nima, who tells us how his family used to have many beautiful old things, until his grandfather's house burned down and they lost everything. He sighs. "Nepal became poorer once we let foreigners in."

My father wants to know why. Nima explains that foreigners bought up the Sherpas' traditional things. At first, they had thought the foreigner's things were better, until they found out that many machine-made things don't last. Nima wishes Sherpas had never sold their handmade things. My mother describes her antiques, bonding again with her newest of sons-in-law.

As the evening wears on, my storyteller spins tales of reincarnation, fortune-tellers, and gods in a world never imagined by my parents. As I listen to Nima talk and hear his conviction for the unseen, I wonder if maybe there isn't something to this mystery of life beyond what I understand. His stories are fantastic, and yet—even my parents begin to believe a little. The evening ends with more questions than answers, just like all conversations with Nima.

Later that evening, Nima and I celebrate alone. He hands me a card:

To my angel wife—my Santa Claus wife. To fifty more birthdays together. Love, your Sherpa. Me

Sunday morning as I write, bored Nima comes into my home office and demands my attention. He strokes my breasts, until passion overtakes us. A rare rainy day in mid-July is our inspiration. Love and thunder. Nima tells me how surprised he is that we just made love without an appointment. I am horrified. We don't make appointments, I tell him. Nima thinks we do. He provides examples, like when he wants to make love and I say, "We'll make love tonight," or tomorrow, or in an hour, or I say, "I'm too busy right now. Later." Isn't that an appointment? In a dreamy state, Nima and I make love well into the afternoon. Love and thunder. The storm continues.

I roll on top of Nima. Our bodies fuse. We are one. Body talk. I like Nima's regained confidence. As Nima changes, I want him to retain his innocent charm. I am intrigued by Nima's simple intelligence, born out of nature and story. Magnificent bolts of lightning strike the horizon. The sky roars. The house shakes. In a sudden summer storm, rain pours down, drives away the smog, and washes Los Angeles' concrete landscape clean.

What makes thunder? Nima asks.

I don't remember, I say, but it follows lightning. What do you think it is? We live near the ocean, so it must be the water dragon.

I thought Nima had been here long enough to know better, or at the very least, to suppress such knowledge. Feeling unself-conscious at this moment, Nima continues: A dragon lives in the ocean, and when he comes out, he roars and shakes water all over us.

I laugh and suggest a shower. Nima is my dragon.

A pattern to our lives is forming. Our social life revolves around friends and food. Nima likes to make Nepalese food and tantalize everyone with his spicy cuisine. Tonight, my colleagues Peter, Mark, and Sandy join us. Mark and Sandy began dating after a hiking trip to Yosemite. Sandy is blonde, small in stature, but large in her ability to focus in on what she wants and give it her undivided attention. Right now, Mark is the lucky recipient.

After dinner, we decide to walk the Strand. It is usually filled with bicycles, skateboarders, roller skaters, strollers, walkers, runners, and dogs, but tonight we five are alone. A mist hides the pier's point of perspective and halos the lights. Fog soaks our clothes and hair. We hear the surf more clearly than we see it. The atmospheric evening does nothing to dampen my colleagues' ire as we discuss our projects, frustrations at work, and office gossip. While the mystery of the night goes by almost unnoticed, I watch Nima grow quiet and sullen as we walk. I worry and later ask him why he kept wandering off during our walk.

All you talked about was work, says Nima. Besides, when people talk fast and interrupt each other, I can't understand them. I try. They don't try. So, I quit.

I suggest that if he doesn't understand something, he needs to ask people to repeat it.

No way. Then they think I'm stupid.

You're not stupid, Nima.

Only foreign people understand this, he says.

Nima's classmate Mohammed works at a gas station nearby, and when he returns from his trip home to Pakistan, he stops by our home to visit. Tall and thin, with angular features that shadow in daylight like the Karakoram Range that crosses his homeland, Mohammed leans toward me: For you, Madame. He hands me a package. I unwrap his gift. I turn over a pale slipper that smells of leather; it is embroidered with gold thread that entwines pink, purple, and green flowers; the simplest triangle of leather makes up the sole. Before he left, he had traced the outline of each of my feet on a sheet of paper, a pattern so my gift would fit properly. Enchanted, I had been curious what he would return with. As I slip his gifts on my feet, I am transported to an exotic land. I thank Mohammed and ask after his family. His wife is good. He speaks with pride. His beautiful daughter is eight months old.

I didn't know you were married, I say.

At my age? he says, surprised. I have to be.

I ask him about the difficulties of separation from his family. Mohammed speaks with passion about how he wants a better life for his family; there are few jobs open to him and no way to improve his standing in Pakistan. He tells me he prays daily that his family will be able to join him in America. His face darkens. His wife is afraid to leave her country and her family. Mohammed stands proud: But she will come. She needs me.

I too struggle with the balance of need versus desire. Nima needs very little. His desires are experiential. I need what I desire, which is the life-style I had when I was single: chic clothes, trendy restaurants, avant-garde culture, and international travel. Although it has been nine months since I returned to work, I remain in debt. Nima has been far more expensive than I had imagined: doctor visits, dentist bills, immunizations he never had, clothes, shoes, food (he still eats like he climbs mountains), and expenses for two. Buddhism teaches that possessions and desires are unnecessary burdens. The religion was not written for a culture like Los earth: Why create a mountain when there are real ones?

Angeles'. We crave. We obtain. We climb. We lust. We reach. We stretch. We obtain. We climb. We crave. We—I just don't want to worry about money.

Tonight I walk the Strand as far and as fast as I have time for. It is dark on my return. I like the dark, the stillness. They are a counterpoint to my stress and allow me to relax when my days overwhelm me with meetings and people and problems. I juggle and keep an unknown number of balls in the air. If one drops, the number only doubles. Sixty-plus-hour work weeks full-throttle only drive me to go faster. I run on empty. I stay late and work weekends. These days, my schedule and Nima's rarely dovetail. When we do go out, I am exhausted.

Clarity comes in seeps or in flashes of startling brilliance, or like a hammer on the head. Tonight, as I walk, I ache from the hammer. I circled the globe, only to come back and return to where I left off. I am terrified. I don't want to return to the person I was when I left, doing the same things and living the same life. I sought change. I did change. I remember Nepal and who I was there. Open. Generous. Curious. Confident without ego. Living large without luxury. Happy. Tonight, I realize the worst.

Not only am I changing back, but I have allowed it to happen.

I have been back from my trip a year, and the novelty of life in Los Angeles is wearing off for me—and for Nima. Although I am Nima's best friend, I cannot compete with his family, friends, and homeland. While Nima does not admit to being homesick, I know that he is. He writes to his parents how the weekends come so fast here and how surprised he is by "the flying time in America." In Nepal, I thought the days went on forever. He writes his parents about our social activities, his job, and how he hardly sees his wife. For his parents, who worked side by side for years on the farm, I imagine this statement will sound strange. Nima reads me what he writes, "I have no one here but my wife, so she is my wife, child, brother, sister, father, and mother." No wonder I am overwhelmed.

Our constant lack of money wears on me. It has been over a year since my return to Los Angeles in late July 1991. I grow afraid, pretend I am not, and live like I have a bank account with a balance. One night in early

August, Nima returns home from work to announce that he needs to find a new job. They cut his hours at the restaurant, and he's scheduled to work only weekends. I am disappointed for him, and for us. Over the next week, Nima looks for work, sort of. He wants to work, but doesn't know how to find a job. I suggest restaurants, the newspaper, his friends. Beyond that, I am unsure how to guide him. He asks questions. Expects me to find him a job. When I tell him he needs to do it himself, his response is that he is new here, so I have to help. I am exhausted by managing two lives, I counter. I'm not an immigrant. I don't know how you find a job.

But—

Try, Nima. Talk to your classmates. Your coworkers. How do they find a job?

But—

Others make it on their own.

But—

A couple of weeks later, it is still the same conversation. But—

No buts! You don't apply yourself in school. You work two days a week. You've got to do something. You've got to—My frustration rises. I watch Nima shut down like a sea anemone, transforming from floating fingers in carefree colors to a stone-gray fist in a poke. He refuses to open.

Nima, you'll find something. He stares ahead. Please say something. He is immobile. Look at me. I wave my hand before his eyes. I love you. Nima is unmoved. Please say something, Sherpa. We sit. I grow worried. Nima? Please? Nima has turned inward. I give him his space, as my pleas only make him go deeper.

Two days later, Nima silently asks for understanding in his own unique way. First, he asks the restaurant owner if he can work weekdays, and he agrees. He leaves me his schedule on the kitchen counter. The next day, Nima comes home too excited to keep silent. Caryl, look what I won for my nephew. A basketball!

Turns out Nima is good at the arcade games at the Redondo Beach pier. That's nice, I tell him, without looking up from my book. After two days of silence, is that all he has to say? Or do? He's won sunglasses for himself. He models them. I look. I fake a smile. I resent him playing stupid games to win cheap prizes. Nima leaves and returns with his hands behind his back.

I won this for you! says Nima, as he hands me my gift. I saw it and knew you would love it! I turn around a tacky blue glass vase with printed-on chrysanthemums on its own plastic cart. I want to cart it to Goodwill. I gush over its beauty and suggest we put it where everyone can see it. I paste on a smile that makes my cheeks hurt. All I can think of is how he wastes our money, and still I pretend. I want Nima back.

One more present, Sherpani. It's so cute. From behind his back, Nima pulls out a red plastic bird and sets it on the table. We need one, he assures me. Nima pushes the bird's head down. The bird's beak grabs a toothpick. This time, I smile at Nima and mean it. We sit in silence and pick our teeth. So cute. The freeze is over.

Tomorrow will be a milestone in my Sherpa's life. Today is practice. After I climb into the passenger seat of his Buick, Nima backs out of our driveway, and we soon merge onto the trails of Los Angeles, which move with a halting, unpredictable rhythm past palm trees, neon, glass buildings, big-box stores, Hondas, Toyotas, Beemers, Mercedes, Jaguars, and Porsches, only to stop within the river of red that flows like blood on a warm day, as we follow the 405 freeway past Marina del Rey, Venice, Santa Monica, and for a moment, only chaparral as we crest the hill, then dive headfirst into a pool of suburbia with a splash at the Ventura Boulevard exit. Nima stops for gas, then merges back into traffic and onto the freeway, heading south, so he can practice on the streets of Santa Monica. Nima drives up and down every street in the neighborhood within a few blocks of the Department of Motor Vehicles. In the chaos of Los Angeles traffic, Nima Gyalgen Sherpa has learned to drive!

In Los Angeles, Nima's connections continue to count. During his driving test, Nima's instructor notices his name is Sherpa and asks if he's climbed Mount Everest. Impressed with his mountaineering skills, and his driving, the instructor passes him. I gain a freedom. Nima gains a pride. Excited over his possession of a California driver's license, Nima calls Jules, then my parents. He picks up Hari Govinda nearby and drives to get gas at the station where Mohammed works, and then on to see his friend Hollywood Sherpa.

"I am like an American now," says Nima. With keys in hand, Nima Gyalgen Sherpa stands ready to unlock the world.

Nima looks like an American.

—*Pasang*

WHEN NIMA LEARNED ABOUT a new Sherpa named Tsering in the San Diego area, visits were quickly arranged, and Nima gained another friend. They look forward to August, when Tsering will join us for the American-Nepal Society camping trip. He is dropped off at our home the evening before we are to leave. Shorter than Nima, he has a curl in his hair. He studied to be a mechanic and now works in a repair shop. Nima, excited to be with another Sherpa, addresses Tsering in Sherpa and leaves me out of the conversation. Only when Nima is busy preparing dinner do I get a chance to talk to Tsering. We talk about his work, and then I ask about his family and where he grew up.

I grew up in India, says Tsering. My father was a Gurkha soldier.

So was I, shouts Nima from the kitchen. I joined the Gurkhas at seventeen.

You never told me that! I say. After a year together, I am surprised to learn that Nima had a military career. What else hasn't he told me? Nima says he and a friend ran away to a Gurkha camp in the south, but the army proved too strict for him, so after three weeks, he deserted. I married a deserter? Tsering assures me that the Gurkhas will not try to track Nima down. Tsering, who had no interest in the army, was schooled in India and became the first in his family to graduate. That explains their differences. Tsering is educated; Nima is wise.

As we enter the Angeles National Forest, our car climbs above 6,000 feet (1,829 m) on a road of narrow switchbacks. We pass chaparral and oaks, then enter a forest of pine, spruce, and cedar. Even at altitude, the terrain remains desertlike, but for trees that keep the August sun off the road and shade our group campsite at Deer Flats. As Nima and I unpack the car, members of the American-Nepal Society pitch tents, gather firewood, and set up the kitchen in a communal display of common purpose so often missing in Los Angeles.

Sonam "Hollywood" Sherpa, master chef, has dinner preparations well under way. Curious about the meal, I stand nearby to watch and see him reach under the bushes and pull out a package wrapped in butcher paper. He places it on the picnic table and unwraps a goat, stored in the shade since morning. On a log near the fire pit, Hollywood lays out the goat, pulls out a *khukuri*, and whacks the goat into pieces. Everything goes into the pot: muscle, bones, stomach, and intestines. I decide to eat vegetarian. While energetic Hollywood is the fulcrum of the barbeque activities, our Tibetan friend Dolma skillfully manages the rest. I help to wash the vegetables and talk to Dolma. Nima chops vegetables and says little, as if to avoid attention. Nima does not go unnoticed though. Like a guard dog, I stick close to him, aware of stares from an attractive Nepalese ingénue.

I am like my father, says Hollywood, who tells stories while he cooks. My father can drink alcohol and not get drunk. My father once told me that there are four kinds of people who drink: snake drunks fight with each other; sheep drunks sleep too much; cat drunks like to wander; pig drunks are happy all the time. He laughs. He and his father are pig drunks—happy all the time.

As dinner cooks in pots over an array of camp stoves under Hollywood's watchful eye, Nima and I walk to the creek. Dust rises from the trail. The air is fire ready. The shade of trees offers a welcome relief. Happy to be out of Los Angeles, I feel myself lighten, ready to rise on an updraft. The electrical energy in the air ignites Nima, who tells me he doesn't like alcohol. His father got crazy when he drank too much. A snake drunk. He'd beat his children with a big stick he kept over the stove. We walk in silence.

Pala would get so mad at me, says Nima. He'd call me dumb. I am not dumb. I just didn't want to say anything if it wasn't nice. He was my father. He created me. I have to respect him. But, I don't have to be like him, be an angry person. So, I never talked or screamed no matter how hard he hit me. And I never cried! He hated me for that. It only made him beat me harder.

And your mother? I ask. Nima looks distressed for a minute.

She never beat me, but she never tried to stop him either. She's my mother. I still must do good karma things for her all my life to pay her back. Grandmother tried to protect us and would bring us to her home, but Pala always found us.

My parents never hit me, I tell Nima. I describe for him my punishments: early to bed for minor misdemeanors, or if delinquent, grounded for two weeks with no TV. I don't mention that I retained my books, games, pets, dinner, and warm bed.

They never beat you? asks Nima, incredulous. No, I tell him, but once my father washed my mouth out with soap for saying a swear word. Nima laughs and wonders if my father believed soap could wash away words. I shake my head. I remember the basket of nettles. Words are like the needles of Nepalese nettles; once they pierce your skin, they scar.

After our grand dinner, the mood is relaxed, digestive. Hollywood and Dolma scrub the metal cooking pots with handfuls of sand and water as if we were in Nepal. The men sip their beers. Mothers take account of their children. The teenagers gather to one side in a quiet circle and decide on dance tapes and who will play the *mondal*. The young man selected places a strap around his knees and the cylindrical double-sided drum on his lap. He begins to softly play. With sticks and stones in dirt, the youngest write words in an alphabet only they understand. In time, drawn in by its warmth, everyone encircles the fire.

The screech of a portable microphone breaks our reveries. Rambhadur, the society's president, welcomes the campers. The intrusion of static and a mechanical voice assaults the audience. The dancers and musicians are eager. Someone strums a guitar. Another taps the *mondal*. A pair of hands clap. Others join in. The clapping crescendos. A young man stands, raises his arms above his head, and begins to dance. Rambhadur, who knows his constituents, concludes his speech to a loud round of applause. No one is shy. Men, women, and children, young and old, Nima and even I, move to the *mondal*. We circle the fire, each of us absorbed in our own movements, the smell of smoke, the long shadows thrown against the forest, and memories evoked by the music.

I remember the night my inhibitions left me. I had gone with friends to a blues bar in South Chicago to hear Clifton Chenier and his Red Hot Louisiana Band play zydeco music, a fast-tempo Creole music. You cannot just listen to zydeco. The music makes you dance. You can't help it. I didn't need a partner. I had music and Clifton and his band. From his wheelchair, Clifton's voice shouted out a song, while he scrubbed his *vest frottoir*, or rub board, with bottle openers. For the first time, I understood that I did not need to wait for others. I could make my own happiness. And so, I danced. I danced to calm my mind, discover my body, and renew my spirit. I danced to be free.

Tonight, we are a community. To dance around a fire under stars in the shadow of mountains recalls an ancient shared past. We transform from individuals into a melded whole with conflicts set aside and differences extinguished. We move in unison. Men show off their athletic prowess. Young girls flirt. Old women raise their arms and sway with a grace I try to match. They nod in approval. Before the musicians, the children hold hands and gyrate, lost in their own imaginations. No one has to look good or be good, just be. Be here. Be dancing. Be free. And so, we dance, until the moon goes down and our legs no longer hold us up.

I sleep well, wake to a crow's caw, and am transported back to Nepal. Should Nima and I have moved to Nepal instead of staying in the States? While the opportunity for him to learn English and American culture has been positive (mostly), life here has been hard on his self-esteem. With the recession, his job search has been difficult, especially with his lack of education. Given the demands of my work, I seldom assist him with his transition. In Nepal, I might have slowed down and remained more in touch with my true nature. What was I afraid of? My relationship with Nima would not work out? I'd kill my career? That a life in Nepal was not how it was supposed to be? I can't answer myself this morning, but what I felt dancing to Clifton Chenier, I felt in Nepal, and I felt last night, and I want to keep it. For now, all I can do is hope to find freedom again, and that each time it will last a little longer.

Morning brings a crisp breeze and perfect skies, so Nima, Hollywood, Tsering, and I decide to hike. Out-of-shape and hungover, we are thankful the dusty trail rises gradually. As we gain elevation, the trees thin out, so by the time we reach the ridgetop, we are above them. Our vista extends out over the Los Angeles basin and into a tree-filled valley below, which inspires a Hollywood story:

One winter, a rhododendron with bent, gnarly branches asked a handsome beech tree to marry her. The beech refused and told her why. She was too ugly. Come spring, when the rhododendron flowered, the beech thought she was the most beautiful thing he had ever seen. This time, the beech asked the rhododendron to marry him. The rhododendron refused and told the beech that if he did not want her in winter, he did not deserve her in summer. The beech, distraught and lovesick, jumped off a cliff into an avalanche couloir. He remains there and grows taller and straighter in the couloirs than in any other place, as he tries to reach the only love of his life, the rhododendron.

Hollywood laments to me how Sherpa parents don't tell, or even know, their stories anymore. Today, Sherpas want their children to go to school and learn from books. I laugh. I want to learn Sherpa stories, I say. Hollywood smiles at me and begins another tale.

Pasang arrives in Los Angeles on Tuesday. Nima, excited to see his younger brother—and to show off his driving skills—picks him up at the airport and drives him to Palos Verdes Estates, where he'll live with Lee and his family. Pasang was living in Hawaii with Lee's family when Nima and I met in Nepal, so I look forward to meeting the last of Nima's siblings.

A couple of days later, Pasang calls for Nima and we talk for the first time. I immediately recognize that Pasang is more fluent in English and easier to understand than Nima. Even on the phone, Pasang brims over with joy as he tells me how happy he is to be back in America.

"Nima looks like an American," says Pasang.

Nima smiles when I share his brother's observation. "Since Pasang and I were little, America was our dream," he says.

When I return home after work one evening, there is Pasang. He is larger than Nima in height and build, but with eyes and smile just as welcoming. The curl of his hair balances the arch of his heavy brows. He carries himself with an easy confidence, as if the world has been kinder to him. *Namaste, Didi*. Pasang bows with his palms together. I return the greeting, happy to meet Nima's brother. Pasang has come with gifts from the family: a Tibetan rug from Tshiring Tendi and Ami, Nepalese lentils from older sister Mingma Futi, two large bags of tea from Uncle Lama Zepa, and Szechwan peppers grown on their farm from Mama. Nima unwraps a small tissue paper package. He lifts a red cord and threads it through the loop of a black braided tassel. He picks up both ends of the red cord and ties it on around my neck.

"A *sangdi* from our lama friend, Sangay Rinpoche," says Nima. "To scare off demons and ghosts." I finger my newfound protection.

The Beverly Hills Hotel has closed, and our project team now works out of a field office in Bungalow Nine at the hotel. We cannot start construction until all the preliminary investigations are done and city approvals are received, but the pressure is more intense than ever, and I feel myself pulled into the "work is everything" trap that I want so much to avoid: As the project moves into the next phase, I must catch up. With a large team to manage through shop drawings, submittals, schedule options, and logistics, not to mention the communications between them all, I work weekends. Our fee for the project is being expended at a record pace, and as manager for my firm's contract, I will be held accountable for any shortfall. I fight to keep the client, owner's representative, hotel's general manager, general contractor, numerous city agencies, historical consultants, neighborhood associations, twenty-plus consultants, four vice-presidents, and the architectural team, all talented professionals, focused on the goal. It is a crazy job, and some days patience drains out of me. People. People. People. Talk. Talk. Talk. Meetings. Phone calls. Meetings. Personnel issues. Meetings. Team reviews. Meetings. I come home exhausted, desirous of solitude.

Nima, being Sherpa, does not understand the concept of "alone," or of "silence." Sherpas are social. He gets angry when I tell him that his brother Pasang cannot spend the night. I am tired of people and talk. Our house is too small. There is no escape. Nima needs to follow me around work for a day; the demands, the multitasking, and the meetings would exhaust him. I need to establish equilibrium.

Although I usually look to the future, on occasion it can be nice to look back. The camaraderie between our project team members and my previous corporate client is evident by the fantastic turnout at Henry's retirement party, held at his home in Pomona in early September. For the three years prior to my trip to Nepal, Henry, my past client, and I worked closely on the details of their new corporate headquarters, and during the two years preceding that, we completed a temporary headquarters project together. Over the five years, we became friends. Although it has been fifteen months since the last project was completed and I left for Nepal, all the key project team members turn out for the celebration. In spite of the challenges, in spite of the economy's failure and the client's decision to vacate the headquarters before all their employees had even moved in, we feel proud to be part of the quality project we delivered to the client. And everyone has now moved on to new opportunities. Sometimes change is forced on us. Those who adapt, evolve.

While I prepared for my journey around the world, this team of people supported my goal. Now they want to travel vicariously with me as I show them slides of my journey. After dinner, Henry sets up the projection screen in the backyard, while dusk settles on the mountaintops behind us and blankets are spread out over the lawn. With wineglasses in hand, all gather in small groups and wait to be transported. To begin, I thank everyone for driving me insane. Crazy! someone shouts. Laughter. Yes, crazy, I tell them. So crazy, I had no choice. I had to take this journey. If things had been easier, I might not have gone. If I had not gone, I would not have met Nima.

A universal "Ahhhhh" rises from the audience. They had been surprised to hear I came back with a Sherpa, but after three years of working together, my project team members trusted my judgment. I am warmed by their continued support. There is no moon tonight, and my images of Asia float in near blackness before silhouettes of the foothills beyond. The beginnings of my new life, our new life, flash before our friends. Nima and I share in the narration. He names the places and peaks, while I tell our story—

"Every story has a beginning. Every story starts with a dream."

In mid-September 1992, I drive to downtown Los Angeles for Nima's final interview with the Department of Justice: Immigration and Naturalization Service to establish his residency based on our marriage and its sustainability. Nima verifies his age, address, marital status, and police record. I confirm our union. Pending paperwork, Nima is approved.

"My dream is reality," says Nima once we are home. "I have my residency, my driver's license, a car, a job, and my brother." I ask if he is missing something. He laughs. "And my best friend, my wife."

With his residency approved, Nima decides to take charge. With no discussion between us, he quits his busboy job. On the phone, he had conferred with Jules, who concluded that he should get paid and get out. He tells me he did it today. He quit. You did what? I say. Nima explains the schedule challenges, the lack of respect he received from the owner, the poor quality of the food and customer service. I wonder why he never shared the depth of his concerns with me before. He tells me he didn't want me to worry. I am okay with his decision, if he focuses on school. I cross my fingers that we'll get by.

Inspired by his brother, Nima signs up for a GED prep class, so he too can get a high school equivalency certificate. Unfortunately, the rigors of school only frustrate a free spirit like Nima. This time around, Nima finds school difficult. Intuitive skills come easy to him. Book learning does not. Paying attention for long proves impossible. His grades are poor. In no time, the novelty of school has worn off. Nima wants to work. I remind him that his school counselor told us it was the worst job market he had ever seen. With his counselor's advice, Nima enrolls in a hotel and restaurant occupation training course at a local community college. Nima likes the idea of "college" and immediately applies his talents to the task. Following his first few classes, Nima calls for me to look at his quick-learned accomplishments. Our cloth dinner napkins, all of them, rise as fans or baskets or birds from wineglasses, barware, and two champagne flutes.

Assigned to work room service as part of the training course, Nima finds it easy. When a guest calls, he presses a button, like "cola," "ham sandwich," or "champagne." When the order arrives, he delivers it. Nima tells me he doesn't need school to learn these things. Nima laughs.

"But, I learn other things! Today, I delivered dinner, wine, and a candle at noon to a Hispanic man and a blonde woman in a negligee. America is amazing!"

The word *Nepal* or *Mount Everest* or *Sherpas* often brings Nima and me into conversations with strangers. Today at the Redondo Beach flea market, I scour old *National Geographic* magazines. As a child, I thought the yellow border contained the world, which accounted for the magazine's weight. I was drawn to the wall of yellow spines that brightened my grandpa's basement sitting area in his house in Connecticut. I would sit on the arm of Grandpa's mohair sofa and lay the world in my lap. Samoans, Somalis, and Sumatrans. Pygmies and Masai. Naked beneath paints made of pigments, or clothed in layers of patterned colors. Bejeweled or unadorned. Deserts, swamps, mountains. Castles or homes or huts. The world was diverse. My neighborhood was not. As I turned the soft pages, a dream began to form. Today, I am living it.

I pick up a reasonably preserved copy of the October 1963 *National Geographic* with the story of Jim Whittaker's climb to the top of Mount Everest. First American to summit Everest, says the seller, who asks if we are climbers. I tell him that Nima is. He's Sherpa. I trek. The seller is surprised. So are we. He traveled to Kathmandu many years ago. Not a climber though, he says. I guessed that. His belly bulges out over his blue jeans and stretches the seams of his navy T-shirt to the breaking point. His hair and moustache are gray. His pale blue eyes follow potential customers who search through his antiques, knickknacks, and old magazines displayed on a faded cotton quilt.

The seller's father was a Swiss mountaineer on the 1922 British Expedition, a buddy of Tenzing Norgay Sherpa, who was the first man on Everest with Sir Edmund Hillary. The seller and his father stayed with Tenzing Norgay once in Darjeeling. Nima is impressed. I want to know more, but the market is busy today. I hand the seller my fifty cents for the magazine. Most people buy them for the Coca-Cola ads on the back, he tells me. Not everyone is a traveler. Imagine. A Sherpa. Small world.

The seller is right. It is a small world. As I traveled, I witnessed a melding of peoples and cultures, evidence of a shrinking world. I want to believe that this melding may one day bring peace, but I am dismayed to see the common denominator being sought, the lack of diversity, and loss of wisdom. Local knowledge adapted to unique living conditions and environments is being traded for global trends and universal desires. History will judge what we have created.

Somehow, Sherpas bring out the best in people. Just before Thanksgiving, I hand Nima the December 1992 *National Geographic* that came in the mail today. "Sherpas: Gatekeepers of the Himalaya" reads the cover. I feel proud to have married into this mythic clan. The story is about the first all-Sherpa expedition up Everest to honor others who have died climbing. It says Sherpas had no schools until Sir Edmund Hillary built the first one in Khumjung in 1961. I am surprised. No schools at all? Nima confirms that the Nepalese government does little in the Solukhumbu. Sir Edmund Hillary and his foundation, The Himalayan Trust, do far more. In the Solukhumbu as a boy, Nima often met Hillary, the New Zealander beekeeper and mountain climber, who came to work on projects, like the first district hospital in Khunde or the Himalayan Rescue Association station at Pheriche. His stature among Sherpas is legendary.

"To Sherpas, Hillary is a god."

Turns out that Nima knows more than one god. Jules, who sponsored Nima to come to the States, stops to visit on his way back from Nepal. Jules's generous spirit matches the Sherpas'. He is easy to be with, and we both enjoy his stimulating conversation, his insight into the Sherpa culture, and his continued support. Jules treats Nima like a son. Nima adores Jules. We all wish we lived closer to each other.

While in Nepal, Jules saw all of our family, except for Nima's mother. Everyone is well. Kandu, Nima's youngest sister, struggles with too much work. As the male family members are all on trek or on expeditions, Kandu must care for both the animals and the farm, which Jules thinks is too much responsibility for a teenager. Jules hands Nima a bundle of letters wrapped in twine from two nephews, his younger sister, two older sisters, his brother Nima Nuru, his parents, and a friend. Eight! Jules digs deeper into his backpack and hands Nima a tape of music from his cousin, dried yak cheese from his aunt, and a computerized dictionary Jules found for Nima in Hong Kong. While Jules shows Nima how the dictionary works, I put the tape in the cassette player. Over the music, Jules tells us stories of his trip, peppered by gossip about family and friends, until well past midnight.

Early the next morning, Nima takes Jules to the Los Angeles airport. When Nima returns home, we both begin letters back to his family.

"Caryl?" I look up. "If you really, really believe, a god helps. Like people. That's our expression." I nod.

I have never given this appellation before to anyone. "Jules is a god." Nima smiles.

One afternoon over the Thanksgiving holiday when Nima is out with his brother, I decide to walk the beach. I leave my shoes near the pier and step barefoot onto the sand. The day is pleasant, but the breeze off the ocean carries winter's chill. At the water's edge, I head south into the sun. The ocean's surf bubbles over my feet, changes moods, and then undermines the sand beneath me. The water's uneven surface gives sunlight a perfect palette for play. The hills of Palos Verdes shimmer through the haze. I follow the wide tire tracks of a beach bicycle and notice the intricate geometry of its tread and the size of its rider's footprints. The tide recedes. Both imprints remain, their edges blurred by water. Seagulls stand to face into the wind. Sailboats heel over as they harness the wind and cut through the waves.

The tide, the wind, and the water suggest a balance, a give and take. I am water. I shape the earth. I leave an imprint. Emotions range from still to calm to insistent to persistent to angry to wrathful. I must balance the energy of my actions. Be aware of the reaction. Know I will not always win. I must stop fighting the forces that come at me. I must not let storms churn me up, crash me over rocks, cast me onto the shore where I drop flotsam and jetsam until I exhaust myself. When the earth resists me, I need to create my own momentum, refuge, shore. I need to find a sheltered cove, so when a deep-down energy is created, I shape my landscape with intention.

But when the alarm goes off Monday morning, I do not get up. I lie there and worry. While our personal financial crisis forces change, it adds a stress level that often brings me to the breaking point. On waking, my first words to Nima are to ask him about his job search and if he ever followed up with the sports shop. When I took him to the store a couple weekends ago, the manager appeared excited to meet a Sherpa and told him he'd transfer the ice-climbing equipment over to him, if he can get him a position. Nima says he called the manager back and was told that he still needed to talk to the mountain shop manager. I want to know what else Nima has done to look for a job. Nima reminds me that the sports shop wants to hire him, then rolls away from me. I point out that they haven't; that he needs to follow more than one job lead at a time; and most important of all, that we have no more rupees. Nima rolls back. None?

I call the office and tell them I'll be in late. Over breakfast, I break out our expenses; share with him our negligible bank balance and our credit card debt. I express relief that no one is coming for Thanksgiving dinner, so we can keep it cheap. Nima insists it's my special holiday, so we have to do it right. Then pay for it with your money, I suggest. He looks away. Things are bad, Nima. Our Christmas presents to my family will be re-gifted possessions. In two weeks, I'm holding a garage sale. Nima doesn't want to sell our things. We're out of options, Nima. Find a job.

I can't, he says. My car battery died two days ago.

When the pressure of life overtakes me, everything is his fault in my mind. Life was simpler without him. My mind goes into overdrive figuring the cost, the time, and the hassle, which I figure will be all mine.

Go to work, Nima tells me. I'll take care of it.

I wish I could believe him.

By the time I get to the office in Santa Monica, I am hysterical. I enlist Juan, a colleague who emigrated from Chile, as my confidant. Juan is solid in all things: his physical stature, his work, and his friendships. Passionate, he doesn't shy from emotions, and as a romantic, he cherishes a love story. Juan has been a supporter of ours from the start.

"How can I keep this relationship going, Juan?" My voice wavers as I tell him how mad with stress I am, and about my frustration over Nima's inability to adapt and figure things out for himself. Even though he's been in America for over a year, he doesn't apply himself at school and barely contributes. Juan lends me his shoulder. Suggests I relax. He understands my frustration, but also sympathizes with Nima. Juan relates his experiences as an immigrant, tells me to keep perspective, and to remember the love we share. Believe in him. In time, things will turn around. More importantly, we must not ever lose sight of our love.

I do believe in Nima, I tell Juan, or I could never do what I am doing. I don't want to fail. I did once. Juan consoles and says I won't again. Our love for each other shows when he sees us together. Be strong. Be kind. I dry my tears.

"Nima is part of me now," I tell Juan. "I don't have a choice."

When I get home from work, Nima tells me his new car battery only cost sixty-five dollars. He got our neighbor Ed to jump the car, then drove it to the gas station. Nima is more resourceful than I give him credit for.

In preparation for our garage sale, I purge with an emotional intensity. I empty closets, drawers, and cupboards of outdated memories and dump them onto the driveway priced to sell. A young woman drives past and notices a painting I did in college. It so haunts her, she comes back for it at the end of the day. Excited to see it still there, she hands me twenty-five dollars. I'm an artist! Clothes don't sell. Antiques sell for pennies on the dollar. My past holds no value without the stories. After two weeks of letting go and six hours in the driveway, I earn two hundred thirteen dollars and twenty-seven cents. I vow to never do a garage sale again. What does not sell, I donate. My mind has released it.

My focus returns to Nima and his job search. He promises to call the sports shop. With school over for the holidays, he has been out early every morning to look for a job. He applied for two pizza-delivery jobs yesterday.

"One day, I'll take care of you, Sherpani." I believe him.

A couple of days later in early December, Nima lands a delivery job with the VFW, tracked down through an ad in the *Los Angeles Times*. He's to deliver promotional merchandise and pick up monetary donations. I assume the job is with the Veterans of Foreign Wars. His first day, he arrives home late, uncertain about his new position. He drove to sections of the city he'd never been in before, got lost, and then scared, until he realized that his profits would be used up in gas. Then, he got mad. One donor was a sex shop in Inglewood with "nasty videos and all these horrible sex things." It humors me to imagine wide-eyed Nima in a sex shop. I am surprised, but I rationalize that vets and their supporters are everywhere. Besides, Nima wants to work, and I need him to work. This type of customer must be a fluke, I assure him. Tomorrow will be better.

A few days later, Nima shatters. Today, he waited four hours for the manager to show up, and he wanted to leave and strange people kept coming and going and he didn't feel safe and didn't know what to do, and once the nasty manager did arrive, he said horrible things to Nima, who shakes as he recalls the abuse.

"I'm never, ever, ever going back!" he says.

I no longer want him to. I imagine the worst. Drug runner? Child pornography enabler? Don't worry about collecting your pay, I tell him. I fear for his safety. Several times a day for the next five days, the "VFW" calls to beg Nima to come back. On the sixth day, we unplug the phone to stop the harassment.

Depression settles over our household. As we prepare dinner, Nima chops fresh vegetables for soup, while I open two packages of ramen noodles. I had never eaten the cheap instant noodles until I met Nima. At twelve dollars a case at the Indian grocery store, they stretch our food budget as hot water extends the curly noodles. As I work beside Nima in the kitchen, I sense an old habit of his has returned. Nima is smoking. When I confront him, he denies it. While doing laundry the next day, I find a can of chew in his pocket. When asked about it, he confirms it is his tobacco, but can say without lying that he is not smoking. I graphically describe the consequences. Nima tells me he'll quit after this can. He just bought it. We can't waste money. For as smart as Nima is, the cause and effect of his actions does not influence his decisions. Nima does not see the future until it arrives. When Nima lies, I question my decision to be with him and wonder if I fell in love with the myth of Sherpas, rather than the man. Myths are infallible. Men are not.

With Nima, there is always something else around the corner. Two days later, he greets me at the door with news that he's had a car accident. No one was hurt. We go to inspect the damage: bumper ripped off on the right side, two smashed headlights, and a dented front fender.

You'll have to fix the headlights and live with everything else, I tell him, as it's not worth reporting to insurance.

Can't I fix it? whines Nima. All smashed, it looks like a poor man's car.

It is, Nima. Get a job.

Nima and his brother Pasang are often together when I get home from work. Tonight, I find them flipping through an unsolicited catalog that came in the mail today.

Pasang points to a *dorje* and a bell, and tells me that Sherpas would never sell religious things in their villages, and that the tourist shops in Pokhara and Thamel sell them for far cheaper than the dharma catalog does.

Buying those religious things doesn't make you a Buddhist, says Nima. He tosses the catalog into the trash. He touches his center. It's here, he says. Monks have nothing. Or hermit monks. Nothing. Like Uncle Lama Zepa. It's here. Inside.

Uncle Lama Zepa is a real monk, explains Pasang. He lives in a rock cave, and when he meditates, no one can see him. Even great lamas live simply.

Nima cooks Nepalese food for his brother. When I offer Pasang more *daal bhaat* he refuses. Sherpas don't ask, they offer, Nima tells me. He demonstrates by extending a spoonful of rice from the bowl to Pasang. *Shey. Shey*, he says. Pasang pushes Nima's hand away. *Shey. Shey.* Both laugh. Pasang again refuses and pushes back Nima's hand. *Shey. Shey.* The rice lands on Pasang's plate.

That's our custom, laughs Pasang. He devours it all.

Over ice cream, my tradition, Nima and Pasang talk about how many young men are moving to Kathmandu or to other countries, forcing their families to hire non-Sherpas to help them farm the land. Their parents had divided up their land among the four boys, but with two in America and one in Kathmandu, only Tshiring Tendi is left to farm. Pasang's property is by the river, but each year, more and more of it washes away in the floods. As the youngest boy is responsible for the parents as they age, Nima Nuru received the most land. Nima describes his own parcel as inland and on top of the bluff.

I never knew we were property owners, Nima, I say. I suggest we stay in Nepal after our Buddhist marriage ceremony and second wedding that Nima has been planning for March 1994, a little more than a year from now. Nima plans to leave ahead of me next spring to make final arrangements for our wedding in Bodhnath. I feel ready to leave Los Angeles.

I like my American life, Sherpani, Nima says.

I used to. Do I still?

I hear no details from Nima about our Buddhist wedding. All I know of Buddhist marriage traditions comes from the book, *Marriage Customs in Nepal*, written and given to me by the Hindu professor who toured me around Kirtipur and Chobar on the back of his scooter. I ask Pasang, who's never been married, and he shares what he knows. A bride's parents may spend years acquiring enough wealth for a proper wedding gift for the couple. For Ang Chokpa, their oldest sister, their parents saved for several years. Tshiring Tendi's wife, Ami, is to receive her gift this summer, ten years after her marriage. The gift ceremony is the final wedding celebration. Traditions apply to women more often, especially arranged marriages, while men are freer to choose their wife.

"My parents arranged a marriage for me once," says Nima.

"They did?"

Nima laughs at my surprise. I don't laugh with him. "Then, will your parents accept me?" I have to ask. Nima assures me they will. Pasang tells me that she wasn't right for Nima. Am I? I don't come with a dowry. Will Nima's parents expect one? As excited as I am to return to Nepal, I worry that his family may impose traditions on us that I cannot accept. Or have expectations about children. Nima insists that they'll like me. What if they don't? Or I don't like them? Nima is vague when I ask. Except for Pasang, their entire family is expected to attend the wedding. With no further counsel, Nima makes plans.

The twenty-first of December is our one-year anniversary, but we are too poor to go out, so Nima makes *daal bhaat* and chicken curry, and we are happy. On Friday, just before Christmas, the owner of a plant maintenance company interviews Nima on the phone. She knows about Sherpas. Nima begins to make plans. He could work days for her, and nights and weekends for the sports shop. We pray they both call. Our checking account balance is thirty-three dollars and eighty cents. Our savings is zero. At forty-one, I live paycheck-to-paycheck. When I charged the Christmas turkey on MasterCard, my purchase was refused, until the grocery store clerk took pity on me and put it through anyway. Happy holidays, she told me with a compassionate grin.

I am determined to celebrate the holiday in style, sort of a crisp cachet frosted with delusion and sprinkled with panache. Cinda and Lance have driven down from San Francisco to share the holiday with us. Recently graduated from college and law school, respectively, and on starter incomes, they understand our position. Cinda and I decide to break with tradition, or create new ones. We open our gifts Christmas Eve, sleep in Christmas morning, and dig deep into our stockings at noon. Our Christmas traditions only baffle Nima. Are Jesus and Santa Claus related? We tell him the tales. Was Jesus a shaman? We try to explain. How do reindeer fly? I tell him, like tigers. To every house in one night?

All Christmas morning, "wannabees" Nima and I lounge around in our new closeout Beverly Hills Hotel bathrobes and pretend we are there, while "loaded" Cinda and Lance relax in their sweats knowing the wealthy have no need to put on airs. Our gourmet brunch, enabled by *Bon Appétit* and prepared by *moi*, is *très bon*. Afterward, Cinda and Nima work on a jigsaw puzzle at the dining table upstairs, while Lance watches the ball game. Downstairs, I curl up on my bed and read. Following dinner, we circle the coffee table and play Monopoly like wildly rich LA developers who buy teardown oceanfront properties, only to build bigger ones that block the neighbors' views. Emotions flare as we cut deals, trade up or out, and pursue the competition with a relentless furor. Tensions rise. Voices crescendo. Values are compromised. The leader falls to a monopoly. Our Christmas spirit falls victim to a game. Money isn't so important, suggests Nima in an attempt to make peace. What does he know? Nima doesn't pay the bills.

The New Year begins on a hopeful note. On December 31, the indoor plant maintenance company calls Nima and offers him a job. The owners will train him and pay reasonably well. They promise to be flexible with his schedule, so he can finish his hospitality training and GED class. Nima's joy spreads around the city, as he drives to different office buildings to maintain and water their indoor plants. He enjoys the professional environment he now finds himself in and the interaction with office workers he meets. It is not hard work, but his territory is wide and his schedule unpredictable.

With a new opportunity ahead of him, Nima expresses disillusionment about his hospitality training class. He's tired of chopping vegetables in the pantry, he tells me, and suggests he could better teach the class. His GED prep class frustrates him, as his tutor is available only an hour per week and tutors six students at a time, each from different countries and at various levels. No one learns. His tutor hands out assignments, gives tests, and never goes back over their work.

"How can I learn when I don't know what I did wrong?" asks Nima.

Nima has never mentioned this to me before. I had thought he liked school. I should have paid more attention to his progress, asked more about his classes, tutored him myself. Does he blame me? I'd thought if he did not complain, everything was okay. I feel disappointed in our system, and even more in myself. Too busy is not an excuse. Nima explains to me how he understands many words when he reads, but doesn't know how to say them or how they should sound, so that when someone speaks, he doesn't always comprehend. He feels isolated. Most students have others who speak their language. At school, Nima has only Hari and his sister who speak Nepali. No one speaks Sherpa.

Our lives go forward, alternating between poverty dinners of noodle soup and opulent occasions financed by others. I use my credit card only when needed to save face. I have to.

In January, we attend the wedding of Chantal and Nick, a work colleague and her new husband, just up the beach in Marina del Rey. Their wedding reception is held on the Wild Goose, a 136-foot (41 m) navy minesweeper once owned by the actor and Hollywood legend John Wayne and formerly harbored in Newport Beach. After he acquired the decommissioned ship, he retrofitted it with plush rooms sized to fit the man. He no longer uses it; he rode off into the sunset over a decade ago.

The evening of the wedding is warm, the breeze still, and in calm waters the harbor lights double their twinkle. At this sophisticated gathering, I enjoy the rare opportunity to share in intellectual conversation and a fine white Bordeaux.

Nima tugs at my arm, certain I'll be as excited as he is. Come see, Caryl, says Nima. I ask him to wait. Nima insists. I am talking, I say. Nima demands. My friend Susan asks him what is so important. Nima promises a surprise. My colleague Mark, always eager for Nima's adventures, suggests we all go. Six of us trot off in a procession, wineglasses in one hand and dainty plates of canapés in the other. We follow Nima across thresholds and through rooms, while the boat gently rocks to the wake of a sea-bound yacht. We step into John Wayne's bedroom and stop at the foot of his oversized bed. Nima points.

Beside the bed is a white antiqued Buddha sporting a fringed lampshade above his head. Party animal, someone begins. Buddha meets bordello. At least, he's enlightened. John or the Buddha? Someone turns the light on and off. Enlighten me. Enlighten me not. Enlighten me. Enlighten me not. We laugh. Not Nima. His focus is on the Buddha. He is in awe. To Nima, the Buddha is never crass, even when someone tries hard to make him so. Nima approaches the Buddha with palms together. He bows. His forehead touches the Buddha. *Om Mani Padme Hum.* We are silenced.

The gods are mad at us.

—Nima

COME EARLY FEBRUARY, Nima and I are ready for a much-needed winter break. I sign us up for the office ski trip to Mammoth Lakes, a ski town nestled in the Sierra Nevada Mountains about five hours northwest of Los Angeles. While most of our group stays in a lodge close to the downhill slopes at the base of Mammoth Mountain, a few of us choose the Tamarack Lodge, a rustic setting near cross-country trails and away from the ski town glamour. On the drive up, Nima tells me he misses the mountains and the exertion they require. He's decided to save his money for skis. I am happy. I love to ski.

My outdoor-loving colleagues are curious about Nima and question him about Nepal and Sherpas as we sit before the fire our first evening. What mountains have you climbed? Nima lists them. What does it take to become a Sherpa? I am Sherpa. What kind of training do you go through? None. Nima looks confused. Some of my colleagues have read of the Himalaya, Nepal, and Sherpas, but others know nothing. Basking in their attention, Nima obliges them with stories of his life, the mountains, and Mount Everest. He begins.

One time, when he was six years old, he and his older brother were taking care of their animals in the jungle (his word for a forest), and he got lost. An older couple found him wandering around the jungle calling out his brother's name. They took him home, gave him supper, and put him to bed. Mountain people help each other, Nima tells us. His older sister Mingma Futi was beside herself when she found him the next day. No problem, Nima told his sister. I just lost myself in the jungle.

Don't go losing yourself in the Sierras, advises Sam.

No problem, says Nima. Now that Caryl found me, she won't lose me.

Everyone laughs. I appreciate their acceptance of him, and even more, their support.

The next day is perfect. Sunshine and fresh snow. While my colleagues stand in lift lines at Mammoth, Sam, Nima, and I ski-climb several thousand feet up Obsidian Dome through sequoias. We sweat from exertion. Nima loves it. His cross-country stride has improved, but downhill remains difficult, for his natural forward stance throws him off balance. Constant falls into deep powder exhaust him. I am glad patient Sam is there to offer Nima advice. Sam, bright and energetic, looks young for his age: tall and lean, sandy blond curls, and an athlete. Nima listens to Sam.

Sam shouts out directions to Nima. Stand upright. Lean back as you go downhill. Like this. Sam demonstrates. Nima positions himself and starts down. He begins to pick up speed.

Bend your knees, Nima! Lean back. More. Like you're going to sit on the back of your skis. No! Don't sit. Only pretend to. Oh no!

Sam and I laugh. How do you do it, Caryl? I smile. I have no idea. When Nima joins us, shaking off his last flurry of powder after a full day of thrills and spills, he announces that he will not be buying skis.

Sam leaves for Los Angeles. Exhausted, Nima sleeps. Inspired, I seek the sacred.

Mysterious Mono Lake north of Mammoth Lakes has tugged on me since I first moved to California. This land is sacred. Ninety percent of California Gulls are born here. I have come to see the tufa. Once underwater, the limestone pillars, or tufa, now rise well above the lake level. The lake is shrinking, because water is sent to Los Angeles faster than it can naturally be replaced. This causes the saline levels to rise, the surrounding ecosystem to change, and the lake to dry up. The tufa are gravestones that mark the former site of water. We dig our own grave. Mono Lake is dying. I have come to pay my last respects.

This looks like Tibet, says Nima as we approach the parking area high above the lake. I imagine both landscapes share a spirituality that we sense as we travel over them. Landscapes can do that—give one a sense of the greater whole. Nima, tired and sore from skiing, refuses to walk with me to the lake. Here, I am glad to go alone.

I hike down a mile to the lake's edge. I relish the quiet. I sense spirits. The tufa emerge above snow-dusted sage, like Gaudi's cathedral towers in Barcelona that reach the sky, but stretch for heaven. The still water doubles the spires to create a white cathedral between a blue heaven and an earth of sulfurous yellows and greens along a sienna shore. A faint haze pastels the sky. All along the water's edge, pungent brine shrimp are a feast for migratory birds. Cradled protectively by snow-covered peaks, the lake bestows her blessing. I stand still and imagine. I too seek substance, as I migrate.

Is this your first time? asks a man as he approaches me.

Yes, and yours? He's been coming here for many years, he says, and finds the lake capricious, different each time he visits. Today is special. A mirrored surface is rare. Most days, the winds whip between the mountains and stir up waves, so the lake's edge is too mucky to get up close.

The man wanders off. Only the breeze generated by the wings of the bountiful alkali flies interrupts the calm.

I am mirrored. Reincarnated at this moment. I shed self. Body. Mask. My old self lies in the lake, not drowned, but in rest, as if returning to the womb. I seek exhilaration, for like Nima, I too am bored. I am like this water, whose downstream filtered version has lost its essence. To gain clarity, I must return to the source.

I rest on cold stones. Since returning from Nepal, I have stalled. Transformations take energy, focus, and commitment. I find it easier to pretend to be the person I was when I left. I know her.

I am mistaken. I am now filled with new teachings. Spirits have entered, but I remain confused about which lessons to retain and which I must discard. I am water. Water finds the path of least resistance. As water, I will find my way.

Who am I? The lake is I. I am blessed to know my pilgrimage continues, as I journey on earth between selves. Among sky and tufa castles, I shimmer with a gentle passing breath and know tomorrow I must change with the wind.

The city's historical process is delaying the hotel project, I explain to Nima, who tries hard to understand what I do. The hotel has been closed for over a year, and we still lack permits. It's a complicated process, and there are many concerns and constituents that have to be addressed. The Beverly Hills Hotel is a famous structure within the city, I say, and important to the history of Beverly Hills. As part of the city approvals, the renovation must meet guidelines set forth by city statutes and the historical review panel, which gets input from the neighborhood histori-cal committee and other interested parties. Without approval, no permits will be issued for construction and the project cannot be built. Nima tells me to be patient, as if it were easy, which only increases my frustration. Through it all, the project team continues to work on newly required surveys and reports on plaster, windows, doors, moldings, and the overall condition, until we know every crack and flaw of this old landmark better than a fading movie star's plastic surgeon knows her face. For over a year, an army of consultants had turned out all her secrets, until what everyone knew before we started is announced: the hotel is an aging starlet, and only a major restoration will return her fame.

While the city deliberates, the indecision and anticipation wear me down. I long for a simpler world. After working on the hotel project for a year and a half, all I have accomplished are notebooks filled with meeting minutes, budgets, schedules, correspondence, and revisions. I circle and bump into myself. I seek a broader dimension, a width that allows me to expand and fill the new spaces I felt open up in Nepal. Until that is possible, I settle for distractions far more mundane.

At home that evening, I enjoy the mindless task of vacuuming, but my workday insists on returning. Our meeting on the hotel went badly this morning. The project is in jeopardy. Will I still have a job? It could go either way. Nima's plant maintenance job is only ten hours a week, even though they promised him more, and he's not paid regularly.

Why don't you vacuum when I'm at work? asks Nima.

Why isn't he cleaning the house?

Once Nima got a job, he told me he was no longer a "house puppy," but a "working man." As proud as I am to see him assert himself, he ignores the fact that I work twelve-hour days with a two-hour-plus commute, clean on weekends, shop whenever, do our paperwork, answer all his questions, and pick up his mess. I move in front of the television. He slides to the other side of the sofa. I vacuum toward him. He lifts his feet and turns up the volume with the remote.

Do it later! shouts Nima over the TV and the vacuum. I don't have "later." Only now. But "now" is a state of mind, and I am not in the now. I am in the past, angry about my week. I am in the future, nervous about something that hasn't happened, may never happen, and is out of my control. Will the project get canceled? Could I lose my job?

You take advantage of me, Nima. You only married me to stay in America!

Nima responds with anger from deep within, and his breath fights to push out words that turn into a hiss. I turn off the vacuum and put it away. Nima turns down the TV. In silence, we keep to opposite floors of the house and sleep on the far opposite sides of the bed. It takes two days for me to clear my mind and my heart. I want to re-craft our relationship. With time and reflection, we go from boil to simmer to silence, and then in an instant, our rage is extinguished.

Happy Valentine's Day, my love, says Nima, as we lounge in bed and listen to the rain.

He moves closer and takes me in his arms. It doesn't matter, he says. You found me. It doesn't matter. I found you. He kisses me and pulls me in to fill his void. I luxuriate at the touch of his silken skin against my body. Nima is warm. I am cool. He raises my temperature. Like mercury, we rise as the day warms. Sunlight peeks through clouds and casts shadows of our entwined bodies onto the patchwork quilt my grandmother made me. As we stitch together our lives with forgiveness, Nima and I create new memories.

On Monday, I hear the magic words: On hold. The hotel project is going nowhere until reports and issues and decisions are read and revised and discussed, then decided on by others. Still in possession of spontaneity and the ability to travel on pocket change, I reserve airline tickets to Naples, Florida, with frequent-flier miles, and book a room at my parents'.

Per usual, everything happens at once. Three potential employers call Nima and ask him to come in for interviews. He phones them back and says he will be leaving on vacation the tenth of March for a week. Two set up appointments for the week he returns. We leave Los Angeles on a red-eye heading southeast toward Florida—and the storm of the century.

Since Hurricane Andrew caused over forty billion in damages and almost forty deaths just seven months ago, the National Weather Service is taking no chances. The public needs to know what is coming and prepare as best they can. The storm now building is gigantic. The day we arrive in Florida, barometric pressure, temperatures, and snow begin to fall fast in the Midwest and along the East Coast. Only Florida is spared the snow. A state of emergency has been called for by several Northeast states. In Florida, on the Gulf Coast, we are not too worried about a nor'easter.

Our first day is peaceful. Mom, Nima, and I drive to Fort Myers to tour the winter homes of Thomas Edison and Henry Ford, which are located next to each other along the Caloosahatchee River. Mother walks with Nima to point out items of interest.

Wow! says Nima, as she shares Edison's and Ford's history of invention.

Wow! says Nima, as we walk their gardens of plants from around the world.

Wow! says Nima, surprised to find out that their homes had electricity and indoor plumbing seventy years ago, while his village still has none.

Wow!

Over breakfast our second morning, we read the March 12, 1993, *Naples Daily News* and learn that the "Storm of the century" is predicted and expected to hit the entire East Coast, from Nova Scotia to Cuba. We are warned: Get ready. This is no hoax. Life-threatening. Alabama has twelve feet (3.7 m) of snow, and it's still snowing!

After Hurricane Andrew last August and the huge drop in temperature yesterday, we believe them. Nima and my father secure windows, doors, and the lanai furniture. Now, all we can do is wait. As they monitor the news, my father asks Nima about his job prospects. My mother worries all day what to cook for him, so I help her in the kitchen. We all follow the storm's path across southern Florida. It's a cyclonic blizzard, nor'easter, says the weather reporter. Up north, air traffic is at a standstill. From the satellite photos, we can see the cyclone build and reach out toward us in a spiral that hides more than a third of the United States. Just before we go to bed, it reaches Naples.

This is not the Florida Nima and I had envisioned for our vacation. Terrible winds and thunder keep us awake most of the night. We open the shades to watch palm trees open and close their fronds as trunks bend toward rooftops. Blasts of cold white light illuminate the street, as if God had flashed a photo. Doors rattle. The wind sucks out the glass, pushes it back, and then sucks again. To be safe, Nima and I crack the windows, close the shades, and move to the twin bed farthest from the window.

On the TV news the next morning, local officials announce the closure of beaches that no longer exist. The white coral sands of Naples have returned to the sea.

Damage in Naples could have been worse. The city is lucky compared to most communities. From tidal surges, record blizzards, and collapsed roofs, many people died along the East Coast. There are trees on houses and cars in Naples, but no one was killed. Nima is restless. He gets up and down and up and walks around the house, as if he were a cyclone. My father thinks Nima has the energy of a ten-year-old. He asks how Nima is doing in school and is disappointed Nima will not re-enroll after this term. My father will never understand how hard Nima struggles with focus and organization. My mother wants to know if everything is okay. She doesn't define "everything," but I know what she means. We're doing great, I tell her. And, mostly, we are.

As soon as the gale-force winds subside, adventurous Nima and I go out to see what is left of the beach. My parents warn us to be careful. The air is electric. My hair flies with such force it stings my face. Nima and I lean forward and press hard into a wind that continues to rip fronds off the palms and snap branches like toothpicks. On the pier, we fight to move forward against the fury, but are an unwelcome obstruction to the raging winds. Below us, like a mad cup of cappuccino, a mocha-colored ocean churns up froth—and sand.

"The gods are mad at us," says Nima, as he points at all the condominiums and parking lots along the beach.

The winds have pummeled the town and uprooted trees. The golf course looked heavily damaged when we drove past. My father told us that the beach had disappeared once before, and the city spent millions to re-create it by pumping sand from the ocean floor. Nima told him that Americans are crazy to think they can shape nature. Nima is right. People disrespected the natural give and take of the shore. We removed sea grapes and sea oats to expose the sand; gave our beaches names like Satellite Beach and Siesta Beach and South Beach; populated them with umbrellas, beach balls, and bikinis; and along their edges built houses, hotels, and high-rise condominiums with no thought of where shadows were cast. We didn't care about the future here. We'd already moved up the coast.

Nature knows what's best, says Nima. People should leave it alone.

Nima has a point. We cannot stop beach erosion any more than we can stop the melting of glaciers. What grew out of ancient oceans slowly returns, like the silt at the deltas of Asia's great rivers. Everything circles.

On our one and only sunny day, I sunbathe by the pool and begin a book, while Nima helps my father fix the sprinklers and cut dead limbs from trees. The weather never clears. Our canoe trip through the mangroves is canceled. Neither of us wants to swim without sunshine.

One day, out of boredom, Nima and I play miniature golf. That night, we dine on stone crabs at home and watch a video. On our last day, my father has Nima climb their grapefruit trees to pick the top fruit. They package them in boxes for everyone in the family and take them to the UPS shipping store. A Sherpa in the family suits my father.

With cold winter across the country, our box of grapefruit arrives in Los Angeles frozen. Over breakfast, we sip ice-cold grapefruit juice and wonder: Will the beaches of Naples ever return?

Since our return from vacation, Nima's job opportunities look promising. Second interviews are scheduled with both a downtown hotel, where he'd work as a bellman with Hollywood Sherpa, and with a nursery in Gardena, whose owner has traveled in Tibet. I want him to work at the nursery, where his hours would be more similar to mine. Nima hopes to work with Hollywood.

Any desire Nima had to pass his GED has vanished. He thought it would be easy. Instead, he moves through the material too fast to comprehend it and has failed another test. His vocabulary and comprehension of concepts is excellent, but he refuses to read directions. He never did in Nepal. Directions are for stupid people. Smart Nima makes up his own. The class is structured on cumulative knowledge, and when he does poorly in one book, he has a harder time in the next. I explain how he must go back to the beginning and learn everything he skipped over. He pouts and asks for my help. I sit down next to him. He wants me to provide the answers. I refuse. Nima tries. He concentrates. He answers correctly. I leave. He reads. He gets bored. He asks questions. I answer. He asks more questions. I get frustrated. We circle.

You need to have a GED, Nima, I say. Even the nurseryman told you that. He sounds like a good man. I hope you get a job there.

I want to work with Hollywood, Nima says. Being a bellman is a good job for me. I have experience.

I ask for an explanation. He reminds me that he began his climbing career as a porter carrying loads. First, on expeditions to Annapurna and

Dhaulagiri Base Camps at age fifteen, as a kitchen boy. He laughs as he recalls an ice storm, his heavy load on an ascent, and tears. His third expedition was a forty-five-day trek to Kanchenjunga. After that, he told his boss that he wanted to be a cook. They don't carry big loads.

"A bellman does." I smile.

"It's different, Caryl. A bellman wears a uniform."

Hollywood calls Nima to tell him he got his dream job, a bellman/van driver/tour-package promoter for Guest Services at a hotel west of Interstate 10, with downtown Los Angeles just on the other side of the freeway. At 4:30 a.m. Monday, Nima and I begin a new routine. I'm not sure who is more excited. I feel the stress drop from my shoulders knowing he has a job, and we still have our weekends. I kiss him good-bye and wish him luck. Two days into his second week, Nima calls me at the office to announce that he made eighty-five dollars in tips! I do the math. He could average eight to ten dollars per hour. That evening, Nima hands me a ten-dollar bill.

"For lunch money, sweetie. I'm the boss now."

At the office, I pick up a "Civil Disturbance Memo" dated April 6, 1993, off my chair. We receive one two days later at the hotel project site. I am unsettled. Riots are anticipated, following the announcement of a federal verdict regarding the four policemen who subdued Rodney King. Last year, news of their acquittal of state criminal charges sparked riots. After the riots ended, the United States Department of Justice decided to investigate and issued an indictment against the four policemen for civil rights violations. The verdict of this second trial will be announced soon. However, the announcement will be held for a minimum of three hours to allow the police, National Guard, and FBI time to get into place. A security officer at the hotel project informs me that the report issued to police departments says intelligence people expect problems in areas with small police departments, and potential casualties of up to ten thousand.

I am ready to move out of Los Angeles. I don't want to live where I feel afraid. I am fed up with the sprawl, the smog, and my office cubicle. I miss days outdoors. I desire a vista, the long view. I want to know nature. Here, I feel trapped, especially this weekend. Nima and Hollywood, nervous about the upcoming verdict, left for Joshua Tree. Before Nima left, he told me he was sick of Rodney King, who has been in the news almost daily since Nima came to the United States. I have a Monday deadline and could not go with them, so remain home alone.

You like being alone, Sherpani, said Nima before he left. Just lock the doors.

I wake up at 2:00 a.m., anxious. I cannot go back to sleep. With all the doors and windows locked, I am suffocating. I long for fresh air. Like the Los Angeles Police Department, my whole body is on alert. I overanalyze every noise. I sleep on and off until morning. Early Saturday, I sit before the TV to listen to the verdict. Two guilty, two not guilty. An even split. Tensions cool. Los Angeles remains quiet.

At the end of April, Jules stops to see us in Redondo Beach on his way to Nepal. Nima, who has been in America two years without a trip home, loves to get news and send news to his family. Jules is often the conduit. Nima gives him letters, small gifts, and money to take to our family. A few days after Jules leaves, we are surprised to get his letter from Nepal. A recently arrived Sherpa from Kathmandu had mailed it from Denver.

Jules will visit again on his return, says Nima. I read the rest of his letter. Typical Jules. His carry-on bag with camera, money, and medicines was stolen in Bangkok. The airlines lost his luggage on the trip over, but found it in Singapore and routed it to Kathmandu, where it arrived after Jules had left for Lukla. It was finally reunited with him there. He bought a new camera in Kathmandu. Poor Jules. I read on:

Enough about the bags … And (this is for Caryl). Nima has always had a happy face but before—every once in a while—I would catch a look in his eyes of kind of faraway suffering and anxiety. Now that look has gone, which means, I guess, that he is really happy—if you didn't need any other proof.

So on that note I will say good-bye again and send you much love and the big hugs that I didn't get to give you before. See you May 17th. Love, Jules

In May, Nima returns from the airport with Jules and all his possessions, minus his replacement camera that disappeared somewhere between the Solukhumbu and Kathmandu, along with photos of Nima's family. Jules throws up his hands, as if it is the will of the gods. Jules has learned to let go. He hands Nima a package of letters and a cassette tape from his family, expressing relief that these are still in his possession. Nima pops the tape into the cassette player and cannot stop grinning. He names each family member as they speak.

Those are my nephews, Bai Tshiring and Nawang Tshiring. So cute, says Nima. I listen to know them. His father says a few words, chokes up, and cries. Mingma Futi, his second-oldest sister, sounds clear and light. Ang Chokpa, his oldest sister, speaks in deep, husky tones. His mother's voice breaks with emotion. His brother-in-law's tenor voice suggests a large man. His older brother's voice is clear. The nephews chatter through it all. A weak male voice finishes the tape.

I worry about my father, says Nima. He's sixty-three. I need to go home.

Jules assures him that his father is still in good health, and then tells me how everyone appreciated my letter. I tell Jules how hard it was to write to people I have never met. Mingma Futi told him that she felt terrible that she couldn't do anything for her new sister-in-law. I express surprise. She wants to, says Nima. That's our tradition. Jules makes clear to us how anxious Nima's family is for his return with his American wife, and that even the nephews told him to say *Namaste* to *Didi*.

"My brother-in-law told me, 'Save money to buy land in Nepal. You have to die in your homeland.' I think he is right," says Nima. So does Jules. So do I.

All week Nima plays the tape. All week it rains. The following Saturday, Nima's chants filter down from above with the incense as I sit on the stairs and sew a button on my sweater. Nima prays and cuts vegetables for *daal bhaat* and talks Sherpa with his brother, Pasang. His chants and chops and Sherpa words mix with the rain. I sit back, close my eyes, and listen. Rain will be good for my garden.

During a sun break, while Nima finishes making lunch, Pasang and

I take up the grass in our small yard. We loosen the earth and amend the soil. Pasang is surprised to learn we fertilize like they do in Nepal, except our dung is steer manure, sterilized and bagged for a price. The Sherpa gather it along the trails or collect it from their own animals, if wealthy enough to own animals. Pasang makes short work of the project, as he cuts in the manure and turns the earth. In the Solukhumbu, they till their fields by hand. He teases me about the size of my urban retreat and says I would starve if this were Nepal. The nurtured soil of the Solukhumbu is black and rich. Vegetables grow well there. My soil is gray and dusty, with nothing to hold it together. Pasang expresses doubts about my garden. This is Southern California, I tell him, where plants somehow flourish in spite of us.

To get to the bird feeder, we create a short redwood path and line it with daylilies and bird-of-paradise flowers. I gather a handful of earth, curb it around each plant, and pat it down. It is good to touch the earth directly. There is an affinity we have for each other, that gets forgotten under concrete and decks and sod. I want to reconnect to the land. Have a hand in rebirth. Witness a miracle. Grow a garden. Create a cycle that nurtures. I like dirt on my hands. Body talk. Skin to skin. I touch the earth. My garden is a chance to reclaim the affection we have for each other.

Over a late lunch, Pasang tells me how he hopes to have his high school diploma by year's end. He likes school in America, where teachers don't torture their students. Nima laughs, then begins Pasang's story.

Their father, Pala, often kept the boys out of school during the day to help in the fields and care for the animals, so he provided room and board to the schoolteacher, who would tutor the boys at night. Their days on the farm began early and ended around five. Their home school began after dinner, no matter how tired the boys or their teacher were. At the smallest infraction or nodding head, the teacher would place a piece of chalk between their third and fourth fingers, and squeeze. Two minutes. Three. Four. Five. Pasang looks visibly disturbed, but stays silent. Nima continues. One day, Pasang couldn't take it any longer, so he beat up the teacher. Nima laughs. Pasang got it bad, he said. Pala kept coiled nettles in one of our copper water pots. The stalks softened, but the thorns remained hard enough to puncture our skin when he whipped us. Pasang got whipped the most. But he worked hard to protect us. He'd cut down all the nettles on our farm with his *khukuri* and throw them into the river. He even dug up the roots, but the nettles always grew back. Ang Chokpa and Mingma Futi, our older sisters, tried to protect us. In many ways, they were our parents.

Why do you think he was so mean when we were young? asks Pasang. Nima shakes his head and reminds his brother that life wasn't easy for their family. When Nima was five, the hay stored below the house caught fire. Everyone got out safely, but the house burned down. The family lived in a black-felt yak herder's tent until Pala built a new house, which was much smaller. Pala's father, their grandfather, traveled extensively and amassed uncommon wealth for a man with no education. Pala, the youngest of a large family, grew up arrogant and spoiled. The house that burned was large, with carved wood windows and so many things from Tibet, India, and China. Then, everything was lost.

That would certainly explain some of his anger, I comment.

Everyone was poor then, says Pasang. He didn't need to be like that.

That's why I ran away, says Nima. The city was safer than home.

I have reservations about meeting Pala, I tell them.

He is my father, says Nima. I forgave him. People were ignorant then.

The next morning upon waking, I look out the window and notice how the acacia we planted last year grew two feet (0.6 m) this spring. California has a fecund climate. Nima reaches over and puts my hand over his heart. I keep loving you more, he tells me. It grows here. I roll on top of him. Skin to skin. Body talk. I touch my earth.

Welcome home.

—*Gelek Rinpoche*

IN LATE MAY, Nima and I circle back to Berkeley to visit my sister Cinda and Lance, and to attend the Himalayan Fair at Live Oak Park. Nima has changed more than I realized. Dolma, our Tibetan friend, tells me that Nima is not as shy or self-conscious as he used to be. She would tell him to hold his head up, be proud, be a man. He's doing it now, she says. I never realized that Nima talked to Dolma about his feelings. He never shared those things with me. She is not surprised. He didn't want to burden me, knowing how hard I worked and how little he could contribute. It takes time to settle into a strange place when you have so much to learn, says Dolma. I note his growing self-confidence once he got his driver's license and his bellman position. Dolma confides that the first years she was here, she cried every day, as she missed her home and her family. We both look at Nima and Dolma's husband, Grant, deep in conversation. Be proud of him, she says. Once his English improves and he meets more people, life will get easier for both of you.

We say good-bye to our friends and move on. The fair is crowded with ethnically Asian, geographically Himalayan attendees, with a wide range of locals mixed among them. As I sit on the roots of an oak tree and slather on sunscreen, Nima tells me that the fairgrounds looks like

Nepal. I agree, for even the sun burns as if we are at altitude.

While we wander among stalls, Nima scans the crowd for friends. When he stops to look at the musical instruments, I look over the clothing. Nima waves to a friend busy with a customer, who waves back. While I skim through books with photographs of Nepal, Nima joins a group of three Sherpas and talks. I move on to a booth of religious artifacts and wonder if Nima would approve of their sale. I want him to look at a *thangka*, a painting of a Buddha Shākyamuni framed in brocades, but he ignores me. When I start to barter, he grabs my elbow and we move on.

The aroma of *momos*, curries, and chai intoxicates me. People intoxicate Nima. He stops again to talk. The men shake hands and smile like they are old friends. Nima makes introductions. *Namaste*. We bow. While the men talk in Sherpa, I pass by Guatemalan, Mexican, and Indonesian imports and companies selling journeys to everywhere, including to your inner self with the help of a psychic healer or palm reader or tarot card diviner. Just as Nima catches up with me, he recognizes the woman in the next booth.

"*Namaste*, Arlene. Remember me?" She draws a blank. "Nima Sherpa. We trekked together in 1983 to Kanchenjunga." The book *Annapurna: A Woman's Place* lies propped up on a stack of books. Arlene Blum is its author. Arlene led the first American and all-woman ascent of Annapurna I, the tenth-highest mountain, in 1978. Her book partially inspired my trip to Nepal. Arlene acknowledges that she and Nima were both younger in 1983, which is why she did not recognize him. He introduces us. I want to share with her how she helped to bring Nima and me together, but friends swamp Arlene, so we drop ten dollars into the jar to support her women's projects in Nepal and move on.

What an interesting life. I want to be like Arlene, I say to Nima, independent, courageous, and committed to a cause.

But you are like Arlene, says Nima. You are both tall, big-boned, and strong.

Drawn to the shade of oaks, Nima and I sit on the grass and watch Indian dancers on stage tell stories with the supple grace of their bodies, their gold and colored-silk costumes a luxurious counterpoint to the hippie/ yuppie inhabitants of Berkeley. Throughout the festival, the dancers, musicians, writers, poets, and storytellers entertain us. Nima tells me how happy he is to be at this festival, suggests I go do what I want, and disappears into the Himalayan diaspora.

Come early evening, Nima returns to Cinda's. After being surrounded all day by Nepalese, Bhutanese, Tibetans, and Sherpas, he cannot stop beaming. I reach for the suntan lotion. Nima has had an especially bright day.

In mid-May, the city of Beverly Hills gave preliminary approval for the hotel project to proceed, with construction to start in June. The project team is elated. News coverage has been lined up for the groundbreaking at the Beverly Hills Hotel. Everyone here supports the project. Slaps on the back go around. The contractors don protective gear and reach for their hammers. The old dowager's facelift begins. The energy of the project team changes, as we transition from ideas and drawings to tangible activities. This positive momentum carries us into our next phase: construction. Scaffolding and tarps surround the structure. Fencing surrounds the site. Demolition begins. After wheels are hosed off and cargo covered, trucks exit under palms, loaded with hotel-room walls that heard stories now never to be told.

With the hotel now under construction, Nima knows I'll be busy, and he wants to be busy too.

I like to be busy, says Nima, who now juggles his work as a bellman in a downtown hotel, his office plant maintenance job, and studies with a private tutor to improve his English pronunciation.

I am not just busy. I am overwhelmed. After the initial euphoria of the hotel starting construction, my hours are longer than ever. I try to relax when I can, like dinner tonight with Nima followed by a stroll out to the pier at sunset, but fail. I continue to put everything work-related first; the business of our lives second; and Nima, third. I have stopped cooking. So has Nima. Our schedules often conflict, so it's not unusual for us to spend evenings alone. Nima wants to spend time together. It's been two months since we were in Berkeley. I tell him I'm too busy. He tells me that I'm always busy, but wonders if what I am busy at is important. So do I. That evening I book an inn at Pine Cove, a mountain town above Palm Springs.

On Saturday morning in August, Nima and I sit on the deck of our cabin and watch the sun come up behind the San Jacinto Mountains. I appreciate that Nima insisted I take a few days off. He's right. I need to enjoy life more. In the cool mountain air, I am warmed by the sun and by Nima's ginger-pepper tea.

We hike ten miles through firs, manzanita, and oaks, among rock outcroppings and slides of boulders, in and out of the sun. I shed self, or rather, the baggage of self. It is too heavy to carry up mountainsides. Like Nima, I have learned to enjoy hiking uphill. The focused effort is a good busy, without the distractions, personalities, and politics of my job. I respond to the earth's terrain as I feel my way toward equilibrium. I respond to the atmosphere, breathing deeply on steep ascents and relaxing on the level. I lighten, as the rarified air cleanses me of toxic thoughts and actions. We move up at a steady pace, with brief stops for water and to enjoy the view. We don't linger. A sustained effort is easier than the stop and go. A sustained effort begets energy. I think about my life in Los Angeles. No wonder I am always exhausted.

To hike uneven terrain requires the earth and me to work together. In the shade of trees, loam cushions my step. My body welcomes earth's gentle side. We stop to pick berries. The earth provides. Stones become steps. Pebbles roll underfoot. My mind recognizes the precariousness of existence. I climb among boulders. I reach to rocks for handholds. My spirit trusts the earth to lead me.

"This looks like Lumding, the other side of the mountain," says Nima, as we look across high-altitude pasture framed by boulders, pine, and low scrub. Fed by multiple creeks, hundreds of wildflowers bloom among ferns. Shooting stars, wild geraniums, butter-and-eggs, Indian paintbrush, purple asters, and yellow lilies. Nima reminisces about his summer home where his family took their animals to high pasture. They had no luxuries, only what was needed: fresh cream, milk, cheese, wild vegetables in season, a root that burns your tongue, wild fruits like kiwi, strawberries in April, fern heads in May, and blackberries all summer. "One day, I'll take you, Sherpani."

We sit on a log to rest. I look at the wildflowers before me. I focus on their shape, color, petals, stamens, leaves, all individual traits. I see an honor in each and a beauty in the whole; a composition that comes of diversity, counterpoint, community. I recall the log bench I sat on in Bhutan the day I trekked alone up to the monastery. I recall my uncertainty and how I had wished for the long view. I turn around and look toward Nima, then past him toward mountains that fade into lighter and lighter shades of purple. I have begun to answer my questions. I married Nima. Change scares me less. When you listen to your heart, all is possible. Passion and commitment lend clarity.

As I squint into the sun, Nima takes my hand. A buck stands regally, sideways to us with his head turned so we see both his elegant crown and white rump. He remains motionless, while a doe feeds. We too remain still. This is all. The earth speaks to us of the now, of love.

Our weekend in Pine Cove, and our return to Los Angeles, makes us even more ready to return to Nepal. After working his hotel job for six months, Nima's hour-long commute to downtown has begun to frustrate him. When he walks in one evening in October, something far worse has Nima in an uncharacteristic rage.

"Downtown is like hell!" shouts Nima. "We need to move from this terrible city."

I ask what happened. For a time he just sits. He has been so excited about his job and working with his friend Hollywood. Nima tells me how he sees so many terrible things at night while he drives guests around downtown in the shuttle van. Once, after he dropped four men off at a restaurant and waited for the light to turn green at Figueroa, several gangs of men came around the corner clubbing each other with big sticks. He pauses between words, as if burdened by them. Terrible. Blood. Violence.

Hate. He was afraid they'd come after him. Nima takes a deep breath, as if at altitude, then whispers, "Last night, while I waited at a stop sign, a guy stuck a gun in my window."

I gasp. Why haven't I heard these stories? All I hear about are the nice people he meets and the fun he has working with Hollywood. He never told me about the dangers. I feel fierce, like a mother protecting her cub. I want him to quit. I want to leave Los Angeles. Now. I want details.

"He kept the gun in my face, leaned in the window, and told me to get out of my car." The culture of Los Angeles has seeped into Nima, for he now knows the allure of possessions. "He wanted my car! I punched him and drove away. Fast! Through red lights. Between cars. Everything!" His rage quiets. "I want to go back to Nepal."

Nima punched a guy with a gun. With a gun! Smart or stupid? Fortunately, it worked. Two years of memories race before me. I love him, depend on his wisdom, and appreciate his endless joy. His car is of little value. Nima, however, has become priceless.

"What else haven't you told me, Nima?"

"Nothing else." I don't believe him, and he knows it. "Nothing, Sherpani." Being a bellman and van driver for a second-class hotel is not worth him getting shot. I suggest he find a new job. Nima is defiant. "But I want to work with Hollywood!"

"And I want you to live!"

Joshua Tree National Monument is our spiritual landscape in America. This time, Nima and I came to say good-bye to a landscape that helped bring clarity to our lives. Nima and I are moving to Michigan in a month, in early January. My firm has decided to open a Detroit office to service two major contracts recently awarded, and I have been asked to manage one account. While I do not want to move back, I do not want to stay in Los Angeles with Nima working downtown, and any other alternative is too great an effort. I agreed to go. I know we will not stay long, for Nima and I are ready to migrate. Michigan will be a default, a stop along the way for two nomads seeking new surroundings.

Nima and I discussed the pros and cons of moving. We both had our doubts, but weighed them against the positives. Family would be nearby, and we could get to know nieces and nephews, husbands and wives, and become reacquainted with siblings and my parents. Family is important to both Nima and me. After the gun scare, a smaller, safer community, like Ann Arbor, appeals to us. And both of us feel ready for change.

The desert wind is fierce today, so we choose the more protected landscape of Hidden Valley to hike. We slip through a slot between stones, hidden behind boulders. It is said that cattle rustlers used this natural pen of stones to hide herds stolen from ranchers. People have lived on this land for over five thousand years, and I wonder aloud how each used this enclosure. Nima knows. As a temple, he tells me. Towering red rocks encircle us, like the menhirs of Stonehenge, but with only one way out. It is a sanctuary, a place of refuge from the wind. There is a comfort in a single point of entry. We do not have to watch our backs. Like in a cave, the earth protects us, shelters us. Perhaps that is the draw, the attraction to this valley. When we have fears, we seek refuge, and instinctively know when we find it.

Mark and Sandy have joined us. As we sit on sun-warmed rocks, I take out our picnic lunch. Mark opens his jackknife to cut cheese and salami. Sandy unwraps the crackers. Nima peels oranges. I open a bag of gorp and pass it around. Mark can't believe we are moving and tells Nima that he'll miss him. Nima says he'll miss Mark and their mountain hikes. Sandy asks about career opportunities after this new account is finished. I tell her we can always return.

Our dream is to start a trekking company, I say to Mark and Sandy, with the goal of getting Nima to Nepal more often, and myself on occasion, and to keep both of us more in touch with Nima's family. I do not share my other plans. I want to change my career, do something less corporate and more creative, something that reaches others, something I can feel passionate about. I want to write.

A cloud covers the sun. My friends wonder about winter and how I'll survive after living in Southern California for ten years. So do I, I tell them. I worry about going home to Michigan. I have changed. Nima tells me that my family will always like me no matter what. I smile. But will your family like me? I say to Nima.

Nima too is going home. We will return to Nepal in March for our second wedding—a Buddhist ceremony with Nima's friends and family in attendance—a trek through the Solukhumbu, and a visit to Chhuserma, where Nima's family lives. Ever since the delicious Chinese dinner with John and Dora, Nima and John have been quietly planning a trek to the Everest region of Nepal. I have been planning a wedding. Until Nima's conditional residency was approved last September, he could not leave the country.

My family will like you, Sherpani.

Mark wants to come and asks Nima about the four-week itinerary. Intense when interested in something, his questions keep coming. Happy to talk about Nepal, Nima stands ready to answer. With Mark and Sandy, Nima shares the details of sites we'll see in Kathmandu, on our trek, and during the planned family visit on our way down the mountain. He mentions the wedding, but gives no details.

I can't take that much time off work, says Mark. Maybe next time.

Sunday morning, an owl's mournful call wakes me. I rise to a chorus of birds before sunrise, in spite of the fact that the coyotes' howls and a relentless rain kept me awake much of the night. Nima slept through it all, and is still sleeping. So are Mark and Sandy. I climb a nearby ridge and sit on a russet stone lit by the first rays of sun. After rain and wind, the desert skies are clear, my vista long. I know where I am going. I look down at a puddle of water cradled by rock. I am mirrored. I shed self. Body. Mask. I have changed, but not all I want to. I seek evolution. In the water, I see an endless sky. And I see me. To return to Michigan is to go home. I made the right decision.

To gain clarity, I must return to the source.

Before we leave for Michigan, a Sherpani named Lhamo calls to introduce herself and tells Nima how excited she is to have another Sherpa in the area. We will live in Ann Arbor, a university town halfway between my office in Detroit and my parents' new home on Crooked Lake. Lhamo and Brad, her American husband, have two children. From Lhamo, we hear about Gelek Rinpoche, who runs the Jewel Heart Buddhist temple in Ann Arbor; we learn of a small Nepalese community; and we receive an invitation to *Losar* at a Tibetan doctor's home. We leave California in January 1994 excited about our new life and a community we can attach ourselves to as soon as we arrive. It seems an auspicious beginning, for a week later, on January 17, 1994, the magnitude 6.7 Northridge earthquake hits southern California, killing seventy-two people, injuring over nine thousand, and causing a couple billion dollars in damage. In the Midwest, we are safe. A week later, we are not so sure.

Doubts about our move begin to surface when the temperature over a two-week period hits a high of -25, or -55 degrees Fahrenheit with the windchill. Two feet (0.6 m) of snow covers the ground, and it is still snowing. Nima and I bundle up in all the cold-weather clothes we own to brave the weather and scrape ice off the windshield of my car so I can drive to work in a blizzard. His breath clouds his face as he tells me how much colder Michigan is than Mount Everest. They climbed in spring when there was sun. Plus, carrying loads makes you hot, says Nima. And even stormy nights on Everest weren't this cold.

While Nima is home in our Ann Arbor apartment with the heat on, I am at the Detroit office with my coat on. The city lost a major transformer, so is on reduced power. In a vain attempt to heat the massive building, two semi-sized generators are parked behind it. All they do is keep the pipes from freezing. The inside temperature drops as the week goes by. By midweek, the inside temperatures are barely in the fifties. We wear coats, hats, and gloves. In poor, mismanaged Detroit, unplowed thoroughfares freeze the ability to do business, and yet I still must go to work.

My twin sister, Caryn, and her husband, Denny, decide that immersion is the best way for Nima and me to adapt to Michigan's winter wonderland, and invite us to an ice festival in Plymouth, twenty-five miles northeast of Ann Arbor. If you live in the north, my sister tells me, you have to get out and enjoy it. In preparation for the occasion, Nima and I buy down coats, heavy gloves, and face masks. The temperature at night is –32 degrees Fahrenheit without the windchill. A surprising number of people mill about the town square, which glimmers with ice sculptures lit by colored lights. When Nima tries to photograph the sculptures, his camera shutter freezes and his fingers show signs of frostbite, so he gives up. The snow crunches beneath our boots in a sign of resistance, as if it too knows that air pockets warm one in this weather. Not one to fight windmills, wise Denny suggests the bar.

Denny wears plaid flannel shirts. He has light blue eyes and sandy curls and is erudite on topics that interest him. He applies his agile mind to testing components for an auto-industry manufacturer. Caryn met Denny at work; they married and settled near Ann Arbor to raise three children. Caryn slowly finished college, while doing childcare in her home, before receiving her teaching certificate. Blonde with blue eyes, she and I have a family resemblance, but people never guess us to be twins. After sharing a bedroom for seventeen years, we have seldom talked since I left home. As time went by, our differences expanded. It will be good to get reacquainted.

The heat inside the bar burns our cheeks. Our fingers ache from the sudden change in temperature. The smell of wet wool, beer, burgers, and cigarettes reminds me that I've come home. I can barely stand to breathe, but resign myself to the fact that to live here, I will have to get used to the smoke, the cold, the snow, and the—How did I ever think I could live here again?

Within weeks of our arrival, Lhamo Sherpa hosts a party to welcome us. Her guests are Nepalese, Indian, Tibetan, and Gelek Rinpoche, a reincarnated lama from Tibet, who heads the Jewel Heart temple in Ann Arbor. I feel myself drawn to him. When he motions for me to sit down at the kitchen table with him, I sense he is a man you do not refuse. He is kind and curious. He tells me how he gave up monk's robes once he arrived in America and now dresses in black pants and turtlenecks to make himself more approachable to Americans. His shaved head and round face glow. His eyes are mischievous and intense. He holds my gaze and asks how Nima and I met. I tell him our story. How I grew up here and have family nearby.

"Are you a Buddhist?" asks Gelek Rinpoche.

"I don't know," I say. Gelek Rinpoche reaches into his pocket, takes my hand between his, and drops a weight into my palm.

"Welcome," says Gelek Rinpoche. He squeezes my hand into a fist. "Welcome home."

I open my fist. The Buddha rests in my palm. He is small, bronze, and seated on a lotus. Time will determine our relationship.

Nima will leave for Nepal in mid-March, a week ahead of me. He will look for a job after he returns. To keep busy, he signs up for a class on computer keyboarding at the local community college. He begins to talk about going back to school. The first few weeks of class, he comes home excited and practices when he can. Then he leaves for class, but no longer speaks of it or practices. Finally, Nima confesses that he no longer goes to class and has been driving around just long enough for me to think he went. His teacher ridiculed him when she couldn't understand his English and called him stupid for not knowing basic computer terms. Not one to disappoint, he lied. I am mad that he lied, but more angry with the school and the teacher.

Now bored, but for television, Nima demands my constant attention. With little overtime required and few other distractions, we have time for each other for the first time since our marriage. We share dinner and a movie, or prowl the used bookstores of Ann Arbor for anything Himalayan, or spend weekends with family in Chelsea or Saline or Sutton's Bay. We cook together, especially after the discovery of an Indian market with spices, basmati rice, and a large stone mortar and pestle. While Nima grinds fresh spices and I chop vegetables, we dream of starting our own trekking company. We both want an excuse to move on. After living and working in Chicago and Los Angeles, I find Ann Arbor quaint, Detroit depressing, and both provincial. I have been on the West Coast too long. I do not belong here. Neither does Nima. In California, with its significant Asian population, Nima did not stand out. He does here, and often comments on his singularity.

One evening after dark, I hear Nima drive up to the back door, then fumble with his key. I unbolt the door, ready to give him a hug, but instead tense up at the look of terror on his face. His whole body shakes. I pull him inside, slam the door, and lock it.

Someone tried to run me off the freeway!

What happened?

They had been tailing Nima for some time, so he got off at an exit hoping to lose them, but they followed. Scared to go home, he drove to the police station. When he pulled into the parking lot, whoever it was took off. Unsure who he could trust, Nima didn't go into the police station. He waited alone in the parking lot for twenty minutes, and then drove home.

"I want to go home to Nepal," says Nima.

Nima now talks constantly about our trip. We both count the days. Our wedding will be in Bodhnath on March 29, 1994, just over three years from the day I met Nima. Nima will leave early to make the arrangements. Our trek will take us through the Solukhumbu to Kala Pattar, a peak with close-up views of Mount Everest. Nima's older brother, Tshiring Tendi, will be *sirdar*, and Nima Nuru, his youngest brother, will come as a guide. Our friend John, who first suggested this trip to Nima, plans to celebrate his seventy-third birthday climbing Everest, and has enlisted his two sons, Allan and Thatcher, to come with him, plus their friend Dean. Jules, who wouldn't miss our Buddhist wedding for anything, will bring his friend Yvonne and her nephew, Chad. Paul, who was on our Annapurna trek, will return to witness the culmination of our romance.

Nima, who so wanted to come to the United States, now wants to go home. America was not what Nima had imagined it to be. Life is not so easy. Americans are not always welcoming. Jobs can be scarce. English words come fast, sentences come more slowly, and sometimes, comprehension does not come at all. Nima has "family," but not family. Lost in the Midwest with no mountains to show him the way, Nima is aimless and uncertain. He needs to reconnect to his family and the familiar, even if only for a short visit. To return to Nepal is to go home. He made the right decision.

To gain clarity, Nima must return to the source.

rain

March – April 1994

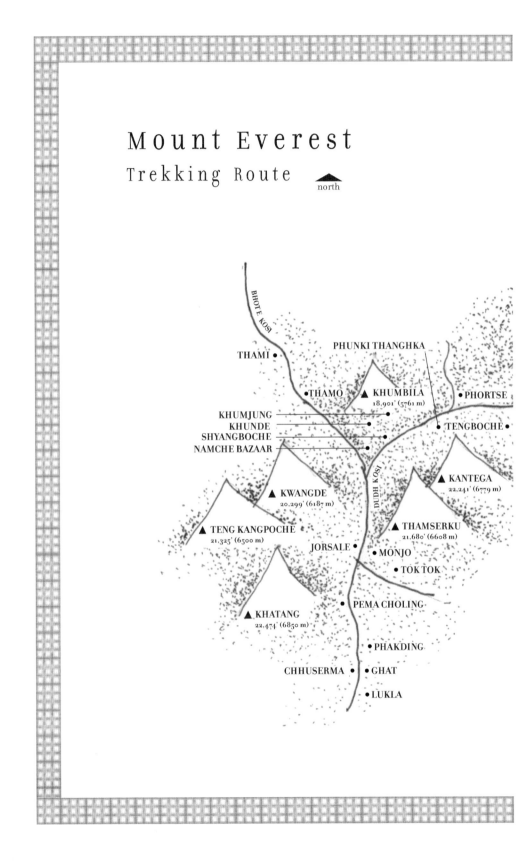

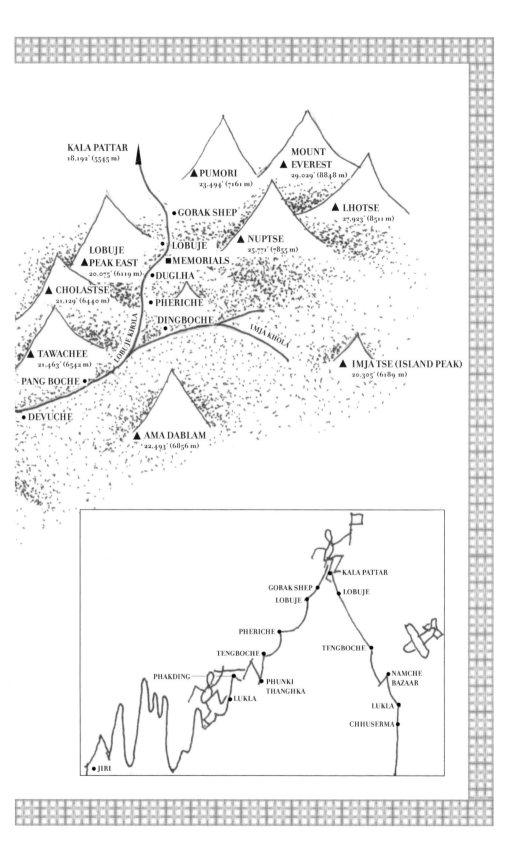

A yak-tail dance finalizes your marriage.

—*Mingma Futi*

A FARMWOMAN NAMED CHANG DOLMA wanted to make a great offering to the Buddha. She asked the local king for his permission, and her wish was granted. The king granted her land the size of a water buffalo skin. Chang Dolma's devotion to the Buddha was far larger, so she cut the skin into one long thread and made a circle outlining her land. The king rewarded Chang Dolma for her ingenuity. She built a shrine with the help of two water buffalo by day and the spirits each night. After she died, her four sons of four fathers from her previous four marriages completed the *chörten*. Her four sons were later reincarnated as great disciples of Buddhism. One of them was Guru Rinpoche, also known as Padmasambhava, who introduced Buddhism to the people of Himalaya.

Chang Dolma attained Buddhahood. Her *chörten* is known as Bodhnath.

The morning of my first day back in Kathmandu, Nima takes me to Bodhnath to do *pūjā*, personal acts of prayers and offerings. As we stand at the *kani*, or entry gate that marks an entrance to a sacred space, a small street lined with tourist shops rises toward the great *chörten* of Bodhnath. I remember the joy I felt when Nima brought me here the morning after our first night together. I am happy our wedding will be within the aura of this sacred space.

At the stone-paved circus of the *chörten*, Nima and I turn left to begin our *kora*, and walk clockwise around the shrine in silence. We spin copper prayer wheels set into niches around the *chörten*'s plinth. Two pilgrims ahead of us do the same, and in added acts of devotion, one spins a hand-held prayer wheel in his left hand, while the other counts prayer beads. Young monks race past us, as if they have somewhere to go. A tourist stops to photograph the scene. We walk around him and back to the wheels.

Bodhnath is Nepal's religious, tourist, and commercial center for all things Tibetan Buddhist. As we circle with the *chörten* on our right, on our left we pass a pastel array of shops, temples, and teahouses filled with colorful distractions: Tibetan rugs, incense and prayer flags for sale, maps, postcards and film, fabrics and shoes, *momos* and chai, international tourists, devotees who perform prostrations, and monks and nuns who send out prayers for us all. Nima and I do the minimum three revolutions of the *chörten*. Each prayer wheel we spin holds a written roll of prayers numbering in the thousands. Our lips move, *Om Mani Padme Hum*. Our vibrations mix with the vibrations of others here today, recognize those who have come before, and anticipate those who will come after. The power of a *kora* protects, purifies, and fulfills us as we cycle through our lives.

Om Mani Padme Hum. Om Mani Padme Hum. Om Mani Padme Hum.

Our marriage will succeed. I feel certain. Millions of prayers were just issued. Nima squeezes my hand, as if to let me know he too believes. Our smiles for each other vibrate with the blessings of Bodhnath.

Nima suggests we go pick up my wedding dress. Near the entrance to Bodhnath, we enter a shop whose ceiling is barely my head height. Two Tibetans stand behind the counter before walls lined with bolts of wool, silk, brocade, and cotton. The shopkeeper recognizes Nima and fetches a package, unwraps it, and holds up an *engi* for my review.

It's gorgeous, Nima, I say.

I love the chrysanthemum pattern, but olive green and pale pink? I'll look like a corpse! I try it on behind a cloth the shopkeepers hold up to offer me some privacy. I step out from behind the calico.

Raamro, says a Nepalese man as he enters.

Zemu, says the Tibetan shopkeeper.

Beautiful, says Nima. Silk brings out a woman's radiance in any color.

At another shop, Nima buys felted Tibetan boots that are tied on at the top. I select a *metil*, the striped apron worn by married women, and a *tsering kinkhap*, the long-life brocade hat with two large flaps and two short flaps, all trimmed in fur. The hat looks handsome on the Sherpas. I look like an animal long extinct.

You look lovely, says Nima. My Sherpani.

Nima Nuru's apartment is in the Lazimpat neighborhood of Kathmandu. As we open the door, I realize this is the same apartment Nima brought me to when I first met his family. Lustful memories come flooding back, and I fight to push them away. Now is not the time. Tonight, I am meeting my in-laws. I explain to Nima how nervous I am, how I don't know what to say, and how I worry no one will understand me. He tells me it's easy. Just smile. I follow him into a living room filled with family. I smile.

Tashi Delek, Tsham, says Nima's youngest brother, Nima Nuru, whom I met here in Kathmandu two years ago. He has matured and exhibits a confidence that comes with knowing something about the world.

Tashi Delek. I bow. To say hello, the Sherpa use the Nepalese greeting *Namaste* in mixed company, but among Tibetans and Sherpas, they use *Tashi Delek.*

Nima makes the introductions. Pala, who sits cross-legged on the floor, is handsome with gray hair, bright eyes, and a lean frame. He leaps up to greet me. Tears come to his eyes as he places his hands together and bows toward me. He appears kind, gentle, and gracious. Not what I had expected. Mama, who has more to lift, rises slowly. Her hair is wrapped in a colorful wool scarf that she fingers often in her nervousness. Mama will not look right at me. Instead, she takes my hands and refuses to let go as she pulls me down beside her onto the sofa. From my seat, I meet everyone else.

Chaa. Iron. Ang Chokpa, the oldest sister, comes in with chai, fills my cup to the brim, and serves it to me with two hands. Attractive, with dark eyes and high cheekbones, she enters a room with a presence that cannot be ignored. As she greets me, I recognize her husky voice from the cassette tape we received last year. *Sa.* Earth. The entrance of Mingma Futi, the second-oldest sister, fills the room with joy. Soft and less sculpted than her older sister, she greets me with a smile. Her laughter and conversation echo around us as she serves a plate of tea biscuits. *Me.* Fire. Kandu, who is fourteen years younger than Nima, refills our teacups. Her movement is boyish, like one active in the outdoors. She nods to me, as we met at dinner two years ago. Her stare is bold, and I feel her gaze. *Shing.* Wood. Fumu, the youngest sister, is shy and quiet, and drifts out of the kitchen only once to meet me. *Chhu.* Water. Lama Nawang, a monk and a cousin, is short and plump. Nima tells me he will preside at our wedding, along with an older monk. While everyone else talks in Sherpa, Lama Nawang chants quiet prayers.

To make astrological calculations, the Buddhist Sherpas use a *kham*, or one of the five elements (*shing*: wood, *sa*: fire, *me*: earth, *chaa*: iron, *chhu*: water), along with one of twelve animal years (Rat, Cow, Tiger, Rabbit, Dragon, Snake, Horse, Sheep, Monkey, Bird, Dog, Pig) for a unique sixty-year lunar calendar. A natal element and animal represent each of us. For Nima's family, I have guessed at them. Nima, he is a rabbit. I am a dragon. Both of us are water. The elements fuse and sustain everything in the universe, and are the natural forces of transformation. Dynamic, they constantly interact and change. Water is a winter sign; wood, spring; fire, summer; and iron, autumn. Earth is the in-between, the all-encompassing, the foundation for the rest of us. Nima is my foundation. Nima is earth. I have recast him.

The two cute boys peeping around the corner are introduced as Bai Tshiring and Nawang Tshiring, the sons of Nima's older brother, Tshiring Tendi. At the sound of their names, they enter. *Tashi Delek, Uru.* At age four and a half, Nawang Tshiring stands taller and looks more serious. Two-year-old Bai Tshiring shows a curiosity when he sits before me and listens while Nawang Tshiring struggles to ask me questions in English.

I admire their round faces, dark eyes, and chapped cheeks. They look endearing in a ragamuffin sort of way, dressed in mismatched clothes washed and mended to make the best possible impression. When a man enters the room, the boys run to him. Tshiring Tendi, the boys' father and Nima's older brother, is introduced as "the one I told you so much about." I want to stand to greet him, but Mama still holds my hand. He nods in understanding. When he smiles, his sculpted cheeks accent dark eyes that shine with a brilliance reserved for the blessed. His lean frame moves with the grace of a body in constant motion and is beautiful to watch.

What begins as an intimate introduction to Nima's immediate family soon becomes a reunion. From out of the bedrooms, kitchen, hall, court-yard, down the street, and across town come cousins, nephews, nieces, aunts, uncles, and relatives once or twice or thrice removed, to welcome their new sister-in-law to the family. As I listen to them talk in a language I do not understand, I recall an afternoon I spent with Nima on the other side of the door curtain following our visit to Bodhnath. The sun poured in the window, and we poured out our love, spilling caresses and kisses all over each other. I felt warm, content, and at peace. That afternoon, I had looked around this room and compared my happiness in this Third World apartment in Lazimpat with my First World experiences. There was no comparison. Happiness had nothing to do with material things. It was inside us. Inside me. Inside Nima. His gift to me is happiness.

Tea is poured often; biscuits and mandarins are served. The Sherpas talk. I smile. I wish I could understand what they say, especially when a group of them turn around to look at me, and then turn back to talk. I sit and smile, and Mama holds my hand. Nima is in and out of the room, excited to see so many relatives in one place. Many came down from the mountains to attend our wedding. Nima is the first in his family to marry a foreigner. While I am exotic here, Nima is in his element.

At dusk, Nima tells his family that we must leave to dine with our trek-king group. His family looks disappointed. I am ready to go—exhausted from the flight that arrived in Kathmandu only yesterday; overwhelmed by my new family; and unsure about what to expect at my upcoming wedding. Each time I have asked Nima for details, he's told me he's taking care of it. For water dragon Caryl, who is energetic and organized, lack of control is difficult.

Our trekking clients receive the same non-answer. All we know is what is on the wedding invitation that Nima passes out over dinner. Two auspicious symbols, a treasure vase decorated with an endless knot, are printed on the red invitation. The treasure vase symbolizes the gods of wealth and holds the holy water of longevity. The endless knot represents the endless cycle of rebirth. Were we husband and wife in a past life? In matters as important as a wedding, Nima's brother Nima Nuru consults a lama, who divined the date for our wedding with the help of astrological charts. March 29 was a good date; not the best date, but a date that fit in with our scheduled trek. For water rabbit Nima, known for his calm, easygoing nature, that would be good enough.

The morning of our wedding, Nima and I escort our trekking group to Bodhnath and its *chörten*, which looks powerful in the soft light of a gray sky, its white dome luminous. Nima and I perform our *pūjā* and walk the *kora* three times. After Nima leaves to complete our wedding preparations, the rest of us have the morning to explore Bodhnath. Before a corner shop, natural incense of leaves or ground powders in earthen colors are piled high in burlap bags folded back at the top. Prayer flags in all sizes for sale in strings of blue, white, red, green, and yellow spill out of an adjacent storefront. Bronze Buddhas, Tārās, bodhisattvas sit peacefully in the windows of several shops, while the wrathful gods who brandish swords hide in the dark interiors and dare you to enter. Down a narrow passage, thick Tibetan carpets hang from the eaves. Inside, the owner lifts one after another from his stack on the floor in hopes of a sale. We have only come to look. *Thangkas* fill every inch of wall space in another shop. Goods of practical use—baskets and brooms of reed, and buckets and flip-flops in plastic—spill out into the street.

I grow anxious when the hour of our wedding comes and goes and there is no sign of Nima. I still have to dress. The trekkers work to calm me. What if he doesn't show up? I leave the others to do a *kora*. Spin. I know he loves me. Spin. Damn him. Spin. Nima, where are you? Spin. The repetition begins to calm me. I focus. I walk. I quiet. Spin.

The book given me by the Hindu professor from Kirtipur regarding Sherpa marriage customs describes a series of required events that could last years before a couple is completely married. Our wedding events are to take place over an afternoon. According to the professor's book, the first step is when the boy's family proposes their son's marriage to the girl's family. If the girl's family accepts their gift of *chhang*, a homemade alcoholic beverage, the marriage events continue. While the community knows of the engagement, neither the boy nor the girl are yet bound to fidelity. Nima and I are way past this stage.

At the second stage, the extended family bedecks and bejewels themselves, and then the bridegroom's party travels in procession to the bride's home to each present a gift of *khata*, a blessing scarf, and *chhang*. The wedding date is determined. The couple continues to live apart. Our families have not yet met, may never meet, our wedding date is today, and we live together. Missed again.

The third stage is scheduled once the couple can support themselves. Property and gifts are exchanged, and the wife is ornamented in jewels in a conspicuous display of her wealth. A lama performs the ceremony. Everyone celebrates. I have no family here. No jewels. The professor's book tells me little about the ceremony other than there are offerings, recitations, blessings, *tikas*, warnings about being faithful to each other, a special dance called a *sillu chumbu*, whatever that means, and a procession where all my wealth is carried by unmarried girls to our new home. That will be difficult.

"Caryl, come quickly," says Nima. "The Sherpanis are asking for you."

"Where have you been?" I give him no chance to answer. "This is my wedding too, Nima. Can't you tell me what's happening? And when?"

"*Zendi*. Wedding, in Sherpa," says Nima. "I want it to be a surprise. Follow me." I start to speak, but think better of it as we race down the street and pass through the *kani* into the enclosed plaza of the Sherpa

Sewa Kendra, their community center. Stone steps lead to large doors that stand open. It looks like a temple, but is secular. Nima and I enter. The day is cool. The hall has no heat. High windows and bare fluorescent strip lights cast a greenish glow over a dim, cavernous room of painted cement with wood columns. Furnishings are nonexistent but for a single dais and low benches along one wall.

"This is my friend Dekyi from Lukla," says Nima, as we enter a room off the main hall. "Go with her." Dekyi smiles.

As I follow her, I notice Dekyi's waist-length black hair is partially clipped into a barrette. She looks young, probably because she barely reaches my shoulders. She wears a blue silk brocade *engi* and a white sweater. She leads me to the next room, filled with women. My wedding dress hangs in the corner. Dekyi motions toward a stool. I sit. When I ask what happens next, she smiles. My inquiry about when I change my clothes solicits another smile. She doesn't understand a word I say. Dekyi smiles once more and leaves the room. I look over at Nima's older sisters, Mingma Futi and Ang Chokpa, in hopes of direction. They acknowledge me and then ignore me, busy with their own preparations. I want to participate, but no one speaks English, and I don't speak Sherpa. The Sherpanis come and go. Every time someone enters the room, I think something will happen. Nothing does. I am cold. I am bored. And once everyone leaves, I am alone. Some celebration. I look at my watch. Noon. I am two hours late for my wedding.

Although there were no details on the wedding ceremony in the professor's book, it did shed light on Sherpa relationships. Polyandrous and polygamous marriages were once practiced to prevent the breakup of family property or to support widowed relations. Divorce is allowed by simple mutual consent, finalized when a thread, held by the husband and one of the wife's relations, is broken. A relationship within the *ru*, or paternal clan, is not permitted. Nonexclusive sexual relationships are tolerated until the final stage of marriage. A couple may have children at any time after their engagement. I find the acknowledgement of human nature in these traditions commendable.

After fifteen minutes alone, I get up to look for Nima. The first room I enter is a crude kitchen. Blackened with soot, the room devours light like Sherpas devour food. A large adobe stove rises from the center of the room. Fire logs spill out from one corner. Piles of vegetables, potatoes, and meat; bags of rice and spices; cartons of beer and Johnnie Walker Black Label all stand at attention like guard dogs on either side of the assembly hall entrance. The cook and his helper enter and begin to arrange pots that lie scattered around the room.

Is this your wedding? asks the cook. I nod. How many people are coming? I ask. His arms reach wide. Many. It's Sherpa, he says.

The food stockpile suggests hundreds. Pleased to find someone who can tell me something, I sit down on a box in the corner.

Come. Come. *Engi*, says Ang Chokpa at the kitchen door.

The dressing room is filled with women changing clothes. As I begin to undress, I am overtaken by the Sherpanis. I am their doll to dress up. I give myself over, just like Kathmandu's Living Goddess, Kumari, whose feet never touch the floor, and who each day blesses her devotees from the upper window of her home, Kumari Bahal, at Durbar Square. Virginity is one of the Kumari's requirements; at menses, when she becomes impure, poor Kumari falls into former-goddess status, becoming an outcast unfit for marriage. And yet, many Hindu families wish for a daughter to be a goddess for the honor it brings them, even if transient. I am happy to not be Kumari.

The Sherpanis' strong, active hands make quick work of my transformation as they remove my American wardrobe and dress me up like them. Mingma Futi folds the collar of my silk blouse, or *raatuk*, over the V-collar of my *engi*, a sort of jumper that ties at the waist. Many hands tuck, fold, and pleat my *engi*. A cousin rolls back my sleeves. Everyone watches as I do my makeup. Each has thoughts about how I should do my hair. I wear it up in a knot at the nape of my neck. I put in pearl earrings. Ang Chokpa reaches around my waist to tie on the Sherpa symbol of wedlock, the apron, or *metil*. Once I am dressed, Mingma Futi pulls me back so the others can take a look at their handiwork. I hear praise in their voices, so I spin and pose and strut to make them happy. The Sherpanis clap and laugh at my runway antics. For a moment, I am one of them. Ang Chokpa asks the others a question. After receiving animated responses, she reaches behind her head and removes her long strand of ancient *zi* beads, coral, and pearls. She steps toward me and slips her entire bank account around my neck. Its weight pulls me forward. My responsibility for it rests heavy on my chest. Tradition suggests that a bride, or *nama*, should bring wealth to her family. I look like I do, even if borrowed for a day.

Zemu, says Ang Chokpa. Beautiful.

Dekyi enters with a black umbrella or *dug*. She tips it toward Mingma Futi, who ties a white silk *khata* to its top. The *dug*, one of the Eight Auspicious Symbols in Buddhism, protects one from the sun like the Buddhist doctrine protects one's spirit. Under the parasol held by Dekyi, we enter the main hall. Nima, the *magpa*, approaches his *nama* from the opposite side of the hall under the parasol's protection, escorted by Gyalbu, his cousin. A procession of family follows each of us. Nima looks regal in his sumptuous purple brocade *chhuba* tied with a fuchsia sash, and his *sogsha* hat with its wide brim and red fringe. As we cross the room to stand together before the monks, I become aware that my marriage is not only to Nima Gyalgen Sherpa, but to his culture.

Both Nawang Tshiring and Bai Tshiring, our young nephews, stand on the dais, as if waiting to receive us. At the back of the dais sits Lama Tenzing, who came from a monastery below Lukla and will perform the service. Next to him, Lama Nawang, Nima's cousin from Tengboche Monastery, will assist. Lama Tenzing looks ancient; his thin long face and sunken cheekbones suggest he holds the wisdom of past lives, and their burdens. Red glasses frame his gentle eyes and match his crimson silk brocade robes. Lama Nawang's bright face exudes a simple joy as he watches Nima and me approach. He wears a monk's simple cotton robes and sits lower on the dais than Lama Tenzing, before a table that holds their ritual instruments. As I move closer, I hear their chants.

Lama Tenzing holds a *dorje*, a symbolic thunderbolt, in his right hand and a *drilbu*, or bell, in his left. In Tibetan Buddhism, the universe arises from the interplay of two energies or aspects, the masculine and the feminine. The *dorje*, which is male, symbolizes both the indestructible energy of the mind of Buddhas and the active aspect of compassion. The *drilbu*, symbol of wisdom, realization of emptiness, and mother of all things, is female. The two are inseparable; one is never found without the other. Only through their union within us is perfect realization attainable.

Nima and I step onto the dais. Lama Tenzing rises and walks over to us. From a brass plate held out to him by Lama Nawang, Lama Tenzing grabs a handful of rice and slowly funnels it from his fist out onto the floor to form a right-turning swastika. He repeats his actions and forms another beside the first. Lama Nawang covers each swastika with a square carpet. We sit on sacred space.

"That symbol means good luck, Sherpani," whispers Nima.

I look out over a low table that holds two china cups, a pitcher, and large bottles of San Miguel beer. Our guests are seated on cushions on the cement floor or on benches along the wall. Dekyi sits besides me, Gyalbu sits beside Nima, and both continue to hold the black umbrellas over our heads. Pala and Mama sit down beside Gyalbu and are followed by Nima's brothers. Ang Chokpa and Mingma Futi stand in for my family beside Dekyi.

"Family beside us ensures long life, happiness, and a good marriage," says Nima.

I would have liked my family here. They were invited, but other family commitments, finances, or frailties kept them from joining us. If they could experience the Sherpas, understand their culture, see Nima in his homeland, and witness the Himalaya, they might better understand my attraction to Nima. While they have learned to enjoy him, my relationship with him remains a mystery to them. At least John and his sons Thatcher and Allan, and their friend Dean, could join us, along with Paul, Jules, and Jules's friend Yvonne with her nephew Chad. Today, they are my family.

Phurba, a more distant cousin, blows the conch shell, or *thung*, to announce Buddha's teaching. The wedding service begins. Lama Tenzing lifts a silver pitcher, a *phumpa*, and stands before us. Nima cups his hands and Lama Tenzing fills them with *tru*, the holy water. Nima touches his forehead to his hands and splashes the water over his head. I repeat Nima's actions. Lama Tenzing chants and dips a peacock feather into the *phumpa*, then rains droplets of the holy water around us.

"To ensure a long life," whispers Nima. As I look out at an audience of well over a hundred guests, I pray I do nothing to offend or bring misfortune to this day. I want their acceptance, and their blessing.

As the monks move around us, they chant and wave ritual objects. I watch with fascination, thankful for the distraction, for my legs feel pierced by hundreds of needles from sitting cross-legged too long. The service continues. The monks chant. I no longer feel my legs. The monks chant. The nephews play on the stage. The audience whispers among themselves. The monks chant. Lama Tenzing stands before us with distant cousin Phurba, who holds a bowl of powdered pigment. As Lama Tenzing chants, Phurba leans over and presents the bowl to Nima, who dabs his finger with vermilion.

"Bow your head and remove your hat, Sherpani." Nima marks my forehead with a *tika*, and then his red finger traces a line across the center of my scalp. *Never underestimate the power of hallowed ground, a holy man, and vermilion.* The monks present me with the bowl, and I do the same for Nima.

"Are we married yet?" I ask.

"Almost, Sherpani."

Lama Tenzing chants. Phurba leans over with a bronze plate of butter. Lama Tenzing runs a line of butter across the center of Nima's head, and then does the same to me.

"Are we married yet?" I ask.

"Almost," says Nima. The monks chant. Nima's two older sisters stand. Mingma Futi fills Nima's cup to the brim with apple juice. Ang Chokpa places three dabs of butter and *tsampa* on its edge. Lama Tenzing offers Nima the cup with two hands. He sips. The monk offers it again. He sips. The monk offers it again. He sips. Nima offers the cup three times to the monk, who does not sip, but instead touches his fourth fingertip to the juice and flicks it three times in succession. The monks chant. Mingma Futi fills my cup to the brim with *chhang*. Ang Chokpa places three dabs of butter and *tsampa* on its edge. Lama Tenzing offers my cup to me. Thrice he offers and thrice I sip, and then I offer it to him. Again, our cups are filled to the brim. Nima offers me his cup. Thrice I sip.

"Same, Nima," says Ang Chokpa, who guides my hands. Thrice he flicks. Thrice I sip. The monks chant. Nima speaks to Ang Chokpa, and then to me.

"We are married, Sherpani," whispers Nima, as he leans back. "Remember. Sherpas don't kiss." We squeeze each other's hands and smile.

After our protectors, Gyalbu and Dekyi, each present us with a *khata*, the ceremonial scarf that demonstrates the pure heart of the giver to the recipient, Ang Chokpa and Mingma Futi are next in line. They offer us *khata* with two hands and bowed head, a blessing for a long life. Nima bows toward Ang Chokpa, and her *khata* slides over his head and onto his shoulders. Ang Chokpa fills his cup to the brim with juice. She is kind to Nima as he sips. I receive a *khata* next, and she fills my cup to the brim with *chhang*. Ang Chokpa raises the cup to my lips, tips it high, and pours the *chhang* into me. I cannot swallow fast enough and *chhang* runs down my chin, over my dress, and into my lap. Her eyes dance. So do Mingma Futi's. I anticipate the same. I vow to be ready to resist any more than a sip of *chhang*. I cannot. A Sherpani's tenacity exceeds even her mountain-climbing husband's.

Pala and Mama come forward, tearful and with shaking hands, to present *khata* and a blessing. Brothers and sisters follow, some gentle, others insistent. Our trekking group, who learn from watching the ritual, do the same. Jules is emotional and delighted. John congratulates us, excited to be part of our exotic happening. Thatcher jokes about the beer. Allan is kind. Dean remains solemn. Chad teases. Yvonne empathizes. Paul cannot believe he was with us at the beginning. And so goes the next hour of our wedding. Each guest presents us with *khata*, gives Nima an envelope, and then fills our cups. I sip thrice. They sip thrice. Some also honor our parents and Nima's siblings in this way. At each stage of the marriage, *chhang* is an essential part of the ceremony. After twenty guests, I no longer care that we share the same cup. After forty, I feel giddy. After sixty, I laugh at everything and am as persuasive with each guest as Ang Chokpa was with me. After eighty, I reek like a barmaid in a beer hall during the final minutes of Oktoberfest. After a hundred, the Sherpas all look alike. After a hundred and twenty, I am smashed. Nima, who doesn't drink alcohol, remains sober.

Distant cousin Phurba, who helped the lamas with the service, has the angular features of a lean man. Dressed in a white shirt and black vest that hangs loosely off his narrow shoulders, Phurba steps out into the center of the hall with a natural grace. The conch bellows. Cymbals crash together in a rhythm that resonates. Phurba picks up a black yak-tail whisk, or *sillu*, and begins to dance. Quick on his feet, he leaps and throws out his arms as he switches the *sillu* between hands. He spins and jumps, and the yak tail flies, and so does Phurba. The cymbals sound. The crowd shouts and demands more, and so he dances on for them, and for us. This ritual wedding dance is traditionally performed when the bride's inheritance is paid to the groom and she moves into his family's home, Nima tells me. As we did not go through the numerous stages of a Sherpa wedding, the Sherpas adapt their traditions. They intuitively understand the dynamic aspect of the universe—change. Through their observations of the sky, their intimate knowledge of the earth, and the continual transformation of the seasons, the Sherpas know change is a constant, and to evolve with it is to sustain.

"*Sillu chumbu*. A yak-tail dance finalizes your marriage," says Mingma Futi to Nima, who translates. "It's danced when the bride says farewell to her family and is given to the groom's family."

"Given?" I have to ask.

"Yes, Sherpani. Caryl Sherpa. Mine."

Mine? I look around at my family. This is going to be interesting.

As our guests line up for dinner, Ang Chokpa and Mingma Futi help me stand. After two hours of sitting, my legs are numb and my balance compromised by *chhang*. Nima and I are a remarkable sight, festooned

282

with a hundred-plus *khata* in shades of white, ivory, and pale yellow silk, a handsome Sherpa in complete control and his drunken American wife, who leans on him to remain upright.

Sherpa occasions are slow to unfold, revolve around food and dancing, and appear to have no one in charge. Jules laughs at the lack of order and tells us it's normal. Guests stop by to talk, but between their broken English and my inebriation, I understand little. Nima has no patience for translation. Besides, he likes the power knowledge gives him in Nepal, after two years of powerlessness in Los Angeles. In time, someone brings me food. I eat. When offered a drink, I refuse. Fortunately, in traditional Sherpa dances, we lock arms in a line, so others can hold me up. I do not dance long. Their steps are too complicated. Instead, I retreat to the bench with my fellow Americans, happy to watch the Sherpas celebrate our *zendi*.

"My family and friends say you are just like a Sherpani," says Nima.

I am honored. I am family. I have a headache. I had wanted to remember every detail of my Sherpa wedding. The next morning, I remember some of the wedding, little of the reception, and nothing of our nuptial night.

A Sherpa must retain his culture.
Best of luck to you both.
—*Sir Edmund Hillary*

O N THE FIRST MORNING of our honeymoon trek, we are
up before sunrise. After an early arrival at Kathmandu's Tribhuvan
International Airport for our flight to Lukla, the launching point of our
trek in the Solukhumbu, our trekking group waits outside the terminal.
No one is in the mood for the pandemonium within the old building
crowded with travelers, except for John, who goes in to look around. He
runs out to tell us that Hillary is inside. Nima expresses doubt.

"There's a big, tall man who sure looks like him," says John. "Come
quick!" He insists his boys follow. We all follow. Once inside, Sir Edmund
Hillary, who stands out above the shorter, slender Nepalese, is spotted
immediately. His gray hair curls over his wide forehead and softens his
long face and nose. His bushy eyebrows dance over animated eyes. John,
who at seventy-three figures he has no time to lose, walks over to Sir
Edmund and asks to have his photograph taken with him. Sir Edmund
Hillary nods in consent.

When Hillary asks John what brings him to Nepal, he points to Nima
and me, and tells Hillary about our wedding ceremony. John also asks
Hillary for a photograph with us. I sit next to Hillary, Nima is beside me,
and then Jules. As everyone takes our photo, guilt nudges at me. I have

removed a Sherpa from the Solukhumbu. I have no doubt that Hillary, when he asks where we intend to live, questions my motives and the feasibility of our relationship. Nima tells him we will live in the States, where he's lived for two years. Nima says he wants to learn English, and then return to Nepal to start a trekking business.

"A Sherpa must retain his culture," says Hillary. "Best of luck to you both." Nima thanks Hillary for his blessing and grins an Everest-size smile.

"So nice man, Hillary," says Nima, as we board the plane.

This journey is a first for each of us: our new trekkers will witness the grandeur of the Himalaya; aging Jules returns for his final trek; Paul, who trekked the Annapurnas with us, will walk in the rain shadow of Everest; I will visit the Sherpa homeland; and after two years in America, Nima will return home.

Before takeoff, the stewardess, dressed in an *engi*, offers us cotton for our ears and a lozenge to suck on, although neither helps much with the noise or the air pressure changes. Only a short time into our flight, the view of red-brick villages and terraced hillsides gives way to a wilder landscape. On occasion, a simple home merges out of the land linked by trails that meander in response to the topography. The valley below us deepens, and then rises as we follow it up. Our plane flies above a narrow pass between mountains before it enters the clouds. Moments later, in a sudden burst of sunlight, the Himalaya emerge. The airplane drops altitude, banks until mountaintops appear out one window and the sharp bluff that marks the edge of the airport comes into view on the other. Between the two is a chasm.

The fun and terrifying thing about our flight into Lukla is the airplane. It is an intimate experience for a small number of people. The open cockpit provides a view of the pilots, the dashboard, and, continuing on, out the front window. As we near the Lukla airport, everyone leans into the aisle and looks past the pilots to watch our approach. The novices can be recognized by their gasps. I am one of them. As the plane tilts down, the runway tilts up. The airstrip ends where the mountain rises at a steep pitch. The plane nearly stalls just before the pilot lands on a well-packed dirt runway, hits the brakes, and tosses us back into our seats. Applause bursts forth from the passengers when we stop just short of the mountainside. We have reached the Solukhumbu!

From the plane window, I see a charming village of stone houses. The villagers, who lined the runway as we landed, run over to meet the plane. I recognize Nima's family, who caught an even earlier flight. After our duffel bags are matched up with porters, we walk into the village of Lukla. Overjoyed, our trekkers stop often to photograph the mountains. As Ang Chokpa's husband, Dawa, and Nima talk, I watch Nima skip down rock steps with a spirited ease, happy to be home.

At the Khumbu Lodge in Lukla, Ang Chokpa welcomes us in and leads us upstairs. Built of stone with a wood roof, her lodge has a pine-paneled interior with carpet-covered benches along the walls and small tables before them. She serves us chai in mugs and tea biscuits on an aluminum plate. I sit back and savor the moment. It is not yet noon. All flights leave early from Kathmandu, as flights into Lukla require visibility, and mornings are typically clearer. I too seek visibility, and insights into my husband of less than two years. By visiting his homeland, I will see how he lived, get to know his family, and better understand his ways. For the last year and a half, Nima has lived in a place so foreign that I now find it hard to fathom how he ever adjusted. Nima grew up not knowing cars, movies, electricity, telephones, central heating, or synthetics, and yet now he lives among all those things as if they have always been a part of his life. Could I shed those same things and live in the Solukhumbu as easily as Nima adjusted to them in America?

While my trek around the Annapurnas began in the semitropical lowlands, we now begin from Lukla at 9,186 feet (2,800 m), with a descent through farmlands and small villages toward Ghat, a village about 820 feet (250 m) below us. We follow the Everest trail along the Dudh Kosi or "Milk River," so named for the glacier silt that clouds its clarity. Steep hillsides along the river limit the livable land. Above the farms, the hills rise sharply and fields disappear into forests. The river runs deep within a canyon between peaks that disappear or reappear depending on one's viewpoint.

Our trek is a family affair. Tshiring Tendi, Nima's older brother, will lead the trek as *sirdar*. Nima Nuru, his younger brother, is our guide. Kandu, their sister, has the toughest job, as the *zopkyok* driver. Portlander Jules has hired Krishna, who works for Tshiring Tendi, to guide him over rocky stretches of trail. A cook and several kitchen staff, including Lhata, who works for Nima's sister Mingma Futi, complete our crew. Our staff speaks limited English, but everyone is eager to learn.

Our trekkers are both friends and new acquaintances. John, who is dark, wiry, and spry, looks Sherpa. His strength, for an older man, surprises the Sherpas, and they treat him with respect. Thatcher is serious, with a dry sense of humor lost on Sherpas who prefer slapstick. He is stockier than his father, with black hair and glasses. Quiet and gentle Allan, who looks like both John and Thatcher, brought a sack of volleyballs for the Jana Sewa Lower Secondary School in Gomela that Nima attended, after learning the kids play it at recess. Nima tells us that Sir Edmund Hillary built his school. Dean, sized like a quarterback, has blond hair, soft eyes, and keeps to himself. After a couple of hard years, Paul is happy to be back in Nepal. Jules's friend Yvonne came for the beauty of the landscape, and to get over her fear of heights. Short brown hair caps her round face and easy smile. Her seventeen-year-old nephew, Chad, is tall, lean, and athletic. Chad will run with the Sherpas.

Beyond the village of Ghat, a towering boulder carved with prayers forces the trail to split and bend around it. Nima reminds us to keep the *mani* to our right. The *mani* stone's white painted Tibetan script emphasizes its prayers. We have already passed a *mani* wall of tablet-size prayer stones, but this one surprises us. Yvonne wants to know if the size of the rock one carves relates to the credit toward one's karmic debt.

"Any work done for the good of others counts," says Tshiring Tendi, "not size."

Nima points out their family farm across the river and how to access it. The lower village is called Chhermadingma; the upper is Chhursema.

rain: A Sherpa must retain his culture. Best of luck to you both.

His family used to live below, but after the flood a decade ago, his parents moved up. The lower land is flat, peppered with boulders left by previous floods and stone walls that define fields. His family's upper land rises to a tall rock bluff and waterfalls that disappear into forests. Mountains rise above that, and the Dudh Kosi flows below. Both above and below, stone and wood houses blend into the mountainside. Nima points out an upper trail that clings to the edge of the mountain, a lower trail that follows the river, and connecting trails between them. Called *milam*, these are mountain trails used by locals. We walk on a *gyalam*, or public trail, and each village is responsible for caring for their section. Trails that zigzag all over the hillsides are called *chhulam*—they're animal trails. *Naalam* are hidden trails that you just have to know. Or you can just say *laam*, which is any trail.

Connections and community are important to the Sherpa. When we pass through Phakding, one of the bigger villages located along the river, friends and family greet Nima, and each invites us to stop for tea. Nima does not refuse. He's missed them and their hospitality. The tea ritual is always the same. Glasses are set out before us. A Sherpani pours chai from a large thermos for the trekkers and me, while she talks and jokes with Nima and his brothers. For the Sherpas, she pours *solja*, the butter salt tea. It's tradition. Everyone insists on cooking for us, but Nima assures them that tea biscuits are enough. While our group is honored by their hospitality, after five stops at various villages along the trail, we are only halfway to camp and drowning in tea. When the frequency of invites does not let up, only Nima and I stop, and the others continue on toward camp. We arrive in Tok Tok late in the day, tired, but not thirsty. *Ch'ah. Solja.* We camp beside a distant cousin's lodge.

The next morning, our group races past waterfalls and rock walls to escape the cold canyon and reach the sunlight's warmth. From here, the forest thickens and villages become less frequent. We are at 9,350 feet (2,850 m) at Jorsale, where we enter Sagarmatha National Park. Sagarmatha is the Nepalese name for Mount Everest. The Sherpa call it Chomolungma, Goddess Mother of the World. In 1856, during Britain's

Great Trigonometric Survey of India, Peak XV was established as the highest point on earth, measuring 29,002 feet (8,840 m). In 1865, the Royal Geological Society named it after the retired surveyor general of India, Sir George Everest. He preferred that a local name be used, but with the borders of Nepal and Tibet closed, none was known. Mount Everest now stands at 29,029 feet (8,848 m) and continues to grow.

While Nima pays our park entry fees at the ranger station, Tshiring Tendi leads us through the entrance gate. At the top of stone steps that drop toward the Dudh Kosi, I pause. An ancient magnolia tree in bloom provides foreground for the dawn's light, which ignites rainbows in the mist of a waterfall before a glimmering rock face. A light fog rises from fields of upturned earth and winter wheat that sparkles with dew. Two small houses hang off the hillside before gardens and pastures. A farmer feeds fodder to two *zopkyok*. A woman bends low to dig up potatoes that her three small children gather into baskets. It is a simple life in a magical land.

I am in the Solukhumbu! Since I first read about Nepal, I have imagined its magnificence. The Annapurnas were one view of Nepal. This is different. This is Nima's home. This is now my home. I too belong. What that means, I am not sure, but after two years of living with Nima, I know it will be revealed. As will the higher mountains as we wind our way up through the foothills toward Mount Everest.

The trail weaves through the valley and crisscrosses the river on questionable bridges of wood and wire. We hike up a hillside, descend to our crossing, only to hike up to an impenetrable rock face that redirects our route. The well-worn trail widens at the water's edge. We walk among stones. The water sculpts stone, carries stone, crushes stone. I hear its rumble, crack, murmur, even when the river disappears. I hear it with increased acuity as I cross a swaying suspension bridge high above rushing water and stride ahead, careful not to step on air where planks have gone missing. I hear bells and hooves echo off canyon walls. I worry about getting across before the oncoming yak train reaches the bridge and begins their stampede toward me. Faded *lungdar* flutter from the center of the bridge. As the bells and hooves grow louder, I begin to pray.

rain: A Sherpa must retain his culture. Best of luck to you both.

Hurry! shouts Tshiring Tendi. He rushes me off the bridge and shoves me up against the stone face of the mountain, just as the yaks clatter down the last stone steps and rush onto the bridge. The Tibetan herders laugh and race after their yaks, while crossing trekkers turn and run for safety.

Yvonne, Jules, and Nima Nuru are behind us, so we wait. Yvonne is terrified of heights. At small bridges she hesitated, but with cajoling, made it across. This one is higher, longer, and less steady. On the far side of the bridge, we see Jules talk to her and Nima Nuru try to take her hand. Yvonne shakes her head and begins to cross alone. A bridge sways less with only one pattern of vibration, so Jules and Nima Nuru hold back people at their end, and we do the same at ours. Yvonne stares straight ahead and does not look down. She walks in measured steps along the bridge and reaches for the railing only when she needs to. She pauses to acknowledge the *lungdar* tied at the center, then moves on, slightly faster. Fear suggests we question our providence. Today, Yvonne has refused to question hers. I admire her boldness. When she steps on land, Yvonne looks radiant with the glow that comes only from living.

After the bridge, the trail to Namche Bazaar goes in one direction. Up. While I struggle to catch my breath as we climb through forests in a demanding ascent, Nima talks like he is on flat land. The Sherpa name for the village of Namche Bazaar is Nawche. The bazaar or market held weekly is called a *haat*. Why must Westerners rename everything. It's not Namche Bazaar, but Nawche or Nawche *haat*. I cannot keep up neither with Nima's ongoing conversation or his fast pace, and I fall back to walk with the others.

A measured speed is important in these foothills, so Tshiring Tendi asks that we follow him. He sets a steady pace that does not tax our bodies. Do not rest, Tshiring Tendi advises. It is better to keep going. We may not all believe him at first, but we follow him with a dogged persistence, step after step after step. We reach the midpoint sooner than I would have thought. From Tshiring Tendi, I learn patience; I learn that tenacity comes in all speeds; and I learn to enjoy the journey.

We arrive at our destination late in the day, after climbing almost

2,000 feet (610 m) to reach Namche Bazaar. The center of commerce for the region, Namche Bazaar is a circular bowl of terraces, homes, and lodges surrounded by snow-covered peaks. A *mani* wall and prayer wheels follow a creek toward a small *chörten* that marks the town center. A *gompa*, or temple, sits high above the village. Trails meander in all directions further into the mountains. Far below us, the Bhote Kosi will soon meet the Dudh Kosi. We camp at the Kala Pattar Lodge owned by Nima's father's cousin. *Ch'ah. Solja.* Exhausted by our ascent, we are happy to rest and have the next day to explore Namche Bazaar. At this elevation, rest days are critical to help one acclimatize.

The village of Namche Bazaar, at 11,286 feet (3,440 m), is the fulcrum of the Solukhumbu, and everything must pass through it. At seven in the morning, our group arrives at the *haat* or outdoor market only to find its narrow mountainside terraces crowded with buyers and sellers. People from throughout the region have come to buy food and household goods. Vendors already sold out are packing to leave.

Namche Bazaar is difficult to reach, so everything must be brought over the mountains on yaks from Tibet, carried up from the lowlands on the backs of porters, flown into Lukla from Kathmandu and brought here by *zopkyok*, or hauled in by locals from their farms. Every week, people and goods circle like the sun so that they arrive in Namche Bazaar by Friday night, in time for the early Saturday-morning *haat*: butter, sugar, flour, beans, lentils, chilies, tomatoes, squash, potatoes, rice, meat, fabric, aluminum ladles and pans, plastic bowls, tins of oil, batteries, baskets, and more.

Near the east entrance to the Nawche *haat*, we stand on an upper terrace and look down on purveyors who have laid out their goods on blankets or in baskets before their instruments of measure: handheld scales, brass or wood cups, and copper bowls. Crowds clamor around an egg seller. The sight and smell of meat being cut up on a stone makes me turn away. A man measures *tsampa* into a bag held open by the weathered hands of a Tibetan. A Sherpani inspects a bolt of wool cloth. Chickens cluck from the confines of bamboo cages; children crow before candy; and villagers preen before friends, for the *haat* is the social event of the week.

From the site of the *haat*, we circle through the village of Namche Bazaar past its *gompa* and turn up over a ridge to head east toward Thami and its seventeenth-century CE monastery, one of the first built by the Sherpa. The trail follows the mountainside high above the Bhote Kosi, past boulders carved with prayers, through forests, villages, and farms. In the early afternoon, we reach the settlement of Thamo, and we are still a couple hours' walk below Thami. Nima's grandfather once owned land here, we learn over a lunch of hot noodles at a distant uncle's lodge. *Ch'ah. Solja.* Nima's grandfather gave his land to the nuns who lived here, so they could support themselves through farming. After Thamo, the land opens up to wide vistas of high himals. The 21,325-foot (6,500 m) mountain of Teng Kangpoche ahead of us marks the gateway to the village of Thami.

Beside us, Kwangde peak at 20,299 feet (6,187 m) spreads out wide and hugs the earth. The boldness of this mountain, and a gradual decrease in altitude, energizes us, and we drop down toward the river at a rapid pace. We stop on a short bridge that crosses a tributary of the Bhote Kosi, where the stream squeezes between rocks with a fury. Carved into organic shapes, these rocks look like Henry Moore sculptures, according to Yvonne, the art curator. Up and around the corner is Thami, which Nima had hoped we'd reach before lunch.

You spent too much time at the *haat* this morning, says Nima. We won't make it to Thami. We'll need to head back toward Namche Bazaar and Mount Everest.

As we turn around, a larger-than-life Green Tārā with a Mona Lisa smile hovers above us. What do these women know that I don't? Etched into a rock face, and then painted, Green Tārā looks down on Nima, who bows toward her with his palms together. His forehead touches stone. Green Tārā bestows her blessing.

"Spirits live in fire, earth, water," says Nima, who tells us how the Green Tārā, the Mother of all the Buddhas, protects the Sherpas.

I like that. I want to live near hallowed ground, know sacred rocks, be protected by water spirits, learn how fire burns on water. I want to nurture the earth, hold it in my hand, understand its essence. I lean forward and bow to Green Tārā. My forehead touches stone. Body talk. Skin to skin. I touch the earth. Green Tārā bestows her blessing.

We climb back west toward Namche Bazaar, skirt above it, and pass through fields of boulders carved with prayers. *Om Mani Padme Hum.* I sense that even those not carved hide blessings. Above the tree line, grass, moss, and small flowers struggle to survive. Autumn-colored lichen covers rocks. I walk among stones. Some stand upright. Others rest in repose. Some sit. A couple dance. Many mingle. Two wrestle. Others sleep. Many carry prayers, carved by Sherpas when they had time after their fields were harvested and before the snow came. Carving builds up a karmic backlog to benefit one's future lives. Carving prayers teaches patience, persistence, and endurance, all skills needed to survive in this rugged environment. Like the Sherpa, I too want to believe that prayers emanating from this field of stones will bring us safely out of the Himalaya.

At dusk, temperatures drop, and we climb the final stretch toward Khunde. A fine frost settles onto the *mani* stones, better revealing their prayers. Yvonne, Jules, and I stop often to admire these stones. Paul and Dean stop to photograph the *mani*. Thatcher and Allan help their father struggle over the rocky trail. Nima and Chad race towards our campsite far ahead. By the time we reach Khunde, it is dark. With no moon, we enter the lodge exhausted, unaware of the wonders around us.

Up at daybreak, we are surrounded by sunlit himals. The crevasses' penumbra creates a contrast to the pink snow and sky, which changes to brilliant white against blue as the sun rises. Wisps of snow blown from peaks sparkle in the light of morning.

Sherpas don't climb Khumbila, says Nima to our group, as we stand in the sun trying to warm ourselves. And they don't allow anyone else to either. At 18,901 feet (5,761 m), Khumbi Yullha, the god of the mountain, lives there. He protects the Sherpa and their land. Nima turns around and points. And that mountain is Kantega, "Horse Saddle Mountain."

It looks like a horse saddle, says Allan. Thatcher and Dean lift their cameras as sunlight grazes its face. I notice Kandu. Oblivious to the mountains, she tosses blankets and saddles onto the *zopkyok*, and then ties on our duffel bags with a self-assured confidence. As I approach her, she looks away. I try to converse. She looks down. I take Nima's advice. I smile. She nods from across the *zopkyok* as she knees one's girth and tightens the packsaddle strap.

Within the Solukhumbu, the adjoining towns of Khunde and Khumjung form a metropolis. At around 12,400 feet (3,780 m), the wide valley above Namche Bazaar and the confluence of the Bhote Kosi and Dudh Kosi is relatively flat, which enables it to support a larger population. At the Swiss bakery, we buy cinnamon buns, and then trek up to the Everest View Hotel for a leisurely breakfast on its terrace with unmatched panoramic views of the Himalaya. Given a perfect day, we linger, happy to enjoy the sun and the dramatic mountains. Nima points out the major peaks: Khumbila, Tawachee, Nuptse, Lhotse, Everest, Ama Dablam, Kantega, and Thamserku. We take photos of the mountains, and each of us before the mountains, and all of us with the mountains as our backdrop. Nima suggests we go. We order more tea and enjoy its warmth in the cool, bright morning. Nima suggests we go. As the sun rises higher, we remove coats and hats and push up our sleeves to feel its heat. Nima insists we go. Like ravens in treetops that seek daybreak, we linger. Only when we begin to feel hungry for lunch do we rise and follow Nima.

We climb down a long dusty trail and drop in elevation surprisingly fast. When we cross the Dudh Kosi at Phunki Thanghka, we are around 1,801 feet (549 m) lower than the Everest View Hotel. Over lunch, our group expresses a contentment not previously demonstrated, as we bask again in the sun. Better adapted to the altitude, we feel strong. We ignore Nima when he tries to rush us and says the hike up will be hard. We want to savor the day. I could see the hilltop and the spire of the monastery's *chörten* as we descended. How far can it be? Midafternoon, Nima finally manages to arouse us.

We soon realize why Nima was concerned. The ascent to Tengboche at 12,697 feet (3,870 m) is a gain of over 2,000 feet (610 m), and the air here holds less oxygen. Unlike the Sherpas, we struggle. Hot sun beats down on our backs. Clouds of dust precede caravans of goats, *zopkyok*, yaks. The narrow trail forces us to climb up rocks to let others pass, slowing our already slow progress. We limp toward the crest of our final hill, marked by a large *chörten* that announces the entrance to the sacred land of Tengboche Monastery. We stop before it to express gratitude at having reached it by dusk.

Situated on a mountaintop plateau encircled by high peaks, Tengboche Monastery was rebuilt after a devastating fire in the 1980s. The crimson monastery building is square with metal roofs, a cupola, and a gold spire that glistens in the sun. Smaller stone houses surrounding it provide lodging for the Tengboche Rinpoche and the monks, and include a private residence for cousin Lama Nawang, who presided at our wedding. The Sherpas have set up camp in the meadow before the monastery. Nima Nuru greets us with a hot lemon drink, then ushers us into the dining tent for popcorn and tea. It's good to rest.

Moments later, Nima pulls back the door flap. Hurry! Lama Nawang will give us a tour.

Is there anywhere along this trail where you don't have family? asks Allan.

Family is good, don't you think? says Nima.

Allan, who is here with his father and brother, agrees. I too nod in affirmation, happy to now be part of Nima's family.

Lama Nawang welcomes us to Tengboche Monastery, and then turns to climb the stone stairs. As he approaches the final flight, he stops, points to two indentations in a boulder, and speaks to Nima, who translates. Lama Sangwa Dorje, who came from Rongphu Monastery in Tibet, founded Tengboche Monastery. He flew over the Himalaya and landed at Pangboche and then Tengboche, where he meditated. Able to see the past, present, and future, Lama Sangwa Dorje predicted that a great monastery would one day be built here. These two indentations are his heel marks, where he slipped in the mud.

First celebrated at Rongphu Monastery, then brought to Tengboche,

rain: A Sherpa must retain his culture. Best of luck to you both.

the Mani Rindup festival is where monks pray and dance to Chenrezi to bring peace and good fortune to the Sherpa. It is a time of *pūjā*—monks make offerings to the gods; the community gives gifts to the monastery; and on the last day of the three-day public festival, the monks dance in costumes for everyone. The dancing monks scared young Nima, except for Mi Tsering, an old man, who teased and played with the children.

Short Lama Nawang looks out of proportion to the oversized red doors of the monastery, as he holds back a curtain used to keep out flies and motions for us to enter. The stone plaza with wood balconies above is empty but for the potted cosmos flowers in tin cans that line the railing and a small monk who peers at us between wood slats. At the side of the courtyard, we climb another flight of stairs to a long, narrow foyer, whose walls and ceiling are bright with paintings of symbols, animals, landscapes, and gods. We remove our shoes and enter the main room of Tengboche.

While the exterior of the monastery looked old for its youth, weathered from winds and rain, the interior looks new and smells of fresh paint. The wall paintings are crisp. New window glass sparkles in the sun. Not all the brightly painted prayer book niches are filled. *Thangkas* and colorful banners hang from rafters. An elevated seat with photos of the Tengboche Rinpoche and his predecessor looks down on raised platforms in rows covered with Tibetan rugs. A red robe lies crumpled in a pile at the seat of each monk, as if to acknowledge his lingering spirit. The walls, columns, ceiling, and beams are painted with stories and symbols. Tengboche is a work in progress, limited by donations and the time it takes to re-create the sacred.

Tell us about the statues, asks Thatcher, as we stand before the altar. Nima speaks to Lama Nawang.

The center one is Padmasambhava or Guru Rinpoche, says Nima. The one with many arms is Chenrezi or Avalokiteshvara, the bodhisattva of compassion who refuses to attain nirvāna and remains on earth to help those suffering.

Nima does three prostrations before Guru Rinpoche, palms together touching his forehead, his lips, his heart, then palms on the floor until he stretches out full length and his forehead touches the floor. I feel self-conscious before the others as I do mine. I have decided to commit to a Buddhist practice and see where it leads me.

Our trekkers are fascinated by the exoticism of Tibetan Buddhism, which pleases Lama Nawang. He motions for us to follow. On the second level, the upper half of the largest Buddha statue any of us has ever seen dominates an intimate chapel. I wonder how locals react in the presence of this golden, bejeweled Buddha Shākyamuni, the historical Buddha. Are they awestruck, as I am? Before a glass case filled with statues, Nima points out Mañjushrī, the Buddha of wisdom; Maitreya, the future Buddha; Milarepa, the—

"Is there more than one Buddha?" asks Yvonne.

"Anyone can be a Buddha," says Nima. "The Buddha has had many lives. Same as us." He speaks with Lama Nawang, and then translates. "There will be one thousand Buddhas. The Bodhisattva Maitreya will be the fifth Buddha, his coming auspicious."

Lama Nawang walks to the wall and removes a prayer book from its niche, carries it to the window, and places it on the sill. He unties its strap and lifts the wood cover from the manuscript. He lays back the cloth wrap and turns a page. The script inscribed on dark indigo paper sparkles in the fading light of dusk. Gold! Jules explains that these ancient texts were some of the few things rescued from the fire.

Those must be sacred words to have created such an exquisite book, says Yvonne. She leans in to better see the craftsmanship. In the last light of day, the gold letters glisten. When read aloud by monks, the vibration of these words alters the earth's energy ever so slightly. Spoken for our enlightenment, we should listen.

I ask Nima to thank Lama Nawang for his tour. He translates. The monk bows. John tells Nima how blessed he feels to know Nima's family. This trip has been his dream. Seventy-three-year-old John came to Nepal to stand on his summit, Kala Pattar, in the presence of Mount Everest. After today, he knows he will reach it.

We may not see *yetis*,
but they see us.

—*Tshiring Tendi*

ON OUR FIFTH MORNING, as we descend to a river, I take no notice of the cold. The rosy glow of sunlit curls of bark bejewels a forest of rhododendrons. Unlike the towering rhododendron trees of the Annapurna area with their dark, forbidding forests, here slender trunks and a sparse canopy create a light-filled sanctuary. Buds burst with red in a struggle to flower. I can relate. I too fight to flower, to express my true nature. While the rhododendron's flowering is seasonal, I hold the power to express my true nature at any time. My only obstacle? Me.

In the valley, at Devuche, we stop at the home of Nima's aunt Ang Futi, his mother's sister, who could not attend our wedding in Kathmandu. She is kind and welcoming. *Ch'ah. Solja.* She honors us with *khata* when we leave. At the nearby nunnery, her sister Yesshe is in meditation and cannot be disturbed. We continue to descend, pass through rhododendron forests, and cross the rapidly moving Imja Khola. The hike up above the river toward Ama Dablam, Lhotse, and the glaciers of Imja Tse, or "Island Peak," looks terrifying, and it is. Narrow trails hang off the mountainside and test us all for vertigo, especially Yvonne. While Jules stays close behind her, she insists on walking it on her own. She is conquering her fear of heights, and I can see the change in her daily, as her power to overcome it grows stronger.

Delighted to be in the Solukhumbu, Nima points out plants he's seen in the States, confident Nepal is their origin; he names villages, rivers, major and minor peaks; he tells stories of climbs; he recalls people from all over the world over with whom he has traveled; he greets friends in passing; he stops in on family; he bows to monks; and he grins at me with pride, pleased to be important and respected again. Based on the reaction of others as I am introduced, his marriage to an American does nothing to diminish his stature.

Tshiring Tendi advises us to watch our step and not look down. He leads to pace us so we do not tire. We climb a trail that appears to disappear into the sky. A *chörten* in silhouette marks the path to heaven. All we need to do is reach the rise and step over. As I struggle up the mountain, the tip of a peak looms ever higher as I ascend. At the crest of the ridge, 22,493-foot (6,856 m) Ama Dablam appears across the valley. A mountain of slender proportion, she looks delicate and vulnerable compared to the granite slabs, ice ridges, and peaks too numerous to name behind her. *Ama Dablam* means "Mother with a Necklace," so named for the mass of ice on her upper slope that Sherpas believe looks like the *dablang*, or charm box, worn by monks, nuns, and laypeople. Farther down the valley stands Mount Everest, framed by Imja Tse, Lhotse, and Nuptse.

At 15,000 feet (4,572 m), we leave behind trees and permanent settlements for shrubs and the seasonal huts of summer pastures. Here, it is easier to shed some of our selves. Yvonne, who has fought hard to overcome her fear of heights, insists on walking mountainside trails alone, although Jules follows close behind. Free-spirited, young Chad races up mountainsides like a Sherpa. We admire John's tenacity. His grown sons, Thatcher and Allan, show the same drive as their father, but with more reserve. Dean, who has been sick with a stomach bug for several days, fights past his fatigue to reach new milestones. Paul, who continues his search for self, has mellowed since his last trek and become an accomplished photographer, finding a positive focus for his intellectual energy. Jules, who knows who he is, sheds stories to anyone who will listen. Divested of his Western ways, Nima reverts to that confident, carefree god of the mountains. I like him Sherpa. I envy his easy transformation, for I must work hard to dispose of my Western persona and take on the qualities of a Sherpani.

We follow a trail that cuts across a mountainside of aromatic bushes. Each brush with my boot stirs up a heady aroma. I bend to rub my hand over the top, then press my face into my palms to awaken the strongest of all memory senses. *Déjà vu*. I have been here. Plants used for incense are called *sang shing*, Nima tells me. Used as an offering, the incense calms angry spirits, like if we argue, or if someone brings an unclean thing into the house. Incense is ancient, I tell him. Perhaps I think I remember this place, when all I recall is the smell. Who knows where I was. Was I with Nima?

"You were here before, Sherpani," says Nima. "That bush only grows above 14,000 feet (4,267 m)."

Lower Pangboche, at 12,664 feet (3,860 m), is poorer and rockier than other Sherpa villages we have passed. At this altitude, boulders grow from fields; fences and homes sprout from stones. At the village center in upper Pangboche, we pass between cedar trees like those that once covered these barren hillsides. The head lama of Pangboche is a Geshe, a scholar of the Buddhist doctrine. He teaches that the trees around the *gompa* are sacred, so the locals leave them alone. The two-story *gompa* is rustic compared to the newly built one in Tengboche. Three brothers, all lamas, built the first *gompas* of the Solukhumbu at Pangboche, Thami, and Rimi Jung, which is known as Pema Choling monastery. Lama Sangwa Dorje, who meditated above Pangboche, built the monastery there. At Pangboche, soot from years of butter lamps dims the once-vibrant painted temple walls, which tell stories of The Old Ways, the Nyingmapa Buddhist legends. The oldest sect of Tibetan Buddhism, the Nyingmapa school was founded by Guru Rinpoche in the eighth century CE. The Sherpa are descendents of his followers. As we tour the temple, Nima tells stories that are more contemporary.

The lama tells us that a yeti served Lama Sangwa Dorje while he meditated, says Nima. When the yeti died, the lama saved the hair-covered skull and hand and placed them in the Pangboche Monastery. They were there up until a few years ago, when someone stole them. Both were bigger than a human's and covered with long, coarse, red hair.

"No way!" exclaims Thatcher, a scientist. "There aren't yetis." Nima Nuru assures him there are.

Jules confirms that he saw the Pangboche skull, actually the top of a yeti head, and hand on previous visits. Yetis may have existed, Jules tells us. Who's to say?

Nima believes they do. He heard one once. Others have found footprints. Or smelled them. Or seen them. About twenty years ago, a Sherpani heard this awful noise one night and went outside to discover a yeti was killing her goats. The yeti chased after her and bit her, but something scared him and she got away. Everyone knows that story. The other Sherpas nod. Thatcher shakes his head in disbelief.

"We may not see *yetis*, but they see us," says Tshiring Tendi.

Can every culture be wrong? Legends abound throughout the Himalaya; they are known as the *almas* in Mongolia, the *barmanou* in Afghanistan and Pakistan, the *yeren* in China, and the Mande Burung in India, while Sasquatch populate the US Pacific Northwest. Yetis may be only a myth, or the last vestiges of Neanderthal man, or the extinct ape Gigantopithecus. The word *vestiges* comes from the Latin word *vestigium*, or "footprint," which is just about all anyone finds of the yeti. Perhaps they are a palimpsest for humankind, ancestors who once roamed the earth and then faded away, leaving behind traces in our DNA, and under the right conditions high up in the Himalaya, a vision of prehumanity.

From Pangboche, we continue up the valley to Dingboche near 14,304 feet (4,360 m). It's a small village of stone houses, where retreating glaciers dumped their payload to produce a landscape of rocks and dirt with little vegetation. Our tents are set up on an upturned field surrounded by stone walls and mountains. Dismayed by the landscape, young Chad wonders what we will do on our day off in Dingboche.

After breakfast the next morning, Paul announces that the wind is perfect for kite flying. If he can photograph his kite before Mount Everest, he might get it published in a kite magazine. Surprised to learn of Paul's extra luggage, we are happy for the diversion.

rain: We may not see *yetis*, but they see us.

Paul unfurls a fuchsia-colored kite, walks to the middle of a field of upturned earth, and releases it. The kite rises. As I watch it lift on an updraft, bright against snowcapped peaks, I wonder how anyone lives in this cold land drained of color and oxygen. Paul hands me the kite string and grabs his camera. The gusty winds that blow off the mountains yank at the kite. To keep it in control requires attention. I watch the kite. I respond. Give and take; action and reaction. Kite karma.

The kite soars, and then dives, only to rise higher, brilliant against the white, gray, and black landscape. Paul runs back and forth across the field, kicking up clods of dirt in his attempts to get the right shot. Suddenly, from out of nowhere, an old man struggles over a stone wall and races toward us waving his arms. I assume he wants to fly the kite. As he nears, we hear his frantic screams. His arms wave like Kali. Does he think we have unleashed a spirit? I hand the kite string over to Allan, so I can run to find Nima if needed. When the old man reaches us, he talks and gesticulates with a frantic helplessness. We look on in empathy and incomprehension. The old man shouts and points toward the land. We are dumbfounded. He bends down and digs in the earth. Allan suggests that he may be looking for a rock to throw at us. We step back. The old man stands up and opens his palm.

"A potato!" says Paul, as he joins us, kite in hand. "At least I got my pictures." Allan expresses regret at tromping all over the man's recently planted field. Food up here must be hard to come by, says Thatcher. And none of us city folks recognized what freshly upturned soil meant, I say. We nod a group apology to the old man who has stood there stoically while we talked in English.

The old man squats and digs a hole in the earth with his hand. He inspects the seed potato, blows the dried earth off it, and solemnly places it in the hole. Both of his hands reach out to slide the earth back over the seed. He pats the land, stands, and wipes his hands. He turns and walks back across his field.

Dean, who has been sick with stomach problems for much of the trek, has lost weight and grown weak, so he struggles at this altitude. Thatcher,

303

concerned for his friend, asks Nima over dinner if there is anything else that Dean can do besides continue to take antibiotics for stomach bacteria. What would a Sherpa do?

The Magar kitchen boy, Lhata, has special powers, says Nima. Thatcher looks skeptical. You have to believe, says Nima. Dean shakes his head, not wanting to be part of any hocus-pocus. Nima responds to them with conviction. Lhata can cure you, he says, but—it only works if you believe.

We are surprised. Lhata can barely hear, so everyone raises their voices when speaking to him, and he responds in an even louder shout. According to Nima, he hadn't used to be like that. One day he got lost in the woods and met a *telma*, a wild man of the forest, a shaman-like fortune-teller oracle. Although Lhata was gone only a couple of weeks, he learned how to see the future. When he returned to Mingma Futi's house, he had changed. The *telma* took most of his hearing for his gift.

How does he heal? asks Dean.

Nima leaves to talk to Lhata, and then returns. You don't have to take anything, says Nima to Dean. Do you want to try?

Dean asks what Lhata will do. Thatcher asks about what medicines he uses. Dean asks if its magic—or witchcraft. Thatcher asks if it works. Dean asks if it's dangerous. They learn nothing from Nima. Powers are performed, not debated. Your part is to believe.

The moonless night is bitterly cold when we leave the dining tent. Dean and Thatcher follow Nima. Those of us who are not allowed to watch Dean's healing pass the time gazing at the stars. The Milky Way is visible. Paul points out constellations, named by the ancients, who had the imagination needed to see them. At home, the artificial glow from our cities has neutralized the constellations, along with our stories about them. Tonight we see stars, think hard to remember their names, and wonder what we have lost.

When Dean returns, his Western-educated mind is uncertain about Lhata's actions and incantations. No doubt embarrassed by the "hocus-pocus," he shares little with us. Thatcher, who doesn't want to say much either, tells us that Lhata read grains of rice in the palm of his own hand

and told them that Dean will get better. Thatcher and Dean, both of whom work in pharmaceuticals, remain skeptical.

At sunrise, we walk the trail out of Dingboche. The crossroads is littered with sticks, food, and flowers in a way that is deliberate, almost ominous. We stop in wonder. Sacred garbage? Nima explains that Lhata left the spirits an offering at the crossroads, to stop evil from entering. Thatcher asks Nima how that works. Nima tells him it just does. Dean does not feel better. There is only one conclusion. Dean did not believe.

Nima respects Lhata's knowledge, no matter what his Western friends say. A *telma* needs a pristine landscape untainted by man, says Nima, and he is worried. These days so many tourists and non-Sherpas come into the Solukhumbu, and despoil the sacred lands. The *telma*, says Nima, will soon disappear.

From Dingboche, we hike back toward the confluence of the Imja Khola and the Lobuje Khola, which is fed from the Khumbu Glacier, and again we follow water. At 13,911 feet (4,240 m), we reach Pheriche. Nima recommends we stop at the aid station, which is run by the Himalaya Rescue Association. While Dean sees a doctor to get medicine for his stomach bugs, we listen to their program on high-altitude sickness. To trek successfully in the Himalaya is simple: be in shape when you come; take time to acclimatize; drink lots of water; avoid alcohol and drugs; and if you get altitude sickness, descend immediately. I have learned that it works. Nima laments that too many people don't follow these simple lessons, and end up putting themselves and the Sherpas, whose job is to help them, at risk.

The trail today traverses alpine tundra, whose color has begun to return as the days grow longer and the weather warms. Snow-covered peaks frame this valley, and between them, rock cairns are common, as if we needed something to remind us that we are not alone. Above Duglha at 15,157 feet (4,620 m), a ridge is lined with small *chörtens* built in the memory of eighteen climbers: Sherpas, as well as several foreigners, who were killed on Everest while supporting two expeditions in the early seventies—the successful Japanese ski down Everest and an American ascent.

After so many rock-strewn trails below, the tundra is a joy to walk on, even if only for a short time. More used to the altitude, and inspired by the himals, we make good time. Above the tree line, the vistas expand and wrap around us in a 360-degree panorama. Nothing in America could have prepared me for the magnitude of this view.

As we approach the terminal moraine of the Khumbu Glacier, we are only halfway up the Himalaya. When shopping for plus 6,000-meter (19,685-foot) peaks, this is the Rodeo Drive of mountain spotting. Just leave your high heels at home. I find it almost impossible to walk, even in hiking boots. Nima leads and I follow him over a massive glacial moraine, a river of rocks in every shape and size left by retreating glaciers. Among this awesome scenery, I am forced to look at my feet. Walking becomes a meditation of sorts: actions focused; concentration singular; awareness heightened. Each step requires attention and resolve. At the sound of a raven's cry, I stop. I look up and see that snowcapped sentinels surround me. Nima turns me counterclockwise and points out for me: Pumori, to the north, who rises to 23,494 feet (7,161 m) before me; Tawachee at 21,463 feet (6,542 m) and Cholatse at 21,129 feet (6,440 m), who look like twins; Ama Dablam at 22,493 feet (6,856 m), Kantega at 22,241 feet (6,779 m), and Thamserku at 21,680 feet (6,608 m), who we passed on our trek from the south. Lastly, up ahead to our right, Lhotse at 27,923 feet (8,511 m) stands tall and imposing while the wide face of Nuptse at 25,771 feet (7,855 m) hides all but the top of 29,029-foot (8,848 m) Mount Everest. I can't wait to see more of her, I tell Nima.

Among the grandeur of this landscape, the forlorn village of Lobuje, at 16,175 feet (4,930 m), is a disappointment. The lodge is a hovel, our campsite mud and rock. In preparation for our big climb tomorrow, we go to bed early, but no one sleeps well, for the air is too thin and our anticipation too great.

"Good morning, *Didi,*" says Nima Nuru, as he pulls back the tent flap. "It looks like a clear day."

It's our ninth day, our summit day. I am glad. I take the cup of tea he offers me and look through sand-crusted eyelids at a star-filled sky above moonlit himals. It is four in the morning. Our plan is to reach the top of Kala Pattar by midmorning, before the clouds come in, except that by the time we are up they hover over the himals and we know they can drop in an instant. Bundled in warm clothes to fight off the cold, we follow Nima up the moraine. The trail is littered with glacial deposits of rock. We fight for balance as we step from stone to stone. Our legs are soon exhausted from rock hopping, and our pace slows. At this altitude, no one can move much faster.

At the top of a ridge, we look down to a tiny village sited near a large depression of sand. That's Gorak Shep, says Nima, which translates to "Graveyard of the Crows." The rock ridge beyond is Kala Pattar, or "Black Rock."

Kala Pattar rises up toward the triangular peak of Pumori like a knee-high child reaching for his mother. Chomolungma, Goddess Mother of the World, rests to the east, her silhouette faintly visible as she naps under a blanket of clouds. Jules, who knows these mountains, says Chomolungma is fickle. She decides when to show herself. It's a two-hour climb up Kala Pattar. The weather could change by then. As we sip tea in Gorak Shep, the optimist Yvonne predicts that Chomolungma will be revealed.

As Tshiring Tendi leads us up Kala Pattar, our breathing is measured. We do not hurry. Step. Breathe. Step. Breathe. Step. Breathe. On a mountainside scattered with rock scree, I test each step. I trust myself, not the land. Nepal loves to surprise. Each step requires confidence. I do not hesitate. I go forward, fearless, yet with a cautious wisdom. Body and spirit align with the land, and we respond to each other with knowledge and respect. Self and the land are never equals, but we give and take and work in unison to reshape our selves in ways as big as my view.

Mountain vistas help me to see. The openness of the land expands my horizons. Space engulfs me. I float. Some may say it is the thin air, but it is the space. Movement requires space. Here I can evolve. Evolution is not linear. Whoever drew that fish that steps from the water and moves in a straight line toward humankind got it wrong. It should have been a spiral, a path of migration, a move toward a deeper understanding of self, unaware of our past and yet knowing, as we circle in toward our center.

As I climb, I learn about this land, and to know this land is to know the Sherpa spirit. Like the Himalaya, we too rose out of an ancient seabed, and continue to evolve. At the top of Kala Pattar, I stand in the presence of Chomolungma. I am humbled by her greatness, awed by her beauty, and infused with her indomitable spirit. When the sun breaks through the clouds, light washes me. The Goddess Mother of the World bestows her blessing.

Our old selves litter Kala Pattar like oxygen bottles litter Everest Base Camp. We have dropped them to lighten our load. On the way up, John refused help from anyone, determined to make it on his own. He stopped often to catch his breath and still his heart, before continuing up. Thatcher and Allan, overcome with emotion, cried as they watched their seventy-three-year-old father struggle to reach the top, at 18,192 feet (5,545 m), and held back to let him go first.

Dean reached his goal in spite of illness and is now ready to go home. Yvonne overcame her demons, her fear of heights, and now treks like a woman who trusts her body. Chad moves with a self-assured boldness that he will take with him into adult life. Jules, at sixty-eight, came to say good-bye. This will be his last high-altitude climb. Jules is letting go, just as young Chad is grabbing on.

Nima came here to rediscover his old self—and now displays a confidence I have not seen since I left him in Nepal two years ago.

Paul disappears behind a boulder. He returned to Nepal with the hope that time in the mountains might help him figure out his future. I have learned that emotions intensify at this altitude as a consciousness difficult to muster in the lowlands arises within me. The essence of life matters here. Self becomes aware. Time becomes now. The "I" becomes a spirit. The earth becomes our mother.

Chomolungma shakes the clouds. A light rain blesses the earth. Life requires the simple compound of hydrogen and oxygen mixed with the right chemical building blocks and an energy source to create water, the original embryonic fluid. The monks understand this, for with their *phumpa* they rain blessings for a long life upon the Sherpas. I remove my hat. Rain wets my hair. I turn my face upward and close my eyes. Blessings streak down my cheeks, as the Goddess Mother of the World watches over me.

Uncomfortable at seeing Chomolungma's guests so emotional, Nima Nuru stands on his head. Allan wants to know how he does it at this altitude, and then follows his lead. Others join them. Laughter bubbles up and erupts in a continual flow. Everyone feels a high. Our new selves are pocketed, too fragile to be exposed for long. We will carry them home and wear them, first in safe company, then, as they become familiar, in public. For now, we want only to enjoy our summit.

John asks to be photographed before Mount Everest reading *The Beach Reporter*, which publishes photos of beach city residents and their travel exploits. Together and alone before Everest, we photograph the moment, either for protection against a failure of memory, when we might forget the heights we once reached and the selves we discarded, or as proof of our exploits, or both. As a cold wind deposits clouds back on Everest, our celebratory spirit dissipates, and all but Paul begin the descent.

I stop just below the summit and kneel. I build a *theu*, a rock cairn, to both mark my passing and celebrate my new self. I now listen as much with my body as with my mind. When a force grabs me and won't let go, I open myself up to it. Instincts honed over eons know more than intellect developed over a few decades. My primitive nature had atrophied. I have begun its resurrection. I can now—sometimes—let go, resist less, lose control, and like it. I can take the long view, or turn inward and go deep, penetrating layers with newfound light. It is a beginning.

I stand. I look toward Chomolungma. She has disappeared. I will remember her.

I kneel. I build a *theu* to honor my union with Nima. I am glad I took the risk and married a man from another culture who had limited education and knew only Third World poverty. With his wisdom, he has brought me riches. With his grace, he has taught me to see beyond myself, helped me to put aside what others thought, encouraged compassion, and taught me to see the sacred in all things. With Nima, I have learned how to climb, not just in the Himalaya, but in all things; and even with his unbridled energy, I have learned stillness. He also has taught me that love, a force and a fate, is beyond my control.

I rise. I am ready to meet my family as a Sherpani.

Far ahead of me, I watch Jules stumble and fall. Nima leaps down the mountain toward him. What happened? Pebbles underfoot caused the fall. He broke his finger. Nima promises to find him a doctor in Gorak Shep. I bandage Jules's hand as best I can.

Jules is lucky, says Paul, who joins us. He saw the whole thing.

When we reach the village, a British physician stands ready to examine Jules's hand. The doctor warns Jules that his injury is serious; he must return to the States immediately or risk losing the use of his right hand. Jules is a writer. He leaves with his guide, Krishna, for the aid station in Pheriche, about 3,000 feet (914 m) below us and twice as far as Lobuje. Jules, an experienced trekker and strong for a man in his late sixties, is determined to get there tonight. Tomorrow, he hopes to reach Shyangboche or Tengboche beyond. Disappointed at not being able to finish the trek and visit Nima's family, Jules gives Nima and me a hug, and without even a short rest, begins to trek back over the glacial moraine with Krishna close beside him.

After hot tea and biscuits, made by the Sherpas, we return to our forlorn camp at Lobuje. Tonight, we sleep like stones.

The Solukhumbu is a *beyul*, a sacred valley
hidden by Guru Rinpoche long ago.

—*Uncle Lama Zepa*

T HE LAST DAYS OF THE TREK, as we retrace our steps, are
uneventful. Before we fly out of Lukla back to Kathmandu, we plan to
spend a few days with Nima's family in Chhuserma. Nima, eager to get
home, keeps racing ahead, only to wait for the rest of us to catch up. An
extra day with his family is important. He pushes us to hurry. As we near
Nima's village, we cross the Dudh Kosi and follow a *milam*, a local trail
that passes by the front doors of Sherpa homes, through their fields, and
past *mani* walls that lead to an ancient *chörten*. Word has traveled down the
trail that Nima and his new wife are near. Friends and relatives stand in
their doorways in anticipation. Nima introduces me when we stop. *Ch'ah.
Solja.* There are many invitations, but Sherpas will not say no, so to refuse
is an artful dance that leaves the other pleased. My family is expecting
their new daughter-in-law, Nima tells the villagers, relatives, and friends
as we pass. They smile at me, then question Nima until he insists that we
continue. Only after accepting their gift of *chhurpi* (yak cheese) or incense
or *khata* can we say good-bye and move on. At each stop, people tell Nima
how excited his parents are to have me as their daughter-in-law. A party is
planned for tomorrow night. Everyone is coming. They all want to meet
me. I am embarrassed by their attention.

311

"I'm not special, Nima."

"Yes, you are," says Nima, who takes my hand. "You are you. That is special."

Yes, I am me. I am special. Nima makes it simple. I make it hard. While I struggle to let go and bring clarity and simplicity to my life, Nima, who is used to bearing burdens, took on Los Angeles with the same fearless tenacity he used to climb the Himalaya. You are you. That is special. The knowledge gives me strength. Nima's Buddhist religion provides him with a foundation to withstand storms and a vision of what is important. Love.

Ami, Tshiring Tendi's wife, dispatched her older son, Nima's nephew Nawang Tshiring, and her field hand out as scouts. They discover us at the Jana Sewa Lower Secondary School that Nima attended, watching the students play volleyball. The school sits on a semi-level area with mountains rising behind and a steep drop to the river far below just beyond the volleyball field. The single-story rectangular school building of whitewashed stone has a corrugated tin roof and five doors that lead directly outside. The teacher sounds an empty oxygen bottle that hangs from the rafters and serves as their bell. The students file into their classrooms. The teacher motions for us to enter a room. Inside, all six surfaces of the room are pinewood. The students, who sit on benches with slate boards on their laps and chalk in their hands, stop their work as we enter. Nima talks to the teacher. I look around the room; there are no books or paper or pencils; an outdated map of the world is nailed to one wall. The only teacher must run back and forth between five rooms. Not much has changed since Nima attended school here in the early seventies.

In the schoolyard, Ami's field hand takes my backpack, while little Nawang Tshiring races home to announce our impending arrival to his mother. It is a short walk, Nima assures us, but with neighbors to visit and two canyons to climb in and out of, it takes us over an hour. We climb the last ridge in the afternoon heat, exhausted. At the sound of Ami's infectious laugh, I feel welcome. Her face is round, with bright eyes and hair pulled back in a bun. Worn with the traditional *engi* and *metil*,

rain: The Solukhumbu is a *beyul*, a sacred valley hidden by Guru Rinpoche long ago.

the silk of her blue blouse glistens in the sun. Only her running shoes are contemporary.

"*Tashi Delek, Tsham*," says Ami, as she takes my arm and escorts me across the stone patio, through the front door, past the *zopkyok* who live below, and up narrow stairs to the living area. Our trekkers follow. Ami motions for us to sit on a bench along one wall. Nima sits next to the fire on a raised seat reserved for the man of the household. Bai Tshiring and Nawang Tshiring, ages two and four and a half respectively, sit on the bed opposite and stare at the foreigners in their home. Pinewood walls, floors, and ceiling surround us. The long storage wall consists of glass-fronted cabinets enclosing stacks of blankets and clothes, and open pinewood shelves that hold large copper storage pots for water, aluminum pots for cooking, and brass plates for eating. Dried chilies and ladles hang from nails among them. Over the wood sink, pastel-colored tea thermoses are lined up like ladies in waiting. Strips of meat hang over the stove to smoke, along with cubes of cheese called *chhurpi* on strings. The bed in the corner is barely big enough for two, below cupboards that display china, glassware, and jars of spices. In the other corner, statues are hard to make out through the smoky glass of their colorful cabinet shrine. A butter lamp burns before it.

Tshiring Tendi welcomes us into his home. He fills the kettle with water plumbed from the creek, which runs constantly into their wooden sink. With the kettle on the fire, he adjusts logs that protrude from a front opening in their adobe fireplace.

We call the fireplace *thapmig*, says Nima. It means "fireplace with eyes." You must never pollute it by tossing trash into the fire or you will offend the spirit, *thaplha*.

Once the water boils, Tshiring Tendi pours it into a tall, slender wood churn trimmed in brass. *Dongmu*, says Tshiring Tendi, who speaks slowly as he points to the tea churn. We repeat. He smiles. Ami adds butter, followed by a handful of salt, fresh butter, and black tea. With strong arms, she churns the contents for ten minutes until froth spills over the side. Tshiring Tendi places two china cups mounted on embossed silver saucers on the table before Nima and me, and removes their coral-topped silver lids.

Thrakya, says Tshiring Tendi to me. I repeat. He corrects my pronunciation. After he pours tea into both cups, Ami fingers a dab of butter and flour on each rim.

That's done to mark the cups' purity, says Nima. *Solja*. Ami hands me a cup with two hands. Along the trail, I was always given a choice. *Ch'ah*. *Solja*. I always chose chai. Out of politeness, I nod in thanks and accept the cup offered me. I handle the cup with care. I sip. I wince. This is awful! The butter tastes gamey and the salt overwhelms me. Everyone watches as I sip again. After my third sip, I force a smile. The Sherpas laugh.

"*Solja* is good for you," says Nima. I begin to gag.

"I can't drink this," I whisper.

"They liked that you tried it," says Nima. "It's tradition." So is Mama's thermos of creamy sweet chai made of milk from her cows and fresh spices. It tastes divine.

Krishna rejoins us the day we arrive at Chhuserma. He had accompanied Jules back toward Kathmandu, and we are anxious to hear about Jules. When they arrived at the aid station at Pheriche, a hand doctor recovering from altitude sickness had just been removed from a hyperbaric chamber. She treated Jules's hand and confirmed his previous diagnosis and the urgency. Poor Jules. Nima feels terrible he wasn't with him as we came down off Kala Pattar. Luckily, Jules caught a flight out of Shyangboche, below Khunde, the afternoon he arrived there and didn't have to trek all the way back to Lukla. As we sip our chai, we take comfort knowing Jules must be back in America by now.

The vastness of the Himalaya points out how small an area we tread upon this earth. From the top of any peak, I look as insignificant as a pebble, lacking purpose. And yet, Jules rolled on one and broke his hand. Perhaps the pebble is our teacher, here to remind us to pay attention. Be present. Be aware. All is significant. Nothing should be ignored. Everything carries karma.

As each of us recalls a story about Jules, Krishna squats on the floor to grate potatoes. The grater is fashioned from a punctured tin can, a

rain: The Solukhumbu is a *beyul*, a sacred valley hidden by Guru Rinpoche long ago.

simple example of the coming together of necessity and invention. When finished, he hands the bowl to Ami, who mixes the potatoes with wheat flour and eggs, and spoons a ladleful onto a hot iron plate that sits over the flame of the stove.

"*Rigikur.* Potato pancakes," says Nima, who tells us how his mother or sisters always made them for him whenever he came home. Allan is impressed so many Sherpa traditions remain intact, but Nima questions for how much longer. Then Nima and I are the first to be served a brass plate of pancakes topped off by a dollop of butter and a spicy cheese sauce. Nima demonstrates how to eat them: he rips off a piece of pancake with his fingers; he mops up the sauce and butter; he bends low over his plate; he shoves it into his mouth; he begins again. Famished, we all devour our *rigikur*, like Nima. It's tradition.

As relatives and friends gather, proud Mama positions herself next to me, so she can show off her new daughter-in-law. I am a rare breed, inspected like one might cattle. I can tell when they talk about me. Nima refuses to translate, except to say they all like me. A neighbor asks Mama a question. With her hand on my back, she pats me up and down. Mama answers. I imagine her response—My daughter-in-law's back is as strong as a yak's. The neighbor nods approval.

As we leave Tshiring Tendi and Ami's home, six bright-yellow tent domes glow in an upturned field. Tshiring Tendi, remembering Dingboche, laughs and assures us that there are no potatoes planted in his field. To reach our tents, we must climb over a dry-stacked stone wall, and over another to get to the outhouse, which isn't so simple—stones shift and shake and unbalance me. I make the best of my tent site by pounding flat the lumps below my sleeping pad, then lie back and close my eyes.

In these Himalaya foothills, the Sherpa are at one with the land. Rocks from mountains create the home's foundation and walls; forests frame windows and entries, and become doors, floors, walls, shelving, benches, and bed. River rocks define fields and fasten down wood shingles. Rushes sweep floors. Rhododendron logs feed fires. Clay from the earth forms hearths. Wool from sheep becomes carpets. Vegetables color the wool.

315

Potatoes, nettles, and ferns simmer in soups. Stream water boils for tea. Cedar smoke purifies. Inside is outside, just tamed. Here, nature quiets the mind, frees the spirit, and makes room for laughter.

The Sherpa live outside more than in. They fetch wood, gather food for a meal, talk with neighbors, and walk to market. Since coming to America, Nima has come inside. He transformed before me and grew tame. His edges have eased. His actions are more refined. His finish has been finessed. In America, I liked the changes. In the Solukhumbu, I am not so sure.

Even Nima recognizes how much he has changed, and is consciously aware of his differences. I see it as he talks to his brother Tshiring Tendi. I suppose anything new tempts for a time, until the new becomes the norm. Unnoticed, we change and do not even know it has happened. Or if we even wanted it to happen. Did Nima? The Solukhumbu has also changed. Only Nima's memories stop time.

"Never leave your shoes upside-down," says Nima as he rights mine and climbs into the tent. "It's bad luck." I question if he still believes that. "Just in case," he tells me, as he lays down beside me for a nap.

Nima is happy to be home, to see his family, and to see me with his family. My acceptance of them, and by them, has weighed on him. I never knew it. I am curious about them, about how they live, about their outlook on the world. His family will give me a view from inside Sherpa culture—and over time, an exotic perspective that will no doubt challenge what I think I know. Our first encounter will be about getting to know each other and finding common ground. Nima always told me his family would accept me, and yet, I worried that because I was his choice and not theirs, his parents might reject us both, after he fought so hard for their love. I didn't want to cause him to lose something so fragile. While painful childhood memories, nightmares, and conflicted family relations continue, I witness reconciliation.

To celebrate our homecoming, a party has been planned. As I enter Nima's parents' house for the first time, I notice Mama has changed her

rain: The Solukhumbu is a *beyul*, a sacred valley hidden by Guru Rinpoche long ago.

plaid wool headscarf for silk. Her *engi* is unchanged, but the shirt she wears under it is the new turtleneck we gave her. Mama makes tea and sets out the cups. Pala sits near the stove, and jumps up to give me his seat when I enter. I refuse. Nima takes it instead. Family, neighbors, and trekkers soon fill their home. Their guests bring produce from the farm, Star Beer, *chhang*, Fanta, and Coke. Nima presents his father with a duty-free bottle of Johnnie Walker Black Label, which Pala places on the shrine. Everyone has a place: father by the fire, the women around the stove or lined up on the bed edge adjacent. Krishna squats and again peels potatoes among them, the guests sit on benches that line the walls, and the children roam freely.

The party preparations are a communal affair: drinks are served and replenished; greens washed; vegetables diced; the kerosene lantern pumped and lit; spices ground; wood fetched; *momos* filled and shaped; children played with; and stories told with laughter. Work is not laborious to a Sherpa. Their agile hands work fast. The young and the old joke, gossip, and tell stories while they prepare the meal together. I like their camaraderie and lack of self-consciousness. A natural sensibility pervades, along with a shyness. Most keep their distance from the other trekkers and me, but remain curious and watch us from across the room. Nima's family is the exception, and they welcome us with a generosity that surprises us all. As the honored guests of the evening, Nima and I are served first, often, and the most. I try to refuse a third helping, but lose the battle.

I am beginning to think that I could live here. It is not as primitive as I thought. I could get used to the outhouse. Solar water heaters are common. Their stoves cook efficiently and take the chill off the house. Their fields produce an abundant harvest. Here, you have space, light, air, mountains—and time. No one hurries. Few wear a watch. None celebrate birthdays. The seasons define their year; the sun and moon, their days; the labors, their hours; the moment, their minute. They come when they come, they leave when they leave, and in between, they are.

Time disappears altogether once Sherpas start to dance. Mingma Futi and Ang Chokpa grab each other at the waist and begin a chant in their low, husky voices. The women line up on one side of them, the men on the other, arms around each other's waist. The resonance of a pine floor, with its creaks and groans and thunder, is the perfect accompaniment to the dancers' monotone voices. Their feet stomp and shuffle in a pattern of steps I try, but fail, to master. Their songs sung in Sherpa provide no clues. I do my best and that is good enough, as we circle in song, in movement, and in spirit.

Traditions and the new blend together here. The Sherpa understand that change is our fate, so embrace it and incorporate it into their traditions. As we sit together and catch our breath, Nima explains that the current song is about the Dalai Lama coming to visit in an airplane. I had thought these were old, traditional songs, I tell him, sung for generations and passed down on nights like this to the next generation.

They are, says Nima. Airplanes aren't so new anymore.

Nepalese disco is new. While the older people danced to the chants, the younger ones respond to the cassette tape that Nima Nuru slips into the player. The music is muddled and jerks in the battery-operated player, so everyone claps to maintain the beat. Tshiring Tendi positions himself in the center of the room and begins to dance. My brother-in-law moves like a cat, with a sinewy grace and a suggestive tease he is unaware of. His hands shape emotions, his body responds, and through it all, his face shouts joy.

Nepalese disco rocks. The children dance among adults. The trekkers dance among the Sherpas. I dance around Nima. I make it up as I go, or watch the others and learn from them as I mimic their movements, only to realize that they watch me and mimic mine. Our jumps and stomps rock the house. The kerosene lantern above our head sways and goes out. Everyone cheers and dances even more ferociously, everyone except Tshiring Tendi, who takes the lantern down, removes the glass shade, and revives the carbon fiber sac with his breath. His life force begets light. Under the glow of the lantern, we dance on, fueled by *chhang*, thin air, and the Sherpa *joie de vivre*.

The next morning, while we trekkers sleep in, the Sherpas feed the

rain: The Solukhumbu is a *beyul*, a sacred valley hidden by Guru Rinpoche long ago.

animals, gather eggs, pick greens, milk the *zom*, and prepare porridge. Over breakfast, Nima proposes a hike up toward Lumding to see red rhododendrons in bloom. The trail is steep and hard to find, he warns. It's a *naalam*, not a tourist trail. Paul is certain he can do it. Allan too. They've been to Kala Pattar. I can't imagine it being much more difficult than what we have done already. Everyone decides to go.

We leave the farm, cross the creek, and turn off onto a path barely visible through the underbrush. The trail rises at a steep angle and grows steeper, and we all feel vertigo as it angles to its steepest. At a short, near-vertical ridge, the Sherpas stop to pull each of us up and over. Branches snag my daypack. Leeches, kept at a safe distance on wider trails, reach for us as we brush overhanging boughs.

Is it like this all the way to Lumding? I ask.

No, Nima assures me. It's harder.

Then I may never see "the other side of the mountain," I say.

Why don't Sherpa trails have switchbacks? asks Thatcher.

They take too long, says Nima.

I think a Sherpa trail reflects a Sherpa. Direct. Straight. The shortest distance, even if it is the hardest. Just go. Go up. Go over. Simple.

We hike straight up for an hour through trees. Our pace is slow and steady. Nothing on Kala Pattar compared to this, even the last stretch to the top above 18,000 feet (5,486 m). We rest often to catch our breath. As the forest opens to an alpine meadow, Nima tells us that this is where they grazed their *zopkyok*. I wonder how their animals stayed upright on the hillside. Yvonne points out how fast one's perspective changes in the mountains, for the Dudh Kosi now looks like a creek. I agree with her and suggest that many more changes take place among mountains.

At a rock outcropping, we stop to rest. "Don't sit down!" shouts Nima, pulling me up. He lifts a spider off the rock and onto the grass. "We need to protect these little creatures too. Otherwise, who else will?"

"It's a spider, Nima."

"To kill even one is bad karma, even if by accident. You don't know who they were in a past life." I sit where the spider once sat. The stone is

319

warm, the sun warmer, and I regret that the spider ended up in the shade. I try to find him, but he is gone.

Across the valley, the triangular peak of Thamserku, or "Golden Mountain," is blessed with snow and sunlight, bright as its name suggests. Nima tells us that the Sherpa define four kinds of mountains. Snow mountains, *khangri*, are sacred, the home of spirits and the source of water. In rocky mountains, *thrakri*, live wildlife and lesser spirits. Only the boulder-covered mountains, *zari*, and the grassy mountains, *pangri*, are inhabitable by man and livestock, along with wild animals and plants like mushrooms, seeds, roots, and greens. In these mountains, the Sherpa can live off the land in summer, like Nima's family did in Lumding.

After a short break, the others continue up, while John, Yvonne, and I wait for them here. We feel off balance, unsure of ourselves at this steep angle, and with no reason to push higher, we are content to sit and enjoy the day. Today, we have time. John is proud of his summit. Yvonne is pleased with conquering her fear of heights. I tell them how excited I am with my new family. John, who left China at age seventeen and did not return for over fifty years, encourages me to bring Nima back to Nepal often. Yvonne advises me to learn all I can about this delightful culture. I tell them that what I need to learn most is the language. Language unlocks a culture.

On the way home, Nima and I linger, as if it might delay our return to America. The others have gone on ahead. As we cross the creek, Uncle Lama Zepa stands at the top of the rise, his crimson robes billowing in the breeze. As we approach, his aged face radiates a calm, in spite of his fur-rowed brow and the gray stubbles that poke out from his chin. He wears the red North Face hat and fleece vest we sent him last year. The lama invites us to visit his cave home before we leave tomorrow. He tells Nima that there is much he wants to learn from me. Given all I could learn from him, I am surprised. Frustrated we cannot communicate, I smile, and we do—a little.

From the folds of his robe, Uncle Lama Zepa extracts a copper and brass pot. He cradles it in his two hands and extends it toward us.

rain: The Solukhumbu is a *beyul*, a sacred valley hidden by Guru Rinpoche long ago.

It's a wedding gift, says Nima, who refuses the pot. He lives simply with so little, he says. But Lama Zepa persists, and after three gestures of offering and three refusals, Nima accepts the pot into his two hands and bows. The tiered copper top is surrounded by a brass band of swastikas for good luck, and fits tight into the bulbous pot.

It's to keep our roasted flour, our *tsampa*, in, says Nima with a laugh. Where will we find that in the States?

When we return home, on the side of his parents' house in a make-shift lean-to, a local craftsman fashions a *dongmu*, or tea churn. It's our wedding present from Pala and Mama, Nima tells me. Curls of wood cover the ground, and the shaped pinewood has been doweled together to make the vessel. Sitting on the ground, the craftsman holds a sliced log with his bare feet, which he uses as a worktable, and with his free hands hammers a leaf pattern into a band of brass used to bind the churn.

"Nima, they really don't know how we live in America, do they?"

"I didn't either, until I got there. There are so many things to have and do in America!"

"I prefer Nepal," I tell Nima. While it may be the mountains that first attracted me to this country, it's the people who make me want to come back. The simplicity of their lives appeals to me. Here, one is part of a community, and I've lost that. The consequences of one's actions are evident. One's footprint does not disappear under thousands of others who stampede behind. Each person stands out and is counted. The Sherpas' connection to their land, their community, and their traditions creates a foundation, a continuity that sustains them.

Back at Nima's parents' home, we sip chai and listen to the Sherpas chatter while dinner is prepared. Pala sits cross-legged beside me, slightly elevated, regal in his demeanor as he looks out over the room: pleased to have a large family and so may hands to help. After spending a couple of days with Nima's father, I struggle with the image I brought with me versus the man I see now. His father is the sweetest man. Each person in the group said that after meeting Pala, all unfamiliar with his past actions. I can't help but wonder if his pious actions are to make up for past actions, like the way he frequently places the palms of his hands together and nods a blessing our way. When a monk came to visit, Pala prepared the altar and recited from the prayer book. Each morning, he fills the incense burner with leaves and adds embers from the fire. When it begins to smoke, he swings it around the house in an act of purification and then hangs it outside under the eaves. There is a self-awareness about him while he does these things, as if he asks us to notice how he atones for his past. Nima and his siblings now care for their parents despite the way their parents cared for them. Nima's family ties are strong. The family is united by adversity, and blessed with the ability to forgive.

On our last morning, Nima and I hike up through the potato fields behind Tshiring Tendi's house and follow a narrow trail that hangs off a cliff above Chhuserma. Up above us, I see Uncle Lama Zepa's cave home protruding from a basalt rock face. Uncle Lama Zepa stands on his sundeck and watches our arrival. When we reach his four-foot-high (1.2 m) front door, he motions for us to enter. His home is no higher inside, and I bend over to cross the foyer to the ladder. I want to investigate his hobbit-like hovel, but he is a lama, so I respect his privacy and climb the ladder to join him. On the deck, he greets us warmly, and then points out the view. Thamserku, the Golden Mountain, is east across the valley and must be seen at sunset, according to Nima. Down below is Lukla. My eyes follow a trail along the steep mountainside. I turn around and look up the bluff behind Uncle Lama Zepa's house. A graphite-colored rock face soars above us, and an ancient spirit catcher and *mani* stones rest on an inaccessible ledge.

The spirits of Nepal have captured me. I am not just curious. I want to know, to understand, to be a part of something greater. Buddhism is a way of life. I want to live that life like the Sherpas, who do not speak of their beliefs, but practice them every day. To show respect for all things living and inanimate, to understand their interconnectedness and recognize all as sacred, will protect their future—and ours. The Buddhist faith is quiet, like an *Om*, a murmur, a wave that travels out and shares its vital energy with us all.

Uncle Lama Zepa notices my interest in the spirit catcher and *mani* stones above. He speaks to Nima, who tells me that the previous lama placed them there for protection. Nima points out a stone cottage with tiny windows and a wood-shake roof engulfed in pink roses, where his deceased aunt, who was a nun or *ani*, once lived.

It's lovely, I tell him. Can we fix it up and live there when we come to visit?

Nima asks Uncle Lama Zepa. They talk in earnest for some time, before Nima relays the response. Uncle Lama Zepa says strong spirits live in this rock. They are powerful, and it is all he can do to protect the family from them. It would be very bad for us to live there. I am wistful, especially after Uncle Lama Zepa walks us past the cottage to a waterfall that drops down the bluff in stages before flowing into a creek that meanders through forests and fields on its way to the Dudh Kosi. As we stand in the glade, Uncle Lama Zepa talks to Nima for some time, and then Nima tells me his story.

The Solukhumbu is a *beyul*, a sacred valley hidden by Guru Rinpoche long ago. Nyingmapa Buddhism, founded by Guru Rinpoche, is the oldest sect of Tibetan Buddhism and is practiced by the Sherpa people. They believe that *terma*, hidden treasures, have been discovered, or will be discovered, by *tertöns*, or treasure revealers. Texts and objects, as well as rocks, earth, water, and sky, all contain ancient human knowledge in the form of *terma*. The Buddhist texts say that when the world is in chaos, a *tertön* will appear, a *terma* will be discovered, and, if a sanctuary is needed for the followers of Nyingmapa, a *beyul* will be revealed to a *tertön*. The Solukhumbu is a *beyul*, opened after a mini ice age to a small group of Sherpa families who left Tibet, most likely to escape religious persecution. Only those with a pure heart can remain in a *beyul*, which is sacred land where negative activities cannot take place without consequences. A *beyul* is a refuge for Guru Rinpoche's followers. There are other *beyul* in the Himalaya, but not all have been revealed. As I stand in this sacred valley, everything I need is here: water, sun, flowers, fields, vistas, rocks, spirits, family, and a home. I could live here.

Could I live in the cottage if I became a nun, an *ani*? I ask. Nima laughs and shares my idea with Uncle Lama Zepa, who responds.

"You would need too many years of practice to live here, even as an *ani*" says Nima. "Uncle Lama Zepa doesn't recommend it. We'll look elsewhere."

I am disappointed, but—I am learning to accept what I cannot see, and to believe what I will never know.

After Uncle Lama Zepa returns to his cave home, Nima and I linger by the pool at the foot of the waterfall. I step onto a stone surrounded by water. I am water. Nima sits on a rock along the shore. Nima is earth. Listen to the water, I murmur. Hear the stones, he whispers. Water and earth converse. It is time for us to move on. Together, we will spiral in one continuous migration, like the water that flows over stones.

This journey has been a broadening of consciousness, a burgeoning awareness. I squat and cup my hands. The water is cold and clear. It smells like earth. I splash my face, the top of my head, and the back of my neck with glacial waters. A drop runs down my spine and I shiver. It feels like fire. I drip a drop onto my lips. The water tastes of rain. I must be water, for to me, Nima will always be earth. Water and earth adapt to each other, reshape each other, enhance each other. Meld porcelain and clay. Like the Himalaya, we are of the elements: earth bound with water, and fused by fire.

As we walk back across Tshiring Tendi's potato field, Nima squats to replant an exposed seed potato. He misses Solukhumbu potatoes, he tells me. They taste better. Each autumn, every Sherpa home fills their potato bin in the lower level to the rafters. Potatoes grow well here in the hot sun, fertile soil, and ample rain.

I should have known what to expect next. It's tradition. When we return to his mother's house, a heaping plate—each!—of boiled red potatoes is placed before us. Nima tells me Sherpas eat a plate a day. Too hot for my fingers, but Nima wraps his fist around a potato, squeezes it out of its skin, and offers it to me with a smile.

I taste fire, earth, rain. I swallow joy!

EPILOGUE

NEPAL WENT FROM MEDIEVAL to modern in Nima's lifetime, and has made drastic changes since I first traveled there in the spring of 1991. Today, the former Kingdom of Nepal is a democracy. Kathmandu is a metropolis; its surrounding farms are suburbs; trekkers can buy North Face or Mountain Hardware or Sherpa Adventure Gear at shops in Kathmandu. The runway at the Lukla airport is paved; hydroelectric power and running water service homes and lodges; cell phone and Internet service reach to Everest Base Camp. Few camp in tents on trek anymore—Sherpa lodges are multistory hotels. Bathrooms have replaced outhouses. In the Solukhumbu, forests have been replanted and bridges rebuilt to prevent the excitement of the dare. The trails are crowded with international trekkers, climbers, and adventure seekers. The Sherpa have become entrepreneurial and worldly, while the monasteries have grown in monks, affluence, and influence. The majestic Himalaya and Sherpa traditions are the Sherpas' continuity.

Nima and I reside in the United States in the Pacific Northwest and look out at Puget Sound and the Olympic Mountains, which some days pretend to be the Himalaya. We return often to Nepal and Tibet to go on trek, go on pilgrimage, and visit family and friends. Three of Nima's siblings reside Stateside. The rest live in Nepal, except for Uncle Lama Zepa, who died several years ago, and Pala and Mingma Futi, who passed on in 2006. That same year, Nima was diagnosed with syringomyelia, a rare spinal cord condition that causes both pain and paralysis. With the help of an excellent neurosurgeon, his support group, his Sherpa friends, and family, he fights hard to maintain his mobility. In 2009, for our eighteenth wedding anniversary, we returned to Nepal. Inspired by the landscape, and with the help of another Sherpa, Nima trekked to Gokyo at 15,584 feet (4,750 m), his Sherpa tenacity intact.

On that trip, I felt I finally received permission from the spirits to live in the Solukhumbu, the *beyul* once hidden in the Himalaya. Nima and I bought land below Uncle Lama Zepa's cave residence, near a waterfall, two creeks, and family. On our land, we will build a home.

May the spirits be with us—and with you.

Caryl Thornton Sherpa
March 2011

GLOSSARY

The topography of Nepal isolates its many ethnic groups, so different languages and dialects continue to be spoken. While it can be confusing at first, this diversity of language and cultural identity also enriches one's experience in Nepal. Its people may be Nepalese first, but their ethnic origins are still reflected in their language.

The Nepali language belongs to the Indo-European language family; it is distantly related to English, French, and German and more closely related to Hindi. It is the national language of Nepal, the lingua franca that helps to unite the many ethnic groups of the country. Nepali is also spoken in parts of India, Tibet, and Bhutan.

Standard Hindi, or Manāk Hindī, of the Hindustani subgroup of the Indo-European language family, is the primary official language of the Republic of India. It was derived from Sanskrit, but since India is at a crossroads of cultures through trade, invasion, and colonization, Hindi has many other language influences.

Sanskrit is the language of Hinduism and Buddhism, and is first known from the Hindu text *Rig-Veda*, which dates to the mid to late second millennium BCE. It belongs to the Indo-Iranian subgroup of the Indo-European family of languages. Nepali, Hindi, and Sanskrit are written in the Devanagari script.

The Tibetan language belongs to the Tibeto-Burman subgroup of the Sino-Tibetan language family. It is thought that Tibetan was an oral language until the eighteenth century CE, when Thonmi Sambhota, a minister of Tibet's King Songtsen Gampo, went to India to study the art of writing, and upon his return introduced the script. Classical Tibetan, a written religious language, has remained virtually unchanged for centuries. However, written Tibetan may vary significantly from the spoken, with its many dialects and changes to pronunciation over the centuries.

The Sherpa language was derived from Tibetan. Sherpa religious practitioners use the written Tibetan script, but spoken Sherpa has evolved from Tibetan in pronunciation and grammar. I have used a roman transliteration that closely represents spoken Sherpa.

Dzongkha, which means "the language spoken in *dzongs*," or monasteries, is the language of Bhutan. Like Sherpa, Dzongkha was adapted from Tibetan. The Nepali, Hindi, Sanskrit, Tibetan, Sherpa, and Dzongkha languages all have origins in the ancient Brahmi script of South Asia.

The spelling of words in these languages, when translated into the English alphabet, varies among references. The selections in this book are my own. The sources I used are listed in "References and Suggested Reading" and noted with a circle (●).

For readers interested in understanding the origins of a word and who might speak it, each word in this glossary is followed by an abbreviation that indicates the language of origin as I heard it on my travels: Dzongkha (Dzk.), Hindi (Hin.), Nepali (Npl.), Pali (Pal.), Sanskrit (Skt.), Sherpa (Shp.), Tibetan (Tib.).

Ādi-Buddha (Skt.) or **Svayambhū** (Skt.)—Primordial Buddha or self-emanating Buddha, the true creator of everything that exists. The Tibetan form of Ādi-Buddha is shown with a naked deep-blue body, symbolizing nothingness, and in union, *yab-yum*, with his white consort. Svayambhū, a blue flame rising from a lotus, is the emanation of the mystic syllable *Om*.

ani (Tib.)—Colloquial term for nun; may be suffixed with honorific *–la,* as in *ani-la*.

Annapurna (Skt., Npl.) or **Parvati** (Skt.)—Goddess of abundance, **Shiva's** consort, **Parvati**, and mother of **Ganesh**.

Avalokiteshvara (Skt.)—See **Chenrezi** (Tib.).

baba or *baba-ge* (Npl.)—Hindu priest. The suffix *–ge* is used as an added sign of respect.

banyan (Skt.)—Indian fig tree (*Ficus benghalensis*) also known as the "strangler fig," whose aerial branches produce roots that become accessory trunks.

beyul (Tib.)—Refuge in which all—plants, animals, people, spirits, the land—is sacred.

Bodh-gayā (Skt.)—City located in present-day Bihar, India, where the **Siddhārtha Gautama**, the historical Buddha, attained buddhahood after meditating for forty-nine days under a *peepul*, or **bodhi tree**; one of Buddhism's four holy sites. The word *bodh-gayā* means "tree of knowledge."

bodhi tree (Skt., Pal.)—A fig or *peepul tree* (*Ficus religiosa*) The bodhi tree became known as the "tree of enlightenment" or "sacred fig" after **Siddhārtha Gautama**, the historical Buddha, meditated and attained buddhahood beneath one.

bodhisattva (Skt.)—Spiritual trainee who, after selfless refusal to leave a cyclic existence and suffering, dedicates his or her life to love and compassion so that all sentient beings might attain enlightenment.

Bönpo (Tib.)—Practitioners of the ancient, pre-Buddhist Bön religion of Tibet, which holds animistic and shamanistic beliefs, some of which were merged with Tibetan Buddhism and certain teachings of the **Nyingmapa** school to form the current Bön religion.

Brahman—Member of a traditional Hindu priest caste considered high class; may or may not have wealth; many are priests.

Buddha, the (Skt., Pal.)—Son of Shākya noble, who renounced his royal status, became an ascetic, achieved enlightenment, and whose teachings became the basis of Buddhism. There are many Buddhas, including the **Bodhisattva Maitreya** who is the future Buddha; the historical **Buddha Shākyamuni**, born as **Siddhārtha Gautama** into the Shākya clan in the sixth century BCE; the **Buddha Mañjushrī**, known as the Wisdom Buddha; and the **Buddha Vairochana**, the Great Illuminator.

chaa (Tib., Shp.)—Iron, one of the five elements in Tibetan astrology.

ch'ah (Npl.) or **chai** (Hin.)—Tea made with milk, water, and spices, most often including cardamom.

chakra (Skt.)—A center of spiritual energy within the physical body; literally translates as "wheel" or "circle." In Indian thought, there are seven spiritual centers, or chakras, within the human body. In Tibetan medicine, there are five: the crown, throat, heart, navel, and secret organ of a person.

Chenrezi (Tib.) or **Avalokiteshvara** (Skt.)—**Bodhisattva** of compassion who selflessly refused to attain nirvāna and instead remained on earth to help others. The most common iconographical form shows him standing with eleven heads and a thousand arms. Patron and protector of "the land of the snows." The Dalai Lamas are believed to be the reincarnations of Chenrezi. Avalokiteshvara's sacred mantra is *Om Mani Padme Hum.*

chhang (Tib., Shp.)—Alcoholic beverage from fermented corn, millet, or rice.

Chhetri—Member of the Hindu warrior caste; second in status to a **Brahman**.

chhu (Tib.)—Water, one of the five elements in Tibetan astrology.

chhuba (Shp.)—Traditional Tibetan or Sherpa man's robe worn over pants and a shirt, and tied at the waist.

chhulam (Shp.)—Trails made and used by animals.

chhurpi (Shp.)—A dry yak cheese.

Chomolungma (Shp.) or **Sagarmatha** (Npl.)—Mount Everest, or to Sherpas, the Goddess Mother of the World.

chörten (Tib.) or *stūpa* (Skt.)—Shrine to the Buddha encasing relics (*zung*) and sacred objects.

daal bhaat (Npl.)—Typical Nepalese dish of rice (*bhaat*) and lentils (*daal*).

dablang (Shp.)—Charm box to hold a holy relic, worn at the chest during travel.

dharma (Skt.)—Primary concept of Buddhism with multiple meanings; one is the Buddha's teachings, the Buddhist doctrine, or "the path"; another meaning is the cosmic law, primarily that of rebirth based on one's karma. The wheel of teaching is known as the **dharma-chakra.**

didi (Npl.)—Older sister, used as a respectful term of address for any older woman.

doko (Npl.)—Woven triangular bamboo basket carried from the forehead by a tumpline.

dongmu (Shp.)—Tea churn for making *solja*.

dorje (Tib.) or *vajra* (Skt.)—Ritual thunderbolt that represents the male aspects of the Buddha mind and translates literally as "lord of the stones" or "with a diamond's hardness"; it symbolizes the indestructible energy of the mind of Buddha and is used by Tibetan Buddhist monks in **Vajrayāna** ceremonies in combination with a *drilbu*, a bell that represents the female aspect. Typically, one is not used without the other.

drilbu (Tib.)—Bell that represents the female aspect or wisdom of the Buddha mind, the realization of emptiness. In **Vajrayāna**, it is used by Tibetan Buddhist monks in combination with a *dorje*, a thunderbolt that represents the male aspect of Buddha. Typically, one is not used without the other.

Druk yul (Dzk.)—Name of Bhutan in the **Dzongkha** language; it means "Land of the Thunder Dragon." The people of Bhutan are called Drukpa.

dudh (Npl.)—Milk, as in the Dudh Kosi or "Milk River."

dug (Shp.)—Umbrella or parasol; one of the Eight Auspicious Symbols; provides protection from pain and suffering. Protects the groom and bride from bad influences during the wedding procession.

durbar (Npl.)—Palace, as in Durbar Marg, which translates literally as "Palace Street."

Dzongkha (Dzk.)—The national language of the Kingdom of Bhutan.

engi (Shp.)—Traditional jumper-like dress a Sherpani wears over a *raatuk*.

Ganesh (Skt.)—Elephant god of luck, remover of obstacles, son of **Parvati** and **Shiva**.

Garuda (Skt.)—Mythical bird, part human and part eagle, ridden by **Vishnu**; occasionally used in Buddhism as a synonym for the **Buddha**.

-ge (Npl.)—Suffix added to a name as a sign of respect, as in **Shiva-ge** or **baba-ge**.

Geshe (Tib.)—Scholar with a doctorate in traditional Buddhist studies; a spiritual teacher.

go (Dzk.)—Traditional robe worn by Bhutanese man; it is similar to the Tibetan or Sherpa *chhuba*, but is often made in brightly colored woven fabrics and worn with knee socks.

gompa (Shp.)—Buddhist village temple or monastery that is community or family owned; spiritual center of the community.

gorak (Shp.)—Raven or crow-like birds.

Gurkha—Nepalese person who today serves as a soldier in the Nepalese, British, and Indian armies, and may also serve former British colonies or with peacekeeping operations around the world. The soldiers now come from almost any ethnic group in Nepal. They are primarily of Indo-Tibeto-Mongolian origin.

Guru Rinpoche (Tib.) or **Padmasambhava** (Skt.)—Guru who introduced Buddhism to the Himalaya regions in the eighth century CE; one of the identifiable historical founders of Tibetan Buddhism who built the first Buddhist monastery in Tibet at Samye. In the **Nyingmapa** school, Guru Rinpoche is known as the "second Buddha." Padmasambhava was a mystic with powers to subdue both spiritual forces and existing religions, so that Buddhism could flourish. Also known in Nepal as **Shiva-ge**.

Gurung—Ethnic group related to Tibetans; the Gurung live in central Nepal and are often **Gurkhas**.

gyalam (Shp.)—Public trail, usually maintained by local villagers.

gyalzen (Shp.)—Sword of victory, often found atop prayer flag poles; also a Sherpa name which may be spelled Gyalgen.

haat (Shp.)—Market or bazaar.

Hanuman (Skt.)—Monkey god who brings success to armies, hero in the Indian epic *Ramayana.*

himal (Skt.)—Mountain or massif.

Jain (Hin., Skt.)—Religion founded in India in the sixth century BCE that teaches salvation by perfection through a cyclic existence and through doing no harm to living creatures.

jiwaa (Shp.)—Danger.

jutho (Npl.)—Belief practiced by the **Brahman** of ritual pollution of home or food by non-Brahman.

Kadrinche la (Dzk.)—Formal form of "Thank you" in **Dzongkha**, the language of Bhutan.

Kali (Skt.)—The god **Shiva's** *shakti* in her most terrifying form.

Kami—Member of a traditional Hindu caste considered low class; many are blacksmiths.

kani (Shp.)—Entrance gate marking a sacred space, placed to remind entrants of their spirituality.

karma (Skt.)—The sum of one's actions in past lives, which determines the fate of one's future lives.

khaa (Shp.)—Snow.

kham (Tib., Shp.)—Any one element of the five elements used in Tibetan astrology.

Kham (Tib.)—Geographic region of eastern Tibet from which the Sherpa are thought to have migrated to Nepal's Everest region at the end of the fifteenth century CE.

khangri (Shp., Tib.)—Snow-covered mountains where gods reside; also, the sacred realm of spirits.

khata (Shp.)—Ceremonial scarf used for greetings, thanks, and blessings for a long life.

khola (Npl.)—Creek.

khukuri (Npl.)—Traditional curved knife of the **Gurkhas** that is now used by all Nepalese.

Khumbi Yullha (Shp.)—Protector deity of the Khumbu area in the **Solukhumbu**, who resides on **Khumbila**. He is shown with a white face, wears a turban and rides a red horse, and was trained by **Guru Rinpoche** to be a protector of the Buddhist religion.

Khumbila (Shp.)—Mountain above Khumjung where **Khumbi Yullha**, the protector deity of the Khumbu area in the **Solukhumbu**, resides.

kira (Dzk.)—Woman's dress in Bhutan; three sections of patterned cloth joined to form a rectangle, folded around the body, pinned at the shoulders, and tied at the waist.

kirtimukha (Skt.)—Face of glory or majesty to Tibetan Buddhists; threshold guardian of the door or passages, depicted by its head and two hands; voracious creature born of **Shiva's** third eye, *kirtimukha* greedily devours jewels.

kora (Shp.)—Circumambulation of a religious shrine or sacred mountain.

Kosi (Npl.)—One of the seven large rivers of the Himalaya region of Nepal. The Kosi is a tributary of the Ganges, emptying into the Bay of Bengal, and a transboundary river flowing through China, Nepal, and India; it includes the Bhote Kosi and Dudh Kosi in the **Solukhumbu**.

Kousouzangpo la (Dzk.)—Formal greeting in **Dzongkha**, the language of Bhutan; literally translates as "You are well."

Kumari (Skt., Npl.)—The Living Goddess, a virgin girl who lives at the Kumari Bahal in Kathmandu until her menses, when a new Living Goddess replaces her.

-la (Shp.)—Mountain pass; also, term of respect, as in Lama-la; also, soul of a person.

laam (Shp.)—Trail.

lama (Tib.)—Tibetan Buddhist religious master or guru; an embodiment of the Buddhist teachings.

Lama Sangwa Dorje—Lama who built Pangboche Monastery and foresaw the building of Tengboche Monastery in the fifteenth century CE. His footprints are found in numerous places in the **Solukhumbu**.

lassi (Npl.)—Yogurt beverage; fruit, such as mangoes or bananas, is often added.

Lho Jong Men Jong (Tib.)—Tibetan name for Bhutan, meaning "Southern Valleys of Medicinal Herbs."

lingam (Skt.)—Symbolic phallus that represents the divine generative male energy and is often seen with a *yoni*, symbolic of the female divine energy.

Losar (Tib., Shp.)—Sherpa New Year, calculated using a lunar calendar; the date varies.

lungdar (Shp.)—Wind-horse flag. Flags are printed by monks with prayers and a wind-horse image. Often strung at a mountain pass or along a ridgeline, the wind and rain carry their prayers out into the world.

Magar—Ethnic group found throughout Nepal; the Magar practice both Hinduism and Buddhism and work as farmers, stonemasons, and **Gurkhas**.

magpa (Shp.)—Groom in a wedding.

Maha Devi (Skt.)—A *shakti* and wife of **Shiva**.

Mahāyāna (Skt.)—"Great Vehicle," the prevalent form of Tibetan Buddhism in Nepal, Tibet, and East Asia; it directs one toward an altruistic spiritual practice embodied in the ideal of the *bodhisattva*.

mahout (Hin.)—A person who works, rides, and cares for an elephant.

Maitreya (Skt.)—Literally translates as "loving one," Maitreya is known as the future Buddha, the fifth and last of the earthly Buddhas. To show his readiness to appear in the world, he is portrayed seated on a raised platform with his feet on the ground, ready to rise.

Manangi—Ethnic group related to Tibetans; the Manangi live primarily north of the Annapurna Mountains and enjoy unique trading privileges originally decreed in 1784.

mandala (Skt.)—Sacred diagram envisioned by Tibetan Buddhists to aid in meditation.

mani (Tib.)—Group of *mantras* or prayers that are printed and placed into a prayer wheel, embossed on a prayer wheel or carved on stones that are often grouped along a rock wall.

Mani Rindup (Shp.)—Religious ceremony that honors **Chenrezi** and includes three days of celebration for the public with masked dances performed by monks. Mani Rindup originated in Rongphu Monastery in Tibet and is performed at all major monasteries of the **Solukhumbu**, including Thami, Tengboche, and Chiwong in the south.

Mañjushrī (Skt.)—"He who is noble and gentle," the **bodhisattva** of wisdom who is iconographically shown with a sword raised above his head and a book over his shoulder. With his sword, he drained the lake that once filled the Kathmandu Valley.

mantra (Skt.)—Sacred syllables spoken as a prayer or chant; in repetition can be a form of meditation. *Om Mani Padme Hum* is an example of a mantra.

me (Tib., Shp.)—Fire, one of the five elements in Tibetan astrology.

metil (Shp.)—Striped woolen front apron, worn by married Sherpani women.

milam (Shp.)—Mountain trail, used primarily by locals.

Milarepa (Tib.)—Student of Marpa (who is credited with translating Buddhist teachings from Sanskrit to Tibetan) and a great eleventh to twelfth century CE poet-saint who endured tremendous hardships during his spiritual quest and attained enlightenment in his lifetime.

Mi Tsering (Shp.)—Old-man character played by a monk at **Mani Rindup.**

momos (Tib.)—Steamed or fried dumplings.

mondal (Npl.)—Two-sided cylindrical drum played with the strap over the drummer's knees and the drum held on the drummer's lap.

motithang (Dzk.)—Meadow of pearls.

mudrā (Skt.)—Symbolic hand gesture or body posture performed in ritual practice by Tibetan Buddhist monks. A characteristic hand gesture is part of the iconography of each Buddha.

Mustangi—Ethnic group related to Tibetans; people of the Kingdom of Mustang.

naalam (Shp.)—Trails that are hidden or hard to follow.

nak (Tib., Shp.)—Female **yak** (*Bos grunniens*), used for milk, meat, and hair and as a pack animal at altitudes above 9,500 feet (2,896 m). See also **yak.**

nama (Shp.)—Bride in a wedding.

Namaste (Hin., Skt.)—Nepalese greeting, "The spirit in me salutes the spirit in you." Alternate translations of this greeting exist.

nirvāna (Skt.)—Literally translates as "extinction," it is the transcendent state in which one is liberated from the cycle of death and rebirth.

nyima (Shp.)—Sun, sacred in Sherpa culture; also, a day of the week; also, a Sherpa name which may have the modern spelling of Nima.

Nyingmapa (Tib.)—Literally translates as "school of the ancients"; first of four main schools of **Mahāyāna** Buddhism, also known as the Red Hat Sect, and practiced by the Sherpa. The Nyingmapa school of Buddhism was founded in the eighth century CE by **Guru Rinpoche**, and then transmitted orally by lay practitioners from one generation to the next.

Nyingmapas (Tib.)—The Old Ones, followers of the **Nyingmapa** school of Buddhism.

Om Mani Padme Hum (Skt.)—Literally, "*Om*, the jewel in the lotus, *hum*"; the **mantra** of **Avalokiteshvara** and the oldest mantra of Tibetan Buddhism.

Padmasambhava (Skt.)—See **Guru Rinpoche**.

pangri (Shp.)—Grass-covered mountains where humans live.

pani (Npl.)—Water.

Parvati (Skt.)—See **Annapurna**.

peepul **tree**—See **bodhi tree**.

phumpa (Shp.)—Sacred pitcher for offering *tru*, usually silver with a peacock-feathered lid with wand; it is used for long-life rituals.

pūjā (Skt.)—An act of worship that involves prayers and offerings, and bestows a blessing on the person performing the act.

raamro (Npl.)—Beautiful.

raatuk (Shp.)—Blouse worn by Sherpa, Tibetan, and Bhutanese men and women.

rakshi (Npl.)—Alcohol made from grain.

ri (Shp.)—Peak or mountain, and home of mountain deities.

rigikur (Shp.)—Potato pancakes.

Rinpoche (Tib.)—Literally translates as "high in value or esteem" and was used in reference to gemstones. In Tibetan Buddhism, the title, "most precious" or Rinpoche, is bestowed on an incarnate lama.

ru (Shp.)—Bone, or paternal clan group; in Sherpa tradition, the father shares bone, and the mother shares blood.

rupees (Skt., Hin., Npl.)—Unit of currency in Nepal and several other Asian countries, as in R100.

sa (Tib.)—Earth, one of the five elements in Tibetan astrology.

saathi (Npl.)—Friend.

sadhu (Skt., Hin.)—Mendicant Hindu holy man.

Sagarmatha (Npl.)—See **Chomolungma**.

sal (Npl.)—Hardwood tree of Nepal's southern foothills and the **Terai**.

Salakha (Shp.)—One of the paternal clan names, or *ru*, of the Sherpa.

samsāra (Skt.)—The cyclic existence of life, death, and suffering based on one's **karma**.

sangdi (Shp.)—A blessing string given by a lama and tied around the neck.

sangha (Skt.)—A community of Buddhist monks, nuns, novices, and laity. See also **Three Jewels**.

sang shing (Shp.)—Incense plant used for purification.

saranghi (Npl.)—Small fiddle made of carved wood and hide with metal strings, played with a bow.

shakti (Skt.)—Consort; also, the dynamic element in the male/female relationship.

Shākymuni (Skt.)—The historical **Buddha**, born as **Siddhārtha Gautama** into the Shākya clan in the sixth century BCE.

shaligram—Fossilized prehistoric ammonite found in the Kali Gandaki River basin and believed to represent Lord **Vishnu**. An English word.

Sherpa or **Sharwa** (Shp.)—Ethnic group of Nepal related to Tibetans, also a Tibeto-Burman language spoken by the Sherpa. The Sherpa live in the Everest region of Nepal and are known for working on Himalayan treks and expeditions. *Sharwa* means "People of the East," and is how the Sherpa people pronounce their name. Sherpa is an anglicized word.

Sherpani (Shp.)—A female **Sherpa**.

shey shey (Shp.)—Sherpa expression commonly used when offering food or drink.

shing (Tib., Shp.)—Wood, one of the five elements in Tibetan astrology.

Shiva (Skt.)—Hindu creator/destroyer god. To many Nepalese, including the Sherpa, **Shiva-ge** is **Guru Rinpoche**, who is considered a manifestation of **Shiva**.

Siddhārtha Gautama (Skt.)—An Indian prince of the Shākya clan who was born in the sixth century BCE in an area that is now part of Nepal. He gave up his noble life to seek spiritual liberation, became enlightened, and began to teach others. His teachings became the basis of Buddhism.

sillu (Shp.)—Yak-tail pom or whisk.

sillu chumbu (Shp.)—Yak-tail dance; a dance with *sillu* that is performed at the end of Sherpa marriage ceremonies.

sirdar (Npl.)—The staff leader/manager of a trekking or mountaineering expedition.

sogsha (Shp.)—Mongolian hat with a wide brim and fringe, worn by Sherpa bridegrooms.

solja (Shp.)—Butter salt tea favored by Sherpas.

Solukhumbu—District of Nepal near Mount Everest combining three areas—listed from lowest to highest elevation, they are Solu, Pharak, and Khumbu.

stūpa (Skt.)—See **chörten** (Tib.).

Tamang—Ethnic group related to Tibetans, the Tamang live in Nepal's middle hills. The Tamang language belongs to the Tibeto-Burman subgroup of the Sino-Tibetan language family.

Tārā (Npl.) or **Dolma** (Tib.)—Goddess referred to as the Mother of all the Buddhas; the Green Tārā offers protection, and the White Tārā offers healing and longevity.

Tashi Delek (Tib., Shp.)—Formal Sherpa greeting used at any time of day.

tato (Npl.)—Hot (temperature), as in *tatopani* ("hot water").

telma (Shp.)—Wild man of the forest; a *telma* is known to be small and strong, and often has shamanistic powers.

Terai—Flat plains in the southern lowlands of Nepal along the Indian border.

terma (Tib.)—Literally translates as "treasure"; religious texts or oral teachings sought after by a *tertön*, or treasure revealer, when the time is right. The search for *terma* is practiced primarily by **Nyingmapa** and **Bönpo**. **Guru Rinpoche** is said to have hidden one hundred and eight *terma* in Tibet.

tertön (Tib.)—Treasure revealer of **terma**.

Thakali—Ethnic group, related to Tibetans, from the Kali Gandaki Valley in the northwest of Nepal; the Thakali reside throughout Nepal and practice a combination of ancient beliefs, Hinduism, and Buddhism.

thangka (Tib.)—Scroll-like Tibetan Buddhist religious painting.

thaplha (Shp.)—Spirit who resides in the **thapmig** or fireplace.

thapmig (Shp.)—"Fireplace with eyes"; an adobe stove with small openings for fuel and for flame.

Tharu—Ancient ethnic group of the **Terai**; the Tharu are peasant farmers and practice a unique form of Hinduism.

theu (Shp.)—Rock cairn or stacked rock marker.

thrakri (Shp.)—Mountains of mostly rock above the tree line.

thrakya (Shp.)—Silver cup stand and lid to hold a china cup, used for respected guests or special occasions.

Three Precious Jewels or *triratna* (Skt.)—Three essential elements of Buddhism and places of refuge from cyclic existence and suffering for a Buddhist: **Buddha** is the ultimate nature, **dharma** is the teaching or true path, and **sangha** is the spiritual community. Also known as wish-fulfilling jewels.

thung (Shp.)—Conch shell that proclaims the Buddha's teachings; a call to prayer for the monks.

tika (Skt.)—Vermilion powder placed at the center of the forehead to symbolize a divine presence.

topi (Npl.)—Traditional Nepalese hat worn by men during formal occasions; its asymmetrical shape represents Mount Kailas in Tibet, the most sacred mountain to Buddhists, Hindus, and Bönpos.

tru (Shp.)—Sacred water, or the nectar of longevity, poured or spattered from a *phumpa*.

tsampa (Shp.)—Roasted barley flour, usually mixed with water, tea, or milk and eaten as dough.

tsering kinkhap (Shp.)—Long-life brocade hat with four flaps trimmed in fur, worn by Sherpas and Tibetans.

tsham (Shp.)—Sister-in-law.

tuk-tuk (Npl.)—Three-wheeled car; *tuk-tuks* are used as taxis in Kathmandu.

uru (Shp.)—Paternal aunt.

Vairochana (Skt.)—Translates literally as "He who is like the sun"; Vairochana, known as the Great Illuminator, is iconographically depicted with the wheel of teaching or *dharma-chakra* and the sun, making the *mudrā* of supreme wisdom.

Vajrayāna (Skt.)—Translates literally as "Diamond Vehicle"; Vajrayāna is a form of Buddhism, an esoteric tradition, with highly developed ritual practices.

Vishnu (Skt.)—Snake god, preserver of life and the world; the king of Nepal is a reincarnation of Vishnu.

yab-yum (Tib.)—Translates literally as "father/mother" and indicates union of the masculine and feminine principles.

yak (Tib., Shp.)—Male *Bos grunniens*, used for meat, hair, and as a pack animal at altitudes above 9,500 feet (2,896 m). See also **nak**.

yeti (Shp.)—Apelike mammal with long red hair and a foul smell; similar to the Abominable Snowman.

za (Shp.)—days of the week: cyclic, with no beginning or end; some are auspicious. Nyima (Sunday), Dawa (Monday), Mingmar (Tuesday), Lhakpa (Wednesday), Phurbu (Thursday), Pasang (Friday), Penpa (Saturday). Sherpa children are often named after the day of their birth. When used as a person's name, variations of the spelling are common.

zari (Shp.)—Boulder-covered mountains.

zemu (Shp.)—Beautiful.

zendi (Shp.)—Marriage or wedding, which in Sherpa tradition involves a number of ceremonies.

zi (Shp.)—Brown, tube-shaped stone bead with white eyes (*zimig*) and lines, origin unknown. They bring the wearer good fortune and protection.

zimig (Shp.)—Eyes of a *zi*; a larger quantity of eyes often increases its value.

zopkyok (Shp.)—Male animal crossbred from a cow and a yak or from a bull and a nak; *zom* is the female crossbreed.

zung (Shp.)—Religious relics, often enshrined in a ***chörten***.

REFERENCES AND SUGGESTED READING

Texts marked with • were used as sources for transliterations and definitions of non-English words in the text and glossary.

• Armington, Stan. *Trekking in the Nepal Himalaya*. 5th ed. Berkeley, California: Lonely Planet Publications, 1991.

Armstrong, Karen. *Buddha*. New York: Viking Penguin, 2001.

Avedon, John F. *In Exile from the Land of Snows*. New York: Alfred A. Knopf, 1984.

Beer, Robert. *The Encyclopedia of Tibetan Symbols and Motifs*. Boston: Shambhala, 1999.

Bernstein, Jeremy. *The Wildest Dreams of Kew: A Profile of Nepal*. Photographs by Claude Jaccoux. New York: Simon and Schuster, 1970.

Blum, Arlene. *Annapurna: A Woman's Place*. San Francisco: Sierra Club Books, 1980.

Blum, Arlene. *Annapurna: A Woman's Place*. 20th anniv. ed. San Francisco: Sierra Club Books, 1998.

Brower, Barbara. *Sherpa of Khumbu: People, Livestock, and Landscape*. Delhi: Oxford University Press, 1991.

Coburn, Broughton. *Nepali Aama: Portrait of a Nepalese Hill Woman*. Chico, California: Moon Publications, Inc., 1991.

• Coleman, Graham. *The Handbook of Tibetan Culture: A Guide to Tibetan Centres and Resources throughout the World*. Compiled by the Orient Foundation. Preface by H. H. The Dalai Lama. Boston: Shambhala, 1994.

Crossette, Barbara. *So Close to Heaven: The Vanishing Buddhist Kingdoms of the Himalayas*. New York: Alfred A. Knopf, 1995.

Cummings, Joe. *Buddhist Stupas in Asia: The Shape of Perfection*. Photographs by Bill Wassman with introduction by Robert A. F. Thurman. Melbourne, Australia, and Oakland, CA: Lonely Planet Publications, 2001.

Dagyab Rinpoche, Loden Sherap. *Buddhist Symbols in Tibetan Culture: An Investigation of the Nine Best-Known Groups of Symbols*. Translated by Maurice Walshe. Foreword by Robert A. F. Thurman. Boston: Wisdom Publications, 1995.

Dalai Lama, His Holiness the XIV. *Becoming Enlightened*. Translated and edited by Jeffrey Hopkins. New York: Atria Books, 2009.

Dalai Lama, His Holiness the XIV and Howard C. Cutler. *The Art of Happiness: A Handbook for Living*. New York: Riverhead Books, 1998.

Deep, Dhurba Krishna. *The Nepal Festivals*. Kathmandu: Ratna Pustak Bhandar, 1982.

Dowman, Keith. *The Great Stupa of Boudhanath: The Tibetan Legend of the Great Stupa*. Translated by Kunzang Tenzin (Keith Dowman) upon the authority of His Holiness the late Dunjom Rinpoche, Yeshe Dorje, and with the assistance of the schoolmaster Nima Norbu of Darjeeling. Jatal Rinpoche, Sangye Dorje, of Ghoom, corrected the manuscript, which was printed from wood blocks in the possession of the Chini Lamas of Boudhanath, and presented to the translator by the

Third Chini Lama, Punya Vajra. Illustrations by Khempo Sangay Tenzin, Gomchen Oleshey, Robert Beer, Keith Payne and Mani Lama. Poulnabrucky, Ballyvaughan, Ireland: Footprint Publishing, 1993.

Farber, Don and the Dalai Lama XIV. *Living Wisdom with His Holiness the Dalai Lama*. Boulder: Sounds True, 2006. DVD, 47 min.

• Fischer-Schreiber, Ingrid, Franz-Karl Ehrhard, and Michael S. Diener. *The Shambhala Dictionary of Buddhism and Zen*. Translated by Michael H. Kohn. Boston: Shambhala, 1991.

Fisher, James F. *Sherpas: Reflections on Change in Himalayan Nepal*. New Delhi: Oxford University Press, 1990.

• Frédéric, Louis. *Buddhism*. Flammarion Iconographic Guides. Paris: Flammarion, 1995.

Fürer-Haimendorf, Christoph von. *The Sherpas of Nepal*. London: John Murray, 1964.

Grimmett, Richard, Carol Inskipp, and Tim Inskipp. *Birds of Nepal*. Helm Field Guides. Illustrated by Clive Byers, Daniel Cole, John Cox, Gerald Driessens, Carl D'Silva, Martin Elliot, Kim Franklin, Alan Harris, Peter Hayman, Craig Robson, Jan Wilczur and Tim Worfolk. Photographs by Carol and Tim Inskipp. New Delhi: Prakash Books, 2000.

Hagen, Toni, Friedrich Traugott Wahlen, and Walter Robert Corti. *Nepal: The Kingdom in the Himalayas*. Berne: Kummerly & Frey, Geographical Publishers, 1961.

Hagen, Toni, Günter-Oskar Dyhrenfurth, Christoph von Fürer-Haimendorf, and Eric Schneider. *Mount Everest: Formation, Population and Exploration of the Everest Region*. Translated by E. Noel Bowman. New York: Oxford University Press, 1963.

Herzog, Maurice. *Annapurna: First Conquest of an 8000-Meter Peak [26,493 Feet]*. Translated by Nea Morin and Janet Adam Smith. Cartographic and photographic documentation by Marcel Ichac with an introduction by Eric Shipton. New York: E. P. Dutton & Company, 1953.

Hunt, Sir John and Sir Edmund Hillary. *The Conquest of Everest*. New York: E. P. Dutton & Company, 1954.

• *Insight Guide Nepal*. 7th ed. Insight Guides. Singapore: Apa Publications, 1989.

Iyer, Pico. *The Open Road: The Global Journey of the Fourteenth Dalai Lama*. New York: Alfred A. Knopf, 2008.

Jerstad, Luther G. *Mani-Rimdu: Sherpa Dance-Drama*. Seattle: The University of Washington Press, 1969.

Lopez, Jr., Donald S. *The Story of Buddhism: A Concise Guide to its History and Teachings*. San Francisco: HarperSanFrancisco, 2001.

Majupuria, Indra, and Trilok Chandra Majupuria. *Marriage Customs in Nepal: Traditions and Wedding Ceremonies among Various Nepalese Ethnic Groups*. Lalipur Colony, Lashkar (Gwalior), India: M. Devi; Bangkok: Craftsman Press, 1989.

Matthiessen, Peter. *The Snow Leopard*. New York: The Viking Press, 1978.

Norgay, Jamling Tenzing. *Touching My Father's Soul: A Sherpa's Journey to the Top of Everest*. With Broughton Coburn. Introduction by Jon Krakauer. New York: HarperSanFrancisco, 2001.

Norgay, Tenzing. *Tiger of the Snows: The Autobiography of Tenzing of Everest*. Written in collaboration with James Ramsey Ullman. New York: G. P. Putnam's Sons, 1955.

Ortner, Sherry B. *High Religion: A Cultural and Political History of Sherpa Buddhism*. New Delhi: Motilal Banarsidass Publishers, 1992.

Peissel, Michel. *Tiger for Breakfast: The Story of Boris of Kathmandu*. New Delhi: Time

Books International, 1990.

Polunin, Oleg, and Adam Stainton. *Flowers of the Himalaya*. Delhi: Oxford University Press, 1984.

• Pommaret, Françoise. *An Illustrated Guide to Bhutan: Buddhist Fort of the Himalayas*. Photography by Françoise Pommaret, Yoshiro Imaeda. Translated by Elisabeth B. Booz. Hong Kong: The Guidebook Company Limited, 1990.

Ridgeway, Rick. *The Last Step: The American Ascent of K2*. Seattle: The Mountaineers Books, 1980.

Rinpoche, Patrul. *The Words of My Perfect Teacher*. With forewords by the Dalai Lama and Dilgo Khyentse Rinpoche. Translated by the Padmakara Translation Group. Boston: Shambhala, 1998.

Schaller, George B. *Stones of Silence: Journeys in the Himalaya*. Chicago: The University of Chicago Press, 1988.

• Sherpa, Ang Phinjo. *Sherpa Nepali English: A Language Guide for Beginners*. Kathmandu: Eco Himal, 1999.

• Sherpa, Lhakpa Norbu. *Through a Sherpa Window: Illustrated Guide to Traditional Sherpa Culture*. Kathmandu: Vajra Publications, 2008.

Snellgrove, David L. *Buddhist Himālaya: Travels and Studies in Quest of the Origins and Nature of Tibetan Religion*. Kathmandu: Himalayan Book Sellers, 1957.

Snellgrove, David L. *Himalayan Pilgrimage: A Study of Tibetan Religion by a Traveller through Western Nepal*. Boston: Shambhala, 1989.

Uchida, Ryohei. *Trekking Mount Everest*. Translation by Japan–Michi Interlingual, Inc. San Francisco: Chronicle Books, 1991.

Yoshida, Toshi with a foreword by Daniel J. Hinkley. *Portraits of Himalayan Flowers*. Portland, OR: Timber Press, 2002.

Zangbu, Ngawang Tenzin. *Stories and Customs of the Sherpas*. As told to the author by the Abbot of Tengboche Monastery. Edited by Frances Klatzel. Translation assistance by Ang Kanchi Sherpa and Passang Thondup Sherpa. Kathmandu: Mera Publications, 2000.

ACKNOWLEDGEMENTS

After my trip to Nepal in 1991, I returned with a story I wanted to tell. In between work and life, it took me fifteen years to learn how to write, another five to pen this book, and the help of many people along the way before it would be published.

The encouragement of my first writing teachers—Barbara Abercrombie, who taught at the community adult education program in Manhattan Beach, California, and Bernard Cooper at UCLA—compelled me to keep writing. A student from Barbara's class, River Montejo, asked me to join her writing group. River, Dee Flacey, Susan Irby, and others became my first writing community, and I will always remember our sessions at the Mermaid Tavern in Hermosa Beach, where I learned to love writing. After leaving Southern California, I found a wonderful literary arts community at Richard Hugo House in Seattle. Through classes and volunteer work at Hugo House, many wonderful writers have provided input on my writing, expressed interest in my story, and encouraged me to continue. Thank you all. It has meant a lot. But it was a few teachers at Richard Hugo House who had the most impact on this project, and I can't thank them enough for their wise guidance and inspiration: Kathleen Alcalá, Rebecca Brown, Jen Graves, Priscilla Long, Barbara Sjoholm, Deborah Woodward, and a special thanks to Dickey Nesenger, who helped me shape the story and find its heart.

I would like to give particular thanks to two readers who edited numerous drafts and helped draw the story into a tight manuscript: my friends Mary Alice Kier and Anna Cottle. You believed in me from the start and that made all the difference. My readers were numerous: you know who you are, and I appreciate the time you took out of your busy lives to provide me with your honest critiques and the prod to keep at it.

As the book took shape, I appreciated the hard work, fact checking, and attention to detail of my editors, Kyra Freestar and Waverly Fitzgerald, as well as my proofreader Anne Moreau, all of whom kept me out of trouble. My cover designer and good friend, Chuck Pennington, designed an eye-catching cover that suggests the mystery and magic of Nepal, and book designer Nina Barnett, created a lovely book to read. A special thanks goes to Robert Peirce, dearest of friends, who drew the maps by hand, and Grace Ericson, who provided the graphics for the maps and did any number of activities to assist me with launching the book.

My heartfelt gratitude goes to Tsering Lama and Anne Jaworski, who provided shelter for my husband and I after we sold our Seattle home, but before we moved to Nepal, as I finalized the book. Food, friends, and laughs. Ahhhhh. So good.

Ben Carlson artfully designed the website—www.carylsherpa.com— set up my blog, and took on the role of social media advisor. The book video trailer, available from the website, was developed by my nephew, the dynamic Derek Klein of Power'd Media, with voice-overs by Brian Butler as both Narrator and Sir Edmund Hillary, Stephanie Riggio as Caryl, Pemba Sherpa as Nima, Pasang Sherpa as himself, Jangbu Sherpa as Gelek Rinpoche, and Phurba Sherpa as Mingma Futi Sherpa.

I am grateful to my Sherpa and Nepalese friends, who have all contributed in their own ways by sharing knowledge about their culture, answering my questions, and supporting my efforts to write about their heritage and traditions. And, I honor most my family in America and my Sherpa family in Nepal, who unknowingly became the characters that populated the tapestry from which I weave my story; and Nima, my husband and guide, who is the thread that binds us all together.